Islam in the Age of Globalization

Religion in the Modern World

Series Editors
Kwok Pui-lan, Emory University
Joerg Rieger, Vanderbilt University

This series explores how various religious traditions wrestle with the dynamic and changing role of religion in the modern world and examines how past changes reflect on today's critical issues. Accessibly and engagingly written, books in this series will look at secularization, global society, gender, race, class, sexuality, and their relation to religious life and religious movements.

Titles in the Series:
Liberating People, Planet, and Religion: Intersections of Ecology, Economics, and Christianity edited by Joerg Rieger and Terra Rowe
The Seven Deadly Sins of White Christian Nationalism: A Call to Action by Carter Heyward
The Hong Kong Protests and Political Theology edited by Kwok Pui-lan and Francis Ching-wah Yip
Race, Religion, and Politics: Toward Human Rights in the United States by Stephanie Y. Mitchem
Modern Muslim Theology: Engaging God and the World with Faith and Imagination by Martin Nguyen
The Politics of Jesús: A Hispanic Political Theology by Miguel A. De La Torre
The Food and Feasts of Jesus: The Original Mediterranean Diet, with Menus and Recipes by Douglas E. Neel and Joel A. Pugh
The Food and Feasts of Jesus: Inside the World of First Century Fare, with Menus and Recipes by Douglas E. Neel and Joel A. Pugh
Occupy Religion: Theology of the Multitude by Joerg Rieger and Kwok Pui-lan
Not God's People: Insiders and Outsiders in the Biblical World by Lawrence M. Wills

Islam in the Age of Globalization

Perspectives and Responses

Asif Mohiuddin

ROWMAN & LITTLEFIELD
Lanham • Boulder • New York • London

Published by Rowman & Littlefield
An imprint of The Rowman & Littlefield Publishing Group, Inc.
4501 Forbes Boulevard, Suite 200, Lanham, Maryland 20706
www.rowman.com

86-90 Paul Street, London EC2A 4NE

Copyright © 2024 by The Rowman & Littlefield Publishing Group, Inc.

All rights reserved. No part of this book may be reproduced in any form or by any electronic or mechanical means, including information storage and retrieval systems, without written permission from the publisher, except by a reviewer who may quote passages in a review.

British Library Cataloguing in Publication Information Available

Library of Congress Cataloging-in-Publication Data

Names: Mohiuddin, Asif, 1988- author.
Title: Islam in the age of globalization : perspectives and responses / Asif Mohiuddin.
Description: Lanham, Maryland : Rowman & Littlefield, [2025] | Includes bibliographical references and in | Summary: "Islam in the Age of Globalization explores the complex relationship between Islam and globalization. From challenging prevailing notions to examining historical influences and contemporary perspectives, this book delves into the multifaceted dimensions of Islam's interaction with international forces"– Provided by publis
Identifiers: LCCN 2024037990 | ISBN 9798881801328 (cloth) | ISBN 9798881801335 (paperback) | ISBN 9798881801342 (epub)
Classification: LCC BP190.5.G56 M64 2025 | DDC 297.2/7--dc23/eng/20240911
LC record available at https://lccn.loc.gov/2024037990

∞™ The paper used in this publication meets the minimum requirements of American National Standard for Information Sciences—Permanence of Paper for Printed Library Materials, ANSI/NISO Z39.48-1992.

Contents

Foreword	vii
Acknowledgments	ix
Introduction: Globalization, Islam, and Muslims	1
PART I: GLOBALIZATION AND ISLAM	**23**
1 Revisiting Globalization: Definitions, Discourses, and Domains	25
2 Globalization and Islam: Exploring the Alternative Paradigm	71
3 From Globalization to Global Islam: Tracing Intersections and Convergence	119
4 Islamic Revivalism in the Era of Globalization: Unraveling the Dynamics of Religion, Culture, and Resistance	165
PART II: ADAPTIVE ISLAM	**189**
5 Embracing or Resisting Globalization? Ali Mazrui's Exploration of Interdependence and the Muslim World's Dilemma	191
6 Islam and the Globalization Paradox: Akbar Ahmad's Reflections on Crisis and Resilience	225

7 Toward a Moral Dimension in Globalization: Umar Chapra's Exploration of Islam's Response to Economic Challenges 250

8 Islamic Thought in the Age of Globalization: Ibrahim Abu Rabi's Perspective on Epistemological, Ethical, and Socioeconomic Changes 275

Conclusion: Islam, Globalization, and Shared Prosperity 303

Bibliography 313

Index 333

About the Author 347

Foreword

With this book, Asif Mohiuddin continues to grapple with one of the most complex, confounding, and urgent issues of our time: how to make sense of, and negotiate, the challenges posed by the various phenomena that combine synergistically to produce what we have come to call "globalization."

As was the case with his previous effort on modern Islamist movements, *Navigating Religious Authority in Muslim Societies*, Dr. Mohiuddin has demonstrated once again his profound grasp of the accumulated data, the various theoretical approaches that have been articulated to organize that data, and the persistent question which haunts us all: *Quo vadis?*

An important global thinker in his own right, Mohiuddin wants to find answers that will contribute to the future well-being of the roughly 8 billion human inhabitants of this planet. As a Muslim, he is particularly concerned with finding answers that will draw upon the wisdom that fifteen centuries of Islamic experience and thought may contribute to that search. And, given the fact that self-identifying Muslims account for about one-fifth of the world's population, he wants to be sure that, in the process, their needs not only as people but as people of faith will be addressed.

I think it is important to stress, however, that his vision is not merely parochial. One of the things I most appreciate about Asif's work is its inclusivity. He wants to see the needs of Muslims considered in the search for answers, and he insists that Muslim proposals for shaping the future should not only be taken seriously but implemented where appropriate. But he fully recognizes that we live in a multiracial, multiethnic, and multireligious *oikumene* for which it is unlikely that "one size fits all." Does this book offer an effective blueprint for moving forward into the future?

That is perhaps too much to ask of any single volume produced by any one author. However, it does offer what we need today: a thorough, thoughtful, and humane voice that gives us much to ponder as the flood tides of globalization continue to rise.

Peter Matthews Wright,
PhD, Associate Professor of Religion,
The Colorado College

Acknowledgments

Bringing this book to fruition has been a journey filled with challenges, growth, and immense learning. As we reach the completion of this project, I am grateful to all those who have contributed their time, expertise, and support. First and foremost, I extend my deepest gratitude to the scholars, intellectuals, and experts who generously shared their insights, knowledge, and perspectives for this book. Your contributions have enriched my understanding of the complex interactions between Islam and globalization, and your dedication to scholarship has been truly inspiring.

I express deep gratitude to Professor Tahir Abbas, Professor Peter Matthews Wright, Professor Jocelyn Cesari, Professor Daniel Brown, Professor Ronald Luckens Bull, Professor Muhammad Hashim Kamali, Professor Ramazan Bicer, Professor Abd Hadi Bin Borham, Dr. Adis Duderija, Professor Rajab Izadi, and Professor Mariusz Maslak for their invaluable contributions to this book. Your expertise, guidance, and dedication have significantly enriched my understanding of the complex interactions between Islam and globalization. Your willingness to share your insights and scholarly perspectives has been instrumental in shaping the content of this work. I am deeply grateful for your support and commitment to advancing knowledge in this important field.

My sincere appreciation goes to the Faculty of Human Sciences at Sultan Idris Education University for their support throughout the research and writing process. Special thanks to all the faculty members who provided invaluable insights, feedback, and encouragement. I am also thankful to the university library for granting access to essential resources that facilitated my research endeavors.

I would also like to extend my appreciation to my editors at Rowman & Littlefield, Dr. Richard Brown and Victoria Shi, for their professionalism, guidance, and meticulous attention to detail throughout the publication process. Their expertise and constructive feedback have played a pivotal role in refining the content of this book and ensuring its quality.

Last but not least, I express my gratitude to the readers who will engage with this book. It is my sincere hope that the insights, perspectives, and discussions presented herein will stimulate further dialogue, reflection, and exploration of the dynamic relationship between Islam and globalization.

Introduction

Globalization, Islam, and Muslims

In contemporary discourse, the articulation of themes related to globalization carries the inherent risk of disseminating knowledge of a less sophisticated nature. Arojomand posits that during the initial years following the collapse of the Berlin Wall (1989–1991), the rise of globalization supplanted postmodernism, emerging as the "master trend of a new era" within the realm of social sciences. This paradigmatic shift not only mandated the delineation of this new era but also marked a pivotal juncture in the transformation of the global landscape, where the advent of the global age filled the preceding void. More broadly, the phenomenon of globalization has occupied a prominent position in scholarly discourses spanning governmental affairs, economic domains, popular culture, and arenas of religious deliberation for a span exceeding a decade. Divergent perspectives prevail, with some contending that the embracement of globalization is imperative for societal contentment, while others ascribe to it the status of being the genesis of myriad predicaments.[1]

In a manner akin to Christopher Hill's examination of the seventeenth-century English revolutions, it can be asserted that the contemporary globalized milieu constitutes a radical or revolutionary paradigm, a "World Turned Upside Down," given the celerity and intensity characterizing the global dynamics. Economically, in the decades leading up to the year 2000, the realms of corporate capitalism and Fordism found themselves encumbered by the vicissitudes of virtual psychocapitalist waves manifesting as futures, derivative products, and the burgeoning dotcom sector.[2] The established paradigm governing religious and socio-ethical interactions is currently undergoing rigorous examination on a global scale, coinciding with discourses on cultural and civilizational warfare, exemplified by the dichotomous narrative of the "West against the rest," thereby exacerbating ethnocentrism in many nations. Simultaneously, radicalized lifestyles and emergent egalitarian (revolutionary) movements are proving inspirational, albeit engendering robust counter-movements of a conservative nature.[3]

Emanating beyond its characterization as an indomitable force, globalization stands as a formidable power that not only erodes the foundations of progressive Enlightenment concepts but also challenges their tenets of authenticity, morality, and veracity. Each facet of these pervasive globalizing influences—encompassing the realms of culture, politics, economy, ideology, and technology—evinces a dual nature, being both a detonation and a collapse. It functions as a detonation, precipitating the dispersal of cultural, structural, behavioral, and communicative elements toward the periphery, while simultaneously constituting a collapse. This dualistic impact is particularly conspicuous in the realm of religion, as each wave of globalizing advancement subjects it to multifaceted criticisms emanating from various quarters, including fundamentalisms, essentialist explications, and grand narratives. The oversimplification inherent in these perspectives contributes significantly to the tensions arising from a number of exceedingly dramatic events. In succinct terms, the consensus among both proponents and detractors of globalization is that the pervasive currents traversing the global landscape, the emergence of global spaces, and the manifold iterations of the new global order possess transformative potentialities. These include the capacity to emancipate individuals, engender innovation, and concurrently exacerbate tyrannical forces grounded in ignorance, immobility, and exclusion. The process of deregulation, notably, has flung open borders, heralding the resurgence of global disparities and exposing humanity to the hazards of maladies, pollution, criminal activities, and the transplantation of localized antipathies and cultural myopia. Concomitantly, the trajectory of globalization has precipitated a significant diminution in the prospects of redistributive and progressive democratic paradigms at the level of the state.[4]

Understanding the intricacies of globalization mandates a recognition of its inherently dynamic nature, characterized by a perpetual state of evolution rather than stasis. Anthony Giddens' conceptualization encapsulates this dynamism, defining globalization as the strengthening of connections between disparate locales. This encompasses the complex interplay between local actions and events, wherein the expansive reach of political, economic, and cultural practices transcends national boundaries.[5] Such a paradigm shift engenders the rise of a global consciousness that, in turn, both shapes and is shaped by events transpiring across extensive geographical territories. Giddens' definition underscores the contemporaneous intensification and expeditiousness with which territorial constraints can be surmounted, epitomized by the rise and prevailing influence of transnational corporations (TNCs). The concept of "decontextualization," articulated within this framework, postulates the obsolescence of localized positioning, thereby denoting the dissolution of geographical borders traditionally demarcating states. This multifaceted definition delineates globalization as a transformative force that renders the world akin to a global village, effecting a reduction in spatial distances by accelerating and deepening the impact of interregional flows and patterns of social interaction. Simultaneously, it induces cultural homogenization, underscores power hegemony (manifested paradoxically in the concentration of power within specific countries or civilizations), and facilitates enhanced modes of communication. Despite advancements in flexible production techniques and labor practices, less developed nations remain ensconced within the orbit of dominance and exploitation orchestrated by powerful states, multinational corporations (MNCs), and financial institutions. These entities, in their pursuit of advancing capitalism and fortifying the ascendancy of the capitalist class, perpetuate a paradigm wherein globalization becomes synonymous with the processes fostering interconnectedness among nations and the cultivation of shared economies and interests.[6]

Much akin to imperialism, the phenomenon of globalization serves as a clarion call to the realization that it is, fundamentally, an exercise in the cumulative transformation, whereby the cultural attributes of the dominant echelon ascend to a position of prominence, undergoing transmission through varied conduits. Foremost among these conduits are the cultural industries, entities intricately engaged in the generation of "social meaning," encompassing domains such as marketing, broadcasting, media, sports, software, and related spheres. This process, in essence, engenders the assimilation of the cultural hegemony of the prevailing group by subordinate entities. In the contemporary world, Western culture, particularly the cultural emanations of the United States, stands as an omnipresent force within the global cultural milieu.[7]

In response to the multifaceted implications of globalization, there has emerged a pervasive need for global governance—a response stemming from the heightened recognition of the complex interconnections characterizing our globalized milieu. This call for governance at a global scale gains traction in the face of pressing challenges spanning the social, political, religious, economic, and environmental spectra. Scholars, cognizant of these developments, contend that the trajectory of globalization assumes a pivotal role in delineating a post-democratic terrain. In this landscape, the rise of capitalist and consumerist forces supersedes the traditional realms of citizenship and politics. The ensuing discourse is characterized by a dialectic between proponents who laud these global shifts as heralding progress and critics who voice reservations, scrutinizing the nature of these transformations and expressing concerns regarding the adaptive capacities of individuals confronted by the evolving contours of the global order.

Some contemporary Muslim scholars, notably Ali Mazrui, articulate a discernibly skeptical stance vis-à-vis the prevailing trajectory of globalization. Within their purview, globalization unfolds as an overarching process characterized by the accentuation of societal uniformity—a phenomenon colloquially termed homogenization.[8] This manifests in the dissemination of common preferences, the ubiquity of a consumption-centric lifestyle, and the proliferation of Western-style fast food, among other elements, permeating diverse global populations. Simultaneously, these scholars underscore the concomitant concentration of power within a select cadre of nations—a phenomenon denoted as hegemonization. In alignment with this critical discourse, Ibrahim M. Abu-Rabi perceives globalization as an advanced phase in the evolution and propagation of Western culture, underscored by its proclivity for hegemonic influence over the broader canvas of Western civilization. His argument posits that the ascendance of capitalism as a preeminent mode of production has functioned as a conduit for the dissemination of Western cultural values, institutions, and political paradigms. This process has engendered an intensification of Western influence, often encapsulated under the rubrics of "Americanization" or "Westernization."[9] Conversely, an alternative intellectual trajectory posits Islam as a potential counterbalance to the predominant contours of globalization. In this vein, Khurshid Ahmad articulates that Islam furnishes a distinct paradigm conducive to human unity based on its universalist ethos. He contends that Islam, through its aspirational creation of a unified global space wherein humanity may partake in mercy, justice, and tranquility and where individuals retain the right to make choices under the aegis of justice, constitutes an intellectual and spiritual foundation for globalization. In this framework, Islam emerges as a catalyst for pioneering a civilized paradigm aimed at achieving universality and unity of purpose.[10]

The theological tenets propagated by the Qur'ān transcend the bounds of particularistic affiliations, extending their universal reach to encompass individuals across disparate corners of the globe. At the heart of Islam lies an unwavering commitment to the unity of God, with its doctrinal purview expressly directed toward all of humanity, irrespective of geographical constraints. In contradistinction to religious frameworks circumscribed within particular communities, Islam, by virtue of its intrinsic ethos, embraces the entirety of the human race, accentuating shared conceptual frameworks such as the unity of humanity. The pivotal role played by Prophet Muhammad (PBUH) in disseminating this universalistic religious paradigm cannot be overstated, as attested by the Qur'ān's verses, which serve as exemplars of the religion's expansive and all-encompassing message, resolutely underscoring its global resonance. The Qur'ān, in its divine injunctions, echoes this expansive outlook, repeatedly employing the term "O mankind" to address the entirety of humanity, exemplified in verses such as: O Mankind! There hath come to you a direction from your Lord and a healing for the (disease) in your hearts,[11] and for those who believe, a guidance and a Mercy.[12] No reward do I ask of you: This is no less than a message for the nations. This is no less than a Message to (all) the worlds.[13] Say: O men! I am sent unto you all.[14] (Al-Quran: 10:57, 34:47, 21:107, 7:158)

An illuminating aspect distinguishing the Qur'ān from other scriptures lies in its consistent use of the term "O mankind" to universally address humanity. In contradistinction to religious traditions that ascribe divinity to specific groups or nations, Islam inherently adopts a universalistic stance from its inception. This distinctiveness is further pronounced when juxtaposed against systems underpinned by exploitation, domination, and self-interest, which often corrode ethical moorings and reduce individuals to mere pawns. Islam's spiritual foundation, conversely, proffers a unique vision of human unity, eschewing the economic and geopolitical interests often pursued by the Western world.

Globalization, Muslim Identity, and Transnational Networks

Within the realm of religious identification, Muslims exhibit a nuanced intellectual and doctrinal heterogeneity comparable to any other societal group. A unified Islamic stance on globalization proves to be an intricate subject, given the multifaceted diversity inherent in this community. The Muslim response to globalization, despite its diversity, manifests along three principal trajectories: traditionalists, Islamists, and reformers. Traditionalism, aptly named, is rooted in a convergence of religious traditions. It is anchored in historical practices, regional idiosyncrasies, and ethno-national customs, reinvigorated and accentuated through rituals and recurrent celebrations. This amalgam thus forms the foundational ethos of traditionalist orientations.

Local practices and traditional Muslim identity find themselves contending for cultural space in a milieu, where such spaces are diminishing precipitously. The immediacy of this threat may be mitigated by the impact of modern processes of cultural globalization, characterized, at times, by the concept of deterritorialization—the dissociation of culture from its "natural" ties to physical and social locales. Despite the ostensibly detached nature of culture from territorial confines, a palpable anxiety permeates many Muslim communities who perceive themselves as engaged in a rearguard action. This perceived decline in social mores is often ascribed to the forces of Westernization or globalization, contributing to a sense of urgency among Muslims to safeguard their cultural heritage. A prevailing misconception regarding globalization revolves around the notion that it is an inexorable process through which the social structures of modernity—namely, rationalism, capitalism, bureaucracy, and individualism—are disseminated globally. This purportedly leads to the obliteration of preexisting cultures and local autonomy. The symbiotic relationship between globalization and Westernization assumes a quasi-synonymous significance, reinforcing the belief that the global dissemination of ideas is inherently aligned with Western values. The genesis of the globalization process in Western economies further accentuates this linkage, prompting inquiries into its underlying motives. Moreover, the globalization process appears to rejuvenate contemporary Western ideals of democracy, individual liberty, and political transparency, raising suspicions of an implicit agenda. From the vantage point of the Muslim world, this may be interpreted as a subtle attempt by former colonial powers to reassert control, coercing Muslim nations to integrate into the global fabric. The skepticism toward globalization is particularly pronounced among orthodox Muslims, who perceive it as a potential threat to their traditional values. However, it is noteworthy that such skepticism is not exclusive to traditional Muslims. A prevailing sentiment of injustice pervades the Muslim world, fueled by perceptions of economic disparity and favoritism toward affluent nations. The skepticism toward globalization thus spans a spectrum of Muslim perspectives, reflecting diverse viewpoints within the Muslim community.[15]

A discernible trend within the Muslim world involves a burgeoning effort to bridge the cultural gap, leveraging the technological strides afforded by globalization to foster connections between Muslim nations and the Western sphere. This movement, emblematic of a conceptualization of Islam as a dynamic and adaptable religious milieu responsive to contemporary exigencies, may aptly be characterized as reformist. The reformist narrative posits

Islam as a living faith capable of harmonizing with evolving circumstances, affirming a conviction in the existence of numerous parallels between Islamic and Western civilizations. Advocates of this perspective contend that modern concepts such as democracy and civil liberties are not only compatible but also congruent with the foundational ethos of Islam. The instrumental role of globalization in facilitating this reformist outlook is evident in the seamless ease of travel, enabling Muslim reformists to traverse between their home countries and Western capitals effortlessly. Similarly, the instantaneous communication capabilities engendered by globalization serve as a catalyst for the formation of "virtual" communities. These manifestations underscore the intrinsic value that globalization, as a facilitative instrument, holds for Muslims navigating the intersection of tradition and modernity. Crucially, the concerns articulated by Muslim traditionalists do not escape the purview of Muslim reformers. The latter share apprehensions about the unabated surge of materialism and the concomitant erosion of moral norms, which appear to accompany the expansive reach of globalization. This perspective reflects a dynamic interplay between tradition and adaptation within the Muslim discourse, encapsulating the multifaceted responses of the Muslim community to the complexities engendered by globalization.[16]

Historical Patterns and Contemporary Global Sphere

In the insightful analyses put forth by some scholars, globalization is perceived not merely as a modern-day phenomenon but as having a lasting historical trajectory, reaching its peak in the current era marked by unprecedented acceleration. Simultaneously, an alternative perspective suggests globalization to be a relatively recent development intricately woven into the sociopolitical and economic ideals of the postmodern epoch. This dual perspective introduces a nuanced distinction, where the focal disparity lies not in the overarching understanding of globalization or its implications for the Muslim world but rather in the divergent interpretations of its historical roots.[17] To navigate this historical puzzle, these scholars assert that the complex mosaic of today's technological and civilizational landscapes results from cumulative outcomes of both harmonious and discordant encounters among civilizations predating the contemporary era. This historiographical perspective aims to contextualize the current manifestations of globalization within a comprehensive continuum shaped by the intricate interplay of diverse civilizations across time.[18]

The origins of these civilizations can be traced back to Ancient Greece when Alexander the Great (356–323 BC) attempted to expand his political influence over neighboring countries, endeavoring to impose the ideals of Hellenistic civilization upon the indigenous populations of the Mediterranean region. However, the territorial confines of these empires and civilizations were inherently precarious and susceptible to factors such as rebellions and coalitions. Owing to fragile alliances, the Romans, who established their civilization on the amalgamation of Greek and Christian traditions, eventually supplanted the Greeks. Consequently, they exerted dominance rather than governance, indicating a lack of standardized authority and control, both in terms of administration and warfare. The propagation of Roman ideals throughout the ancient world engendered discord between the Romans and their counterparts, particularly the Persians. This geopolitical confrontation between two formidable empires of the time—the Byzantine and the Persian—persisted until the emergence of Islam as a transformative political force in the seventh century.

Islam positions itself as a doctrinal paradigm transcending borders, offering guidance of universal relevance that resonates across racial spectra and addresses the entirety of the human race. This outlook, emblematic even in the embryonic phases of Islam's rise in Arabia, underscores the egalitarian principles within its teachings—advocating unity and equality among individuals, regardless of their diverse ethnic backgrounds, whether Arab, Persian, Ethiopian, Black, or white. The prophet accentuated the primacy of devotion and virtuous character, elevating them above superficial distinctions. As Islamic civilization burgeoned geographically, witnessing the rapid ascension of the Islamic state and the establishment of Islam as a global religious phenomenon, it entered a distinctive phase of "globalization," characterized by dynamic interactions and exchanges with other civilizations.[19] Within the confines of the Muslim world during this epoch, a fluid nexus of human knowledge and affiliations facilitated perpetual interactions among Muslims, engendering encounters with the cultural legacies of antecedent civilizations. This enabled them to metamorphose into a seminal wellspring of knowledge.[20] In the span between the seventh and thirteenth centuries, Muslim scholars exhibited a profound reverence for the intellectual legacy of their forebears. Exploiting this reservoir of knowledge, they orchestrated the establishment of an extraordinary civilization, nurturing a scientific, philosophical, and artistic culture intricately woven into the foundational tenets of Islam.

The task of constructing the foundation of this traditional Muslim civilization unfolded successively under the stewardship of the Arabs, followed by the Persians, culminating in the contributions of the Turks. By the thirteenth century, Africa and the Indian Subcontinent had emerged as pivotal loci of

Muslim civilization. Concurrently, in the Malay-Indonesian region, Muslim kingdoms took root and the influence of Chinese Muslims permeated various regions of China.[21] Historical narratives of Western civilization, reflective of early Islamic periods, often erroneously contend that mass conversions did not accompany the territorial conquests. However, scholars now recognize that the surge in conversions occurred later, as Islam gained ascendancy in the political sphere, fortified by its substantial material achievements and the allure of inclusive civic rights extended to all adherents of the faith. This revision challenges the Orientalist narrative asserting the forcible spread of Islam, emphasizing instead that conversions proliferated when Islam evolved into a comprehensive way of life, providing guidance for all Muslims.[22] George Bernard Shaw even foresaw the acceptability of "the faith of Muhammad" in the future Europe, a testament to the virtues of Muslim civilization and the harmonious interactions fostered by its forebearers.[23]

In the intricate fabric of history, Islamic civilization once exuded a resplendent global vitality; however, the echoes of its magnificence began to wane in the seventeenth century. This marked a pivotal juncture when the Ottoman caliphate embarked on a prolonged journey of territorial fragmentation spanning over two centuries. As the twentieth century unfolded, a new narrative emerged, demarcating the planet into distinct categories: the developed, the developing, and the less developed. Within this paradigm, the term "Third World" materialized, devoid of geographical confines, serving as a delineation for regions beyond the spheres of influence held by both Western powers and the enigmatic Soviet Union. The Muslim nations, assessed through the lens of their poverty, weakness, and perceived "backwardness," found themselves enveloped within the framework of the Third World. This political categorization marked the conclusion of Muslim globalization and paved the way for Anglo-Saxon globalization to rise to prominence.[24] Under the sway of this new phase of globalization, numerous facets of Islamic civilization commenced a process of disintegration. This transformation gained momentum when European imperial forces penetrated Muslim nations, assuming control over their natural resources, converting substantial segments of the local populace into wage laborers for foreign masters and substituting *sharī'ah* laws with secular ones to regulate the vertical relationships between colonizers and the governed, ostensibly to maintain peace and order.

In the unfolding narrative of this century's events, we can discern three distinctive chapters of Anglo-Saxon globalization. The initial chapter unfolded as European imperial powers expanded their dominion, colonizing Third World nations and imposing their political, cultural, and economic ideologies. This wave cascaded over the nineteenth and early twentieth centuries, leaving an enduring imprint. The second chapter surged forth during the icy grip of the Cold War, marked by a relentless tug-of-war between two superpowers, while nations such as Palestine, Korea, and Vietnam found themselves entangled in the crosshairs of geopolitical strife. As the Cold War's embers settled, the third chapter emerged with the fall of the Soviet Union, ushering in a seismic shift in the global political landscape. The mantle of authority now predominantly rests upon the United States, steering the course of the "New World Order," signifying a new era in the ongoing saga of Anglo-Saxon globalization.[25] This political transition marks the commencement of the third stage of Anglo-Saxon globalization, which has cleaved the globe into a "core" (United States) and a "periphery," empowering the former to imprint its ideals on the latter. Those who dare to dissent from its global strategy are labeled as members of the "axis of evil" or adversaries of civilization and democracy.[26] This perspective echoes the sentiments of several Muslim intellectuals who perceive the current iteration of Anglo-Saxon globalization as "neo-colonialism" or a process of Westernizing non-Western nations at the expense of their indigenous cultural traditions. To gain a comprehensive understanding of how younger Muslim generations perceive the overarching topic of globalization, we must closely examine three distinct groups.

Amid the milieu of Muslim intellectuals, a discernible subset emerges, consisting of individuals whose academic pursuits transpired within Western institutions, whether domiciled in their native lands or abroad. This group aligns with the first category, distinguished by an earnest enthrallment with Western civilization. At the crux of their conviction is the belief that by assimilating Western values and principles, they can play a pivotal role in the advancement of their "underdeveloped communities." Consequently, their initiatives are oriented toward the Westernization of their nations, spanning both structural facets of the state and normative aspects of society. The historical narrative of Kemal Ataturk stands as an illustrative exemplar, wherein he executed a sweeping agenda encompassing secularization, de-Islamization, and the cultural and political nationalization of post-Ottoman Turkey, epitomizing the ethos inherent to this intellectual paradigm.

The second faction within this discourse espouses the notion of an "inside" reformation of the Muslim community, displaying a lesser inclination toward governmental upheaval in their respective nations. Examples of this can be seen in the manifestos of *Jamā'at al-Tabligh* and the everyday conduct of leaders within certain Sufi orders.[27] Within the paradigm of Anglo-Saxon globalization, members of the third category are more amenable to embracing certain principles when they align with the goals of *sharī'ah* law.

This faction contends that such an approach enables the reconciliation of traditional Islamic institutions and beliefs with contemporary sociopolitical realities, paving the way for the resurgence of Islamic principles as the most efficacious catalyst for the development of Muslim communities. To achieve this goal, they have built a wide network of grassroots organizations covering politics, society, finance, education, and philanthropy. Simultaneously, they find themselves embroiled in overt confrontations and intense rivalries with the governing bodies of their nations. This struggle culminates in the formal recognition of their political presence as pressure organizations or opposition parties. In certain instances, a few among them have achieved triumph, securing control and instituting various Islamist regimes, as exemplified by the cases of Iran and Sudan. This work undertakes a comprehensive exploration of the responses of Muslim scholars to the prevailing Anglo-Saxon globalization, with a robust emphasis on delineating their distinctive position within this transformative landscape.[28] The ensuing analysis reveals the intricacy of categorizing all Islamic revivalist groups as rejectionist or reactionary toward Western civilization. Some among them manifest moderate, pragmatic dispositions, willing to engage with globalization as long as it preserves the fundamental tenets of their Islamic identity.

Intersections, Impacts, and Alternatives

Throughout history, Muslims have encountered a diverse array of challenges and obstacles. In various parts of the Muslim world, a profound and pervasive sense of desolation, despondency, and indignation has taken root, casting an extensive shadow. However, in contemporary times, the gravity of these challenges has surged exponentially due to a sequence of pivotal, transformative events, actions, and reactions. The prevailing scenario in numerous sectors of the Muslim world is characterized by an overwhelming dependence on foreign military technology, hardware, and weaponry. Additionally, there is a substantial reliance on the massive importation of products and services, coupled with a profound engagement with Western economic and educational institutions, along with their accompanying ideological paradigms.[29] This situation highlights a noticeable lack of a self-reliant attitude and cultural ethos, compounded by an unfortunate dearth of professionalism, entrepreneurship, inventiveness, and strategic long-term planning.

The challenges confronting the Muslim world have perpetually constituted a focal point of scholarly inquiry throughout history. However, recent years have borne witness to an unparalleled surge in scholarly endeavors dedicated to exploring alternative developmental paradigms and discourses across the realms of politics, economics, culture, and religion. Within contemporary Islamic thought, debates are predominantly centered around pivotal topics, with a notable emphasis on delineating how Muslims should adeptly navigate and respond to the multifaceted challenges of the present era, particularly those emanating from the forces of globalization. Furthermore, scholars are directing their attention toward the strategic construction of nations and communities, aligning these endeavors with preexisting knowledge paradigms.

As Muslims in the twenty-first century grapple with increasingly profound issues and challenges, a discernible acknowledgment has emerged regarding the imperative for innovative approaches that resonate harmoniously with their dynamically evolving environment and evolving needs. Despite the commendable efforts of Muslim scholars, duly recognized for their substantial contributions in comprehending the nuanced predicaments of Muslims and proffering solutions contextualized to specific temporal and spatial conditions, the challenges stemming from globalization within the Islamic world persist. These challenges, compounded by the pervasive affliction experienced by the Muslim community, confront hindrances embedded in diverse obstacles. Consequently, an unmistakable need manifests for an impartial, intellectually stimulating, and efficacious response. It is discerned that the Muslim world currently lacks the depth of thoughtful reflection and objective evaluation requisite for a comprehensive understanding of the prevailing global situation, its latent potentialities, and the impediments obstructing the realization of these opportunities.

Amid the complex responses to the challenges presented by globalization, the Muslim world exhibits a diverse range of attitudes. Some seem oblivious to the swiftly shifting global landscape, while others display complacency and self-righteousness, anchored in notions of righteousness. Hypersensitivity and defensiveness often emerge, creating protective barriers against perceived threats. Unfortunately, collective self-introspection remains elusive, with discord and division fracturing unity, impeding coordinated action amid turbulent currents. However, within this complex panorama, a stirring resurgence of Islamic consciousness unfolds. This resurgence is marked by the growth of local associations, the rise of transnational Islamic movements, and active Muslim participation in faith-based communal initiatives and transformative programs. In this complex scenario, the Muslim world adeptly navigates globalization's challenges, skillfully blending tradition and adaptation as it seeks new pathways toward a dynamic and sustainable future.

In the contemporary global milieu, the exploration of the Muslim perspective and the solutions proffered by Muslim scholars in the context of globalization stands as a salient and imperative research endeavor. This academic pursuit underscores several key areas, each instrumental in comprehending the multifaceted nature of globalization. Globalization, in its current trajectory, unfolds as a unique opportunity for Islam and the Muslim community to propagate the message of Islam in its authentic context. This prospect, however, hinges on the willingness of Muslims to engage in a critical evaluation of their current circumstances. The Muslim world finds itself in a rather dismal state, grappling with the challenge of reconciling traditional beliefs with the forces of modernity and progress, exacerbated by the absence of a centralized organizational structure or leadership. Beyond economic and developmental concerns, Muslims contend with apprehensions regarding health, education, and the cultural ramifications of globalization.

The pursuit of economic and political growth underpinned by Islamic principles poses a formidable challenge for individuals residing in both Muslim-majority and Muslim-minority nations. Navigating a middle path between capitalism and communism, especially in the face of international bodies and perceived Western dominance, introduces complexities. Despite these challenges, globalization has ushered in improved communication and access to information for many Muslim populations. The less privileged have experienced benefits through foreign aid in the realms of social and health sectors. However, for some, globalization represents the resurgence of historical specters, particularly in underdeveloped countries where memories of colonialism remain distressingly recent. Hence, Muslims necessitate a strategic approach grounded in adherence to and respect for global norms and ideals. A cautionary note is sounded against globalization propelled by hegemonic economic and political ambitions and a myopic, nationalistic worldview, which is perceived as inherently perilous for humanity. The potential for globalization to flourish and become a boon for mankind lies in its alignment with shared universal principles, coupled with a steadfast dedication to procedures and traditions fostering tolerance for diversity and the genuine acceptance of variation and differences.

In the contemporary phase of globalization, a conspicuous lacuna prevails—a void where a just and universally embraced legal, political, and economic framework should reside. The current state of global affairs unveils a misalignment within the world's legal, political, economic, and financial systems, deviating from the requisites essential for a robust, fair, and sustainable global trajectory. Of paramount significance to both the global community and individual nations is the imperative of good governance. To surmount this predicament, a paradigmatic shift becomes imperative, one that can give birth to viable resolution and infuse a renewed vision of harmony into the global order. This new paradigm, poised to underpin a healthy and equitable phase of globalization, fostering universal and shared wealth, must be constructed upon a foundation of principles. The principles encompass freedom, responsibility, individualism, competition, collaboration, compassion, efficiency, rule of law, accountability, and fairness. The inclusion of these prerequisites justifies a substantial paradigm shift away from the prevailing Western civilizational paradigm, recognized for its inherent bias, even in its partial reality. The West, often perceived as one-sided, places emphasis on freedom, individualism, profit pursuit, competition, liberalization, and power, neglecting the complementary coordinates of responsibility, solidarity, collaboration, accountability, justice, and compassion.

It is postulated that fundamentalist and sectarian groups have emerged in response to globalization, giving rise to persistent conflicts within the Muslim world. This ideological manifestation underscores the complex interplay between globalizing forces and the rise of identity-based movements within the Muslim milieu. A credible response to the challenges posed by globalization necessitates urgent attention from Muslim intellectuals. Their task involves addressing the intellectual vacuum through conceptualization and reconceptualization of key issues, extending beyond the confines of Muslim communities to encompass relevance for humanity at large. The endeavor entails the development of ethical and moral principles as an alternative to capitalism. Such endeavors underscore the pressing necessity for a systematic exploration of future solutions, avoiding haphazard approaches. The world stands in dire need of innovative and positive engagement in this regard. The proposal articulated in this book, outlining an Islamic paradigm on globalization, is poised to offer substantial insights into this critical and pressing topic.

The pivotal discourse concerning the future trajectory of Islam and the Muslim *ummah* in the contemporary era of globalization represents an evolving yet underutilized initiative. This discourse encompasses ongoing and substantial revival and reform endeavors within Muslim societies. An imperative task arises, prompting a meticulous exploration of alternative trajectories for Islam and the *ummah*, especially in the context of globalization. This involves a systematic examination of choices and responses, with the goal of devising models that address concerns related to the burgeoning anti-Islamic sentiment. These transformative changes introduce novel challenges and opportunities, necessitating a thorough investigation into how Islam and the *ummah* can navigate this shifting landscape. It becomes crucial to proactively handle these complexities to foster mutual respect and peaceful coexistence within the global community. This examination not only aims to comprehend the multifaceted implications of globalization on

Islamic societies but also strives to devise proactive strategies that contribute to the positive evolution of Islam in the contemporary global milieu.

A multitude of scholars and researchers hailing from diverse academic disciplines have collectively acknowledged the profound and far-reaching influence exerted by globalization on the contemporary world. Yet, there are still many unanswered questions about how the world has become more interconnected over time. In this work, we embark on a quest to fill the gaps within the theoretical literature, challenging the notion that globalization and the Islamic world are inherently at odds. Existing definitions of globalization, for the most part, suffer from ambiguity and inconsistency, or they simply employ the term as a convenient shorthand for more conventional concepts. Our work attempts to formulate a comprehensive conceptual framework for globalization, delving into the intricate realms of definition, causality, and effect.

This work asserts the harmonious coexistence of Islam with the principles of global engagement. We posit that the prevalent features of contemporary globalization, often reinforcing Western hegemony in politics, media, economics, and cultural values, deviate from the authentic essence of global interconnectedness. These imbalances endow powerful nations with the capability to dominate weaker economies and undermine their national capacities. By scrutinizing religious scriptures and cultural heritage, a stark reality emerges: Islam inherently possesses a global nature, persistently aspiring to transcend geographical boundaries throughout its historical trajectory. It consistently challenges the historical pattern of oppressive forces seeking control, a motif recurring across ages. We aim to demonstrate that Islam unequivocally aligns with the principles of authentic globalization, grounded in voluntary collaboration rather than the forceful imposition of Western ideals upon the Eastern world. Our research culminates in proposing recommendations to cultivate a balanced and equitable approach, upholding moral universal values while safeguarding cultural integrity and averting the dominance of one culture over another.

Islam delineates values rooted in social solidarity, reciprocity, and the advancement of human welfare.[30] It commands individuals to engage in collaborative efforts, promoting helpfulness with kindness and piety while discouraging egregious forms of assistance. This principle, vividly embraced at the local level by Prophet Muhammad PBUH, extends seamlessly to the global arena. Central to this ethos is the concept of the brotherhood of mankind, underscored by the acknowledgment of brotherhood among Muslims in the Qur'ān.[31] This global perspective envisages neighboring countries not merely in geographic proximity but rather as nations with regular political and economic ties to the Islamic world. Islam's acceptance and its influential role in the globalization process are further accentuated by the dissemination of Arabic. For centuries, Arabic served as a linguistic franca, facilitating significant advancements in mathematics, astronomy, and medicine. This linguistic legacy proved instrumental to European intellectuals during the Renaissance, marking a testament to the integrative power of Islamic societies that transcended political borders.

Some argue that globalization cannot be exclusively characterized as a Western phenomenon, given that the agents propelling globalization are not exclusively European or rooted solely in the Western sphere.[32] The scope of Westernization extends beyond politics and economics, encompassing a broader array of exports to the rest of the globe, including technology and languages disseminated across most regions. This challenges the notion of a unidirectional flow, where Westernization implies a one-way influence from the West. Instead, the process of globalization should be perceived as a mutual, albeit unequal, infiltration, with the West penetrating other regions and vice versa. Amartya Sen contends that Europe would have been considerably poorer had it not embraced the globalization of mathematics, science, and technology from the East.[33] This underscores the importance of distinguishing between the outcomes of Westernization and the contributions of globalization. The enduring impact of globalization, facilitated by world-spanning technologies like the internet, has introduced various elements such as neoliberal capitalism, imperialism, and disequilibrating social changes. These elements, despite their contested consequences, have played a role in transforming local marketplaces into significant consumer markets on a global scale, contributing to the enrichment of Western-based businesses eager to meet global consumer needs. Within the discourse surrounding Islam and globalization, numerous misguided assessments have given rise to fallacious interpretations concerning the role Islam plays in our interconnected world. These misjudgments not only disregard the historically fruitful contributions of Islam but also cast doubt on its potential for ongoing prosperity in the future. A stark and unfounded claim that Islam stands in opposition to modernization and globalization risks undermining the vast impact Islam has had on the global stage, posing a threat to the world's potential deprivation of its immeasurable contributions.

In the complex discourse surrounding Muslim responses to the challenges posed by globalization, this work aims to delve into the perspectives of Muslim scholars. It seeks to scrutinize how these scholars navigate and respond to the forces of globalization, endeavoring to find solutions that address local issues within specific regional, national, global, and local contexts. While existing scholarship has extensively explored the multifaceted dimensions of globalization, a critical examination of the viewpoints expressed by both Muslim and Western scholars becomes imperative. This inquiry is essential for determining whether the trajectory of globalization leans toward hegemonization or homogenization and whether these trends align with the inclusive ethos advocated by Islam.

This work grapples with pivotal questions that probe the role of Islam in the era of globalization, the potential impact of Muslims on the future of globalization, and the unique opportunities that globalization presents for both Muslims and Islam. It further explores whether Islamic fundamentalism can be construed as a reactionary response to the challenges posed by globalization. Additionally, the study attempts to unearth the alternatives or remedies for globalization that have been proposed by Muslim scholars. The thesis advanced in this work posits a profound disparity in perspectives between Muslim scholars and their Western counterparts within contemporary Islamic thought. This disparity extends beyond fundamental assumptions, encompassing the very direction and orientation of their viewpoints. Throughout the research, it is argued that the outcomes and consequences diverge significantly, challenging the attempt in the debate to draw parallels from selected thematic ideas articulated by Muslim scholars.

Organization of Chapters

This work is divided into two parts. Part I focuses on globalization–Islam debate, with a particular focus on challenging the prevailing notion that Islamic revivalism is merely a reactive response to the forces of globalization. The introductory chapter serves as the foundation, setting the stage for a nuanced exploration that encapsulates the dynamic interplay between Islam and globalization. Central to our endeavor is the recognition of the profound imperative of our contemporary era to bridge the intellectual void. This entails a genuine quest to conceptualize and re-conceptualize crucial themes that emerge in direct response to the complex challenges posed by the phenomenon of globalization. In the first chapter, we explore the discourse on globalization, tracing its roots back to ancient times when our early ancestors ventured across continents over a million years ago. While recognizing the limited scope of globalization in that prehistoric era, we discuss the lasting impact of Islam, reaching beyond the seventh and eighth centuries and shaping social, political, and economic interactions. Transitioning to economic and political dimensions, we explore the evolution from Keynesian to neoliberal principles governing governments and markets. The chapter navigates through theories suggesting a decline in the authority of nation-states. Shifting focus to culture, we examine the global impact of cultural industries before concluding with an exploration of local alternatives to the social, political, and cultural facets of globalization.

In chapter 2, a comprehensive exploration ensues into the complex relationship between globalization and Islam. This chapter delves into the foundational underpinnings of an Islamic paradigm regarding globalization. It argues that Islam inherently aligns with globalization, albeit diverging from the Western conceptualization and practice. Grounded in contextual analysis, the chapter sheds light on this discourse by drawing upon the Qur'ān and dissecting the multifaceted dimensions of this relationship. From the essence of *ummah* to institutional aspects and the *shuratic* viewpoint, each facet undergoes scholarly scrutiny. Chapter 3 explores the multifaceted relationship between Islam and the global landscape, spanning historical archaic globalization to contemporary global Islam. It examines Islam's pivotal role in early globalization, emphasizing the Umayyad dynasty's integration of Islamic principles. Transitioning to the Golden Age of the Muslims under the Abbasid dynasty, it highlights a commitment to knowledge and intellectual vibrancy. The exploration extends to contemporary global Islam, addressing cooperation and conflict dynamics in modern globalization and manifestations of Muslim universalism in the postcolonial era. It delves into postcolonial identity formation within the Islamic framework and the complexities of the global Muslim diaspora. The chapter scrutinizes the multifaceted relationship between Islam and global governance, exploring the roles of Muslim-majority states in international structures. It concludes by synthesizing these threads, emphasizing the enduring impact of Islamic principles on global dynamics, and prompting contemplation on Islam's evolving role in our interconnected world. Chapter 4 explores the nexus between globalization and Islamic revivalism. It uncovers why Islamic revivalism is happening, as people strive to change what they see as a problematic status quo that does not align with genuine Islamic traditions. Looking back at history, this chapter shows how fundamentalist groups have strongly influenced how people view Islam and Muslims, with lasting impacts on our collective understanding. By navigating through history, it untangles how these groups evolved, revealing the complex factors that have shaped our present situation.

Part II focuses on the thoughts of prominent Muslim thinkers—Ali Mazrui, Akbar S. Ahmad, Umar Chapra, and Ibrahim Abu Rabi. Through their insightful scholarship, these intellectuals unravel the impact of globalization on academia, society, and social movements. Exploring their ideas, we discover a shared understanding that globalization serves as a channel for expressing concerns, judgments, inquiries, and keen observations about the profound changes in our contemporary world. While diverse views exist on the exact nature of these shifts, Muslim intellectuals are steadfast in the belief that communities worldwide grapple with significant challenges of immense scale and geographic scope.

Chapter 5 delves into Ali Mazrui's perspective on globalization. Mazrui asserts that while the term "globalization" is relatively recent, the processes leading to global interdependence and interchange began centuries ago. He identifies religion, technology, the economy, and empire as the four main influences on globalization. Focusing on the homogenization thesis, which suggests increasing resemblance among nations, Mazrui acknowledges the rise in global similarity but also points to an undue concentration of power among a select few nations (hegemonization). The chapter argues that globalization, marked by increased interdependence and brisk commerce over long distances, diminishes the relevance of national boundaries, accelerates migration, and contributes to a smaller, more homogenous society globally. While Mazrui acknowledges the damaging effects of hegemonization and homogeneity on the Muslim world, he raises the question of whether Islam can benefit from homogeneity, suggesting that Islamic values need to become universal. Mazrui contends that countering Western hegemony requires more than the infiltration of Muslims and Islam into the Western culture; a substantial Muslim presence in the West may limit the homogenization of civilizations, fostering a clash of values, competing preferences, and converging opinions on the global stage.

Chapter 6 provides an insight into Akbar S. Ahmad's perspective on globalization. Ahmad observes a dichotomy among people's reactions to aspects of life in developing nations tied to globalization—simultaneously fascinated and repulsed. While some desire economic growth and local production, others may feel alienated and harbor negative perceptions due to exposure to diverse cultures through global media. The chapter contends that while globalization brings people together and offers benefits, it also divides societies, leading to conflict when individuals resist perceived external threats. In the age of globalization, the chapter highlights the dangerous notion of a perpetual Clash of Civilizations and discusses three Muslim reactions—modernists seeking harmony with Western modernity, literalists drawing limits around Islam in response to perceived attacks, and Sufi mystics advocating peace transcending borders. Ahmad argues that, post-9/11, the preference for literalists over mystics and modernists in the Muslim world reflects a belief in Islam being under attack by the West.

Chapter 7 outlines Umar Chapra's critique of globalization. Chapra contends that globalization should prioritize equitable prosperity for both developed and developing countries, stressing the need for social and political integration alongside economic aspects. He introduces a moral dimension to address unfair wealth distribution, aligning with Islamic economic theories that prioritize interconnected development. Chapra highlights the importance of *maqasid al-sharī'ah*, protecting religion, the soul, intellect, lineage, and human property. He advocates for applying Islamic economics to reduce wealth concentration and restructure financial conditions. Chapra acknowledges the promising focus on global development to combat poverty and unemployment but notes a decline in the worldwide saving rate. Contrary to the idea that unemployment solely results from this decline, he sees it as a significant factor. Chapra proposes a moral foundation to boost investment, create jobs, and reduce crime and conflict. He warns against overemphasizing self-interest without considering moral standards, advocating for the crucial role of morality in promoting societal and household harmony for effective governance and market functioning.

Chapter 8 presents Ibrahim Abu Rabi's critique of Western-dominated globalization, focusing on the state of contemporary Arab and Islamic thought. The chapter offers critical remarks on these perspectives and provides recommendations for navigating the intricate changes in politics, economics, science, and ethics brought about by globalization worldwide. It acknowledges that many proponents of globalization have not seriously considered the Islamic perspective on the economy and community, emphasizing the lack of in-depth examination from an Islamic standpoint. Abu Rabi notes a political backlash against Western modernity in many Muslim countries but highlights the longstanding need for a Muslim intellectual response to globalization's challenges. He suggests that the West, having a unique position to reflect on globalization, should assist the Muslim world in understanding the risks posed by neoliberalism and market forces. However, he criticizes intellectuals for not offering sufficient clarity on the subject, asserting that the entire Muslim world is impacted. Abu Rabi identifies a prevalent focus on issues related to identity, ancestry, and authenticity and argues for advancing beyond the conceptualizations of nineteenth-century Muslim intellectuals. He calls for a new Islamic way of thinking that responds imaginatively to critical philosophical and ethical reasoning, especially regarding the complex issue of globalization.

In this expansive view, a fervent quest emerges, seeking global solutions for localized predicaments and aiming to bridge the gap between the local and the global. The focus extends to various dimensions of globalization, covering social, cultural, and economic aspects. This involves the dynamic exchange of people, ideas, capital, information, and imagery, along with the dissemination of scientific knowledge and religious ideologies. As the investigation concludes, the work advocates for a balanced and nuanced (*wasatiyyah*) approach to understanding and acknowledging the intricate circumstances and potential consequences of globalization. Emphasizing the importance of moral universal values, the work suggests that culture should be guided by a robust ethical framework to prevent the undue dominance of one culture over another. Finally, it offers a set of crucial recommendations, paving the way for further exploration and implementation.

Notes

1. Sa'īd Arjomand, "Social Theory and the Changing World: Mass Democracy, Development, Modernization and Globalization," *International Sociology* 19 (2004): 321–353.

2. Z. Bauman, *Globalization: The Human Consequences* (Cambridge, MA: Polity, 1999), 2.

3. Catarina Kinnvall and Paul Nesbitt-Larking, *The Political Psychology of Globalization: Muslims in the West* (London: Oxford University Press, 2011), 3.

4. Kinvall and Nesbitt-Larking, *The Political Psychology*, 4.

5. Anthony Giddens, *The Consequences of Modernity* (Cambridge, MA: Polity Press, 1991), 64.

6. Ali A. Mazrui, "Globalization, Islam and the West: Between Homogenisation and Hegemonisation," *The American Journal of Islamic Social Sciences* 15, no. 2 (1998): 3–4.

7. Abu Sadat Nurullah, "Globalization as a Challenge to Islamic Cultural Identity," *The International Journal of Interdisciplinary Social Sciences* 3, no. 6 (2008): 46.

8. Mazrui, "Globalization, Islam and the West," 3–4.

9. Ibrahim M. Abu-Rabi', "Globalization: A Contemporary Islamic Response?," *The American Journal of Islamic Social Sciences* 15, no. 3 (1998): 15–43.

10. Khurshid Ahmad, "Globalization: Challenges and Prospects for Muslims," *Policy Perspectives* 3, no. 1 (2006): 1–11.

11. Al-Qur'ān, 10: 57: "O Mankind! There hath come to you a direction from your Lord and a healing for the (disease) in your hearts, and for those who believe, a guidance and a Mercy."

12. Al-Qur'ān, 6: 90: "Say: No reward for this do I ask of you: This is no less than a message for the nations.

13. Al-Qur'ān, 38: 87: "This is no less than a Message to (all) the worlds."

14. Al-Qur'ān, 7: 158: "Say: O men! I am sent unto you all."

15. Shahram Akbarzadeh, "The Globalization of Islam," in *An Introduction to International Relations: Australian Perspectives*, ed. Richard Devetak, Anthony Burke, and Jim George (CambridgeUK: Cambridge University Press, 2008), 308–309.

16. Akbarzadeh, "The Globalization," 310.
17. Hasan Hanafi and Sadiq Jalal al-Azm, *What is Globalization?* (Damascus: Dar al-Fikr, 2000), 17–23.
18. Abdullahy Y. Zalloum, *Painting Islam as the New Enemy: Globalization and Capitalism Crisis* (Kuala Lumpur: Crescent New, 2003), 107.
19. Qur'ān, 7:157; and 34:28. Dayf Shawqi, *The Universality of Islam* (trans. El-Affendi, Abdel wahb) (Rabat: ISESCO, 1998), 10.
20. Ismail R. Al-Faruqi and Lois Lamya al-Faruqi, *The Cultural Atlas of Islam* (New York: Macmillan, 1986), 23.
21. Al-Faruqi and al-Faruqi, *The Cultural Atlas*, 24.
22. Carlton J. H. Hayes, Marshall Whitehead Baldwin, and Charles Woolsey Cole, *History of Western Civilization* (New York: Macmillan, 1962), 140.
23. Fawaz A. Gerges, "Islam and Muslims in the Mind of America," *The Annals of the American Academy of Political and Social Science* 588 (2003): 73–89.
24. R. R. Palmer and Joel Colton, "The Advance of Democracy: Third French Republic, United Kingdom, German Empire," in *A History of the Modern World*, 3rd edition, ed. R. R. Palmer and Joel Colton (New York: Afred A. Knopf, 1978), 605–617.
25. Barry Buzan, "New Patterns of Global Security in the Twenty-first Century," *International Affairs* 67, no. 3 (1991): 431–451.
26. The phrase "axis of evil" was used by George W. Bush, when he was delivering his state of the Union Address on February 18, 2002.
27. Ahmad, S. Maqbool, "Madrasa System of Education and Indian Muslim Society," in *India and Contemporary Islam: Proceedings of a Seminar*, ed. S. T. Lokhandwalla (Shimla, India: Indian Institute of Advanced Study, 1971), 60–69.
28. Nasser Momayezi, "Islamic Revivalism and the Quest for Political Power," *The Journal of Conflict Studies* 17, no. 2 (1997). https://journals.lib.unb.ca/index.php/JCS/article/view/11753/12527. Abdul Rashid Moten, *Revolution to Revolution: Jamāt-e-Islami in the Politics of Pakistan* (Kuala Lumpur: Islamic Book Trust, 2002), 34; Abdel Wahab Affendi, *Turabi's Revolution: Islam and Power in the Sudan*, (London: Grey Seal, 1991), 13.
29. Ahmet Rumeli, "Moral and Material Values Versus Technological Development of the Muslim World," *Journal of Islamic Academy of Sciences* 4, no. 3 (1991): 181–183.
30. Al-Qur'ān, 5:2.
31. Masudul Alam Choudhury, "Financial Globalization and Islamic Financing Institutions: The Topic Revisited," *Islamic Economic Studies* 9, no. 1 (2001): 37.
32. Jonathan Xavier Inda and Renato Rosaldo, "Introduction," in *The Anthropology of Globalization, A Reader*, 2nd edition, ed. Jonathan Xavier Inda and Renato Rosaldo (Maiden, MA: Blackwell, 2008), 24.
33. Amartya Sen, "How to Judge Globalism," *The American Prospect*, January 5, 2002. Accessed April 12, 2024. https://prospect.org/features/judge-globalism/.

PART I

GLOBALIZATION AND ISLAM
DYNAMICS, PARADOXES, AND ALTERNATIVES

CHAPTER 1

∼

Revisiting Globalization
Definitions, Discourses, and Domains

Introduction

For myriad reasons, a considerable number of discussions pertaining to globalization remain ensnared within historical disagreements surrounding fundamental premises encompassing its definition, orientation, scope, chronology, and multidisciplinary framework. In the realm of definition, scholars, academics, and writers have recurrently sought to conceptualize globalization within diverse theoretical frameworks, thereby engaging in contentious debates from the very beginning. Varied perspectives on the scale of globalization have been posited, spanning from staunch ultra-skeptics, who adamantly refute any form of globalization, to certain observers asserting, from the opposite spectrum, that we presently inhabit a thoroughly globalized milieu. From a chronological point of view, disparate historical accounts trace the roots of globalization to antiquity, while others employ sweeping characterizations, attributing its origins to the recent past few decades. In terms of an explanatory framework, analysts have delineated significantly disparate social, economic, and political dynamics inherent in globalization. Some analysts have forged connections between globalization and nearly every purported contemporary social transformation, advancing arguments about the emergence of an information society, the political marginalization of the nation-state, the waning influence of traditional cultures, and the onset of a postmodern era.[1]

Viewed through a normative lens, some scholars have linked globalization with notions of peace, prosperity, and advancement. Conversely, for others, the globalized landscape has precipitated significant consequences, including deprivation, disasters, and heightened income inequality. Given the expansive and varied body of literature on globalization, coupled with its continuously increasing prominence in both political and academic spheres, it is reasonable to anticipate its diffusion into diverse and distinct disciplinary discourses.[2] The fundamental discussions on globalization within the realm of religion, encompassing both a general perspective and a specific focus on Islam, center around four key dimensions: deterritorialization, spatial considerations, homogenization, responses to globalization, and the phenomenon of Islamic revivalism. These scholarly conversations aim to probe the complex relationship between transnational religious phenomena and territorial boundaries. They systematically assess the impact of Westernization on indigenous religions, particularly Islam, and examine the diversification of religious practices in a global context. Furthermore, these studies delve into the ways in which globalization prompts religious reactions and poses challenges to established nation-states.[3] Each of the aforementioned themes will be comprehensively examined in subsequent chapters. However, prior to delving into detailed discussions, this chapter will undertake an exploration of the historical trajectory of globalization. Subsequently, it will elucidate how globalization, conceived as a conceptual tool, has exerted influence across diverse domains of human existence, encompassing the social, economic, political, and cultural spheres. In an effort to introduce clarity amid the analytical disarray stemming from various interpretations or appropriations of globalization, the initial step involves addressing a foundational matter—the precise definition of the object of study: globalization.

Definitions

Despite attempts to systematically delineate an analytical framework for globalization, it is crucial to acknowledge that, in its mundane and commonplace usage, globalization stands as a fundamentally contested concept. A plethora of diverse works purporting to engage with the discourse surrounding globalization attests to the absence of a universally accepted definition, with some opting to concentrate on specific dimensions, designating them as pivotal concepts. For instance, a politically oriented definition accentuates the waning influence of the nation-state and the traditional circumscriptions that constituted the fundamental unit of analysis in the realms of modern politics, international relations, and sociology.[4] In contrast, economically centered definitions pinpoint capitalism and a free-market economy as the principal driving forces propelling the globalization process. Globalization is commonly construed as a legal façade or ideological construct—a constellation of convictions that selectively distorts reality to advance particular interests. Within this contextual framework, Schirato and Webb characterize globalization as a "discursive regime," portraying it as a mechanistic entity that voraciously assimilates anything and anyone in its trajectory, thereby encapsulating a formidable ideological apparatus with transformative potential.[5]

They assert that globalization operates as a set of texts, ideas, objectives, values, perspectives, and prohibitions—an unquestionable paradigm for appraising practices that is imbued and influenced by the interests of those who wield access to it.[6] Moreover, globalization is envisaged as a material reality in the present-day world. This reality is occasionally perceived to be singularly dominated by a specific aspect, as illustrated in the ensuing definition from *The Social Sciences Encyclopaedia*, wherein the economic dimension takes precedence in the conceptualization of globalization:

> The development of the world economy has a long history, dating from at least the sixteenth century, and is associated with the economic and imperial expansionism of the great powers. By globalization we refer to a more advanced stage of this process of development.[7]

Ali Mazrui portrays globalization as a convergence of complex processes propelling the world toward intensified interdependence and the expeditious exchange of goods and ideas across expansive spatial dimensions. Despite the contemporary coinage of the term "globalization," Mazrui posits that the foundational mechanisms facilitating global interdependence and exchange have been operative for centuries. Within this paradigm, he discerns four elemental forces serving as primary engines propelling globalization: religion, technology, economy, and empire.[8] In an alternative paradigm, proponents advocate for a more expansive conceptualization—one that encapsulates the broader flow of ideas, effecting a transformative reconfiguration of political institutions and cultural values. Chandra Muzaffar encapsulates this nuanced perspective:

> Globalization ... is a process by which capital, goods, and services and sometimes labour cross national borders and acquire a transnational character. It is often accompanied by the flow of related tastes, ideas and even values across boundaries thus helping to reshape local political institutions, social relationships and cultural patterns. It is a process, it is argued, which will lead inevitably to a single global system and global unity.[9]

In Ibrahim Abu Rabi's conceptualization, "globalization is not a new phenomenon; it emerged with the triumph of laissez-faire capitalism in the post-Industrial Revolution era and the expansion of European imperialism." He contends that European imperialism engendered profound structural, economic, cultural, and religious transformations in the Third World, fostering heightened interaction between the North and the South.[10] Conversely, for Akbar S. Ahmad and Hastings Donnan, globalization pertains to "the rapid developments in communication technology, transport, and information which bring the remotest parts of the world within easy reach."[11] Zygmaunt Baumann characterizes globalization as a manifestation of time–space compression, encompassing communication, transport, and the acceleration of production. Roland Robertson defines it as "the crystallization of the entire world as a single place."[12] The divergent labels employed in these definitions potentially invite confusion and may lead to circular definitions lacking explanatory depth. To establish meaningful analytical distinctions between causes and effects, a relatively open and expansive conceptualization of globalization appears more suitable. Michael Mann's definition aligns with this approach, defining globalization as the expansion of social relations across the globe.[13] This resonates with David Held's and Anthony McGrew's perspective, framing globalization as the augmentation of world connectivity, or succinctly put:

> globalization denotes the expanding scale, growing magnitude, speeding up and deepening impact of interregional flows and patterns of social interaction. It refers to a shift or transformation in the scale of human organization that links distant communities and expands the reach of power relations across the world's major regions and continents.[14]

Having delineated certain fundamental attributes of globalization, it seems fitting to proffer the ensuing conceptualization:

> Globalization refers to a multidimensional set of social processes that create, multiply, stretch, and intensify worldwide social interdependencies and exchanges while at the same time fostering in people a growing awareness of deepening connections between the local and the distant.[15]

This definition encapsulates globalization within the framework of four fundamental concepts: the augmentation of social relations, intensification of flows, heightened interpenetration, and the establishment of global infrastructures. Although we have now attempted to present an adequate definition of globalization by focusing on some of the common insights provided by different scholars, we must not lose sight of the fact that there still remain many areas of contestation.

Globalization: Conflicting Views and Evolving Paradigms

Given the inherently uneven nature of globalization, commentators have elucidated the foundational social processes, driving it in various, often conflicting, ways. Scholars not only harbor divergent perspectives on multiple definitions of globalization but also exhibit discordance regarding its causation, consequences, policy implications, scale, and historical trajectory. A notable point of academic contention revolves around the scale of globalization, specifically whether it is a singular or differentiated process.[16] Even among scholars who assert that globalization is a unified process, disagreements persist regarding which process constitutes the essence of this phenomenon. Some emphasize economic processes, while others accord priority to political, social, cultural, and environmental dimensions. Consequently, scholars engaged in discussions on globalization are categorized into three overarching groups: globalists, skeptics, and transformationalists. Rooted in three broad waves of analysis, this tripartite classification serves as a foundational framework for comprehending the general contours of scholarly perspectives on globalization, acknowledging its fluidity rather than imposing a rigid structure that encapsulates all intellectual viewpoints seamlessly.[17]

Globalists

Globalists perceive the advent of globalization as a transformative phase in history, characterized by the diminishing authority of nation-states, largely driven by the denationalized dynamics inherent in global markets. This perspective, often leaning toward economic analysis, acknowledges that the economic shifts associated with globalization have far-reaching cultural and political consequences. From the globalist viewpoint, the traditional role of nation-states is considered to be overshadowed by the ascendancy of global institutions like the United Nations (UN) and the International Monetary Fund (IMF), as well as by transnational social movements that adopt a global orientation. In the analysis of globalization by globalists, a spectrum of perspectives emerges, encompassing both optimism and pessimism. Optimists contend that the forces of globalization contribute to the advancement of democracy, foster increased mutual understanding among nations, and elevate living standards on a global scale. On the other hand, pessimistic globalists argue that globalization tends to serve specific political and economic interests, leading to the propagation of cultural homogeneity, instances of violence, widespread dislocation, and exacerbated global economic disparities. This dualistic interpretation within the globalist framework reflects the diverse and complex nature of the ongoing global transformation.[18]

Skeptics

Skeptics of globalization view it primarily as an ideological construct, a plausible myth that serves to justify and legitimize the neoliberal global project. This project involves the establishment of a global free market and the consolidation of Anglo-American capitalism within major economic regions worldwide. According to Held and McGrew, skeptics see globalization as a "necessary myth" that state authorities use to discipline their populations to participate in the global marketplace.[19] The widespread dissemination of globalization discourse aligns with the timing of the neoliberal project's consolidation, marked by deregulation, free markets, structural adjustment programs, and limited state intervention. This shift gained prominence within key Western countries and international institutions like the IMF.[20] It is noteworthy that the skepticism toward globalization is not limited to Western scholars; many prominent Muslim scholars and intellectuals, including Ali Mazrui, Ibrahim Abu Rabi, 'Abd Allah Balqaziz, Husayn Ma'lum, Naguib Mahfuz (Nobel Laureate), 'Abd al-Wahhab al-Masiri, and Dr. Salim al Awwa, share a similar perspective. This reflects a commonality in critical views on globalization among scholars from diverse cultural and intellectual backgrounds.[21]

Transformationalists

Transformationalists introduce a more nuanced and complex perspective on globalization, contending that it transcends a simple escalation in intensity. According to this view, globalization is not merely an economic phenomenon but a process with profound structural consequences, reshaping political, social, and economic landscapes. In contrast to the binary outlook of globalists and skeptics, transformationalists assert that globalization instigates a re-articulation of cultural, economic, and political power dynamics. A pivotal concept in the transformationalist paradigm is the "reconfiguration of political power." This concept defies easy categorization as either globalist or skeptic, embodying the transformationalist stance that globalization is not a one-dimensional process of either convergence or divergence. Instead, it is portrayed as a dialectical force, capable of both integration and division, resulting in the emergence of both beneficiaries and marginalized entities.

A distinguishing feature of the transformationalist perspective is its recognition of the multidisciplinary nature of globalization. It extends beyond the economic realm to encompass political and cultural dimensions. Scholars within this framework often dissect the globalization process into distinct categories such as political, cultural, and economic globalization. Within this multifaceted approach, discussions on the role of religion frequently unfold within the context of cultural globalization, highlighting its profound impact on the global cultural tapestry.[22] In summary, transformationalists offer a comprehensive understanding of globalization, emphasizing its transformative nature and complex interplay across various societal dimensions. This perspective urges a departure from a narrow focus on economic aspects, encouraging the recognition of the broader and interconnected implications of globalization on diverse facets of human societies.

Globalization through the Ages: From Ancient Trade Routes to Modern Networks

Although the term "globalization" gained widespread usage in academic and popular literature in the late 1980s and early 1990s, the roots of the forces propelling this trend can be traced back to prehistoric times. The complexity of globalization and the multitude of its dimensions necessitate scholarly analyses that acknowledge the inevitable disjunctions arising from the vast characterizations of this phenomenon. While many perceive globalization as a recent development, particularly emerging after the collapse of the Soviet Union, some scholars challenge this viewpoint as an example of intellectual short-termism. An alternative perspective suggests that numerous features of contemporary globalization were already in motion during the latter half of the nineteenth century. Manfred Streger offers a valuable framework for understanding globalization, dividing it into four distinct phases. The first phase, prehistoric globalization, encompasses the period from 10000 BCE to 3500 BCE. This is succeeded by the premodern period, spanning approximately from 3500 BCE to 1500 CE. The subsequent phase is the early modern period (1500–1750), followed by the modern phase (1750–1970). Each phase represents a distinctive stage in the evolution of globalization, highlighting the continuity and transformation of this complex process throughout human history.[23]

The initial phase commenced around 10000 BCE when small groups of gatherers and hunters reached the southern tip of South America, marking the culmination of a lengthy process initiated by hominid African human ancestors over a million years ago. Although some major islands in the Atlantic and Pacific remained uninhabited until recent times, the global dispersion of human species was ultimately realized. During this era, most migrating groups initially covered relatively short distances from their original locations, with long-distance movements evolving over time due to population shifts.[24] Evidence suggests that some Native Americans rapidly traversed the Pacific Coast, originating from the Siberia–Alaska route and the American northwest, utilizing coastal routes to reach various parts of South America. While this migration brought diverse groups of people to various places, there was no substantial return, resulting in limited regional interaction patterns beyond encounters between natives and migrants on the spot. In contrast, trade emerged as a transformative force over considerable distances, fostering interactions for the exchange of assets or profit. The exact origins of trade are not entirely clear, but according to some sources, seashells from the Indian Ocean reached Syria around 5000 BCE, possibly indicating gift exchanges of ornamentation and suggesting movement across the Middle East. However, it remains uncertain whether this represented a consistent form of interaction or if the shells gradually moved from one area to another.[25] This phenomenon intensified during the second phase of globalization, marked by the escalation of interregional trade facilitated by primitive shipping across the Persian Gulf region by at least 4000 BCE. In the words of Peter Stearns:

> Several of the early river valley civilizations developed inter-regional trade. Mesopotamia, at the mouths of the Tigris and Euphrates rivers, exchanged with Harappan society in northwestern India (today Pakistan). Not only goods, but artistic symbols were part of this exchange, and there may have been cross-fertilization in religious ideas as well. Egypt began to launch shipping in the Red Sea by 2500 BCE, reaching the Arabian Peninsula (present-day Yemen) and also farther down the Indian Ocean coast of Africa. Egyptians received gold, ivory and slaves from Ethiopia, in exchange for manufactured goods. Trade with the Middle East emphasized spices, some of which had been shipped over from India. Here was an example of somewhat longer-distance trade that did not however involve direct connections; that is, it operated in shorter inter-regional hops rather than direct contact, in this case between Egypt and India. Several centers in the Persian Gulf, notably a center called Dilmun (present-day Bahrain), also served as transmission hubs for goods, such as precious stones, produced elsewhere. By the 2nd millennium BCE, a trading ship in the Mediterranean might carry goods from sub-Saharan Africa and northern Europe, as well as the Middle East or India, showing the range of contacts that sustained a lively commerce.[26]

Early intercivilizational interactions played a crucial role in shaping a prototypical global orientation within various premodern contexts. A case in point is the genesis of ancient Greek society, which emerged from a complex amalgamation of Indo-European, Phoenician, Egyptian, and Aegean influences. The second century CE marked the onset of sustained interactions among diverse populations spanning Eurasia, from China to Spain, facilitated by the renowned Silk Road extending from China to Turkey. This extensive network of contacts significantly contributed to the expansion of trade and commerce, extending its reach along the east coast of Africa. According to Scholte, premodern indications of globalization manifested in diverse activities. Notably, a series of "dollars of the Middle Ages" served as currencies across the Mediterranean world. This sequence included the Byzantine solidus from the fifth to seventh centuries, the Muslim dinar in conjunction with the solidus from the eighth to the middle of the thirteenth century, and the fiorino of Florence during the subsequent 150 years.[27] These monetary transitions exemplify the multifaceted nature of premodern globalization, encompassing economic, cultural, and geopolitical dimensions.

During the seventh and eighth centuries, Arab engagement in Indian Ocean trade assumed a distinctive significance, marked by the extensive utilization of diverse trade routes and an elevated intensity and scope of commodity exchange. Arabs strategically founded trading settlements along the African coast, fostering an intricate network of connections that entailed the active participation of both merchants and local elites. This complex interplay culminated in the emergence of a unique linguistic and cultural milieu, exemplified by the development of Swahili as a language for this transnational trading community, elucidating the cultural dimensions intricately intertwined with the consolidation of more stabilized commercial exchanges. Moreover, the advent of Islam, the prevailing religion among Arab traders, served as a profound religious linkage within this commercial paradigm. Islamic tenets, which underscored the value of commerce and merchant endeavors, played a central role in shaping the ethos of this trading network. Prophet Muhammad PBUH, himself a trader, extolled the intrinsic value and gratification associated with a merchant's life, ranking it second only to religious pursuits. While debates among Islamic scholars ensued regarding the ethical implications of commercial activities, expressing concerns about the integrity of endeavors aimed at improving economic conditions, Islam exhibited an unparalleled tolerance toward the merchant vocation compared to other religions, including Confucianism in China. This historical context underscores the complex interplay between religion, commerce, and cultural evolution during this pivotal period of Indian Ocean trade.

Within the framework of Islam, the stature of honest merchants was often elevated to a level akin to prophets and martyrs. The confluence of trading activities and profit generation was deemed congruent with religious values, provided that certain ethical and moral obligations were diligently adhered to. These included the principled rejection of interest-based loans, coupled with the faithful fulfillment of other religious obligations, notably prayers and charitable endeavors. Remarkably, merchant capital not only augmented the capacity for charitable initiatives but also served as a means to undertake the sacred pilgrimage to Mecca, thereby accentuating its religious merit. Moreover, the expansion of interregional trade facilitated missionary activity, intertwining economic and religious motivations within the broader Islamic ethos. The propagation of Islam and the Arabic language concurrently promoted various trading assets. This engendered a notable pattern, wherein the economic sphere not only facilitated the conversion to Islam but also catalyzed the expansion of the Islamic faith. This phenomenon extended not only along the African coast but also across portions of the Indian Subcontinent and other regions of Asia. Consequently, this facilitated the establishment of robust commercial relations between Arab traders and their local merchant counterparts who shared the same religious affiliations.[28] This complex interplay between economic interests and religious dynamics underscores the multifaceted nature of Islamic influence in the realm of interregional trade.

Travel and trade emerged as integral components of Arab culture, gaining prominence in the centuries preceding 1000 CE. Scholars posit that the expansion of Islam, underpinned by a fundamental belief in the unity of the Muslim community across geographical boundaries, constituted an early example of a global community. The Muslim community, known as the *ummah*, lacked a defined political boundary but embraced all believers, fostering genuine Islamic ties across Asia. Shared commitment to fundamental Islamic beliefs, coupled with a common religious identity, formed robust bonds within the Muslim world, particularly within the boundaries of the Arab caliphate. While recognizing that the *dar al-Islam* (the Muslim world) did not encompass the entire Afro-Eurasian expanse, Muslims identified an abode of war, *dar al-harb*, outside Islamic jurisdiction, often referring to non-Islamic lands such as Europe and East Asia. Despite this, the sense of a common identity forged vital links for Muslims and provided a broader context for extensive exchanges.[29] This concise elucidation underscores that the notion of global integration did not emerge solely in recent centuries. According to Wallerstein, starting from the sixteenth century, the pursuit of endless wealth accumulation fueled a necessity for continuous technological exchange and a perpetual expansion of frontiers—geographical, psychological, intellectual, and scientific.[30] For an extended period, hegemonic powers, such as the Dutch, the British, and America, dominated the interstate system. They established the rules of the geopolitical game, wielded political influence with minimal use of power (despite its substantial strength), and articulated the prevailing cultural paradigm through which the world was understood. The early modern period (1500–1750) witnessed European expansion and voyages by the Spanish and Portuguese to Africa, Asia, and the Americas. These navigations facilitated exchanges of diverse products, including ivory, sugar, pepper, silver, and gold, as well as the transmission of slaves, diseases, and ideas.[31]

During this time period, Europe played a pivotal role in propelling the forces of globalization, with its social practices serving as primary accelerators of this transformative process. While Europe had made modest contributions to scientific and technological advancements, its immense gains were derived from the diffusion and adaptation of technological innovations originating in the cultural spheres of Islam and China. Despite the diminishing political influence of China and the Fertile Crescent (Islam), European powers encountered challenges in penetrating the interior regions of Africa and Asia, prompting a redirection of their efforts westward in pursuit of new, lucrative voyages to India. In the early 1600s, corporations such as the Dutch and British East India Companies were established with the explicit objective of establishing trade posts abroad. As these entities expanded their operational scope, they acquired the capacity to govern a substantial portion of intercontinental economic transactions. In the process, they implemented social and cultural practices that laid the groundwork for later colonial powers to assert direct political control over these regions. The year 1648 marked the emergence of nation-states within the Westphalian state system, and as the modern period neared its conclusion, interdependencies among nations intensified, precipitating political and military transformations.[32] In the subsequent modern period (1750–1970), Europe and its descendants assumed a self-assigned role as custodians of universal law and morality on a global scale. This period witnessed a consolidation of European influence, marked by a pervasive impact on legal and ethical frameworks that shaped the trajectory of international relations.

The persistent claims of civilizational ascendancy by European powers coexisted with a remarkable disregard for the entrenched racial beliefs and pervasive inequalities that permeated both Western and Eastern societies. This lack of awareness persisted despite their proclamations of superiority. The elevation of Western capitalist institutions was propelled by a continual influx of materials and resources from diverse global sources. This economic transformation prompted influential entrepreneurs and their allies to disseminate a philosophy centered on individualism and self-interest, extolling an idealized capitalist system ostensibly grounded in the concealed mechanisms of the open market and its imperceptible hand. Under the guidance of multinational financial institutions, capital traversed borders with notable fluidity, facilitated by the sterling-based gold standard that enabled the global circulation of currencies like the British pound and the Dutch guilder. The imposition of colonial rule across various regions in the Global South became a strategic imperative for securing independent resource bases. However, the rise of Europe and the subsequent establishment of global interconnections would have been inconceivable without the parallel explosion of science and technology. This scientific and technological surge played an instrumental role in shaping the trajectory of global development, underpinning the complex web of interdependencies that characterized the evolving landscape of the modern world. Certainly, the rise of nascent industrial powers mandated the acquisition of innovative power sources, prominently exemplified by the imperative reliance on oil and electricity. However, the unregulated exploitation of these resources bore deleterious consequences, manifesting in the eradication of numerous plant and animal species and the widespread contamination of entire regions. Concurrently, the modern era unfolded amid a backdrop of heightened political fragmentation, juxtaposed with a revival of global flows and exchanges. This multifaceted historical landscape delineates intricate patterns of sociopolitical and economic transformations. As noted by Manfred Streger:

> The defeat of the axis powers in 1945 and the process of decolonization slowly revived global flows and international exchanges. A new political order of nation-states anchored in the charter of the UN raised the prospect of global democratic governance. During the 1950s, however, such cosmopolitan hopes quickly faded as the Cold War divided the world for four long decades into two antagonistic spheres: a liberal capitalist camp dominated by the United States, and an authoritarian-socialist realm controlled by the Soviet Union. For the first time in human history, the spectre of a global conflict capable of destroying virtually all life on our planet had been raised.[33]

When contemplating the contemporary phase of globalization, it becomes imperative to bring together the protracted historical trajectory of globalization with a more discerning perspective highlighting substantial transformations in global interconnections witnessed over recent decades. Various attempts have been made to encapsulate this change, spanning from assertions that this phase has ushered in novel patterns of mobility and fluidity, to an emphasis on the network society and globalization as emergent forms of modernity. Amid these contentions, the usage of the term "postcolonial" introduces a nuanced perspective that does not readily align with broader discourses in a linear fashion. The emphasis on the postcolonial paradigm assumes significant relevance when examining the East–West relationship dynamics. However, it faces a pivotal objection concerning the resurgence of imperialism in recent times. Huntington's concept of the "Clash of Civilizations" between the West and the emerging Islamo-Confucian bloc casts doubt on whether the United States has forsaken imperial aspirations characteristic of European agendas in the early nineteenth century. Instead, there is a discernible revival of the notion of a hegemonic system or political configuration, portraying a negative trend necessitating a coalition against hegemony. This quasi-imperialist nexus is instrumentalized by the American government and its allies, purportedly to combat terrorism, often irrespective of global bodies' or the European Union (EU)'s endorsement.[34] Another dimension of contemporary globalization is the notion of a global civil society, a term whose precise delineation remains elusive but has gained prominence as a conceptual framework for contemplating social and political processes operating beyond top-down state initiatives and market-based dealings. It encompasses a spectrum of international institutions such as Amnesty International and Friends of the Earth, along with intricate networks extending from politically motivated individuals to various spheres encompassing religion, music, multicultural societies, and migration patterns. Some perceive these activities as an alternative counterforce to contemporary globalization or as agents propelling globalization from grassroots levels.[35] Given the multifaceted nature of globalization comprising diverse and simultaneous processes operating across multiple levels, it becomes imperative to see these interactions and exchanges as constituent elements of an intricate mosaic characterized by overlapping processes and actions. Thus, employing analytical distinctions becomes necessary to contextualize the complex web of global exchanges and interdependencies. The next sections will delve into identifying, assessing, and evaluating the patterns of globalization in economic, cultural, and political domains, considering its operation as an integrated whole.

Beyond One Globalization: Understanding Plural Perspectives

A fundamental tension pervades the ongoing discourse on globalization, revealing a dialectic between proponents of capitalism who perceive it as an unstoppable force and adversaries envisioning new avenues for extending transnational capitalism through advancements in information and communication technology. The ostensibly linear and immutable characterization of globalization is increasingly unveiled as an oversimplified narrative, incapable of adequately encapsulating the complex and multifaceted nature of the global system. This simplistic portrayal serves a limited ideological agenda, overlooking the nuanced details of the world's intricate social and economic milieu. The inherent inconsistencies and conflicts in these perspectives underscore that the term "globalization" encompasses a diverse array of unique processes, some inherently at odds with one another. In essence, what is colloquially termed "globalization" is a convergence of different social interactions giving rise to interconnected phenomena, warranting the recognition that "globalization" should be conceived in plural terms.[36] The historical narrative of globalization is often articulated by the winners, further perpetuating their perspective in public discourse.

As an interdisciplinary concept, globalization spans a multitude of dimensions, including economic, political, technological, cultural, and environmental factors. Despite the absence of a universally agreed-upon framework to comprehensively encapsulate its intricacies, an exploration of these foundational dimensions provides valuable insights into the diverse facets of globalization. Delving into the economic, political, social, and cultural dimensions facilitates a comprehensive understanding of the profound changes and challenges characterizing our increasingly globalized world. Recognizing the interconnected yet distinctive characteristics and dynamics within each dimension is crucial, as globalization continues to shape our world. A critical analysis of the complexities, opportunities, and challenges within the economic, political, technological, cultural, and environmental dimensions is imperative for navigating the intricate terrain of globalization and working toward a more inclusive, sustainable, and equitable global future.

Economic Globalization: Impacts, Controversies, and Alternative Movements

Within the vast literature on globalization, economic globalization emerges as the most scrutinized, discussed, and contentious issue, exerting a profound impact on the dynamics of culture, politics, and the burgeoning alternative globalization movement. In this discourse, the contemporary phase of globalization is seen as a historical trajectory wherein the economic sphere attains autonomy and exerts substantial influence over other realms, such as culture, politics, and society. The roots of contemporary economic globalization can be traced back to the formulation of a new international economic order, a watershed moment following World War II, orchestrated during a seminal conference held at Bretton Woods. Confronting the currency instability prevalent in the interwar period, the architects of Bretton Woods devised a gold exchange standard. Under this framework, the value of each country's currency was linked to gold and the U.S. dollar assumed the pivotal role of a key currency. The dollar, theoretically redeemable in gold at a fixed rate of $35 per ounce, instituted a system of steadfast exchange rates between nations, effectively countering the competitive devaluations that marked the interwar era.[37]

However, with the acceleration of the global financial system compounded by the oil crisis of the early 1970s and the declining position of America ushered in a period of volatility in the relationship between the dollar and gold, the pivotal shift occurred when the United States, confronted with its first balance of trade deficit in 1971, made the decision to remove the convertibility between the dollar and gold. This strategic move marked a departure from fixed exchange rates, with currency values becoming contingent upon market forces, thereby heralding a new era. Concurrently, this time period witnessed a gradual upswing in capital flows. The historic Bretton Woods conference, beyond its immediate post-World War II imperatives, not only addressed the exigencies of the time but also laid the groundwork for an enduring international economic order. This act facilitated the establishment of two institutions—the International Bank for Reconstruction and Development, later known as the World Bank, and the IIMF. Conceived as integral components of a tripartite structure for global economic institutions, these institutions were entrusted with the formulation of a comprehensive framework for postwar reconstruction and enduring prosperity.[38]

The IMF, initially designed to regulate monetary exchanges and extend short-term loans to countries grappling with balance-of-payments challenges, underwent a transformative evolution over subsequent years. Critics contend that, particularly since the tumultuous 1980s, the IMF's focus shifted toward scrutinizing the economic development of nations and offering loans contingent upon the adoption of structural adjustment programs.[39] This evolution, according to detractors, signified a departure from the institution's original mandate. The subsequent years were marked by global economic instability, characterized by high inflation, sluggish economic growth, elevated unemployment rates, and an energy crisis stemming from the Organization of the Petroleum Exporting Countries (OPEC)'s considerable control over a substantial portion of the world's oil supply. This tumultuous period witnessed a shift in political dynamics, with conservative political factions championing a neoliberal approach to both economic and social policies, thereby eclipsing the dominance of political forces in the East aligned with the paradigm of controlled capitalism. The collapse of the Soviet Union further bolstered the legitimacy of the neoliberal economic approach. Since then, pivotal developments in financial globalization have revolved around the internationalization of trade and finance, the rise of transnational corporations (TNCs), and the global influence wielded by institutions such as the IMF, the World Bank, and the World Trade Organization (WTO).

The intertwining of global financial integration with the principles of free trade has yielded advantages for nations, yet persistent concerns linger about the equitable distribution of these gains. Numerous studies underscore widening income disparities resulting from the liberalization of trade and finance. Critics attribute some of the most detrimental consequences of globalization to the neoliberal policies embraced by influential institutions like the IMF, the World Bank, and the WTO. These institutions adhere to the "Washington Consensus," a neoliberal economic paradigm originating from policies implemented in Latin America during the late 1980s. This neoliberal perspective, often criticized for exacerbating income inequality, underscores the complex interplay between financial globalization, free trade, and the policy orientations of influential international institutions. The principles encapsulated in the "Washington Consensus" encompass enforcing fiscal responsibility and managing budget deficits, reducing public spending (especially in the military and public administration), and implementing comprehensive and well-enforced tax reform. In addition, it advocates liberalizing finances with market-determined interest rates, fostering competitive exchange rates for export-oriented growth, eliminating import licensing, and reducing tariffs for trade liberalization. Furthermore, the "Washington Consensus" promotes foreign direct investment, enhancing efficiency and performance through the privatization of state enterprises, while also easing regulatory controls on the economy and safeguarding property rights.[40] These principles form the bedrock of neoliberal economic policies and have sparked extensive debate and critique within the discourse on globalization.

The nomenclature "Washington Consensus" for this program is not coincidental, as the United States has been the predominant force within the IMF and the World Bank from the outset. Despite the intentions behind loans granted by these institutions, a considerable portion has either lined the pockets of authoritarian leaders or advanced local organizations and the Northern corporations they typically serve. In terms of the global distribution of wealth, scholars highlight the striking disparity, noting that the West, representing only 22 percent of the world's population, consumes 70 percent of total global resources. They emphasize the escalating wealth disparities between the "haves" and "have-nots." In 1960, the gap between the top 20 percent and the bottom 20 percent was thirty times, reaching ninety times by 2000. Chandra Muzaffar underscores the alarming statistic that the total income of the world's richest individual surpasses that of the entire sub-Saharan Africa, and the combined income of the three wealthiest individuals exceeds that of forty-eight of the world's poorest countries. Simultaneously, half of humanity struggles to survive on $2 a day and one-fifth remains illiterate without access to basic healthcare or modern sanitation. The grim reality persists, with approximately 10 million children succumbing annually to preventable diseases like cholera, typhoid, and polio.[41]

Former Malaysian prime minister Mahathir Mohammad asserts that globalization primarily revolves around opening up existing markets and maximizing profits. He goes further, identifying a conspiratorial element propelling financial globalization:

> It is clear that the developed countries wish to use the [World Trade Organization] to impose conditions on the developing countries which will result, not in improving human rights or labour practices or greater care for the environment, but in stunting their growth and consequently the suffering for their people . . . Already, the developed West has shown they are not interested in these matters in themselves, but are interested in these only in those countries which pose a threat to the West. If these countries are absolutely poor and producing nothing that constitutes a threat to the developed countries of the West, the plight of their people in terms of human rights or labor practices or environment matter not at all. But if these countries are competing with the West in any way then their records are scrutinized and threats issued. The net effect is to prevent the development of these countries and their emergence as newly industrializing economies.[42]

Mahathir expounds on the impending inundation of small business enterprises in the East due to financial globalization. He predicts that economic globalization will lead to the deterioration of small companies based in developing countries, as large TNCs from the global North assert dominance. Manufacturing, telecommunications, trading enterprises, and banks will amalgamate and be operated by financially robust companies from the developed world. Consequently, small enterprises in developing countries will be absorbed and eventually cease to exist.[43] Examining the D-8 members—Bangladesh, India, Malaysia, Egypt, Iran, Indonesia, Pakistan, Nigeria, and Turkey—Mahathir notes that despite their combined population representing almost 17 percent of the world's population, they only hold a 4 percent share in world trade. The formation of this group was, in part, a reaction to economic globalization.

Political Globalization: Redefining Power and Governance in a Changing World

The term "political globalization" encompasses the acceleration and expansion of political interactions on a global scale. This phenomenon not only influences the contours of state sovereignty and the roles of intergovernmental organizations but also prompts a reevaluation of political structures beyond the traditional nation-state framework, challenging the established conceptual paradigms. Throughout history, human societies have delineated political differences based on territorial boundaries, fostering a sense of identity tied to specific geographical regions. This division of the global social space into domestic and foreign realms has cultivated exclusive identities, creating a dichotomy of "us" versus "them." This artificial division has provided the psychological and cultural underpinnings of the modern nation-system, instilling a sense of security and historical continuity while demanding unwavering national allegiance. In the context of contemporary globalization, these territorial boundaries are being gradually weakened, transcending conceptual limits and blurring religious lines of demarcation.

In the discourse surrounding political globalization, a prevalent assertion is that it leads to the marginalization of the nation-state, encapsulated in notions like a progressing "borderless world" and a "hollow state." The emergence of global finance and TNCs, the cultural fragmentation of national populations, the emergence of effective governance entities at transnational and local levels, citizens' detachment from politics, and the rise of civil society are all considered factors eroding the power or authority of the state. Globalists argue that since the late 1960s, there has been a fundamental "deterritorialization" of politics, governance, and rule.[44] However, skeptics challenge these assertions, emphasizing the enduring relevance of the nation-state as the political container of modern society. While acknowledging the evolution of regional spheres as new forms of territorialization, skeptics reject the idea of the demise of the nation-state in a post-statist or regionalized world. Chris Delanty and Chris Rumford argue against the notion of a zero-sum position, where states vanish due to the internationalization of markets or are replaced by global governance structures. They posit that states persist as robust actors but in a more complex form that they do not fully control.[45]

For proponents of globalization, the realm of political authority and governance is undergoing a transformative shift from a predominantly national order to an increasingly global or transnational order. According to this perspective, global politics is no longer primarily centered around states and traditional conceptual distinctions between local and international, and territorial and non-territorial, are losing relevance, gaining intellectual traction both at the national and transnational or global levels. Ulrick Beck articulates this shift by asserting that national spaces are experiencing a process of denationalization, rendering the national no longer strictly national, just as the global is no longer strictly global.[46] This suggests a simultaneous erosion of the power foundations of nation-states from both internal and external forces. Supporting this viewpoint, several factors can be considered: nationalism faces challenges from global allegiances based on diverse factors; states increasingly find themselves beholden to the authority of powerful and mobile capital interests, particularly in the face of significant deficits; sub-state actors seek greater autonomy, bypassing state authority; regionalization, exemplified by entities like North American Free Trade Agreement and the EU, and global governance through institutions like the UN or the WTO, is on the ascent; and new actors within global civil society have emerged.[47]

To synthesize the foregoing discussion, the argument for the diminishing influence of the nation-state seems compelling, though it is important to note that this does not imply the state is simply becoming a nostalgic fiction.[48] Nor does it signify a simple collapse of the state in response to the rise of TNCs and the growing prominence of global financial markets. Critics emphasize a transformative trend in the reconstitution of power and governance, rather than the state's outright demise in the face of capitalist growth. Castells contends that the contemporary landscape involves a continual sharing of sovereignty in regulating significant issues such as security, environment, and finance. He envisions states as nodes within a broader power framework.[49] In this perspective, political power undergoes repositioning, recontextualization, and partial transformation due to the rise of other groups or power systems, with state power being just one crucial attribute of power.[50] Scholars propose the emergence of a new paradigm of global governance as states grapple with regulating the flow of ideas and commodities amid the expansion of global processes and international treaties and organizations consolidate their operations. The result is the unfolding of transnational politics, where nation-state power is redefined, intricately woven into global processes and flows. Abu Rabi' contends that these transnational developments have significantly influenced the advanced center, which champions the democratic ideal expected to foster genuine democracy in the South. However, the era of globalization has given rise to a novel association between political actors and economic forces, particularly multinational corporations. In the Muslim world, this shift has translated into enhanced repressive powers for the tribal, quasi-constitutional state, typically dominated by the same family or clan.[51]

Cultural Globalization: The Power Dynamics of Global Flows

Cultural globalization signifies the intensification and extension of cultural interactions on a global scale. Culture, being a broad concept, involves the symbolic construction, articulation, and dissemination of meaning, gaining particular significance within the context of globalization. The complex network of cultural interconnectedness in recent decades has led scholars to assert that cultural patterns play a central role in the contemporary processes of globalization. It is noteworthy that cultural globalization did not originate solely with the global diffusion of consumer culture. As previously mentioned, civilizational interactions have a long historical trajectory. Nonetheless, the cultural transformations witnessed in the contemporary period surpass those of earlier phases. Fueled by the internet and various communication channels, the dominant systems of meaning in our age—such as consumerism, individualism, and critical discourses related to religious and secular lifestyles—spread more freely and extensively than ever before. In the premodern era, cultural globalization primarily revolved around transnational religions like Buddhism, Christianity, and Islam. In contrast, the modern era, marked by the intense diffusion of capitalism, democracy, and industrialization, has seen cultural globalization manifest through the dissemination of secular ideological narratives such as liberalism, nationalism, and socialism, along with the proliferation of values and practices associated with the modern scientific method. In the present era, cultural globalization is prominently characterized by the increasing influence of cultural products, the growing dominance of cultural corporations, the seemingly pervasive nature of Western culture, and the resultant impact on identity stemming from these various sources. Consequently, the contemporary phenomenon of globalization is interpreted through the concept of deterritorialization, signifying the diminishing natural connection of culture to territorial and social contexts.[52] Scholars in this field navigate a broad thematic landscape, and the questions they pose have captured the attention of numerous observers, analysts, and researchers across diverse academic disciplines. Discussions surrounding the idea of global culture often focus on the omnipresence of American popular culture and scrutinize its implications for local cultures and other communities.

Opinions have coalesced into two distinct assumptions concerning cultural globalization: one posits it as the transformation of worldwide diversity into a globalized Western culture, akin to a pervasive global pandemic culture; the other conceptualizes cultural globalization as a process of hybridization, involving continuous cultural exchanges and adaptations that result in the perpetual reformulation and rejuvenation of cultural forms. The former places a predominant emphasis on the global aspect, asserting that cultural globalization entails the intermixing of various cultures to the extent that the relevance of distinct cultural entities becomes obsolete. In contrast, the latter perspective accentuates the local dimension, portraying cultural globalization as a process of "maturation" that leads to the continual evolution of cultural expressions.[53] Furthermore, a prominent characteristic of contemporary globalization is the dissemination of deleterious ideas and practices, contributing to the erosion and obliteration of diverse cultures. In this context, a form of cultural imperialism emerges as a conspicuous feature of the contemporary phase of globalization. This cultural imperialism, as articulated by Mackay, manifests through the flow of cultural goods to diverse regions, predominantly inculcating U.S. or Western values in the recipient nations. This initial cultural influence, according to Mackay, serves as a preparatory phase for the subsequent importation of additional Western goods, exemplifying the intricate entwining of cultural and economic dimensions within the globalized cultural landscape.[54]

The concept of cultural imperialism finds expression in terms such as "Disneyfication," "Coca-colonization," and "Westoxification," encapsulating the idea that cultural influence is not evenly distributed but predominantly wielded by the West, particularly the United States. The anticipated outcome of extensive global cultural exchanges is posited as cultural homogenization, signifying a worldwide standardization of modus vivendi.[55] This homogenization is often regarded with lament, reflecting a convergence toward what Benjamin Barber terms "McWorld," a phenomenon he envisions as emerging triumphantly. Barber contends that a soulless consumer capitalism embodied by McWorld is rapidly transforming global populations into a uniformly bland market. In this paradigm, the primary function of social organization becomes profit-making, with the individual elevated primarily to the status of a consumer. Barber's analysis of cultural globalization also acknowledges the significant recognition that the imperialistic tendencies of McWorld elicit political and cultural reactions in the form of *"Jihād"*—an opposing force that vehemently rejects the homogenizing influences of the West wherever they manifest. The cultural struggle between *Jihād* and McWorld, as described by Barber, unfolds as a bitter contest for political allegiance.

Importantly, both forces stand opposed to participatory forms of democracy, as they are inclined to attack civil liberties, thereby undermining the potential for the widespread dissemination of democratic values.[56]

In his seminal work, Samuel P. Huntington argued that following the end of the Cold War, the trajectory of international politics underwent a notable transition away from its Western-centric phase. A pivotal shift occurred, with the primary focus redirected toward the interaction dynamics between the Western world and non-Western civilizations, as well as among non-Western civilizations themselves.[57] Huntington expanded the scope of his argument into a sweeping characterization of culture, contending that all distinctions among civilizations find their determinants in the overarching concept of "culture." This thesis, however, proved contentious on multiple fronts. From an academic perspective, Huntington's demarcation of the world into contentious civilizational blocs was critiqued as an inaccurate portrayal of global cultural phenomena. The intricacies of Huntington's terminology, particularly the use of "civilization" and "culture," necessitated the substantiation of his thesis through the presentation of supporting facts, aligning with his assumption of cultural complexities. Despite the inherent ambiguity in his usage of the term "civilization," his deployment of "culture" rested on an assumption of cultural homogeneity. Notwithstandingly, Huntington achieved the notable feat of rejecting prevalent notions of both hybridization and homogenization. Instead, he advocated for a paradigm of civilizational conflict, a stance characterized by its political dogmatism, intellectual absurdity, and empirical indefensibility. According to Nederveen Pieterse, the conspicuous amalgamation of security interests with a rudimentary portrayal of civilizational difference distinguishes Huntington's position, rendering it demagogic in nature.[58]

Appadurai delves into the contemporary dynamics of global interactions, framing the central challenge as the interplay between cultural homogenization and heterogenization.[59] While a prevailing view among globalization scholars leans toward an increasing trend of heterogenization, the widespread diffusion of American consumer culture and fast-food restaurants suggests a simultaneous rise in homogenization. In essence, both perspectives can coexist, signifying a nuanced reality where certain dimensions of lifestyles experience heightened homogenization, while others witness greater heterogenization. This dual trajectory aligns with Giddens' characterization of globalization as the intensification of global social relations, intricately connecting distant localities and shaping local events through events occurring miles away.[60] Within Robertson's ideal-typical conception of the global human condition, there emerges a recognition that cultural uniformity and the shared commonality of mankind can be accorded equal importance.[61] This sentiment finds resonance in Friedman's assertion that ethnic and cultural fragmentations, coupled with modernist homogenization, represent foundational trends in global reality.[62] This acknowledgment underscores the intricate interplay of forces influencing the evolving landscape of global interactions.

In addition to the homogenizing and hegemonizing tendencies associated with cultural globalization, certain commentators present an alternative perspective, linking globalization to the emergence of novel forms of cultural expression. Within this discourse, Robertson posits that global cultural flows possess the capacity to rejuvenate local cultural practices. He contends that the impact of cultural globalization on local contexts is not tantamount to cultural homogenization, advocating instead for the concept of "glocalization." This concept encapsulates the complex and reciprocal relationship between the global and the local, acknowledging the dynamic interplay between the two spheres.[63] While Robertson's assertion that local cultures persist in the face of global processes holds merit, observable phenomena, such as the proliferation of fast-food restaurants and the ubiquitous use of credit cards, underscore the profound homogenizing effects that these processes exert on local cultures. This discussion thus affirms that the contemporary phase of globalization does not entail the dominance of any singular civilizational metanarrative but rather its dispersion. The global culture, in this context, assumes a chaotic character—integrated and interconnected, yet lacking coherence or centralization. The flows of resources, encompassing material, ideologies, and people, traverse the globe, interconnecting all components of this intricate cultural landscape.

As per Featherstone, the interplay of global flows contributes to shaping a distinct configuration for globalized culture. Primarily, these flows establish connections among previously independent and culturally homogeneous niches, compelling each to undergo a process of relativization in relation to others. Secondly, they foster the emergence of transnational cultures that transcend the confines of nation-state boundaries, exhibiting characteristics that may be novel or syncretic.[64] The accelerated pace of these flows corresponds to an intensified manifestation of globalization. In alignment with Harvey's perspective, the recent decades signify another phase in the continual annihilation of space through time—a phenomenon inherent to the dynamic nature of capitalism. Harvey argues that advancements in satellite communication, resulting in reduced costs relative to distance, along with diminished international freight rates and the global dissemination of images through television, have effectively transformed the world into a unified field where capitalism operates. This has caused economic flows to become increasingly attuned to specific spatial locations.[65]

Malcolm Waters interprets globalization as a direct consequence of "the expansion of European culture across the planet via settlement, colonization, and cultural mimesis. It is bound up intrinsically with the pattern of capitalist development as it has ramified through political and cultural arenas".[66] Consequently, every religious or social group is compelled to relativize itself, consolidate its position, harness its intellectual potential, and establish relevance in relation to the West. However, the impact of cultural globalization in the Muslim world is resulting in a form of cultural hybridization, leading to the diminishing relevance of Islamic culture. This phenomenon poses a significant challenge to the preservation and revitalization of local cultures, with the cultural influences of globalization permeating throughout the Muslim world. In the current context, Islamic culture finds itself in conflict with two distinct cultures: one is the modern popular culture disseminated through media outlets and the other is Western culture, particularly the American variant, driven by modernization, which introduces certain alien values into Islam.

Through its dominant cultural forms, cultural globalization serves to advance a society free from religious influences, ultimately diminishing the role of Islam and eroding Islamic cultural values. This trend is facilitated by global industries that supersede traditional methods of cultural creation and dissemination, giving rise to a transnational civilization that fosters the convergence of consumer tastes and preferences. Rooted in the American–Western cultural experience, these industries are primarily driven by the pursuit of greater wealth. Consequently, global culture assumes a hegemonic character, exerting dominance worldwide and assimilating diverse populations, with Muslims being no exception.[67] Chandra Muzaffar emphasizes the detrimental effects of cultural globalization, asserting that it goes beyond mere homogenization of cultural diversity. He contends that globalization is culpable for propagating a superficial American culture that tantalizes the senses but dulls the spirit. This culture, centered around television singers and movie stars, is characterized by a momentary absorption that discourages reflection and contemplation. Muzaffar draws a distinction between contemporary globalized entertainment culture and the music and plays of earlier religious civilizations, which often sought to elevate the moral consciousness of the community.[68]

Glocal Dynamics: Power, Meaning, and Identity in a Connected World

In accordance with the dictionary's definition, the terms "glocal" and glocalization" signify the amalgamation of global and local aspects. Glocalization is defined as the "creation of products or services designed for the global market, yet customized to align with local cultures."[69] Taking a holistic perspective on globalization, the notion of "locality" or the "local" emerges as a byproduct of global processes. It is rare to find cultures that exist in isolation or remain unaffected by global dynamics. Robertson did not perceive globalization as a contemporary phenomenon, nor did he attribute it solely to modernization. The globalization of business operations and the concept of a global strategy surfaced in the early 1980s. Levitt is often acknowledged as the first to discern the inclination toward globalization.[70] He asserts that companies must adeptly function as though the world were a unified market, disregarding superficial regional and national distinctions. Furthermore, he contends that companies failing to adjust to the emerging global realities will succumb to those that do.

In their analysis, Jeannet and Hennessey assert that the pursuit of a global strategy and the globalization of business activities encounter numerous impediments.[71] These challenges encompass market characteristics, industrial conditions, marketing institutions, and legal restrictions. Robertson's conceptualization of globalization in the twentieth century emphasizes the "interpenetration of the universalization of particularization and the particularization of universalism."[72] Expanding on Robertson's framework, Khondker advocates for a perspective that sees globalization or glocalization as an interdependent process. This involves addressing the dual processes of macro-localization and micro-globalization, tackling the simultaneous globalization of the local and the localization of globality.[73] The concept of a society governed by the mechanism of free and voluntary trade, achieving economic integration on a global scale, did not emerge solely from our relatively brief experience of globalization, much of which transpired in the 1990s. Instead, this notion traces its roots back to classical economic thought. Effective economic integration, grounded in the market, was already well underway a century ago, only to experience a significant setback.[74] The history of economic integration in large regions, built on diverse foundations and punctuated by periods of deglobalization, provides further evidence that this cycle is indeed possible.

While globalization primarily influences economic integrations, it also poses challenges for numerous cultures globally, stemming from the conflict between human relationships and the excessive exploitation of resources, as well as the maximization of competitiveness in liberalized markets.[75] As noted before, one perspective is encapsulated in the "clash of cultures" viewpoint, articulated in terms of the Clash of Civilizations. The second perspective finds its most apt expression in the concept of the "McDonaldization" of the world. This viewpoint implies a homogenized world, dominated by a singular culture that eradicates distinctions among local cultures. The third perspective is that of "hybridization" (or synthesis). Much of the cultural evolution in human history involves exchanges, diffusion, and cross-breeding, where adaptation to local needs was commonplace.[76]

Thus, a product can be designated as internationalized when its development is geared toward meeting the diverse needs of a global community without specific tailoring to a particular region. The process of tailoring to a specific region is termed "localization."[77] Glocalization, a term formed by amalgamating globalization and localization, has emerged as the predominant standard for augmenting the positive facets of global interaction. This encompasses various elements such as textual translations, localized marketing communication, sociopolitical considerations, and more. The approach of glocalization adheres to a structured process, incorporating local customer considerations right from the inception into market offerings through collaborative bottom-up efforts. This all-encompassing strategy involves the research and integration of cultural, linguistic, political, religious, and ethnic affiliations, resulting in a cohesive and holistic solution. This ensures active participation of the intended market throughout the entire process, not merely at the final outcome.[78] However, what is fundamentally needed are globally applicable concepts that facilitate the examination of processes of social transformation intricately connected with global changes.

Globalization is characterized by transnational and transregional processes that exert influence over numerous local communities. Scholars in area studies may have overlooked the significance of global forces due to a misinterpretation of the geographical distribution of cultural areas. The concept of macro-localization involves expanding the boundaries of locality and globalizing specific local ideas, practices, and institutions. Examples of macro-localization can be found in the emergence of global religious or ethnic revivalist movements. Conversely, micro-globalization entails integrating certain global processes into the local context. This is evident in social movements like feminism or ecology, as well as the adoption of new production techniques and marketing strategies originating in a local setting but spreading far beyond to encompass a broader spatial and historical dimension. Industries such as print or computers, initially localized, have evolved into global phenomena. Overcoming spatial limitations defines globalization. From this standpoint, globalization aligns with the concept of glocalization. However, glocalization is fundamentally transforming this reality, allowing individuals to depart and return home while maintaining the familial and national ties that have traditionally defined them.

The glocalization thesis has been broadened to present a more comprehensive view of globalization, influenced by increasing research across diverse disciplines.[79] According to Khondker, glocalization can be regarded as an advanced form of globalization, encapsulating the following principles: Diversity is intrinsic to social life, and not all distinctions are eliminated. History and culture operate independently, shaping unique experiences for various groups, be they cultures, societies, or nations. This perspective on glocalization alleviates concerns that globalization acts as a sweeping force erasing all distinctions.[80] Over time, Robertson has embraced the perspective that sees globalization as inherently self-limiting.[81] This viewpoint aligns with Turner's "enclave society" thesis, suggesting that globalization does not lead to global integration but, instead, results in the fragmentation and establishment of various enclaves. These enclaves isolate a neighborhood, suburb, or other units from their immediate surroundings while connecting them to distant places.[82] Consequently, globalization entails not only the creation of new units for integration but also the systematic fragmentation of existing units. It involves the formation of new units and groups behind new barriers that restrict communication and movement. In essence, globalization brings about a multitude of fragmentation, making it, in effect, a form of glocalization.

At its essence, this interpretation views "globalization as glocalization." Glocalization and globalization are analytically merged, or, to phrase it differently, glocalization is encompassed within globalization. This formulation enables Robertson to maintain a cohesive theme throughout his body of work spanning several decades, avoiding the need for explicit breaks. This transition has not gone unnoticed; Ritzer observes that "Robertson and White imply that glocalization is globalization" and that precisely encapsulates the idea.[83] By blurring the conceptual boundary between the two, Robertson can sustain continuity without undergoing a major overhaul. However, this approach proves to be immensely challenging. Robertson's body of work has developed in tandem with, and to some extent in response to, the world polity or world society perspective formulated by sociologist John W. Meyer and his collaborators at Stanford since the 1970s. Initially centered on notable commonalities in international discourses, this perspective has expanded to encompass a diverse range of topics, from human rights to environmentalism.

While variations exist in specific details, these commonalities represent widely shared assumptions that serve as universal templates, fostering uniformity among nations. Thorough empirical research has illustrated the top-down process through which global models and discourses permeate into nation-states, particularly those with robust international organizational ties. This uniformity across societies, or isomorphism, is explained as adherence to prevailing, legitimate perspectives.

Cultural frameworks, which encompass traditional ideas about governance, organizations, science, or education, function as guiding templates defining what is considered normal or appropriate for nation-states, organizations, or institutions. These frameworks extend globally, contributing to the widespread dissemination of ideas and policy models. The world society perspective emphasizes the historical development of international organizations and structures that institutionalize these cultural frameworks. The uniformity observed in these frameworks is credited to institutional isomorphism, the propelling force behind the establishment of contemporary global culture.[84] Lechner and Boli posit that, despite inherent tensions and contradictions, this cultural influence saturates various aspects of social life, ranging from law, organizations, religion, and national identity, to even anti-globalization movements. Advocates of the world society theory argue that globalization results in the standardization of culture.[85]

Robertson introduces a significant departure from the core principles of the neo-institutional perspective by proposing that globalization not only unifies but also generates differences. This idea is closely associated with the introduction of glocalization into the vocabulary of social science. The concept of globalization brings forth the challenge of global social integration, reviving the age-old inquiry into whether societies exhibit convergence or divergence in their developmental trajectories. However, if globalization is inherently self-limiting, it becomes inherently incomplete, thereby implicitly questioning the assertions of the world society perspective. However, the extensive evidence presented in world society scholarship strongly supports the reality of institutional isomorphism. This leads to a complex problem, one that only arises when accepting the thesis that globalization is synonymous with glocalization. The intricacy is swiftly unraveled by embracing the notion of glocalization's analytical autonomy.

George Ritzer's examination of "grobalization" and Victor Roudometof's effort to map power dynamics within the glocal sphere by evaluating their "capacity to initiate or resist waves of globalization" affirm the enduring importance of power in glocalization theory.[86] However, there is a need for a more targeted and comprehensive approach to the convergence of glocalization and power, potentially exploring connections with other influential factors in the glocal context. An evident example is the concept of global consciousness, deeply embedded in Robertson's conceptualization of globalization/glocalization. Expanding on previous research in this domain, there is a necessity to shed light on the various ways in which shifts in collective consciousness can impact the glocalization process.[87] Another aspect connected to the cultural realm involves the prioritization of certain glocal formations based on perceived similarities between global and local cultures, as if certain global concepts were somehow "preconceived" in local cultures.[88] In simpler terms, glocalization is always the outcome of translation processes. These translations are, at best, imperfect and frequently lead to actual misunderstandings or cultural betrayals. These processes are ingrained in cultural dynamics, and the immediate global dimension facilitated by contemporary media only accentuates them: both the comparison and dialogue with other cultures, as well as those within a particular lifeworld, give rise to networks of synonyms and homonyms, equivalences without identity or identity without equivalence.[89]

Consider the multitude of diverse flags that contribute to the translocal recognition of state-national identity, forming a global formula for the creation and recognition of the local.[90] On a contrasting note, envision the same flag being utilized by different actors in varying discursive realms and practices, so diverse that it fragments into numerous objects brimming with local, incomparable significance. In doing so, it presents its identity as an avenue for global misunderstanding. Alternatively, contemplate a more foundational example, the body, hailed as the quintessential glocal matrix: consistently subjected to discourses and rituals that position, define, and categorize it—deemed "the most local of globalized sites"—yet perpetually involved in tangible forms of envisioning communities, worlds, and universes—recognized as the most global of the localized sites.[91]

Just like turning an object in a prism, we should consistently examine the items in our possession. This practice allows us to recognize that we are constantly encountering glocal interconnections marked by both similarities and differences. These interconnections facilitate the circulation and sharing of meaning, yet simultaneously result in dispersion, confusion, and distortion—and vice versa. This introduces us to a paradoxical mechanism compelling individuals to undergo a double transformation through contact with otherness: absorbing figures or structures while using the same contact to reaffirm their distinctiveness in the process. The history of cultural relations consistently provides instances where cultures, despite appearing homogenized in practice, differ significantly in self-perception. Conversely, we can unearth instances of cultures perceiving their daily lives through the lens of repetition, imitation, or commonality with other cultures, regardless of temporal or spatial remoteness. These phenomena, described as specters of comparison, dynamic amalgamations of practical and ideological identities, and diverse layers of forms of existence and belief, become crucial considerations, especially when analyzing contemporary politics, which is often fragmented by the very posts and tweets that initiate and propagate forms of global contagion of ideas and trends.[92]

Determining when and to what degree these processes of generating locality, entailing an incessant and diverse global repositioning, occur intentionally or unintentionally—whether in a strategic or tactical manner, in the terms of de Certeau (1980)—poses a complex challenge approached through various perspectives.[93] However, if translation serves as both the starting and concluding point for glocalism, it becomes valuable to identify the translation operators—whether human or nonhuman, in the form of discourses or rituals—that execute it. Additionally, it proves beneficial to delineate the translation networks—whether horizontal or vertical, or explosive or implosive—that, throughout history or within unrestrained contingencies, disrupt and reconstruct the hierarchies of meaning shaping the fabric of everyday life. Comprehending glocality within the realm of daily existence thus necessitates the ability to perceive this intricate structural narrative.[94]

A narrative comprised of amalgamations—akin to hybridizations and creolizations, potentially already assimilated—along with intersections and connections—akin to the evolving forms of dialogism—and compositions and embeddings—encompassing the implicit dimensions of dominance, whether more or less consensual or contested, inherent in every isomorphism.[95] It is crucial to reiterate that within these structures operates the meta-structure of self-description, involving the selection of differences (more or less imaginary) aiming to synthesize the dynamic plurality constituting each collective and guide the collective's identifications and conflicts.

If we earnestly consider the interconnected essence of the global–local binary, scrutinizing this mechanism should transcend a mere focus on the inherent qualities of specific ideas coursing through global currents. Instead, it necessitates acknowledging the interactive character of glocalization and its repercussions in terms of power, meaning, and self-definition for diverse participants. Undertaking a thorough analysis of these and other potential facets of glocalization and their interplay is undeniably an ambitious undertaking, likely requiring a multidisciplinary approach and the collaboration of scholars spanning various domains and global regions. Nevertheless, at this juncture in the discourse, such an endeavor would undoubtedly fortify and deepen glocalization theory, contribute to its practical implementation, and furnish a more nuanced elucidation of the everyday implications of the glocal. Undoubtedly, this undertaking could draw upon an array of conceptual strategies and resources. Here, we can only present a few instances of theoretical frameworks that hold potential for this task, as elucidated in our contributions to this special issue. From a semiotic standpoint, for instance, a Lotmanian perspective could provide an advantageous vantage point. This perspective appears to facilitate a productive exploration of glocal dynamics in terms of translating communications/signs from one semiosphere to another, with a particular focus on the role of semiotic borders as bilingual mechanisms.[96] From a perspective aligned with the social sciences, a pragmatist approach presents another promising starting point for the integrated analysis of cultural resonance and other factors underpinning glocal processes. This approach is noteworthy for its emphasis on the assertion that these dynamics invariably result from social relations and interactions.

The Interplay of Globalization and Social Identity

The theories surrounding globalization suggest that a key aspect of this phenomenon is the transcendence or compression of space and time in human interactions. The core of globalization is perceived as the gradual elimination of physical barriers to interpersonal connections, driven by widespread technological progress. The impact of these changes extends across a broad spectrum of activities, simultaneously influencing various spheres of human relations. While the issue of geographical distance is undeniably central to globalization, different theories place varying emphasis on this aspect. Early definitions broadly characterized globalization as the "intensification of worldwide social relations linking distant localities in such a way that local occurrences are shaped by events happening many miles away, and vice versa."[97]

Alternative conceptualizations highlight the need for these connections to be either transnational or transcontinental.[98] Some theorists take it a step further, contending that the essence of globalization is best encapsulated by the concepts of "deterritorialization" or "supra-territorialization" in human relations. According to Scholte, globalization involves the proliferation of transplanetary and supra-territorial connections between individuals, leading to a reduction in barriers to transworld contacts.[99] In this view, people gain increased physical, legal, cultural, and psychological capacity to engage with each other in a unified world. Supra-territorialization, the defining characteristic, renders the spatial location of connected individuals irrelevant. For example, in the realm of the internet, a supra-territorial space, two people can connect regardless of their physical location as long as they have access to the network. In global trade, products from any corner of the world, including cultural items like Hollywood blockbusters, can reach an individual in another country, given their participation in the international trade network.

Certainly, globalization should be viewed as a progression toward the aspirational state of supra-territorialization, rather than a static condition universally realized across all relevant domains. Our fundamental hypothesis is that the social, cultural, economic, and psychological involvement inherent in globalization brings about a transformation in an individual's social identity. Social identity, in this context, refers to "that part of the individual's self-concept which derives from his knowledge of his membership of a social group (or groups) together with the value and emotional significance attached to that membership."[100] Social identity hinges on categorization, the psychological process of assigning individuals to categories; identification, the process by which an individual associates themselves with specific groups; and comparison, the process of evaluating one's own group in relation to others.[101]

A fundamental distinction exists between the "ingroup" and the residual category referred to as the "outgroup." An ingroup can be characterized as a group with which an individual (i) associates themselves, (ii) categorizes as part of their identity, and (iii) uses for comparisons with other groups. Turner et al. introduced three possible levels of self-categorization, with categorization at the level of humankind being the most comprehensive.[102] At the intermediate level, differences between one's ingroup and outgroup, as well as similarities within one's ingroup, contribute to shaping the self. At the lowest level, the differentiation from other ingroup members molds an individual's identity. Existing research on social identity has predominantly concentrated on the intermediate level of ingroup–outgroup categorization, investigating the circumstances in which "ingroup favoritism," the inclination to treat ingroup members more favorably than outgroup members in strategic interactions, emerges. Little attention has been directed toward exploring the highest level of self-categorization.[103]

Through theories that posit opposing "ideal types" resulting from the globalization process—specifically, the "cosmopolitan" individual and the "reactant" individual—the connection between globalization and social identity becomes apparent. The former suggests that individuals engaged in global networks undergo an intensified global social identity experience, expanding the ingroup boundary outward to include groups once considered part of the "outgroup." In extreme cases, this process may encompass all of humanity.[104] Examples of the diffusion of a "cosmopolitan" individual can be seen in the proliferation of various "global" social movements addressing issues such as human rights or the environment, as well as the increasing significance of global humanitarian relief operations. Conversely, the "reactant" individual hypothesis anticipates heightened attachment to traditional loyalties, such as local and national communities, as an outcome of globalization.

According to this framework, globalization exacerbates the division between ingroup and outgroup, eliciting a negative response from individuals toward the global flow of objects, commodities, people, and ideas. This reaction may result in a retreat to the state-nation community or even alignment with fundamentalist movements.[105] Within the ingroup–outgroup model, the presence of an "other" becomes more pronounced for ingroup members, thereby reinforcing the narrow parochial boundary between "us" and "them." Buchan et al. discovered evidence aligning with the "cosmopolitan" ideal type. Individuals more engaged in global networks showed a significantly greater inclination to cooperate with global counterparts compared to less globalized individuals. Connecting with the concept of the "world as a whole," the unique idea of a shared destiny among many individuals globally due to increased interconnection is a vital facet of globalization. Individuals who exhibit a stronger identification with the "world as a whole" in comparison to national and local communities are more likely to collaborate with global counterparts.[106] Notably, these findings indicate a shift in motives and values from self-interest to group interest and concern for the group's well-being. This transformation implies that heightened global social identity correlates with increased cooperation within the global collective. Importantly, this positive impact of global social identity on cooperation extends beyond expectations regarding the behavior of others in the group.

The Rising Tide of Anti-Globalization Forces

There has been a significant upsurge in opposition to globalization on several fronts. Increased protectionist policies, the deconstruction of the WTO's dispute settlement process, and public demonstrations directed at international financial institutions, such as the IMF, are all examples of this pushback. Political globalization is also being resisted by people and politicians, who are opposing the constraints placed on national sovereignty by international organizations. This backlash goes beyond economic globalization. Notable member nations have left a number of international organizations, including the EU, the International Criminal Court, and UN Educational, Scientific, and Cultural Organization (UNESCO). There are several obstacles in the way of initiatives to create new international accords. Additionally, there is a growing opposition to social and cultural globalization, manifested through anti-immigrant rhetoric, protests against tourism, and a general unease regarding the preservation of local cultures in an increasingly globalized world.[107]

Examining the various facets of globalization is crucial, given their inherent interconnectedness. For instance, actions like the dismantling of the WTO dispute settlement system resist both economic and political globalization. Similarly, opposition to the European Court of Human Rights reflects a combination of resistance to political and sociocultural globalization. Paradoxically, resistance in one aspect of globalization may coexist with support for increased globalization in other domains. Consider the climate youth movement, which, while skeptical about the environmental impacts of international trade associated with economic globalization, advocates for enhanced political globalization to foster a more coordinated global response to climate change. Conversely, figures like market-liberal Brexiteers object to the constraints imposed on national sovereignty by political globalization but strongly endorse free trade and, consequently, economic globalization.

A prevailing narrative asserts that the backlash against globalization stems from the broader public, where an expanding segment of those adversely affected by globalization is increasingly expressing discontent with its various forms. The election victories of nationalist figures like Donald Trump in the United States and Jair Bolsonaro in Brazil, along with the Brexit referendum vote, stand out as prominent examples of this populist backlash. This narrative paints a picture of substantial shifts in public sentiment, particularly against trade, international cooperation, and immigration. However, a closer examination reveals a more nuanced reality than this narrative implies regarding a widespread change in public preferences. Comprehensive studies exploring shifts in globalization-related public opinion over time are relatively scarce and offer inconclusive findings. While some studies identify a trend of increasing negativity toward globalization, including more adverse attitudes toward international and supranational organizations, others present evidence that attitudes toward globalization remain surprisingly stable and, in some cases, even become more positive over time.[108]

Across various dimensions, we observe an increasing skepticism toward certain facets of globalization while witnessing contrasting attitudes on other fronts. Notably, respondents exhibit heightened skepticism regarding the advantages of free trade, yet their positivity toward restricting imports has diminished. Similarly, while there is a decrease in support for international organizations enforcing solutions, it remains generally high. Concerns about immigration and the endorsement of more national content on television have grown, but these shifts are not particularly pronounced. Notably, there is intriguing divergence between more and less developed countries, as well as between European and non-European nations. However, there is no compelling evidence to suggest that the perceived backlash against globalization, if it exists, is confined to developed countries or Europe. Instead, skepticism in developed nations has primarily intensified in relation to sociocultural globalization and, to a lesser extent, economic globalization. In contrast, less developed and European countries have seen a notable increase in skepticism, particularly concerning political globalization. There is no distinct evidence of a backlash against economic globalization in any of these country groups. Despite this variation, the data do not strongly support a significant shift in public opinion against globalization. Although a substantial portion of the general public is skeptical, these sentiments have remained relatively stable over the past two decades.[109]

In addition to these developments, it is crucial to note that discontent with globalization has also found expression in civil society mobilization. Since the 1990s, there has been significant activism, with movements like ATTAC (the Association pour la Taxation des Transactions financières et l'Aide aux Citoyens/Association for the Taxation of Financial Transactions and Aid to Citizens) gaining prominence. Instances of protest, such as the 2001 G20 summit demonstrations in Genoa, highlight the tangible expressions of dissatisfaction. More recently, the use of online platforms, including petitions, has proven effective in rallying civil society against major international trade agreements like the Transatlantic Trade and Investment Partnership and the Canada–Europe Trade Agreement. These evolving targets of discontent, which now include protests against overtourism, emphasize that dissatisfaction with various aspects of globalization has persisted and continues to be mobilized over time.[110]

What prompts the current global backlash against globalization? The prevailing view in the literature attributes its emergence to significant structural changes over the past three decades. These changes encompass the rapid pace of globalization, deindustrialization, technological advancements, and growing inequality. Moreover, noneconomic shifts, including the end of the Cold War, heightened immigration rates, cultural value shifts, and the expanding influence of international organizations in domestic politics, contribute to this phenomenon.[111] This perspective aligns with insights from economic history, which indicate that the initial backlash against globalization during the late nineteenth and early twentieth centuries was similarly rooted in structural transformations, such as the integration of commodity markets and mass migration.[112]

The significance of these structural shifts becomes evident through numerous studies that provide compelling evidence of a more pronounced backlash against globalization in communities most adversely affected by these changes. Regions facing heightened trade competition, particularly with low-wage countries like China, witness increased success for radical right-wing parties.[113] In these areas of the United States, there is a surge in ideological polarization, stronger endorsement of protectionist measures and restrictive immigration policies, and legislative support for more protectionist trade policies. Similarly, during the United Kingdom's 2016 Brexit referendum, communities more exposed to the "China shock" and experiencing heightened immigration levels displayed significantly higher Leave votes.[114] The impact of financial globalization is also noteworthy: Radical right parties tend to thrive in the aftermath of international financial crises, communities facing more significant repercussions from international financial shocks and crises exhibit stronger support for nationalist populist parties, and the influence of trade shocks on voting behavior has been intensified by the global financial crisis and the euro crisis.

Trade, with its potent distributive consequences, has been identified as a catalyst for inequality and a source of grievances in both developed and developing nations.[115] These findings strongly indicate a growing tendency toward a backlash against globalization in response to regional shifts caused by the process. However, the primary driver of this backlash remains a subject of debate. Some argue that globalization, while influential, is not the sole or even primary force behind the backlash; other socioeconomic transformations play equally, if not more, crucial roles in fueling this opposition. For instance, research indicates that support for radical right parties and nationalist endeavors, such as Brexit, is propelled by exposure to automation and the digital revolution.[116] A recent study by the IMF (2019) even concludes that the impacts of technology on local labor markets are more pervasive and enduring than those of trade shocks. These significant economic transformations have led to increased regional disparities and socioeconomic inequality. Furthermore, the decline in corporate, income, and wealth taxes, driven by financial globalization, has not only contributed to rising inequality but has also constrained the state's capacity to compensate those adversely affected by these changes.[117] These multifaceted developments have created fertile ground for the emergence of backlash sentiments.[118]

There is a growing concern that the resistance against globalization may evolve into a profound challenge for the current international order. This prospect becomes more imminent when societal, policy, and international responses inadvertently strengthen the backlash and its underlying grievances, setting in motion self-perpetuating dynamics. These dynamics can manifest in various ways, and on the societal level, several potential reinforcement mechanisms exist. In terms of voters, numerous studies reveal that a successful backlash against globalization, marked by widespread antiglobalization mobilization, electoral victories for globalization-skeptical parties, or effective policy reversals, has the potential to heighten voters' anti-globalization attitudes and preferences. For instance, providing information to individuals about the increased use of capital controls by other countries tends to make them more supportive of restrictions on international financial flows.[119] Concerning the backlash against political globalization, research indicates that voters who perceive Brexit as successful for the United Kingdom are significantly more inclined to support an EU exit for their own country. The electoral triumphs of radical parties and figures, such as Donald Trump, legitimize their perspectives, thereby encouraging those who share similar views to express them more openly.[120]

Further dynamics contributing to the reinforcement of the globalization backlash can also be observed at the policy and international levels. Policy-wise, instances of successful anti-globalization measures, whether in the form of trade restrictions or immigration controls, may embolden policymakers to pursue more restrictive policies. This reinforcement dynamic is evident in the fact that policy successes in curtailing globalization can foster a continuous pursuit of such measures, perpetuating a cycle of restrictive policies. On the international stage, the responses of countries to the globalization backlash can contribute to a self-reinforcing cycle. Instances where countries witness perceived benefits from resisting globalizing forces may encourage other nations to follow suit, creating a domino effect. Moreover, if international organizations and agreements face challenges or experience setbacks due to anti-globalization sentiments, it may fuel skepticism and provide justification for further resistance.

These policies often echo on the international stage. One repercussion is that other nations are inclined to retaliate against protectionist measures. Additionally, protectionist policies in one country can diminish support for pro-globalization measures, such as being open to foreign investment abroad. Negative discourse about trade can undermine confidence in the overall trade regime, tempting other states to violate trade rules.[121] Attempts by one nation to renegotiate more favorable terms of international cooperation can trigger similar demands from other governments.[122] Ultimately, governments skeptical of globalization, like successive pro-Brexit British administrations and the Trump administration, have effectively undermined and dismantled existing institutions and structures fundamental to the contemporary global order. However, they have struggled to replace these institutions with effective alternatives. The question remains as to who will step in to fill the void and what the reactions to the newly emerging structures will be. For instance, one potential scenario is that major businesses may seize the opportunity to shape new rules in their favor.[123]

One potential scenario involves a more pronounced role for China.[124] These dynamics have the potential to heighten the grievances linked to the globalization backlash, perpetuating the very forces fueling the politicization of globalization at the societal level. In addition, there are responses at the international level to counteract the effects of the globalization backlash. Confronted with domestic skepticism toward globalization, governments frequently adopt a more cautious approach in international negotiations, prioritizing responsiveness to the interests of their constituents.[125] While this strategy may address local concerns about globalization, it introduces complexities in decision-making on the global stage. The challenges faced in successfully concluding the 2019 Madrid climate summit and formulating EU-wide responses to the euro, refugee, and COVID-19 crises serve as illustrative examples. Moreover, international organizations have the capacity to strategically react to the globalization backlash. For instance, the European Court of Justice has become more restrictive in its rationale and rulings to align with the growing public opposition to the free movement of people.[126] Simultaneously, the European Commission more frequently withdraws legislative proposals when encountering backlash. However, these responses pose a dual challenge as they may invite further opposition in the long term by compromising the input and output legitimacy of these institutions.

Conclusion

With regard to theoretical issues and empirical indicators, this chapter has tried to offer some light on the ongoing globalization discussion. We have made an effort to show that the debate's extreme diversity may, in part, be due to the participants' diverse backgrounds and extremely varied contributions to the discussion. This discussion is in fact cross-disciplinary in that regard. The fact that the protagonists' conceptual frameworks are so dissimilar, however, also attests to the challenges that such a discussion entails. In our discussion of economic globalization, we have explored a wide range of topics, including neoliberal restructuring, international banking, multinational corporations, and urban settings. Economic globalization undoubtedly affects a wide range of issues, many of which are very complicated.[127] We think that the effects of economic globalization have frequently been negative, with a propensity for commercialization, polarization of life prospects, and damage to the environment. On all of these points, there are qualifications to be made and plenty of examples to the contrary, but one of the big challenges with globalization, in our opinion, is that economic development and profitability have become so much more important than social justice and equality issues.

This is consistent with the current domination of neoliberalism as economic common sense. In this chapter, we have agreed with the transformationalists in asserting that the monopoly of the relationship between territory and power has been shattered and that governance has become more multidimensional, albeit not totally and consistently. The state is still a crucial player, but it confronts difficulties that necessitate considerable changes in how power is used and how politics is conducted. The expansion of the influence of MNCs and markets is a significant factor in this. New suprastate concerns, pressures, and institutions, from environmental difficulties to groups like the WTO and the EU, provide a significant challenge.[128] The local scene has also been the center of fresh political attention. Although a lot of ground is covered here, including the cultural industries, cultural imperialism, identity, nationalism, and the Clash of Civilizations thesis, the issues raised here center on interpretations of cultural globalization that, depending on the interpretation, emphasize homogenization, hybridization, or polarization. These broad assessments of the cultural effects of globalization each present persuasive, though by themselves inadequate, arguments.

Advancements in technology propel globalization, breaking down physical barriers in human interactions. Diverse theories underscore the growing interconnectedness in various aspects of human relations, offering varying perspectives on the nature of these connections. The impact of globalization on individual social identity, marked by categorization, identification, and comparison processes, is transformative. Two prototypes emerge: the "cosmopolitan," engaged in global networks and cooperation, and the "reactant," reinforcing ties to traditional loyalties and potentially retreating to local communities.[129] The former aligns with global cooperation, while the latter may seek refuge in more localized affiliations. Empirical evidence indicates that individuals actively involved in global networks tend to exhibit greater cooperation with their global counterparts. This cooperative behavior reflects a shared destiny among globally interconnected individuals, contributing to an increased focus on group interests over self-interest.

The global pushback against globalization is observable through various means, including an increase in protectionist policies, resistance to international organizations, and mobilization in civil society. This resistance cuts across economic, political, and sociocultural realms. Notably, skepticism is evident in developed nations concerning sociocultural aspects and in less developed nations regarding political globalization.[130] Key drivers of this resistance include rapid globalization, technological progress, and growing inequality. The potential challenges stemming from this resistance raise concerns about its impact on the international order. The role of China is acknowledged as a potential force in the evolving global landscape. Governments, responding to domestic skepticism, may adopt cautious approaches in international negotiations, complicating global decision-making. The chapter emphasizes the importance of effective responses to prevent enduring consequences for the international order.

To summarize, globalization, fueled by technological advancements, reshapes the dynamics of human interactions. The theories surrounding this phenomenon highlight the evolving interconnectedness in human relations and the diverse responses it elicits, ranging from active global engagement to a retreat into local or national affiliations. The evidence suggests a shift toward increased cooperation and a collective emphasis on shared global interests resulting from this interconnectedness.

Notes

1. Jan Art Scholte, *Globalization: A Short Introduction* (New York: Palgrave Macmillan, 2005), 14–15.

2. Colin Hay and David Marsh, "Introduction: Demystifying Globalization," in *Demystifying Globalization*, ed. Colin Hay and David Marsh (New York: Palgrave Macmillan, 2000), 1.

3. Veronique Altglas, "Introduction," in *Religion and Globalization: Critical Concepts in Social Studies*, ed. Veronique Altglas (London: Routledge, 2011), 3.

4. Chamsy O. Jeili and Patrick Hayden, *Critical Theories of Globalization* (New York: Palgrave Macmillan, 2006), 12.

5. Jeili and Hayden, *Critical Theories*, 14.

6. Tony Schirato and Jen Webb, *Understanding Globalization* (London: Sage, 2003), 199–200.

7. Kooru Yamamoto, "Educational Psychology," in *The Social Sciences Encyclopedia*, ed. Adam Kuper and Jessica Kuper, 2nd edition (London: Routledge, 1996), 234.

8. Mazrui, "Globalization, Islam and the West," 1.

9. Chandra Muzaffar, "Globalization and Religion: Some Reflections," in *Globalization: The Perspectives and Experiences of the Religious Traditions of Asia Pacific*, ed.

Joseph Camilleri and Chandra Muzaffar (Kuala Lumpur: International Movement for a Just World, 1998), 179–190.

10. Mazrui, "Globalization, Islam and the West," 20.

11. Akbar S. Ahmed and Hastings Donnan, "Islam in the Age of Postmodernity," in *Islam, Globalization and Postmodernity*, ed. Akbar S. Ahmed and Hastings Donnan (London: Routledge, 1994), 1.

12. Johann P. Arnason, "Nationalism, Globalization and Modernity," in *Global Culture: Nationalism, Globalization and Modernity*, ed. Mike Featherstone (London: Sage, 1990), 220. Zygmaunt Bauman, *Globalization: The Human Consequences* (Cambridge: Polity, 1999), 10.

13. Michael Mann, "Globalization and September 11," *New Left Review* 12 (2001): 51–72.

14. David Held and Anthony McGrew, *Globalization/Anti-Globalization* (Cambridge: Polity, 2002), 1.

15. Manfred B. Steger, *Globalization: A Very Short Introduction* (London: Oxford University Press, 2003), 13.

16. Steger, *Globalization*, 14–16.

17. Robert J. Holten, *Making Globalization* (New York: Palgrave Macmillan, 2005), 5.

18. David Held, "A Globalising Society?," in *A Globalizing World? Culture, Economics, Politics*, ed. David Held (London: Routledge, 2000), 22–24.

19. David Held and Anthony Mcgrew, "Introduction," in *The Global Transformations Reader: An Introduction to the Globalization Debate*, 2nd edition, ed. David Held and Anthony Mcgrew (Cambridge: Polity Press, 2003), 5.

20. Held and Mcgrew, "Introduction," 5–6.

21. Fauzzi Najjar, "The Arabs, Islam and Globalization," *Middle East Policy* XII, no. 3 (2005): 91–96.

22. Lauren Movius, "Cultural Globalization and Challenges to Traditional Communication Theories," *PLATFORM: Journal of Media and Communication* 2, no. 1 (2010): 7–8.

23. Anthony Gerald Hopkins, "The History of Globalization and Globalization of History?," in *Globalization in World History*, ed. Anthony Gerald Hopkins (London: Pimlico, 2002), 28.

24. Steger, *Globalization*, 20.

25. Peter N. Stearns, *Globalization in World History* (London: Routledge, 2010), 13–14.

26. Sterns, *Globalization in World History*, 15.

27. Scholte, *Globalization: A Short Introduction*, 88.

28. Stearns, *Globalization in World History*, 33.

29. Stearns, *Globalization in World History*, 34–35.

30. Immanuel Wallerstein, *World-Systems Analysis: An Introduction* (Durham, NC: Duke University Press, 2005), 2.

31. Wallerstein, *World-Systems Analysis*, 58.

32. Steger, *Globalization*, 29.

33. Steger, *Globalization*, 35
34. Holten, *Making Globalization*, 48.
35. Holten, *Making Globalization*, 49
36. Holger Daun and Reza Arjmand, "Islam, Globalizations, and Education," in *Handbook of Islamic Education*, ed. Holger Daun and Reza Arjmand (New York: Springer, 2018), 333–355. See also Asif Mohiuddin, *Navigating Religious Authority in Muslim Societies: Islamist Movements and the Challenge of Globalization* (New York: Palgrave Macmillan, 2023), 24.
37. Kathleen R. McNamara, "A Rivalry in the Making? The Euro and International Monetary Power," *Review of International Political Economy* 15, no. 3 (2008): 441.
38. Marc Williams, "Multilateral Economic Institutions," in *An Introduction to International Relations: Australian Perspectives*, ed. Richard Devetak, Anthony Burke, and Jim George (Cambridge: Cambridge University Press, 2007), 238.
39. Theodore H. Cohn, *Global Political Economy*, 6th edition (New York: Pearson, 2012), 141.
40. Jeili and Hayden, *Critical Theories*, 55.
41. Chandra Muzaffar, *Human Rights and the New World Order* (Penang: Just World Trust, 1993), 13.
42. "Globalization: What it means to small nations", Speech by the former Malaysian Prime Minister Dato Seri Dr. Mahathir Bin Mohamad at the Inaugural Lecture of the Prime Ministers of Malaysia Fellowship Exchange Programme, Kuala Lumpur, July 24, 1996. Accessed April 13, 2024. https://twn.my/title/small-cn.htm.
43. Peter G. Riddell, "Globalization, Western and Islamic, into the 21st Century: Perspectives from Southeast Asia and Beyond," *Asian Christian Review* 2, no. 2 and 3 (2008): 133–134.
44. Jeili and Hayden, *Critical Theories*, 89.
45. Gerard Delanty and Chris Rumford, "Political Globalization," in *The Blackwell Companion to Globalization*, ed. George Ritzer (Oxford: Blackwell, 2007), 416–417.
46. Ulrich Beck, "The Terrorist Threat: World Risk Society Revisited," *Theory, Culture and Society* 19, no. 4 (2002): 53.
47. Jeili and Hayden, *Critical Theories*, 96.
48. Malcolm Edey, "The Global Financial Crisis and Its Effects," in *The Globalization Reader*, ed. Frank J. Lechner and John Boli (Oxford: Blackwell, 2000), 208.
49. Manuel Castells, *The Information Age: Economy, Society and Culture — The Power of Identity* (Oxford: Blackwell, 2000), 304.
50. David Held, "Realism Versus Cosmopolitanism: A Debate between Barry Buzan and David Held," *Review of International Studies* 24, no. 3 (1998): 387–398.
51. Rabi', "Globalization: A Contemporary Islamic Response?," 23.
52. John Tomlinson, *Globalization and Culture* (Chicago, IL: The University of Chicago Press, 1999), 107.
53. Marwan M. Kraidy, *Hybridity, or the Cultural Logic of Globalization* (Philadelphia, PA: Temple University Press, 2005), 16.
54. Held, "A Globalising Society?," 48.

55. Tomlinson, *Globalization and Culture*, 89.

56. Benjamin R. Barber, *Jihad Versus McWorld: How Globalism and Tribalism are Reshaping the World* (New York: Ballantine Books, 1996), 8.

57. Kraidy, *Hybridity, or the Cultural Logic of Globalization*, 19–20.

58. Jan Nederveen Pieterse, "Globalization and Culture: Three Paradigms," *Economic and Political Weekly* 31, no. 23 (1996): 1389.

59. Arjun Appadurai, "Disjuncture and Difference in the Global Cultural Economy," in *Global Culture: Nationalism, Globalization and Modernity*, ed. Mike Featherstone (London: Sage, 1990), 295.

60. Anthony Giddens, *The Consequences of Modernity* (Stanford, CA: Stanford University Press, 1990), 64.

61. Roland Robertson, *Globalization: Social Theory and Global Culture* (London: Sage, 1992), 132.

62. Jonathan Friedman, "Being in the World: Globalization and Localization," in *Global Culture: Nationalism, Globalization and Modernity*, ed. Mike Featherstone (London: Sage, 1990), 311.

63. Robertson, *Globalization: Social Theory and Global Culture*, 173.

64. Malcolm Waters, *Globalization: Key Ideas*, 2nd edition (London: Routledge, 2001), 186.

65. David Harvey, *The Condition of Postmodernity* (Oxford: Blackwell, 1989), 293.

66. Malcolm Waters, *Globalization* (London: Routledge, 1998), 9.

67. Abu Sadat Nurullah, "Globalization as a Challenge to Islamic Cultural Identity," *The International Journal of Interdisciplinary Social Sciences* 3, no. 6 (2008): 47.

68. Chandra Muzaffar, "Globalization and Religion: Some Reflections." Accessed April 12, 2024. https://www.angelfire.com/ms/MOHDFARHAN/3/globalization.html.

69. Joachim Blatter, "Glocalization," *Encyclopedia Britannica*, February 23, 2022. Accessed April 13, 2024. https://www.britannica.com/money/glocalization.

70. Theodor Levitt, "The Globalization of Markets," *Harvard Business Review* 61, no. 3 (1983): 92–102.

71. Jean-Pierre Jeannet and Hubert D. Hennessey, *Global Marketing Strategies* (Boston, MA: Houghton Mifflin Company, 1992), 34.

72. Robertson, *Globalization: Social Theory and Global Culture*, 100.

73. Habibul Haque Khondker, "Globalization Theory: A Critical Analysis," Department of Sociology Working Paper, National University of Singapore, Singapore, 1994.

74. Harold James, *The End of Globalization: Lessons from the Great Depression* (Cambridge, MA: Harvard University Press, 2001), 31.

75. Robert Boyer and Daniel Drache, *States Against Markets: The Limits of Globalization* (London: Routledge, 1996), 34.

76. Habibul Haque Khondker, "Glocalization as Globalization: Evolution of a Sociological Concept," *Bangladesh e-Journal of Sociology* 1, no. 2 (2004): 12–20.

77. John Robertson and Ellis Tallman, "Vector Autoregression and Reality," *Federal Reserve Bank of Atlanta, Economic Review* 84, no. 1 (1999): 4–18.

78. Saskia Sassen, "Territory and Territoriality in the Global Economy," *International Sociology* 15 (2000): 393.
79. Khondker, "Glocalization as Globalization," 13.
80. Khondker, "Glocalization as Globalization,"14.
81. Roland Robertson and Kathleen White, *Globalization: Critical Concepts in Sociology* (London: Routledge, 2003), 21.
82. Bryan S. Turner, "Enclave Society: Towards a Sociology of Immobility," *European Journal of Social Theory* 10, no. 2 (2007): 287–304.
83. George Ritzer, "Introduction," in *The Blackwell Companion to Globalization*, ed. George Ritzer (Oxford: Basil Blackwell, 2007), 1–14.
84. Ritzer, "Introduction," 15.
85. John W. Meyer, "World Society, Institutional Theories and the Actor," *Annual Review of Sociology* 36 (2010): 1–20.
86. Victor Roudometof, *Glocalization: A Critical Introduction* (London: Routledge, 2016), 29. Marshall Sahlins, "Goodbye to Tristes Tropes: Ethnography in the Context of Modern World History," *The Journal of Modern History* 65, no. 1 (1993): 1–25.
87. Ugo Dessì, *The Global Repositioning of Japanese Religions: An Integrated Approach* (London: Routledge, 2017), 44.
88. Franciscu Sedda, "Glocal and Food: On Alimentary Translation," *Semiotica* 211 (2016): 105–125.
89. Ugo Dessì and Franciscu Sedda, "Glocalization and Everyday Life," *Glocalism: Journal of Culture, Politics and Innovation* 3 (2020): 1–13.
90. Arjun Appadurai, "The Production of Locality," in *Counterworks: Managing the Diversity of Knowledge*, ed. Richard Fardon (London: Routledge, 1995), 208–229.
91. Arjun Appadurai, "Dead Certainty: Ethnic Violence in the Era of Globalization," *Public Culture* 10, no. 2 (1998): 225–247.
92. Dessì and Sedda, "Glocalization and Everyday Life," 11.
93. Ugo Dessì, *The Global Repositioning of Japanese Religions: An Integrated Approach* (London: Routledge, 2017), 51.
94. Juri M. Lotman, *Culture and Explosion: Semiotics, Communication and Congnition* (New York: Mouton de Gruyter, 2009), 65.
95. Saskia Sassen, *Territory, Authority, Rights: From Medieval to Global Assemblages* (Princeton, NJ: Princeton University Press, 2006), 37.
96. Franciscu Sedda, "Semiotics of Culture(s): Basic Questions and Concepts," in *International Handbook of Semiotics*, ed. Peter P. Trifonas (Berlin: Springer, 2015), 675–696.
97. Sam McFarland, Matthew Webb, and Derek Brown, "All Humanity is My Ingroup: A Measure and Studies of Identification with all Humanity," *Journal of Personality and Social Psychology* 103, no. 5 (2012): 830–853.
98. David Held, Anthony McGrew, David Goldblatt, and Jonathan Perraton, "Rethinking Globalization," in *Global Transformations: Politics, Economics and Culture*, ed. David Held (Cambridge: Polity Press and Stanford, CA: Stanford University Press, 1999), 67–74.
99. Scholte, *Globalization: A Short Introduction*, 17–18.

100. Henri Tajfel, *Human Groups and Social Categories: Studies in Social Psychology* (Cambridge: Cambridge University Press, 1981), 34.

101. John C. Turner, *Rediscovering the Social Group: A Self-Categorization Theory* (Oxford: Basil Blackwell, 1987), 9.

102. Turner, *Rediscovering the Social Group*, 11.

103. Gianluca Grimalda, Nancy Buchan, and Marilynn Brewer, "Social Identity Mediates the Positive Effect of Globalization on Individual Cooperation: Results from International Experiments," *PLoS ONE* 13, no. 12 (2018): 1–25.

104. Grimalda, Buchan, and Brewer, "Social Identity Mediates the Positive Effect of Globalization," 12.

105. Jeffrey Jensen Arnett, "The Psychology of Globalization," *American Psychologist* 57, no. 10 (2002): 774–783.

106. Nancy R. Buchan, Marilynn B. Brewer, Gianluca Grimalda, Rick K. Wilson, Enrique Fatas, and Margaret Foddy, "Global Social Identity and Global Cooperation," *Psychological Science* 22, no. 6 (2011): 821–828.

107. Stefanie Walter, "The Backlash Against Globalization," *Annual Review of Political Science* 24 (2021): 421–442.

108. Matthias Mader, Nils D. Steiner, and Harald Schoen, "The Globalization Divide in the Public Mind: Belief Systems on Globalization and their Electoral Consequences," *Journal of European Public Policy* 27, no. 10 (2019): 1526–1545.

109. Stefanie Walter, "The Backlash Against Globalization," *Annual Review of Political Science* 24 (2021): 421–442.

110. Sophie Meunier and Rozalie Czesana, "From Back Rooms to the Street? A Research Agenda for Explaining Variation in the Public Salience of Trade Policy-Making in Europe," *Journal of European Public Policy* 26, no. 12 (2019): 1847–1865.

111. Pippa Norris and Ronald Inglehart, *Cultural Backlash: Trump, Brexit, and Authoritarian Populism* (New York: Cambridge University Press, 2019), 77.

112. Maurice Obstfeld, "Globalization Cycles," *Italian Economy Journal* 6, no. 1 (2020): 1–12.

113. Christian Dippel, Robert Gold, and Stephan Heblich, "Globalization and its (dis-)content: Trade Shocks and Voting Behavior," NBER Working Papers, No. 21812. Accessed April 13, 2024. https://www.ifw-kiel.de/publications/globalization-and-its-dis-content-trade-shocks-and-voting-behavior-23145/.

114. Matthew Goodwin and Caitlin Milazzo, "Taking Back Control? Investigating the Role of Immigration in the 2016 Vote for Brexit," *The British Journal of Politics and International Relations* 19, no. 3 (2017): 450–464.

115. Valentin F. Lang and Marina Mendes Tavares, *The Distribution of Gains from Globalization* (Washington, DC: International Monetary Fund, 2018), 23.

116. Italo Colantone and Piero Stanig, "The Trade Origins of Economic Nationalism: Import Competition and Voting Behavior in Western Europe," *American Journal of Political Science* 62, no. 4 (2018): 936–953.

117. Dani Rodrik, "Populism and the Economics of Globalization," *Journal of International Business Policy* 1 (2018): 12–33.

118. Thiemo Fetzer, "Did Austerity Cause Brexit?," *American Economy Review* 109, no. 1 (2019): 3849–3886.

119. Stefanie Walter, "The Backlash Against Globalization," *Annual Review of Political Science* 24 (2021): 421–442.

120. Daniel Bischof and Markus Wagner, "Do Voters Polarize When Radical Parties Enter Parliament?," *American Journal of Political Science* 63, no. 4 (2019): 888–904.

121. Allison Carnegie and Austin Carson, "Reckless Rhetoric? Compliance Pessimism and International Order in the Age of Trump," *Journal of Politics* 81, no. 2 (2019): 739–746.

122. Stefanie Walter, "The Mass Politics of International Disintegration," CIS Working Paper No. 105, Center for Comparative and International Studies (CIS), Zürich, 2020. Accessed April 13, 2024. https://ethz.ch/content/dam/ethz/special-interest/gess/cis/cis-dam/CIS_2020/WP%20105%20Walter.pdf.

123. Leslie Johns, Krzysztof J. Pelc, and Rachel L. Wellhausen, "How a Retreat from Global Economic Governance May Empower Business Interests," *Journal of Politics* 81, no. 2 (2019): 731–738.

124. Jessica Chan Weiss and Jeremy L. Wallace, "Domestic Politics, China's Rise, and the Future of the Liberal International Order," *International Organization*. Accessed April 13, 2024. https://papers.ssrn.com/sol3/papers.cfm?abstract_id=3671848.

125. Christina J. Schneider, *The Responsive Union: National Elections and European Governance* (New York: Cambridge University Press, 2019), 20.

126. Stefanie Walter, "The Backlash Against Globalization," *Annual Review of Political Science* 24 (2021): 421–442.

127. Agus Dwi Nugroho, Priya Rani Bhagat, Robert Magda, and Zoltan Lakner, "The Impacts of Economic Globalization on Agricultural Value Added in Developing Countries," *PLoS One* 16, no. 11 (2021): 1–23.

128. Austin Sarat and Stuart A. Scheingold, "State Transformation, Globalization, and the Possibilities of Cause Lawyering: An Introduction," in *Cause Lawyering and the State in a Global Era*, ed. Austin Sarat (New York: Oxford University Press, 2001), 3–32.

129. Mirsad Kriještorac, *First Nationalism then Identity: On Bosnian Muslims and Their Bosniak Identity* (Ann Arbor, MI: University of Michigan Press, 2022), 34.

130. Catherine Eschle, "Constructing the Anti-Globalization Movement," *International Journal of Peace Studies* 9, no. 1 (2004): 61–84.

CHAPTER 2

Globalization and Islam
Exploring the Alternative Paradigm

Introduction

The relationship between globalization and Islam constitutes a terrain replete with new possibilities and concomitant challenges, given the diversity of the global Muslim populace and the confluence of salient factors such as multiple geopolitical conflicts, revolutionary upheavals, persistent power struggles, and extensive worldwide population movements. Undoubtedly, these events and demographic factors have necessitated diverse interpretations, sparking contentious debates concerning the tumultuous zones of conflict and instability they have engendered.[1] Central to the ongoing academic discourse is the proposition that Islam remains impervious to the transformative forces of globalization. The focal point of the discussion revolves around the idea that Islam is inherently bereft of the requisite capacity to occupy the "hermeneutical space" emergent within the nexus of intersecting forces generated by the profound economic, political, and cultural exchanges characteristic of our contemporary late-modern globalized era. However, this inquiry adopts a delimited and contentious perspective, forsaking a comprehensive, interdisciplinary approach that dismisses the intricacies inherent in the Islamic dimension of the broader discourse on globalization.

The historical period, commencing with the fall of the Roman Empire, delineates a momentous reorientation of the globalized world's epicenter, gravitating toward the Indian subcontinent and extending its influence as far as China. From the vantage point of proponents of neoliberalism, this scholarly investigation propounds a captivating yet surreal narrative, constituting an extension of conceptual enclosures that permeate the very fabric of the economic realm itself. In the eyes of certain observers, Islam emerges as a direct contender against certain principles propagated by advocates of transnational, neoliberal free-market capitalism, as well as proponents of an economically dominant system. Nevertheless, Islam acknowledges an economic order informed by a distinctive form of globalization, one grounded in human values and an ethical approach to political and economic matters. This conceptual framework serves as a complex network of possibilities, intricately connecting concepts and realities within a globalized paradigm, with the objective of fostering a more comprehensive understanding of Islam. This expansive approach seeks to transcend the realm of political boundaries, encompassing authoritative expressions over communities of faith and thereby aspiring to eradicate substantial portions of the discursive and ideological landscape of potentialities. The inherent dynamism and adaptability within Islam, evidenced by its continual evolution and responsiveness to external influences and pressures, manifest across its ideological, legitimizing, and structural dimensions. It is this remarkable quality that imparts to Islam a specific orientation, endowing it not only with resilience but also with the capacity to actively contribute to globalization.

The objective of this chapter is to conduct a thorough examination of the alternative paradigm that situates Islam within the framework of globalization. By delving into diverse dimensions, encompassing the foundational tenets of an Islam, the role of the *ummah*, the *shurātic* perspective, and the application of Islamic methodologies to technological advancements, the chapter attempts to explicate a nuanced comprehension of Islam's interaction with the globalized milieu. Furthermore, the chapter seeks to underscore Islam's dedication to justice, equity, and sustainable development. It delves into the domain of Islamic finance, revealing how sustainability principles intricately permeate financial practices. The environmental challenge is also addressed, emphasizing the Islamic imperative for responsible stewardship of the Earth. In its exploration of the dimensions of cultural diversity and pluralism within the globalized landscape, the chapter envisions Islam as a unifying force actively fostering mutual understanding and cooperation. The alternative paradigm presented herein demonstrates Islam's capacity to adapt and endure modern challenges, facilitating peaceful coexistence beyond cultural, technological, and environmental boundaries.

The Foundations of Islamic Paradigm

Globalization transcends the mere expansion of trade and capital across borders; it creates a complex web of interactions. It not only champions progress and the pursuit of an ideal society but also embraces a positivist and scientific ethos, challenging conventional realist views on power dynamics while fostering innovative models of collaborative organization. Intriguingly, when scrutinized in its most literal sense, globalization—the intensification of interconnectedness and interdependence among individuals and nations—is not a new concept.[2] For centuries, individuals and, subsequently, institutions have partaken in cross-border processes such as interregional trade, technological dissemination, and population migration spanning borders and distances. However, in the context of the Muslim *ummah*, its existence finds its roots in concise, credo, practical rituals; moral considerations; and legal precepts. These elements provide the intellectual and conceptual underpinnings for globalization.

Embedded within the rich discourse of Islamic tradition lies the concept of *tawhīd*, encapsulating the essence of God's unity. This concept transcends a mere acknowledgment of monotheism; it embodies a comprehensive understanding of harmonious integration and cohesive oneness, constituting the bedrock of Islamic philosophical thought. In the Islamic framework, *tawhīd* assumes a significance unparalleled in Judaism or Christianity, standing as the pivotal force that binds together the entire belief system, surpassing its role in other faith traditions. Islam provides a resolute and distinct perspective on *tawhīd*, affirming the unequivocal proclamation that there exists only one Supreme Being (Allah), the Lord of all worlds, and the sole creator of the heavens. Islam steadfastly rejects the notion of competing governing forces, such as the Trinity in Christianity, or the existence of multiple eternal creative entities as portrayed in process theism, as described in certain scriptural accounts.

At the core of Islamic faith lies the concept of *shahadah* also referred to as the *kalimah* or Islamic creed. This proclamation serves as a testament to the Muslim conviction in the unity of God and the Prophethood of Muhammad (PBUH), as eloquently articulated by Shabbir Akhtar in the following words:

> In the kalimah (word, statement) of faith, Muslims profess: "I testify that there is no god except the only God and I testify that Muhammad is the messenger of the only God" (LāilāhāillāAllāh, MuhammadunRasulAllāh). Both parts of this double testimony are in the present tense: believers affirm God's continuing uniqueness and endorse Muhammad as his current envoy. The creed does not claim that Muhammad is God's only messenger since Islam reveres all earlier prophets. Surprisingly, however, it does not claim his finality even though the prophetic office is abolished after the Arabian Messenger's universal mission (see Q: 4:79;21:107; 34:28). Belief in Muhammad as the seal of prophets (Q: 33:40) entails that he brought ultimate truth and confirmed it (Q: 37:37). This controversial claim about the finality of prophethood defines and distinguishes

Islam. It terminates divine revelation and implies that the prophetic office is the optimal method for the divine tuition of humanity.[3]

The Islamic system of belief substantiates the legitimacy and cogency of the Prophets preceding Prophet Muhammad PBUH. The Qur'ān explicitly attests that these Prophets and their adherents collectively form one *ummah*, a global community rooted in shared faith and the adherence to its legal precepts. The Qur'ān unequivocally asserts that while human beings naturally organize into tribes and nations, this has been done to serve collective interests, as opposed to conforming to contemporary perspectives that perceive national communities as elite-engineered constructions.[4] These collective interests encompass ecumenical values devoid of ideological codifiers attempting to rigidly define the meaning of core unifying concepts, fostering reciprocal identification and encouraging collaboration.

Islam, as articulated in the Qur'ān, establishes the equality of all human beings, irrespective of their racial, ethnic, or national distinctions. This stands in contrast to articulating personal identities primarily in racial terms. The Qur'ān emphasizes that superiority is not contingent upon factors such as origin, color, tribe, nationality, ideological modalities, or leadership. In the eyes of God, the sole criterion for superiority lies in an individual's piety. The Qur'ān clarifies:

> O mankind! Lo! We have created you male and female, and have made you nations and tribes that ye may know one another. Lo! The noblest of you, in the sight of Allah, is the best in conduct. Lo! Allah is Knower, Aware.[5]

Equality, a principle entrenched in both the beginning and end phases of legal procedures, stands as a fundamental tenet in Islamic law. This principle, significant in concepts of justice and the legal landscape across various religious traditions, is accentuated in Islamic law by emphasizing the transcendental origin of humanity and the essence of human brotherhood.[6] Such emphasis reinforces the comprehensive equality of individuals, irrespective of language, race, gender, or social standing. While there is clear evidence within Islam affirming the concept of equality in basic rights and duties among all Muslims, real-world observations suggest a world structured to simmer with nightmarish injustices. The evidence, however, is somewhat inconclusive regarding whether this equality extends universally to all members of the human race. This lack of clarity arises from sources that permit different interpretations and from circumstances during the formative period of Islamic law. Nonetheless, the historical culture of Muslim societies, rooted in universal values, articles of faith, and principles, staunchly upholds a fundamentally monotheistic vision of Islam. This vision, despite variations, serves as an exemplary moral and intellectual foundation for a coherent and sustainable conceptual framework for globalization.

For some Muslim scholars, the alternative paradigm of globalization constitutes an epistemology rooted in the complete, universal, and singular foundation of knowledge, encompassing concepts such as *tawhīd* (unity), *khilafah* (trusteeship), *"ilm* (knowledge), *halal* (praiseworthy), *haram* (blameworthy), *"adl* (social justice), *zulm* (tyranny), *istislah* (public interest), and *dhiya* (waste).[7] The primordial "Beginning" gives rise to the fundamental belief in God (*tawhīd*) as the all-encompassing, perfect, pure, and complete One. God stands alone, without intermediate agency, affirming that the Beginning of God's Domain of knowledge is a metaphor for the uncreated open Beginning. Nevertheless, God creates everything through absolute divine command and will—"Be, and it was." This knowledge structuring the nature of the unity of the divine law for everything is exogenous. The carriers of the original episteme of *tawhīd*, the unity of God (i.e., the divine law) in the Qur'ān, are primarily the Sunnah. The Sunnah represents the interwoven fabric of Islamic life, intricately linked to how the nature, objectives, and methodology of Qur'ānic revelation are conceptualized. Apart from the practice-based component of the Sunnah, which includes sayings, actions, and the outspoken moral valuations of the Prophet, it comprises elements such as *fiqh* (jurisprudence), *'aqidah* (creed), *akhlaq* (ethics), and *'ibadah*. These elements are methodologically and epistemologically independent of *hadīth* but organically linked to a specific type of Qur'ānic hermeneutic.[8]

Secondly, with the Qur'ān and the Sunnah as the core foundational elements of knowledge unity, the discursive mechanism of a democratic society is subsequently established, along with its institutions and enforcing tools. The primary goal of this discursive mechanism is to exert effort in explicating the rules of diverse interpretations of laws, methodologies, and applications, referencing the canonical sources of knowledge, the Qur'ān and Sunnah. *Tawhīd*, serving as the episteme of the oneness of God, intricately influences the coherence of the mind, subject, and psyche at a detailed level. This influence extends to the transmission of the episteme, allowing it to be extracted, perceived, and infused into all aspects through the mechanism of evolutionary learning. This learning process involves synergistic interrelations between systems and their discursive subjectivities. The inherent challenge in this relational learning lies in the vagueness of knowledge within the human and inanimate cosmos. The dynamics of learning within this evolutionary cosmos are driven by perpetual causal looping between representative entities. The notion that a foot rule cannot precisely measure the cosmic pyramid discourages us from acknowledging limitations in understanding the divine law and constructing a framework based on imperfect and evolving knowledge. In contrast, *tawhīd* underscores the broader Islamic unity of thought, action, and values across humanity, nature, individuals, and God.

Khilafah, a traditionalist political theory, articulates the establishment of a coherent community aiming to fulfill the needs of the emerging religious community. This is achieved by significantly reducing the expectations placed on the deputy, while maintaining the legitimacy of the supreme authority of God as the lord over all. Khilafah asserts that ownership of the Earth lies with God and humans operate in a stewardship role, preserving the social order on Earth rather than causing harm.[9] The core of the Islamic worldview centers on justice, referred to as *'adl*, which encompasses rationality, ethics, law, natural law, equity, and the consequences for breaching ethical standards. Justice is considered a moral virtue and an intrinsic aspect of human character that prioritizes the broader welfare of people, known as *istislah*. According to Suhail Umar, *'ibadah*, denoting worship or contemplation, marks the initial and essential phase. Through profound reflection and observation, both internal and external, emerges the knowledge or *'ilm* of oneself, others, and the natural world. Consequently, one's actions align with being halal, commendable, rather than haram, blameworthy. Within this framework, the squandering of individual and collective potentials, labeled as *dhiya* (waste), and tyranny, defined as the dominance of a few or one over many, or the imposition of a narrow ideology over the unity within plurality advocated by the Islamic paradigm, is averted. The resultant science does not adopt a reductionist and objective approach; instead, it is synthetic and rooted in values, driven by an emotional commitment to comprehend the world as ordained by God.[10]

In contrast, the ensuing discourse introduces an alternative conceptual framework within Islam. This perspective envisions an *ummah*, a unified community that embraces the entirety of humanity, encompassing both believers and nonbelievers. This transnational paradigm puts forth an alternative approach that seeks recognition. At the core of Islam's fundamental essence is the ambition to reinstate unity by reintegrating individuals into the natural fabric of existence. It advocates for a comprehensive understanding of the Islamic world as a cohesive entity, inseparable from the prevailing social structure and an intrinsic component of the interconnected whole. While Western civilization, guided by prevailing notions of Eurocentric and orientalist power discourse, has historically waged battles against the tyranny of royalty (from the Magna Carta to the Glorious English Revolution), for Muslims, the most formidable struggles have been against the imperial dominance of colonial cultures, sparking a humanistic spirit. Thus, the vision of the *ummah* must transcend cultural subjectivity and embody the idea of universal values. Before delving further into this point, however, it is imperative to clarify the term *ummah*, especially in light of Qur'ānic precepts.

Ummah

As previously highlighted, the fundamental theological element of the Muslim faith is *Shahādah*, constituting the profession of faith. Integral to the concept of *Shahādah* is what Muslim scholars identify as *tawhīd*, signifying the doctrine of the oneness of God. This fundamental tenet asserts that everything existing within the confines of the universe originates from the ultimate source (God) and will ultimately return to Him. Marranci posits that the term *"ummah"* is mentioned in the Qur'ān sixty times with varying, and at times contrasting, meanings. These meanings include the acolytes of the Prophet, a religious congregation and a minority community within a majority religious group. Given that each individual species is considered an *ummah*, the Qur'ān does not confine the concept of *ummah* (derived from a single source, "umm") to human beings alone. According to the Qur'ān, human beings are the only creatures on Earth, after God, characterized by free will, which, nonetheless, results in diversity. Despite its multifaceted meanings, the term predominantly refers to a nascent Muslim community, serving as both a political and religious entity, which emerged under the leadership of Prophet Muhammad PBUH in Madinah.[11]

Al-Faruqi argues that the term *"ummah"* denotes a religious community united by faith, transcending all other identity markers such as national, racial, or geographic divisions. However, certain Islamic movements have broadened the significance of the *ummah*, moving beyond its purely religious characteristic. For these movements, the political structure of this community was conceived as informal, distinct from the conventional concept of church and state. Instead, they firmly recognized the Islamic sense of community, where people with shared interests formed the fundamental identification of Muslims.[12] El-Awaisi observes that these Islamic movements acknowledged the practical reality that mankind is divided into people and tribes. Consequently, they considered Muslims to belong to two nations: the nation of their birth and the nation of Islam. Both of these nations imposed obligations that Muslims were expected to fulfill.[13] With regard to the historical evolution of the *ummah* and its socio-legal, religious, and political dimensions, Ishtiaq Hossain argues:

The Compact of Madinah (Sahifat al-Madinah, circa. 622 CE) not only formed the constitutional foundation of the political community established by the Prophet Muhammad (Peace be upon him), but according to Luay Safi, also laid down the following as the five main features of the Ummah: Firstly, a political society, open to all individuals committed to its principles and values, and ready to shoulder its burdens and responsibilities. Secondly, individual norms and the scope of political action within the new society can be created by preserving the basic social and political structures prevalent in tribal Arabia. Thirdly, guaranteeing religious autonomy, based on the freedom of belief, for all members. Fourthly, subjecting all social and political activities to a set of universal values and standards that treat all people equally in a society where the sovereignty does not rest with the rulers, or any particular group, but with the law founded on the basis of justice, maintaining goodness, the dignity of all and condemning injustice and tyranny. Fifthly, introduction of rights for all individuals, Muslims and non-Muslims, such as (1) rights to be helped, if oppressed; (2) rights not be liable for an ally's misdeeds; (3) rights to practice respective religion; and (4) rights to free movement from and to Madinah ... At close examination of the features, it seems that with its emphasis on community feelings, individual rights (of the members), and freedom of movement the Ummah is compatible with Bull's conception of an international society. Mention should also be made that the Compact of Madinah is also a guidance for Islamic approach to conflict resolution, and that many of the mediation techniques utilized by the Compact continue to be practised today.[14]

From a sociological perspective, the concept of *ummah* underwent a transformative evolution within the Arab tribes, shifting their supreme tribal loyalty to a new Islamic identity following the establishment of the first Muslim state in Madinah during the seventh century. Hasan further elaborates on this transformation, asserting that *ummah* became a transformative concept as it altered the identities of Arab tribes into a unified Muslim identity. As Islam expanded to non-Arab lands, various groups of Muslims underwent a similar transformation, coalescing into a community of believers. *Ummah*, in this context, acquired a political dimension as well.[15]

In political terms, Prophet Muhammad PBUH laid the foundation for the concept of *ummah* with the establishment of the first Islamic state in Madinah, documented in the Madinah Constitution, also known as the Charter of Madinah. Through this charter, the Prophet formulated a peace treaty, employing reason, discussion, contemplation, and drawing upon the principles of unity, respect, love, and tolerance to forge a cohesive pluralistic community. The mere formulation of the Charter and the establishment of peace were remarkable achievements. The content of the Charter itself reflects how the Prophet combated *Jahilliyah*, or ignorance—the mindset fostering violence and endorsing any system, ideology, or institution based on values other than those referring to God. Safi posits that the Madinah Charter, particularly Article 30, inclusively designates Jews as part of the same community as the believers. According to Safi, this inclusion serves to "define the political rights and duties of the members of the newly established community, Muslims and non-Muslims alike."[16] On the contrary, al-Ahsan proposes that the Charter was developed in multiple stages and initially excluded non-Muslims. However, due to security considerations, an offer was extended to the Jews to grant them citizenship, transforming the Charter into a "defense pact." Ultimately, the Charter included nonbelievers, indicating the original *ummah* of Madinah accepted the inclusive vision. Sachdina introduces additional dimensions to the concept of *ummah* by referencing Qur'ānic verse 5:48. This verse suggests the supremacy of Muslims as the ideal or best community, characterized by a shared way of life, a common legacy, and a common role and aim. The intention is for Muslims to affirm and be reminded of their religious and human unity, emphasizing their membership in a single universal community.[17]

In this context, the existence of the Muslim *ummah* does not negate the presence of other communities, as depicted in Qur'ānic verse 2:143:

> And thus we have willed you to be a community of the middle way (*ummatan wasatan*), so that you might be a witness (to the truth) before all mankind, and that the Apostle might bear witness (to it) before you. And it is only to the end that We might make a clear distinction between those who follow the Apostle and those who turn about on their heels that we had appointed (for this community) the direction of prayer. (Qur'ān 2:143)

Al-Ahsan, in interpreting this verse, suggests that *ummah* refers to the "followers of Muhammad as a group of people with a physical identity of direction to pray, which is the Ka'bah, thus explicitly indicating to the Muslims." The significance of this verse becomes apparent when compared to verse 5:48, where the Qur'ān acknowledges the supremacy of Muslims while projecting *ummah* as an inclusive term. Although implicitly emphasizing the centrality of religion, it nonetheless recognizes the entirety of humankind and includes them as part of the global community.[18]

As previously discussed, Islam incorporates various agents and systems of thought, institutions, and the socio-scientific order through the unifying principle of God's unity (*tawhīd*). The concept of the unity of God is perceived as a dynamic process that aims to reduce all systems to an irreducible reality, capable of unifying them through interactions based on the Islamic divine law (*sharī'ah*) grounded in this unity. Within this framework, the process of globalization entails the emergence, conduct, and intersection of continuous cycles of discourses among agents from multiple systems, fostering comprehensive reflection and realization of *sharī'ah*. The axiom of *tawhīd* remains the unchanging foundation of these transformative dynamics.

To illustrate, applying this principle of globalization to the subjective realm of human resource development implies the cultivation of a complementary and synergistic epistemology across all disciplines, skills, and training (see figure 2.1). This epistemology, derived from the nature of *tawhīdi* dynamics, has evolved through relevant instruments of the knowledge process, integrating the normative essence of *tawhīdi* episteme with the positivistic essence, thereby reinforcing the methods and disciplines of learning. Now, let us delve into the institutional aspect of such a globalization methodology, focusing on conflict resolution and the continuity of inter- and intra-systems.

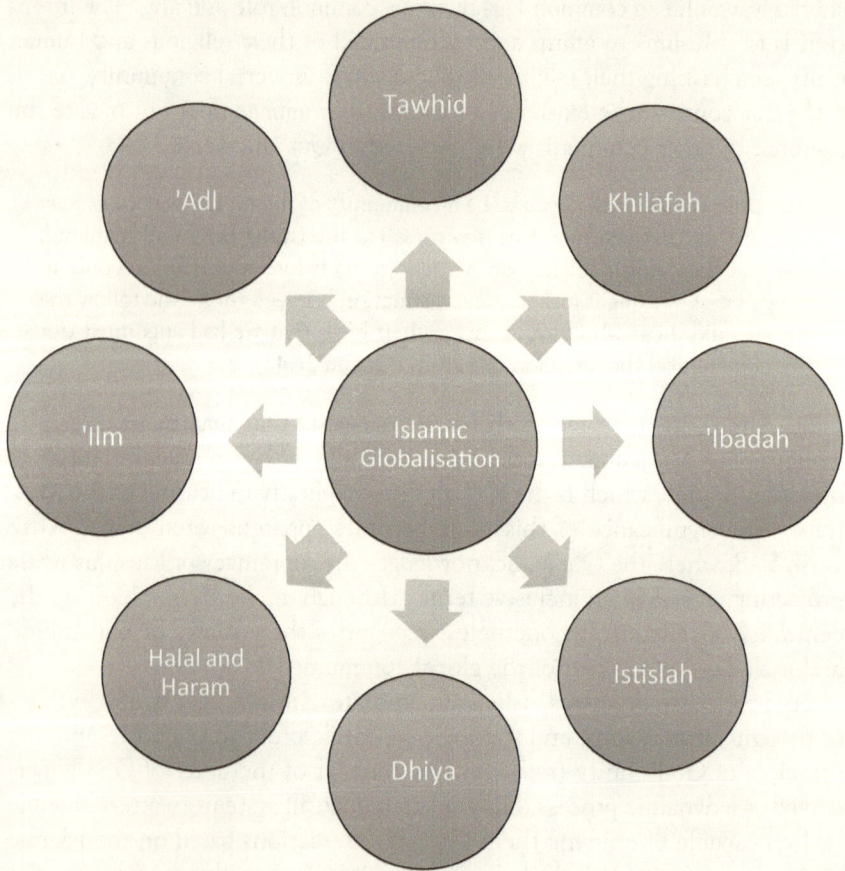

Figure 2.1 Islamic Paradigm of Globalization. *Source:* From the author.

Islamic Perspective on the Institutional Aspect of Globalization

In the Islamic context, we encounter the foundational textual reference to *sharī'ah*, with its principles applying to the nature and challenges of any given knowledge structure. This textual reference, often termed a *shuratic* interpretive reference in polity, permeates both inter- and intra-systems (trans-political). Its primary role is the formulation of rules of life (*ahkām*) and the transformation of the fundamental activities and behaviors within the socioeconomic order.[19] It is essential to note that neither *ahkām* (representing a polity's preference based on the understanding of acquired knowledge, characterization, and delivery of the rule) nor the *shūrā* can be imposed. Instead, these principles gain strength through the voluntary acceptance of their truth and contribution to the well-being (*islāh* and *falāh*) of the entire system. The system consists of two integral parts: the polity (*shūrā*) and the socio-scientific order (such as the market functioning as a subset of ecology). The *ahkām*, representing a preference of polity (*shūrā*), is directed at transforming the fundamental activities and behaviors within the socioeconomic order. The market activities encompassing consumption, production, and distribution are thus targeted for transformation under the influence of *ahkām*. The socio-scientific order, in turn, contributes to the provision of a social good. Consequently, the preferences of polity undergo scrutiny, acceptance, revision, or rejection by the socio-scientific order. The resulting preference of the socio-scientific order represents interactively generated preferences, forming a dynamic relationship with those of *ahkām*. These responses, viewed as interactive preferences from the socio-scientific order, undergo post-evaluation as part of the learning process within polity (*shūrā*) ... Consensus or majority rule is established through partial or complete *ijmā* (qiyās), as circular interactions persist between polity and the socio-scientific order. This continuous circularity of *sharī'āh* and *ahkām*, facilitated by interactions and integration, is perceived as the recreative essence of the *tawhīdi* episteme, manifested through the instruments and institutions of change. The entirety of this circular process, perpetually established and sustained between the socio-scientific system as a universally pervasive and embryonic entity, is referred to here as the *shuratic* process.[20]

Application of *Shurātic* Perspective

By employing the *shurātic* approach, which incorporates both trade and institutionalism, we can formulate a well-organized framework that encapsulates the authentic Islamic essence and methodology of global integration within the context of a pervasive democratic process of growth and transformation. Nevertheless, this requires a fundamental reorientation of our thinking, aligning it with a *tawhīdi* worldview in the socio-scientific domain. This transformative shift will inevitably result in the development of grassroots democratic institutions, establishing a cause-and-effect relationship as a natural outcome of the *shuratic* process.

The Qur'ān explicitly declares that God has made the sea subservient, allowing ships to traverse its waves. This arrangement enables people to embark on journeys in search of God's bounty, providing them with reasons to express gratitude. The interpretive scope of this verse suggests the emergence of beneficial diversity that mirrors the Divine Essence. The Qur'ān explicitly declares that God has made the sea subservient, allowing ships to traverse its waves. This arrangement enables people to embark on journeys in search of God's bounty, providing them with reasons to express gratitude.[21] The interpretive scope of this verse suggests the emergence of beneficial diversity that mirrors the Divine Essence.[22]

The *shūrā*, in this context, represents an institutional paradigm interconnected in a bottom-to-top-to-bottom manner, forming an extensive network of micro-shuras that reflect the interactive–integrative preferences of these shuras. This, in turn, underscores the persuasive relevance of the intra-shurātic process in polity. The socio-scientific order of trade, guided by principles of balance, well-being, purpose, and truth, implies the unification of such a paradigm through the ummatic model, given the antipathy of the Eurocentric model to a *tawhīdi* worldview. Consequently, a trade system with evolutionary linkages, characterized by technological change, complementarity, diversity, and participatory financial instruments, is developed. Subsequent trade with the non-Muslim world, albeit on a second-best basis, is conducted on the *shurātic* foundation without compromising the self-reliant development, complementarity, and growth arising from *ummatic* diversity. In this context, commodity prices, determined based on the aforementioned *ahkām*, are naturally established to counteract free ridership on excess supply to the dominant West, fostering open and purposeful trading principles globally from grassroots upward and downward.

This would engender interactive preferences between the grassroots institutional paradigm, exemplified by the Islamic World Trade Organisation and the extensive network of micro-shuras representing the *ummah* at large. Such interaction perpetuates the *shurātic* worldview of globalization, fostering orders characterized by balance, growth, goodness, purpose, and distributive equity. M.A. Chaudhury contends that through the Ahqām and the process of its delivery via precept and institutions/instruments, such ends become complementary because the Unification Epistemology of Tawhīd constitutes the unique essence of the Worldview. Consequently, the shurātic process model of international trade, globalization, and privatization is distinct and polar to the occidental process.[23]

Thus, Islamic thought, methods, behavior, institutions, and socio-scientific paradigm can substantially imbue the market economy with ethical considerations, providing an authentically Islamic orientation to the twin concepts of privatization and globalization. This model operationalizes global Islamic integration by promoting intra-communal relations and opening the paradigm of globalization to the rest of the world.[24]

Contrary to this paradigm, the process of globalization has garnered its prevailing aura of inevitability and abstract perfection over many centuries of theoretical endeavors aimed at integrating the world, primarily championed by the rulers of nations, empires, and their prominent intellectuals. However, contemporary globalization theories fall short of elucidating the implications of an ideology rooted in global conquest, shaped by a history of successful expansion and immersion within the processes of globalization that predates the evolution of the West. Some Muslims embrace a form of globalization that incorporates the *shuratic* practice and envisions an international community extending beyond Arab and non-Arab boundaries. They do not endorse the currently Western-dominated practice and interpretation of the process. Therefore, to understand the dialectical relationship between globalization and Islam in the present context, it is imperative to transcend the contemporary time frame established by recent studies and underscore the significance of historical contexts that shape the corpus of reference for contemporary actions and beliefs. In this process, an attempt is made to broaden the debate on Islam and globalization by mapping out different knowledge and practice terrains, particularly focusing on the effects of globalization that have become increasingly noticeable throughout the Muslim world in recent years. The next section examines the relationship among economic development, innovation, and entrepreneurship within the Islamic worldview. This discussion lays the groundwork for understanding how Islamic principles influence these aspects and sets the stage for exploring the Islamic paradigm of globalization. It suggests that the ethical framework derived from Islamic teachings extends to global economic interactions, shaping how Muslims engage with the broader global community.

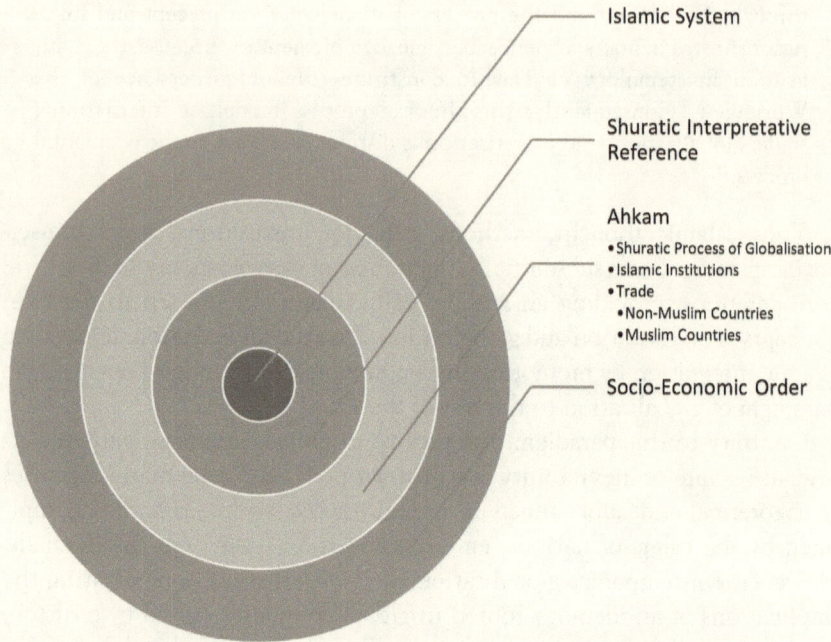

Figure 2.2 **Islamic Perspective on the Institutional Aspect of Globalization and Its Application.** *Source*: From the author.

The Islamic Paradigm: Ethics, Innovation, and Economic Development

Theories underpinning economic development and strategic management underscore the indispensable nature of innovation for institutions. At its core, innovation entails the identification and exploitation of new opportunities to create value for users while generating profits for the firms involved. This perspective places a premium on innovation not only as a means of enhancing the financial performance of individual firms within a given industry but also as a vital factor in sustaining the industry as a whole over the long term. Furthermore, it posits that the robust growth of firms plays a pivotal role in advancing the overall economic development, yielding advantages for both consumers and businesses in the process.[25] The ongoing dialogues, while informative, exhibit a notable deficiency in systematically tackling the intricacies of social development and well-being concerning the economic advancements arising from innovation and entrepreneurship in various industries. This conspicuous gap holds substantial implications for the societal fabric and ethical evolution of the communities in which these innovative and entrepreneurial endeavors unfold. Instances of detrimental innovations and excessive resource wastage serve as exemplars of endeavors that lack ethical values or moral considerations in the application of science and technology.

Rectifying these oversights necessitates the incorporation of values-based principles, with the Islamic worldview standing out as a noteworthy example. Rooted in a comprehensive perspective on life, the Islamic worldview encompasses facets such as equitable economic practices and just social development. Adopting this holistic understanding can pave the way for the formulation of solutions that foster congruence between socio-economic development and ethical considerations. From an Islamic point of view, the intrinsic purpose of human existence resides in the execution of religious duties (*ibadah*) and the assumption of the role of vicegerent on Earth.[26] These intertwined responsibilities serve as the conduit for individuals to achieve their ultimate aspiration—*mardhatillah*, denoting the pleasure and blessings bestowed by God.[27] The realization of *mardhatillah* mandates steadfast adherence to the *sharī'ah*, an encompassing guide governing Muslim conduct in all facets of life, coupled with the unwavering commitment to Islamic ethical principles. Furthermore, individuals are compelled to earnestly direct their actions, imbued with sincerity (*ikhlas*), toward the pursuit of perfection (*ihsan*). Hence, the practices of innovation and entrepreneurship, when grounded in Islamic teachings, find their boundaries delineated by the *sharī'ah* and ethical principles. This delineation serves to facilitate inventors, entrepreneurs, and managers in fulfilling their religious obligations and attaining *mardhatillah*, as elucidated in the Qur'ān:

> O ye who believe! Obey Allah and obey the Messenger and those charged with authority among you. If ye differ in anything among yourselves, refer it to Allah and His Messenger if ye do believe in Allah and the Last Day: that is best, and most suitable for final determination.[28]

Scientific cognition, characterized by its methodical and objective approach to inquiry, serves as a cornerstone in the pursuit of knowledge. This mode of investigation, grounded in meticulous observation and systematic methodologies, forms the scaffolding of understanding natural and human phenomena. The amalgamation of worldview, disciplined inquiry, and adept modes of reasoning constitutes the foundational elements nurturing the genesis of scientific thinking. It is these elements that sustain and propel thinking styles throughout the diverse phases of scientific advancement. Conversely, the absence of scientific thinking or the decline of inventive cognition is a consequence of the inefficacy of the aforementioned factors. The evolutionary trajectory of scientific thinking across history is not solely aimed at fostering new knowledge about existing phenomena; rather, its paramount objective is the reconfiguration of prevailing ideas and hegemonic modes of thinking.

Inspiration for great ideas and modes of creative thinking emanates from intellectual prowess guided by Divine Wisdom. The initiation of the Islamic mission, as outlined in the Holy Qur'ān, underscores the call for a reconstruction of the worldview. The directive, "Read by the name of your Lord who created," signifies the fundamental method of appreciating the Creator through the study and understanding of nature and the entire created world.[29] This Islamic perspective, rooted in pure *tawhid* ("unity of God"), cultivates an innovative power of thinking and creative insights within the community of believers, fostering exploration and understanding of the natural world. The *tawhidic* worldview not only introduces a new vision of nature but also instills a fresh spirit of enthusiasm in Muslim scholarship, motivating scientific research and contributing to societal development. Consequently, the Holy Qur'ān and the Sunnah of the Prophet (PBUH) stand as the primary sources of inspiration for scientific thinking within Islamic scholarship.

The Qur'ān serves as the cornerstone for intellectual thinking, encouraging inventive and evaluative reasoning through its thought-provoking queries like "Are the blind man and he who sees are equal? You don't think?," (You request others to conduct rightly while you forget to practice it yourselves and yet you are studying the Scripture? Do you not understand? [2:44]).[30] These inquiries, posed by the Qur'ān, are not intended for simplistic answers but rather to stimulate innovative and discerning thinking. The Qur'ān advises against unquestioning acceptance of others' perspectives without substantiated evidence. Allah, as depicted in the Qur'ān, invites individuals to scrutinize societal norms, freeing them from unexamined conformity.[31] The Qur'ān encourages people to transcend personal desires that might hinder the pursuit of truth, prompting them to ponder the meaning of life, the inevitability of death, and the nature of existence beyond life. The Qur'ān underscores the importance of contemplating the origins and sustenance of the universe, guiding individuals toward the realization that the intricate design and harmonious plan observable in the world are reflections of Allah Almighty's creative power. Thus, within the Islamic worldview, intellectual freedom operates within the framework of faith (*Iman*), offering a guiding principle for the entire scientific enterprise.

The Qur'ānic Approach to Creative Methodologies

Al-Karasneh and Saleh originally proposed four methodologies—traveling, observing, listening, and deliberation—derived from their Qur'ānic analysis to stimulate creativity. Expanding on these insights, Khairul Akmaliah Adhama et al. introduced two additional approaches to enhance the creative process.[32] The first approach involves exploring scientific knowledge as unveiled in the Qur'ān, emphasizing the Qur'ānic role as a foundational source for scientific knowledge and innovation in Islam. This approach draws on verses such as Yunus-10:5, Yaseen-36:38–40, An-Nahl-16:66, Ar-Ra'd-13:4, Qaf-50:7–8, and Al-Muminun-23:13–14, providing insights into astronomy, zoology, botany, geoscience, and creationism. These verses contribute to a profound understanding of human creation and underscore Allah as the supreme Creator. The second approach focuses on drawing insights from historical narratives, utilizing the Qur'ān's narration of significant past events to extract valuable lessons. Surah Yusuf-12:111 emphasizes that these narratives are not mere tales but detailed expositions, serving as guides and sources of mercy for believers. This historical knowledge, acting as a guide and source of innovation, aligns with the Qur'ān's directive to learn from the past.[33] Surah Al-Ankabut-29:20 encourages traversing the Earth to witness Allah's creations, emphasizing *tawhīd*—the acknowledgment of God's power over all things. This directive underscores the importance of travel in acquiring knowledge across diverse fields, including botany, zoology, humanities, and geology. Surah Al-Imran-3:137 associates the travel directive with a cautionary reminder for those who disobey Allah, highlighting the crucial role of exploration and knowledge acquisition in shaping a holistic understanding of the world.

An alternative and noteworthy approach involves the act of seeing and observing, as explicitly emphasized in diverse verses of the Qur'ān.[34] Notably, Al-Baqarah-2:164 impels individuals to contemplate the intricate creation of the heavens and the Earth, the rhythmic alternation of night and day, the maritime ventures of ships, the life-bestowing descent of rain, the manifold diversity of creatures scattered across the terrestrial expanse, the dynamic shifts in winds, and the ethereal procession of trailing clouds—an eloquent call to engage in profound reflection and to acknowledge the boundless magnificence of God.[35] This particular method advocates for humanity to perceive the cosmos through a lens of novelty, thereby nurturing sentiments of awe and reverence and prompting the remembrance of Allah's unparalleled grandeur.[36] The subsequent verse, Al-Baqarah-2:259, further urges individuals to witness the manifestations of God's dominion over life and death, encouraging contemplation on the ephemeral nature of existence.[37]

The Qur'ān, with an emphasis on the methodological significance of seeing, issues directives for individuals to keenly observe God's intricate craftsmanship evident in the creation of the universe and heavens, thereby fortifying their faith in God.[38] Az-Zumar-39:21 intricately interweaves the acts of seeing, thinking, and wisdom, instructing the observation of God's creations. Al-Ghashiya-88:17–20 guides individuals to scrutinize the intricacies of God's creation, imparting insights into diverse realms such as zoology, astronomy, and geography, accompanied by *tawhidic* reminders.[39] This series of instructions underscores humanity's ultimate return to Allah (Al-Ghashiya 88:25). Furthermore, Qaf-50:6–8 implores mankind to actively observe the marvels of Allah's creations, with Qaf-50:8 supplementing these observations with *tawhidic* reminders. An-Nur-24:44 elucidates Allah's orchestration of day and night, presenting it as an illustrative model for those endowed with vision. These scriptural directives advocate for meticulous observation and contemplation, acting as catalysts for the cultivation of innovative ideas.[40]

In the creative process, the Qur'ān emphasizes the pivotal role of attentive listening through various verses. The scriptural directive urges individuals to listen attentively when the Qur'ān is recited, highlighting the potential for blessings and profound comprehension.[41] Muslims are actively encouraged to engage in contemplative listening during the recitation, as this intentional auditory engagement serves as a conduit for remembrance and comprehension of Qur'ānic verses, ensuring blessings in both the present world and the hereafter. Sayyid Qutb's commentary further elucidates that attentive listening stimulates piety, prompts self-correction, and instills tranquility, underscoring its instrumental role in fostering contemplation, positive attitudes, and heightened creativity. Another verse underscores the ongoing importance of listening and discerning sound advice.[42] Sayyid Qutb expounds on this, asserting that the act of listening and embracing sagacious counsel propels individuals toward divine guidance, creating a cyclical reinforcement of attentive listening and adherence to the best counsel. This dynamic process ultimately leads to an increased reception of divine guidance. In the realm of innovation or creativity, this divine guidance becomes a preeminent source, where listening and embracing sagacious counsel serve as conduits for profound guidance, as highlighted in a subsequent verse (Qur'ān, 2:285).[43] This verse unequivocally emphasizes that listening is the ultimate manifestation of adherence to *tawhīd*, seamlessly followed by obedience and a genuine plea for forgiveness. For actively listening Muslims responding to the calls and regulations of God, this practice becomes a tangible manifestation of *tawhīd* in their conduct.

Scholars have elaborated on numerous Qur'ānic verses, including surah An-Nahl-16:10–11, 13, 68–69, Ali Imran-3:191, and Al-Baqarah-2:164, that advocate contemplation.[44] The central theme is that the call to contemplate aims to empower individuals to unearth the ultimate truth about themselves—pertaining to their purpose in this world and their relationship with God. This identified truth serves as a foundational basis for a deeper comprehension of God. The *tawhidic* dimension assumes a pivotal role in fostering innovation, positing that innovators embracing *tawhīd* are inherently more motivated to develop innovations for the betterment of mankind, driven by their belief in the rewards in the Hereafter.[45] The concept of *tawhidic* science underscores the necessity for *tawhidic* methodologies in the research and innovation process. The analysis discerns that the Islamic methodologies for innovativeness are prescribed in the Qur'ān and inherently possess *tawhidic* attributes. The pursuit of "creation" or innovativeness can be realized through six methodologies, fundamentally constituting a form of deliberative technique with a pronounced *tawhidic* emphasis in their procedural application. This implies that the concept of innovation in Islam serves to bring Muslims closer to comprehending their raison d'être in this world and their connections with God.[46]

While these methodologies are predominantly evident during the stage of developing the idea, they retain applicability in making creative decisions across all phases of the innovation process. For instance, deliberation can be employed when determining the optimal course of action for a product launch. The methodologies advocated by God extend beyond the Western perspective of creativity and innovation, which predominantly relies on scientifically validated knowledge, disregarding divine revelation as a source. Western perspectives often emphasize the entrepreneurial context, cognitive reasoning, and prior experience as primary sources of creativity and knowledge for innovation. In contrast, Islam recognizes creativity and innovation as a continuous process, prescribing methodologies within the Qur'ān.

Sharī'ah Objectives and Utility in Technological Innovation

Within the discourse of technological innovation, especially concerning its deployment, Islam advocates a prescriptive framework encapsulated in the *maqasid* of *sharī'ah* (objectives of *sharī'ah*) and *maslahah* (utility). The conceptualization by Al-Ghazali defines *maqasid al-sharī'ah*, delineating its essence as the preservation of religion, life, intellect, progeny, and wealth. In tandem, *maslahah* encompasses any means or elements safeguarding the *maqasid as-sharī'ah*, with its implementation following prioritized categories: necessities (*darruriyyah*), conveniences (*hajiyyah*), and refinements (*tahsiniyyah*).[47] Hence, transcending conventional considerations in technology deployment, Islamic teachings underscore the imperative to align innovations with the objectives of *sharī'ah* and the utility concept. Within an Islamic societal framework, innovations must align with the *sharī'ah* objectives safeguarding quintessential human elements. Innovations conflicting with this protective stance are deemed discredited and disapproved. Consequently, the entire spectrum of innovation, spanning scientific research and research and development (R&D), necessitates a comprehensive integration of the *maslahah* concept and the fulfillment of objectives. Moreover, the establishment of production priorities within the milieu of social and economic progress is paramount. These priorities should address the basic needs of individuals (*darruriyyah* and *hajiyyah*). Any pursuits surpassing the realm of *tahsiniyyah*, especially innovations leading to inappropriate and harmful products or those promoting self-indulgence, are unequivocally disapproved within the Islamic framework.[48]

In addition to fostering bidirectional communication between technology deployers and their intended users, Islam establishes the principle of *tawhīd* to fulfill the vicegerency roles of entrepreneurs and managers within organizations. This principle posits that product innovation, along with its associated promotion and packaging strategies, is oriented toward augmenting customers' comprehension of . This, in turn, is envisioned to influence and mold their subsequent behaviors and actions. When contemplating innovation and entrepreneurship as manifestations of *ibadah* (worship), inventors, entrepreneurs, and managers are enjoined to aspire to "doing good deeds" and striving for perfection, as articulated in Surah Al-Mulk:

> Blessed is He in Whose hand is the Sovereignty, and, He is Able to do all things. Who hath created life and death that He may try you which of you is best in conduct; and He is the Mighty, the Forgiving. (Qur'ān, 67:1–2)[49]

In interpreting the abovementioned verse, Sayyid Qutb underscores the incumbent duty of a Muslim to maintain vigilant oversight over both intentions and actions, persistently endeavoring to attain the apex of "best conduct" (*ihsan*) in the sight of God.[50] The mandate for *ihsan* finds further affirmation in the *hadith* of Prophet Muhammad PBUH, particularly in the second *hadith* of *Hadith* Arba'ain, where the Prophet responds to Jibril's inquiry about the meaning of *ihsan*. Prophet Muhammad PBUH expounds, "It is to worship Allah as if you see Him, for though you do not see Him, surely He sees you." This articulation within the *hadith* emphasizes God's command that *ibadah* must be executed with *ihsan*. The practice of *ibadah* imbued with *ihsan* is explicated by Imam Ahmad ibn Hanbal, who posits that it not only instills *tawhidic* values in Muslims but also fosters sincerity (*ikhlas*) in worship and a resolute commitment to perfecting one's *ibadah*.[51]

Expanding the scope, *ihsan* entails the unwavering pursuit of perfection within the domains of innovation and entrepreneuring. While conventional literature discusses the notion of continuous improvement as an end in itself, the concept of *ihsan* is distinctively tethered to *tawhīd*, emanating directly from the commandments of Allah. In the seventeenth *hadith* of Hadith Arba'ain, Abu Yaala Shaddad bin Aws conveys Prophet Muhammad PBUH's assertion: "Verily, Allah has prescribed ihsan in all things" (related by al-Imam Muslim). Some scholars interpret ihsan as "the act of doing well." In the context of innovation, this implies that commendable deeds and the meticulous refinement of those deeds must constitute integral aspects of the inventive process.[52]

Toward Economic Justice and Global Sustainability

The international economic landscape has undergone a transformation into a cohesive structure with the establishment of various economic and trade agreements, including entities and regional alliances. This interconnected network poses a significant challenge to the Muslim world, particularly concerning the economic standing and competitiveness of Islamic nations against the Western and developed counterparts. Many of these trade agreements were crafted during a period when numerous Muslim countries were under colonial domination, leading to their exclusion from active participation and consent. Consequently, the Muslim world became enmeshed in an obligatory economic relationship within a polarized trade framework, allowing for the exploitation of their economies by the developed capitalist world. Despite holding over 70 percent of the world's oil reserves, most Muslim countries struggle to leverage these resources for economic development.[53]

It is crucial to acknowledge that historical trade agreements were often self-serving during the colonial era, exacerbating economic challenges for Muslim nations. This historical context has resulted in a stark disparity, where only a handful of countries within the Muslim world, such as Saudi Arabia, Qatar, the United Arab Emirates, Malaysia, Indonesia, and Brunei Darussalam, have successfully avoided impoverishment and economic stagnation. Applying theoretical frameworks to this context, the systems theory of international relations underscores the complex interplay among global nations within semiautonomous yet coordinated subsystems, encompassing economic and various other domains. The advent of a unipolar hegemonic global power dynamic has the potential to cultivate a fragile international relationship framework, wherein the preeminent superpower may tighten its influence over weaker states to advance its vested interests. This dynamic is observable in the contemporary globalization landscape, particularly in the interactions between the United States, its allies, and the Muslim world.[54]

Conversely, Qutb's articulation of the Jahili society doctrine posits that the imposition of Western economic systems on the Muslim world, accompanied by colonialism, has plunged the Muslim *ummah* into a state of Jahiliyyah, unparalleled in world history.[55] This transformation is attributed to the incorporation of detrimental Western economic paradigms involving usury, capitalism, and inequality. Nevertheless, acknowledging the undeniable economic advantages accrued by the Muslim world in the era of globalization is imperative. Notably, the global acceptance of the Islamic financial system by non-Muslim nations, as an economic alternative to mitigate depression and recession, stands out as a significant development. This adoption has remarkably contributed to elevating the principles and economic values of Islam on a global scale. Moreover, the globalization era has facilitated foreign investment and technology transfer, particularly benefiting strategically positioned Islamic countries. The economic landscape has witnessed positive transformations as a result of these endeavors.

Islam advocates for economic fairness and an equitable distribution of wealth. At the core of the Islamic economic system lie fundamental principles of impartiality, fairness, and communal obligation. It perceives wealth not as an ultimate goal but as a tool to nurture societal welfare and alleviate poverty. At the heart of Islamic teachings lies Zakat, a mandatory practice that involves donating a portion of one's wealth to support the destitute and those facing hardship. Zakat functions as a mechanism designed to redistribute wealth and bridge socioeconomic disparities. Its effective application enables societies to methodically address the essential needs of all individuals, fostering social harmony and curbing the widening gap between the prosperous and the marginalized. The Islamic economic framework stands as a model that prioritizes the collective welfare, underscoring the importance of equitable wealth distribution to enhance communal well-being.[56]

The primary aim underlying the dissuasion of conspicuous socioeconomic disparities within the Islamic paradigm is the establishment of a moral framework that cultivates reciprocal sentiments of altruism and compassion among the inhabitants of a given societal or communal milieu. As an ideological construct, Islam fervently espouses the virtues of social cohesion, fraternal amity, and the weaving of a harmonious societal fabric. Accordingly, disparities in socioeconomic status that have the potential to engender animosity, malevolence, or acrimony are deemed antithetical to the Islamic ethos and necessitate rectification. The Islamic doctrine prescribes for the impoverished not to resort to seeking alms from their peers, but rather to exert themselves while supplicating divine assistance. Concurrently, the affluent are enjoined to partake in *ihsan*, signifying the provision of comprehensive support to those in need, with the promise of spiritual recompense in the afterlife. The Qur'ānic mandate directs humanity to allocate surplus wealth for the amelioration of the destitute, thereby securing divine favor. Within the Islamic sociopolitical framework, the potential emergence of egregious inequalities is mitigated through the eradication of exploitative mechanisms.[57]

In its pursuit of an equitable social order, Islam adopts a dual-pronged strategy that encompasses the attenuation of economic disparities and the cultivation of social unity. It advances a set of ethical guidelines for resource allocation, grounded in the principles of *'Adl, Insaf,* and *Ihsan*, aimed at synthesizing meritocracy and necessity as the foundations of justice. This synthesis, in turn, ensures societal equilibrium and fosters positive interpersonal relationships as the culmination of these ethical precepts. In its efforts to mitigate pronounced disparities, Islam introduces moral safeguards. While Islam refrains from specifying a predetermined income ratio between minimum and maximum thresholds, it unequivocally discourages the propagation of extreme economic differentials. The institution of Zakat emerges as a pivotal mechanism within the Islamic faith, dedicated to resource redistribution and the amelioration of exacerbated wealth gaps. Zakat, a foundational tenet of Islam, serves as a conduit for poverty alleviation and wealth reallocation. Its meticulous administration addresses the scourge of absolute poverty, obligating the affluent to contribute a designated proportion of their wealth to deserving members of society.

The eligible beneficiaries of Zakat span across a range of categories, embracing eight distinct groups: the destitute (*fuqara*), the impoverished (*masakin*), individuals appointed by the state to collect Zakat, those whose hearts require reconciliation (*muallafat-alqulub*), individuals seeking emancipation from slavery (*fi-al-riqab*), individuals burdened by debt, contributors in the cause of Allah (*fi-sabil al-Allah*), and wayfarers (*ibn-al-sabil*). Within the realm of Muslim jurisprudence and scholarship, a consensus prevails concerning the specified categories of Zakat recipients. Nevertheless, there exists a divergence of scholarly opinions regarding the specific activities for which Zakat funds can be allocated within these categories. Remarkably, six out of the eight categories predominantly concentrate on alleviating the suffering of the impoverished and meeting their fundamental needs.

While various religions advocate for voluntary contributions to collective funds aimed at diminishing poverty levels, such acts are generally regarded as manifestations of goodwill rather than being elevated to the status of worship or religious obligation. In stark contrast, Islam formalizes such philanthropic endeavors through Zakat payments, designating them as obligatory contributions for the collective well-being of the impoverished and needy. The discourse on social justice in the Western context is primarily characterized by a philosophical orientation, diverging significantly from the Islamic approach grounded in legal and judicial dimensions, broadly guided by the precepts outlined in the Qur'ān and Sunnah. In contradistinction to the Western philosophical discourse, often immersed in considerations of rationality and theoretical paradigms, the juristic approach of Islam places paramount importance on the formulation of a normative framework that encapsulates a diversity of perspectives. This approach prioritizes the examination of each case based on its individual merits rather than rigidly adhering to a predefined philosophical standpoint.[58] The payment of Zakat stands as a cornerstone within Islam, representing an act of worship (*'ibadah*). In the sphere of Muslim governance, authorities wield the legal authority to prosecute individuals who neglect to fulfill their Zakat obligations or choose to abstain from the mandated contributions. Notably, during the nascent phase of his leadership, the first Caliph, Abu Bakr, invoked *jihād* against those who resisted the payment of Zakat.[59]

For scholars immersed in the exploration of the Islamic viewpoint on psychological and cultural phenomena, a discernible correlation emerges between psychological and social maladies and the manifestation of counterfeit, adverse, and inequitable economic conditions. These maladies encompass characteristics such as miserliness, narcissism, aggression, exploitation within primary groups, and a spectrum of mental pathologies. Hence, the imperative of sound economics and just governance policies stand as a cornerstone for the stability of any society. The degree of equity embedded within an economic system correlate directly with the harmonious nature of interpersonal relationships. The Islamic perspective on distributive justice transcends mere material considerations, drawing from spiritual foundations. It advocates values and behaviors that, when assimilated into any cultural milieu, serve to rectify unwarranted economic disparities and foster comprehensive human development.

In Western societies, the distribution of wealth is predominantly dictated by market forces, a paradigm susceptible to manipulations. The ostensibly free conditions required for the operation of a free-market system are rarely immune to such manipulations. Consequently, individuals within this system, particularly the economically disadvantaged, face enduring hardships and a dearth of opportunities. This outcome is a product of the Darwinian mechanism underpinning the system, where the survival of the fittest dictates the rules of engagement, ultimately exacerbating the plight of the impoverished while consolidating wealth among the affluent. In stark contrast, Islam propounds a multifaceted distribution system with diverse objectives. The aim extends beyond the eradication of poverty and the prevention of wealth concentration exclusively in the hands of the affluent. The Islamic system also attends to the needs of various segments facing hardship, including travelers, individuals in debt, and one's own relatives. This system is not solely dedicated to the establishment of justice but is equally committed to nurturing mutual affection and kindness within the community.[60]

The Islamic system for administering Zakat, a compulsory wealth deduction from the prosperous for the purpose of fair redistribution among the destitute, actively promotes the injection of wealth into economic consumption channels. The resulting effects on production, facilitated through exchanges and resource allocation across different sectors, are inherent but presently not fully recognized due to the absence of Islamic management frameworks and existing operational challenges. The Zakat deduction acts as a natural deterrent against the tendency to hoard idle financial resources and other assets, simultaneously serving as a powerful spiritual, moral, and economic incentive for investment.[61] The imposition of Zakat acts as a strong restraint on the inclination to accumulate stagnant capital, thus providing a dynamic impetus for investment. Increased investment, sanctioned within the Islamic framework, leads to heightened profits for the affluent while concurrently creating employment opportunities for the workforce in impoverished communities. The interdependent relationship between consumption and production underscores Zakat's ability to stimulate production to meet the consumption needs of the impoverished, thereby encouraging the development of new avenues of trade. Moreover, the revenues generated from Zakat can be prudently allocated to provide opportunities or enhance the productivity of the economically disadvantaged. Over an extended period, this strategic use of Zakat funds promotes the self-sufficiency of the impoverished, thereby reducing the national burden associated with expenditures on social security initiatives.[62]

Islamic economics hinges on the premise that Islam provides a moral archetype capable of steering diverse dimensions within an economic framework—encompassing consumption, production, and distribution. It crystallized as a conceptual framework, in part, as an endeavor to assert Islamic identity within the economic domain. While some proponents maintain that Islam, being a comprehensive code of life, prescribes a unique Islamic economic system, an alternative perspective involves seeking guidance from Islamic teachings to inform the construction of an economic system through human intellectual endeavors. This approach entails a departure from the pursuit of a meticulously detailed economic or financial system within the primary sources of Islam. The Qur'ān, while containing few specific economic directives, imparts guidance to individual conduct by shaping behaviors, incentives, constraints, and choices. Key elements of the Islamic worldview, including the sovereignty of God, societal responsibility, and the fervent promotion of social justice and equity, play pivotal roles in influencing economic perspectives.[63]

Islamic teachings actively discourage the practices of waste, extravagant consumption, and unfair trade. The yardstick for evaluating the fairness of transactions lies in their ability to prevent unearned gains or undeserved losses. Anchored in the principles of sustainable development, the Islamic approach to development aligns itself with the preservation of individuals' wealth, intellect, and future generations. Serving as a distinct alternative to both capitalism and socialism, Islamic economics strives for a nuanced equilibrium between competing considerations. While individual freedoms are upheld, their exercise is contingent upon and subservient to the collective welfare.

The Islamic economic model not only embraces aspects of a market economy but also expresses deep-seated concerns about potential negative social externalities. The framework accommodates the pursuit of individual interests, profit maximization, market competition, and personal freedoms, provided that these endeavors remain in consonance with the broader well-being of the community. In congruence with this ethos, while Islamic jurisprudence permits private ownership of property, this entitlement to asset ownership is circumscribed by a notable caveat. According to Islamic precepts, the ultimate proprietorship of all assets rests with God, and humanity is entrusted with the right to ownership with the overarching imperative of promoting societal welfare. Fundamentally, the Islamic economic paradigm pivots on achieving equilibrium amid conflicting considerations: the dichotomy between amassing wealth and redistributing it, the interplay of individual motivations and communal welfare, the juxtaposition of spiritual and material pursuits, the exigencies of the present generation weighed against the imperatives of posterity, and the nuanced navigation of the realms of the immediate versus the eschatological.[64]

The literature on Islamic economics and finance places a significant emphasis on socioeconomic justice, encompassing the equitable distribution of economic wealth and opportunities. A central concern within this domain revolves around the prevalent issue of heightened wealth concentration and the concomitant limited access to financial opportunities. Contemporary banking systems and capital markets often exhibit a proclivity for lending practices that favor the affluent, thereby contributing to the concentration of wealth and opportunities, which subsequently fosters inequality and social maladies. In stark contrast, Islamic finance advocates for a paradigm centered on risk-sharing in asset ownership and entrepreneurial ventures. This approach is poised to disseminate economic opportunities more broadly, ensuring that finance remains aligned with the imperatives of the real economy. Within the framework of Islam, market-based risk-sharing mechanisms in financing emerge as pivotal instruments for advancing economic justice within the financial system.[65]

This does not mean that the favored modes of Islamic financing, characterized by principles of profit-sharing and risk-sharing, are immune to injustices. An illustration of this could be a party in a transaction reserving a disproportionately excessive share of profit, surpassing what is considered reasonable. Additionally, profit-sharing ventures, even within permissible business domains, carry the potential to inflict substantial harm on society and the environment, such as instances of water pollution. Conversely, interest-based financial transactions, such as conventional microcredit, might contribute to economic opportunity. Nevertheless, the discourse within Islamic finance literature tends to perceive interest-based lending of money and the trading of risk as inherently problematic. This perception holds true, if not at the micro level in the short term, then for the broader economy in the long term.

From a financial standpoint, a 2018 report by the Islamic Financial Services Board indicates that the Islamic finance service industry, encompassing banking, capital markets, and *takāful*, had a combined value of approximately U.S.$2.05 trillion in 2017. These figures highlight a substantial opportunity within the Islamic finance sector, offering Organisation of Islamic Cooperation (OIC) member countries a means to bridge the significant financing gap for sustainable development investments. In terms of Islamic funds, despite a slight reduction in their number to 1,161 in 2017, the assets under management (AuM) exhibited a notable surge of 19 percent, reaching U.S.$67 billion. It is noteworthy that twenty out of the thirty-four domiciles of Islamic funds are situated in non-OIC countries like Ireland, the United States, and Luxembourg. Collectively, these non-OIC countries command an

AuM share nearly equivalent to 20 percent of the overall total. This emphasizes the critical need for Muslim countries to embrace effective institutional reforms and frameworks, aligning with principles advocated in Islam. These recommendations resonate not only within the Islamic context but also align with broader political reform agendas beyond the Islamic sphere. A realistic timetable for transitioning to representative governments accountable to their constituents is underscored as a shared principle.[66]

Economic, Environmental, and Social Sustainability in Islamic Finance

The notion of financial stability transcends mere functionality; it signifies a state where the components of the economic structure, comprising financial markets, institutions, and associated infrastructures, operate cohesively, resilient to systemic disruptions. This state reflects an environment, where each facet of the financial system demonstrates optimal flexibility in responding to potential shocks, thereby fostering continuous functionality and financial intermediation conducive to sustainable economic growth.[67] Within the realm of Islamic finance, a profound potential for sustainable development unfolds. This trajectory aligns with a higher objective that prioritizes the maximization of positive value creation while mitigating adverse impacts on stakeholders and the environment. However, this evolution necessitates seamless integration with the *maqasid al-sharī'ah*, a framework initially articulated by Abu Hamid al-Ghazali in the twelfth century. The *maqasid al-sharī'ah* delineates objectives centered around preserving religion, life, family, intellect, and property, with the overarching aim of preventing harm and realizing benefits. Subsequent scholarly contributions have expounded on the *maqasid sharī'ah*, framing it as the attainment of good, welfare, advantage, and benefits, along with the prevention of evil, injury, and loss. Modern scholars have delved into the dimensions of righteousness and justice within this framework. Contemporary discourse within Islamic law acknowledges human development as a paramount expression of *maslahah* (public interest) across all economic activities. This nuanced understanding emphasizes the intricate balance required for Islamic finance to serve as a catalyst for positive change while upholding the fundamental principles ingrained in the *maqasid al-sharī'ah*.[68]

Upon achieving alignment with the five *sharī'ah* objectives, the operations of Islamic Finance culminate in the realization of economic, environmental, and social sustainability. This posits the argument that the *maqasid al-sharī'ah*, serving as the bedrock of Islamic Finance and the broader Islamic economy, embraces a more comprehensive outlook in the pursuit of public interests. Its overarching goal involves fostering prosperity without leaving any segment of society behind, thereby contributing to the construction of a cohesive and resilient societal framework. Consequently, it can be posited that Islamic finance exhibits a high degree of sustainability, particularly when juxtaposed with the conventional system, owing to its proximity to the real economy. The array of Islamic banking products and services further underscores this sustainability, distinguished by their equity-based nature rather than reliance on loans. Moreover, these financial instruments are more intricately linked with environmental concerns, social considerations, and actual production processes. This nuanced approach not only positions Islamic finance as a robust economic system but also accentuates its potential to contribute meaningfully to broader societal and environmental objectives.[69]

The development of Islamic finance is contingent upon its steadfast commitment to three pivotal realms: economic sustainability, environmental sustainability, and social sustainability. Economic sustainability necessitates the comprehensive alignment and equilibrium of diverse elements within wealth creation, spanning micro and macroeconomics, public and private finance, and social finance. The realization of economic sustainability encompasses a multifaceted strategy, including the implementation of a rigorous *sharī'ah* screening process for income purification, the equitable allocation of profit and loss based on the sharing principle, and the fortification of Islamic social finance instruments such as the Zakat payment system, Qard Hasan, charity (Sadaqah), and Waqf. Moreover, the transparent disclosure of non-halal earnings emerges as a crucial facet in fortifying economic sustainability within the landscape of Islamic finance.[70]

The potential impact of Islamic banking and finance on environmental sustainability is significant. Rooted in Islamic values that prioritize the preservation of natural resources and respect for all living entities, the relationship between humanity and the environment is approached with profound consideration. Upholding environmental sustainability requires the formulation of comprehensive policies for green lending and investments, underpinned by a rigorous analysis of environmental risks and adherence to national ecological regulations. This encompasses the promotion of green products, services, and investments in environmentally-friendly projects. Moreover, the pursuit of social sustainability in Islamic finance involves the cultivation of human resources, the facilitation of scholarships, and active engagement in R&D. These initiatives are essential elements for continuous improvement and the enduring achievement of sustainable growth.[71]

Environmental Crisis and Management

The escalating environmental challenges, spanning issues like global warming, freshwater depletion, biodiversity loss, and ozone layer depletion, have prompted a surge in scholarly investigations probing the environmental insights embedded within the Qur'ān. Scholars have conducted research to unravel the ethical policy implications arising from these intricate relationships. An analysis grounded in the teachings of the Qur'ān underscores the Islamic perspective on the environment, anchored in the fundamental belief that Allah assumes the dual roles of Creator and Sustainer of the universe.[72]

Al-Jayyousi's research scrutinized environmental deterioration as a poignant indication of moral and ethical disorder. The natural equilibrium has been disrupted by human decisions and actions, characterized by the excessive exploitation of natural resources. Consequently, it is imperative to responsibly manage natural resources, demonstrating thoughtful consideration for the well-being of all living things. In alignment with this perspective, Islamic scholars and other Muslim leaders wholeheartedly endorse the 2015 "Islamic Declaration of Istanbul" on climate change. This declaration urges people and leaders worldwide to promptly phase out greenhouse gas emissions, stabilize atmospheric concentrations of greenhouse gases, and steadfastly commit to addressing the environmental challenges we face. In 2015, Al-Jayyousi advocated for a paradigm shift from the prevailing secular environmental model to a resurgence of the holistic Islamic approach. This approach, rooted in sustainability principles encompassing environmental, social, and economic dimensions, draws inspiration from the Islamic concepts of harmony, the "natural state" (*fitra*), and the principles of balance (*mizan*) and proportion (*mikdar*) inherent in the systems of the universe.[73] Furthermore, Al-Jayyousi proposed the rejuvenation of the Green Endowment Fund (Waqf) as a pivotal instrument to facilitate the transition to a sustainable economy. The Waqf, in this context, would actively support endeavors such as green activism, innovation inspired by both nature and culture, and the adoption of a sustainable green lifestyle.[74] In light of the anticipated escalation of disasters due to climate change in numerous OIC member nations, the OIC 25 agenda advocates for the implementation of prudent environmental management practices. The primary objective is to mitigate disaster risks and ameliorate the adverse impacts of climate change. In addressing the critical matter of augmenting water productivity, particular emphasis is placed on enhancing the technical efficiency of water utilization and ensuring the judicious allocation of available water resources amid competing demands.[75] Moreover, within the Islamic framework, there exists a tenet that underscores the establishment of an inclusive and equitable economic system. This system is designed to safeguard the rights of workers, ensure the provision of fair wages, and prohibit exploitative practices such as usury (*riba*) and the accumulation of wealth through hoarding. Islamic finance emerges as a proponent of alternative models that endorse ethical investment, profit-sharing, and risk-sharing. These financial paradigms contribute substantively to the cultivation of economic stability and the facilitation of sustainable growth.[76]

Fostering Global Diversity, Pluralism, and Interfaith Cooperation for Mutual Understanding

Unquestionably, the contemporary era unfolds within an unprecedented wave of globalization. The undeniable reality is that our world today is more intricately interconnected than it was just a few decades ago, not to mention a century past. We assert that the trajectory of globalization will persist, projecting that our future world will surpass our present one in terms of interconnectedness. This ongoing trend toward heightened globalization is underpinned by a powerful combination of material and human factors. Advancements in communication and transportation technologies, economic interdependence, and educational paradigms collectively drive the relentless momentum propelling our world into an intensified state of globalization.[77] The unprecedented flow of individuals across national and continental boundaries, facilitated by these three primary factors, instigates profound shifts in the demographic and cultural cartography of the world. To grasp the irreversible trajectory of this phenomenon, an in-depth exploration of globalization's intrinsic nature becomes imperative. Globalization unfolds as a dynamic process, wherein the global human community steadily advances toward heightened interconnectedness and interdependence. This progression is intricately woven through the complex interplay of diverse forces—both natural and human—across each of the six dimensions previously outlined. Furthermore, it epitomizes a global process, wherein the coalescence of unity and diversity in human life and thought assumes unprecedented visibility.

The effects of globalization manifest across our contemporary world in myriad material and human dimensions, presenting numerous and often formidable challenges. The impact of globalization extends both positively, contributing to the prospective well-being of humanity, and negatively, posing significant challenges to contemporary human existence. Extensive discourse has been dedicated to unraveling the virtues and vices inherent in the phenomenon of globalization. This ongoing dialogue, occurring on national, regional, and global platforms, is accompanied by an evolution in the diverse facets of globalization. Among its most consequential outcomes is the progressively pluralistic character that permeates our world.[78]

Undoubtedly, well before the advent of the contemporary term "globalization," the global landscape has perpetually been characterized by pluralism, embracing multifaceted ethnicities, religions, cultures, and civilizations from the earliest historical epochs. However, the human comprehension of this inherent diversity has undergone evolution. Presently, within our modern era, there exists an amplified consciousness regarding our existence within an inherently pluralistic world. This heightened awareness of cultural pluralism predominantly stems from the influential forces shaping contemporary globalization—especially media, telecommunications, and transportation technologies—granting individuals the firsthand observation of increasingly heterogeneous and pluralistic compositions within various human societies.[79]

In transforming our world into a materially unified "global village," technology has played a pivotal role. However, despite this material homogeneity, we find ourselves grappling with the challenge of peaceful coexistence within a culturally diverse village. As our world inexorably advances toward greater and more intricate pluralism, we are compelled to confront and navigate the intricate reality it presents. Effectively addressing the multifaceted contemporary phenomenon of cultural pluralism demands a thoughtful and patient approach. In my perspective, a key strategy for overcoming the challenges posed by cultural pluralism lies in highlighting the significance of cultural dialogue in the pursuit of the common good. This approach recognizes that peaceful coexistence in a diverse and pluralistic world hinges on cultivating cultural dialogue as an ingrained way of life. Through ongoing dialogue, the objective is to discern shared values, strengthen them, and identify differences with the aim of minimizing them to their irreducible essence. Subsequently, we turn to education as a means to instil the spirit of respect and tolerance for these inherent differences.[80]

Throughout history, the world has borne witness to a multitude of tragic events documented by scholars. Events such as the 9/11 attacks, the Israel–Palestine conflict, turmoil in the Middle East, and Muslim–Buddhist contentions in Thailand and Myanmar manifest as palpable and pressing scenarios.[81] Paradoxically, these incidents, with their profound implications, seemingly stand in stark contrast to the foundational tenets of religious beliefs in general.[82] While the teachings of every religious tradition espouse the principles of universal love and advocate compassion toward fellow human beings, paradoxically, acts of egregious violence often unfold in the name of religion, claiming the lives of numerous innocents. This disconcerting reality underscores the imperative to delve into the root causes of this conundrum and to devise comprehensive solutions that foster unity among individuals from diverse religious and cultural backgrounds. A pivotal avenue for effecting positive change lies in engaging in meaningful interreligious dialogue, a collaborative endeavor aimed at advancing the greater interests of humanity. Recognized as an indispensable tool, interreligious dialogue serves as a means to assuage the tensions that persist between different religious communities on a global scale.[83]

Islam, as a global faith, imparts teachings that revolve around love, tolerance, and compassion for the entirety of humanity.[84] Muslims, since the time of the Prophet, have played a pivotal role in advancing interreligious harmony.[85] The Qur'ān serves as an invaluable repository of instances illustrating dialogue and interreligious relationships, vividly portrayed in verses such as 49:13, 5:48, and 16:125. Notably, the Qur'ān presents dialogues involving the Prophets with God, Angels with God, Prophets with their respective communities, and even dialogues with the devil.[86] The exemplary conduct of the Prophet of Islam serves as a paradigm for positive engagement, pre-dating his prophetic calling. An illustrative case is the resolution of tribal disputes in Mecca through the replacement of the Black Stone (*Hajar al-Aswad*), a manifestation of the Prophet's constructive involvement five years prior to embarking on his prophetic journey.

For this reason, individuals bestowed upon him the titles of al-Amin, "the trustworthy" and al-Sadiq, "the truthful." The annals of Islamic history are replete with instances illustrating harmonious interreligious relationships. A compelling historical illustration is found in the context of Islamic Jerusalem under early Muslim rule.[87] Furthermore, the Common Word initiative of 2007, endorsed by 138 esteemed Muslim scholars, stands as a testament to the Islamic stance on non-Muslims. In the contemporary landscape, Islam has encountered misconceptions primarily stemming from a deficiency in accurate Islamic knowledge. Researchers have diligently addressed this issue to dispel misunderstandings.[88]

The world unfolds in its inherent diversity, a landscape shaped not by human hands but by the divine will of God, as elucidated in Islam for the collective benefit of humanity. The Qur'ān, in stating "If God willed, He would make you one community" (Al-Qur'ān 5: 48), underscores the intentional diversity in God's plan. Another verse, "If God willed, all human beings would believe. So will you (O Prophet) compel them to believe?" (Al-Qur'ān 10: 99), emphasizes that diversity is intrinsic to God's design. Muslims, in accordance with these Qur'ānic teachings, are obliged to acknowledge that not all individuals or groups will adhere to their religion.[89] They are called to coexist with these differences with love, cooperation, and mutual understanding.[90] Islam, as a guiding principle, advocates for peace and harmony, manifest in the Muslim greeting *"As-salamu-'alaykum"* (peace be upon you).[91] The Prophet of Islam is revered as *"rahmatan lil-'alamin"* (mercy for the entire world) (Al-Qur'ān 21:107), portraying the universal compassion inherent in Islam. The divine title *"rabbil 'alamin'"* (the cherisher of the entire world) (Al-Qur'ān 1:1) further accentuates the inclusive nature of God in Islam. Muslim scholars unequivocally acknowledge the legitimacy of all revelations.[92]

In adherence to Islamic teachings, there exists no singular system designed for the entire human populace. Instead, divine guidance entails the dispatch of a Prophet to each distinct community, with diverse Prophets appointed for various societies. The divine message, encompassing the absence of discrimination among these Prophets, resonates globally (Al-Qur'ān 22:67; 2:285).[93] Fundamental to Islamic tenets is the imperative belief in embracing faith in all Prophets, a doctrine expounded in the Qur'ān (Al-Qur'ān 4:136; 4:164).[94] Islam ardently posits that rejection of God and His Prophets, coupled with discriminatory attitudes toward them, invites a retribution deemed debasing (Al-Qur'ān 4:150–151).[95] Islam views itself as a seamless continuation of preceding revealed religions. Notably, Prophet Noah earned the designation "submitter" (Muslim) (Al-Qur'ān 10:72), and Prophet Ibrahim (Abraham) was similarly identified as a Muslim in the Qur'ān (Al-Qur'ān 3:67).[96] Hence, Islam embraces all antecedent Prophets as integral to its own prophetic lineage. As posited by Cole (2019), the term "Islam" found in the Qur'ān originates from the Aramaic *mashlmānūtā*, subsequently translated into Greek as paradosis, denoting "Tradition." The influence of Greek usage on Arabic is discernible in the Qur'ānic usage of Islam, signifying the prophetic tradition of monotheism that encompasses all monotheistic religions.[97]

Islam aims to create a world characterized by tranquility, extending its vision beyond the well-being of its own followers to encompass individuals of varied faiths and cultures. This overarching objective is rooted in the promotion of peace, harmony, and coexistence among diverse religious traditions, all contributing to the collective welfare of society.[98] An examination arises, seeking to understand the causes or mechanisms that have led to the deterioration of interfaith relations and the association of intolerance toward non-Muslims within the framework of Islam. Current scholarly inquiries into the dynamics of interfaith relations underscore that the underlying causes contributing to the observed intolerance within specific segments of the Muslim population are multifaceted. Principal among these factors is the ideological politicization intertwined with the postcolonial dissemination of political Islam. This endeavor seeks to address the multifarious societal, economic, and political constraints prevalent in Muslim-majority nations. The manifestation of this phenomenon, prominently exemplified by the widespread influence of Islamist fundamentalism, arises as a response to both internal political restrictions and external military interventions during the latter part of the twentieth century.[99] A second pivotal dimension involves the rise of religious extremism, epitomized by the global proliferation of Salafism since the 1970s. This theological orientation contributes substantially to the observed climate of religious discord. Lastly, the phenomenon of radicalization is intricately linked to the repercussions of Western military engagements in Muslim-majority regions, encompassing nations such as Afghanistan, Iraq, Libya, and Syria. Additionally, the protracted occupation of Palestine by Israel, coupled with substantial financial and military backing from the United States, exacerbates tensions and contributes significantly to the phenomenon of radicalization.

Critics have scrutinized the Islamic *"dhimmi"* system, a term rooted in Arabic denoting covenant, contract (*"al-aqd"*), protection, guarantee, safety, custody, and more.[100] Classical Muslim jurists defined *"dhimmi"* as indigenous non-Muslims, specifically those from Ahl al-Kitāb and Zoroastrians, who establish permanent residence within Islamic territories.[101] This concept represents a contractual agreement between Muslims and non-Muslims in an Islamic state, ensuring the protection of non-Muslim citizens.[102] However, critics argue that Islam relegates non-Muslims to second-class citizenship through the *dhimmi* status. In contrast, Al-Buti contends that Islam rejects class distinctions, emphasizing the equality of all individuals before the law and their equitable standing in the community, with equal citizenship rights. Kurucan and Erol explain that Islam guides its adherents to engage with all citizens based on principles of social justice.[103]

It is fundamental to recognize that the core tenets of Islam repudiate any form of discriminatory governance between Muslims and non-Muslims cohabiting in Muslim territories. In this context, we may refer to the initial state in Madinah during the time of Prophet Muhammad PBUH. It was characterized by a diverse community that included Jews, showcasing religious and cultural diversity.[104] Following the Prophet's era, both constitutional religious texts and jurisprudence (*fiqh*) underwent evolution driven by economic, political, and social considerations. Importantly, medieval Islamic jurisprudence sources offer diverse interpretations of *dhimmi* law.[105] In contemporary discourse, scholars such as al-Qaradāwī, Fahmi Howeidi, Salim al-'Aawa, and Rashid Ghannoushi have revisited the Document of Medina.

Their examination reveals that individuals from the people of the book and non-Muslims enjoyed comprehensive citizenship rights in alignment with the principles laid out in this historical document. Consequently, various Muslim jurists and scholars are actively reevaluating classical dhimmi law, seeking to develop an updated *fiqh* that can effectively address the nuanced challenges of the dhimmi concept in the present context.[106]

In the aftermath of the Cold War and the dissolution of the Soviet Union, a paradigm shift was anticipated, transitioning from military-centric rivalries to a Clash of Civilizations, as articulated in the renowned thesis by Huntington. The notion of a Clash of Civilizations implies not just a confrontation between cultural entities but, more specifically, a clash between Islam and the West. This theory has evoked diverse reactions and rebuttals, including responses from Islamic scholars who have contested the concept of such a clash. In contrast, they advocate for the promotion of interfaith dialogue or, in a broader context, dialogue encompassing intercultural and intercivilizational dimensions (*al-hiwar baina al-hadarat*). Introduced by the President of the Islamic Republic of Iran, Mohammad Khatami, a resolution unanimously adopted by the UN General Assembly on November 4, 1998, formally designated the year 2001 as the UN Year of Dialogue among Civilizations.[107] This pivotal resolution has since catalyzed extensive discussions and deliberations on "Dialogue among Civilisations" in diverse conferences and international forums. Scholars in the domains of International Relations and Political Theory have shown limited engagement in delineating and explicating the potential significance of "Dialogue among Civilisations" as a prospective framework for the evolution of international relations. This shortfall is particularly disheartening, considering Khatami's explicit articulation of this vision with a specific objective in mind.

In his inaugural address as the Chairman of the eighth Summit Conference of the OIC convened in Tehran, Mohammad Khatami delivered a speech before an assembly of more than fifty heads of Muslim states. Khatami implored the *ummah*, the Muslim community, to acknowledge historical missteps, glean insights from others, and foster unity and support within the *ummah*. According to Khatami, the imperative for engaging in a dialogue of civilizations was essential for the revitalization of Islam. This was considered a strategy to transcend the "painful state of passivity" in relation to the prevailing dominant civilization and to reintegrate with the "once illustrious human civilisations" whose accomplishments and remnants remain commendable and to which the prevailing world civilization owes a genuine debt. Khatami underscored that an understanding of one's own culture should precede participation in the dialogue of civilizations; otherwise, a dialogue between an alienated imitator and others becomes devoid of meaning and certainly lacks any inherent good or benefit.[108]

Further elaborating on the complex relations between the Islamic world and others, Khatami pointed out the presence of mistrust, misunderstanding, and misconceived perceptions. He identified historical roots and hegemonic power dynamics as contributing factors, as well as the deliberate cultivation of enduring misunderstandings by dominant forces. To address these challenges, Khatami emphasized the need for dialogue among civilizations and cultures, with intellectuals playing a pivotal role. The goal is to establish the conditions for a fundamental understanding that underpins genuine peace, rooted in the recognition of the rights of all nations. This, in turn, aims to neutralize the grounds for the influence of negative propaganda in public opinion.

In his address, Khatami urged Muslim leaders to engage in deliberations regarding the contours of a "new and just world order." He juxtaposed this vision with the prevailing discourse on American supremacy in the post-Cold War era. Khatami highlighted the inadequacy of American politicians' attempts to assert their dominance as the remaining pole of power, attempting to position the world around their interests. He asserted that international relations are undergoing a transition from the previous bipolar system to a new stage in history. From his perspective, a new order, rooted in pluralism, is emerging globally, and he expressed the hope that it would not be monopolized by any single power. Khatami, however, acknowledged the challenges inherent in realizing this envisioned world order. He did not assert that the dialogue of civilizations would serve as a panacea for every problem, recognizing the complexity of the task ahead.[109]

The accepted interpretation of dialogue among cultures and civilizations is poised to initiate a robust discourse on contemporary global issues. In the current era, humanity earnestly yearns for justice, peace, freedom, and security, reflecting historical aspirations. The realization of peace is integral to the materialization of dialogue among civilizations, and conversely, the sustained achievement of peace can be facilitated through such dialogues. According to Khatami, the dialogue of civilizations holds the potential to transcend cultural misconceptions among participants. Furthermore, it acts as a catalyst for an Islamic revival, urging Muslims to adhere to the Islamic path while simultaneously assimilating insights from other civilizations. The Summit Conference concluded with a declaration, discussed subsequently, advocating for the commencement of a dialogue of civilizations.[110]

The discourse surrounding the agenda of the dialogue of civilizations, serving both as a mechanism to alter Islam's portrayal in the international arena and as a perspective on international relations, gained significant traction in the subsequent OIC summit conferences. As the notion of the dialogue of civilizations garnered broader international acceptance, the OIC experienced an augmentation of its perceived importance and legitimacy. Evidently, the OIC appears to assimilate the dialogue agenda as a defining attribute in its interactions with broader Islamic entities and within the realm of Christian–Muslim Relations.[111] The commencement of the ninth Session of the Islamic Summit Conference (Doha, Qatar, December 2000) was marked by a self-congratulatory tone, emphasizing the OIC's achievements in promoting the dialogue of civilizations. Notably, there was commendation for the UN's Declaration of 2001 designating it as the UN Year of Dialogue Among Civilizations.[112]

The Declaration of the 2000 OIC Conference commenced by extolling Islam, expressing "great pride" in the recognition that the noble tenets of the religion provide optimal solutions to contemporary challenges faced by human societies. It underscored Islam as the embodiment of love, justice, tolerance, progress, and respect for human rights and dignity.[113] Transitioning to the promotion of the dialogue of civilizations, the Declaration hailed this initiative as a novel paradigm and universal vision for constructing an equitable international order. This vision, grounded in principles of inclusion, participation, mutual understanding, and tolerance among diverse peoples and nations, was endorsed as pivotal.[114] According to the Conference participants, the dialogue of civilizations held significance in disseminating the "true image of Islam" and accentuating its foundational role in human civilization. This was deemed crucial, especially considering the prevalent misrepresentations of Islam through various means. The attendees of the Doha meeting went further to adopt the Global Program of Action on Dialogue among Civilizations. Additionally, they established an Islamic Committee to facilitate the ongoing dialogue among Member States within the UN.[115]

The OIC has strategically leveraged the discourse on the dialogue of civilizations to articulate its stance against Islamic extremism. During the third Extraordinary Session of the Islamic Summit Conference in Mecca (December 7–8, 2005), the OIC framed the "Dialogue of Civilisations" within the broader context of disseminating accurate perceptions of Islam as a religion characterized by moderation and tolerance. Simultaneously, this initiative was positioned to protect Islamic values, beliefs, and principles, serving as a bulwark against extremism and narrow-mindedness. The conference declaration unequivocally condemned extremism in all its forms. The comprehensive report, "Ten-year program of action: to meet the challenge facing the Muslim ummah in the 21st century," delved into intellectual, political, developmental, socioeconomic, and scientific dimensions. This multifaceted approach aimed to contribute to the *ummah's* renaissance over the ensuing decade.[116]

Within the "intellectual and political issues" category, the emphasis on "Islam – the religion of moderation and tolerance" stands out as a crucial element, outlining specific actions for the dialogue of civilizations. This particular segment underscores the paramount importance of inter-civilizational dialogue, built upon the foundations of mutual respect, understanding, and equality among people. It highlights these as essential prerequisites for fostering international peace and security, promoting tolerance, enabling peaceful coexistence, and establishing effective mechanisms for sustained dialogue. The report strongly encourages member states to endorse "inter-religious dialogue" and foster "common values and denominators" among various religions. It envisions active participation from the OIC and its specialized bodies as proactive partners in dialogue among civilizations and religions, urging initiatives and efforts in this direction. Moreover, the report calls on Muslim states to strategically employ mass media to champion the causes of the Muslim *ummah*, propagate the noble principles and values of Islam, and rectify prevailing misconceptions.

In conjunction with political figures such as Khatami and institutions like the OIC, several notable Muslim religious leaders have embraced the discourse on civilizations, offering theological justifications for its incorporation into Islamic political thought through interfaith dialogue initiatives. This marks a significant and transformative departure from the historical trend where major interfaith endeavors, until the mid-1990s, were primarily driven by Christian organizations. The initiation of modern interfaith and interreligious dialogue can be traced back to the inaugural meeting of the World's Parliament of Religions in Chicago in 1893, where diverse faith and religious communities convened. As the twentieth century unfolded, the World Council of Churches (WCC), a more conservative Christian ecumenical body rooted in Protestant religious communities, actively engaged in interfaith dialogue. The WCC's Interreligious Relations and Dialogue department became particularly involved in Muslim–Christian dialogue starting in the 1970s.[117] Concurrently, the Vatican, through the Second Vatican Council (1962–1965), also advocated for interfaith dialogue. The declaration "Nostra aetate" underscored shared beliefs and practices, aiming to stimulate interfaith dialogue and cooperation.

In its treatment of Islam, Nostra aetate (Nostra aetate, promulgated in 1965 by the Second Vatican Council, specifically addresses the relationship between the Catholic Church and non-Christian religions). It codified and promoted a stance of dialogue and reverence toward the principal non-Christian religions globally.[118] Cassidy identified shared tenets, including monotheism, the virgin birth of Christ, and the anticipation of judgment day, along with common religious practices like prayer and fasting.[119] The document refrained from providing commentary on the authenticity of the Qur'ān or the prophethood of Muhammad (PBUH). The Pontifical Council of Inter-religious Dialogue played a crucial role in promoting initiatives for interfaith cooperation. Nevertheless, these endeavors led by Christians encountered challenges in establishing meaningful connections with the Muslim community. The absence of a formalized Muslim institutional counterpart to established Christian organizations contributed to this limitation, coupled with a general lack of enthusiasm and interest among Muslims in interfaith dialogue during the 1970s and 1980s. When Muslims did participate, they often assumed a "guest" role rather than that of hosts, exhibiting reluctance to take the lead in initiating interfaith meetings.[120]

The reticence of Muslims to engage in interfaith dialogue may be attributed to multifaceted factors, encompassing institutional challenges, political complexities, historical reverberations, and religious considerations.[121] However, during the 1990s, a discernible shift occurred as an increasing number of Muslim leaders embraced interfaith dialogue, and in the subsequent decade, Muslims took prominent roles in leading major interfaith initiatives. Interpretations of the Qur'ān, *hadīth*, and Islamic history conducive to dialogue became integral to the perspectives on Islam advocated by diverse scholars and Islamic movements. Since the mid-1990s, Muslim religious leaders have propagated a religious discourse that accommodates the religious "other" and actively participates in various interfaith endeavors. These religiously oriented initiatives not only fortified but also expanded the dialogue agenda, grounding it in religious concepts and thereby securing legitimacy within Muslim organizations and the broader populace. The endeavors of these religious elites directly addressed a public grappling with the reconciliation of religious commitment and the reality of religious diversity.

Conclusion

In exploring the alternative paradigm at the intersection of globalization and Islam, this chapter has engaged in a thorough examination of the foundational elements constituting the Islamic standpoint on globalization. A central theme that has surfaced revolves around the profound significance attributed to the *ummah*, the worldwide community of Muslims, and the *shurātic* perspective in shaping responses to the institutional dimensions of globalization. These fundamental concepts not only function as guiding tenets for individual adherents of Islam but also furnish a collective framework for comprehending and navigating the intricacies of a globalized milieu. The *ummah*, emblematic of the unity and solidarity ingrained in the Muslim community, holds integral importance in the Islamic approach to globalization. Its scope extends beyond the individual realm, accentuating a shared responsibility and a sense of interconnectedness among Muslims globally. This communal approach underscores the paramountcy of collaboration and mutual support in addressing the challenges and opportunities posed by globalization. Consequently, the *ummah* emerges as a consolidating force that transcends geographical confines and cultural distinctions, nurturing a shared sense of purpose in light of global transformations.

Concurrently, the *shurātic* perspective, grounded in the Islamic ethos of consultation and collective decision-making, assumes a pivotal role in influencing reactions to the institutional facets of globalization. This perspective champions the ideals of deliberation and consensus-building, harmonizing with democratic principles while presenting an ethical framework rooted in Islam. Through the integration of *shurā* into decision-making processes across various echelons, Muslims can adeptly navigate the intricacies of global governance structures, ensuring that their involvement is informed by Islamic values and principles.[122] The interaction between the *ummah* and the *shurātic* perspective signifies a responsive and flexible approach to the institutional dimensions of globalization, underscoring Islam's dedication to furnishing ethical and just resolutions to the challenges posed by a swiftly evolving global landscape.

It is crucial to highlight that the Islamic commitment to advancing justice, equity, and sustainable development within the framework of globalization extends its influence across diverse realms of Islamic practice, including the financial domain. The examination of Islamic finance in the context of globalization unveiled a nuanced strategy that intertwines financial practices with sustainability principles. In contrast to conventional financial systems, Islamic finance operates within a framework that prioritizes ethical considerations, ensuring that economic activities align with overarching principles of justice and equity.[123] This distinctive approach marks a significant departure from profit-centric models commonly associated with globalized financial systems. In the discourse on sustainable development, we probed into the multifaceted challenges confronting the contemporary world.[124] Acknowledging the imperative of responsible stewardship of the Earth, Islamic principles advocate for an environmental ethic that aligns with the goals of sustainable development. The environmental challenge is not perceived merely as an isolated concern but is intricately linked to broader ethical considerations embedded in Islam. This perspective promotes a holistic approach to sustainable development, encompassing economic, social, and environmental dimensions.

Acknowledging the necessity of conscientious Earth stewardship, Islamic principles advocate for an environmental ethic that aligns seamlessly with the objectives of sustainable development. The environmental challenge is not perceived in isolation but is intricately interconnected with broader ethical considerations ingrained in Islam. This viewpoint promotes an all-encompassing strategy for sustainable development, taking into account economic, social, and environmental dimensions.[125] The exploration of justice, equity, and sustainable development within the framework of an Islamic paradigm emerges as a crucial perspective for evaluating and responding to the ramifications of globalization. It underscores the interrelatedness of economic, social, and environmental facets, underscoring the imperative for a comprehensive and ethically guided developmental approach.

The principles enshrined in Islam advocate for dialogue and collaboration, fostering an atmosphere where diverse cultures can coexist harmoniously. This seamlessly aligns with the overarching theme of interconnectedness prevalent in the era of globalization. The alternative paradigm delineated in this chapter positions Islam as a vibrant and adaptable force within the globalized context. It stands as a testament to Islam's ability to confront contemporary challenges while steadfastly upholding its foundational principles. This exemplifies Islam's resilience and pertinence in navigating the intricacies of a swiftly evolving global landscape. As we traverse the complex intersections of globalization and Islam, this paradigm functions as a guiding principle, advocating for a harmonious coexistence that transcends not only cultural boundaries but also extends to encompass technological advancements and environmental considerations.

It is crucial to underscore that critiques of globalization within the Muslim world do not necessarily endorse a shift toward increased localization or regional alternatives. Notably, Muslim scholars, whether adhering to modernist or Islamist perspectives, channel their efforts toward the fundamental sources of Islam to construct an alternative narrative in response to globalization. Within the framework of Islam itself, various narratives on an alternative globalization surface, encompassing realms such as politics, society, economy, and culture. The exploration of these diverse narratives gains significance against the backdrop of the broader global resurgence of Islam. Despite Islam providing new avenues for globalization, political elites often limit it to a reactive politics that stifles diversity and creative thought.

Nonetheless, Islam holds the potential to align with other competing discourses, envisioning an alternative transnational society—a moral reality of globalization. Achieving this vision, however, requires positioning Islam as an alternative to the Western project, promising a more balanced society grounded in unity of thought, innovative epistemology, and an alternative paradigm spanning economy, politics, and society.

Notes

1. Ebrahim Moosa, "Muslim Ethics in an Era of Globalism: Reconciliation in an Age of Empire," in *Solidarity Beyond Borders: Ethics in a Globalising World*, ed. Salamon Janusz (London: Bloomsbury Publishing), 97–113.
2. Mohammad Hashim Kamali, *The Middle Path of Moderation in Islam: The Qur'ānic Principle of Wasaṭiyyah* (Oxford: Oxford University Press, 2015), 203.
3. Shabbir Akhtar, *Islam as Political Religion: The Future of an Imperial Faith* (London: Routledge, 2011), 16.
4. Al-Qur'ān, 23:52: "And lo! This your religion is one religion and I am your Lord, so keep your duty unto Me." Al-Qur'ān, 21:92: "Lo! This, your religion, is one religion, and I am your Lord, so worship Me." Al-Qur'ān 4:1:

> O mankind! Be careful of your duty to your Lord Who created you from a single soul and from it created its mate and from them twain hath spread abroad a multitude of men and women. Be careful of your duty toward Allah in Whom ye claim (your rights) of one another, and toward the wombs (that bare you). Lo! Allah hath been a watcher over you.

Prophet Muhammad PBUH said: "The origin of man is from one couple and the entire humanity is one family." See Khurshid Ahmad, "Globalisation: Challenges and Prospects for Muslims," *Policy Perspectives* 3, no. 1 (2006): 1–11.
5. Al-Qur'ān 49:13.
6. A. Christian Van Gorder, *Islam, Peace and Social Justice: A Christian Perspective* (New York: James Clarke & Co, 2015), 15.
7. Ziauddin Sardar, *Islamic Science: The Way Ahead* (Islamabad: OIC/COMSTECH, 1995), 39.
8. Adis Duderija, "Toward a Methodology of Understanding the Nature and Scope of the Concept of Sunnah," *Arab Law Quarterly* 21 (2007): 1–2.
9. Antony Black, *The History of Islamic Political Thought: From the Prophet to the Present*, 2nd edition (Edinburgh: Edinburgh University Press), 84.
10. Sohail Inayatullah, "Islamic Civilization in Globalization: From Islamic Futures to a Post-Western Civilization." Accessed April 13, 2024. https://www.metafuture.org/Articles/islamic-civilization-globalization.htm.
11. Gabriele Marranci, *The Anthropology of Islam* (Oxford: Berg, 2007), 108.
12. Maysam J. Al Faruqi, Umma, "The Orientalists and the Qur'ānic Concept of Identity," *Journal of Islamic Studies* 16 (2005): 1–34.

13. Abd Al-Fattah El-Awaisi, "The Conceptual Approach of the Egyptian Muslim Brothers towards the Palestine Question, 1928–1949," *Journal of Islamic Studies* 2 (1991): 225–244.

14. Ishtiaq Hossain, "Muslim Ummah, International Organisations, and Human Development in the MMCs," in *The Muslim World in the 21st Century: Space, Power, and Human Development*, ed. Samiul Hasan (London: Springer, 2012), 302–303.

15. Riaz Hassan, "Globalisation's Challenge to the Islamic Ummah," *Asian Journal of Social Science* 34, no. 2 (2006): 311–323.

16. Mubashar Hasan, "The Concept of Globalisation and How this has Impacted on Contemporary Muslim Understanding of Ummah," *Journal of Globalisation Studies* 2, no. 2 (2011): 145–159.

17. Abdullah Al-Ahsan, *Ummah or Nation? Identity Crisis in a Contemporary Muslim Society* (London: The Islamic Foundation, 1992), 15.

18. Hasan, "The Concept of Globalisation," 148.

19. Al-Qur'ān 42:51–52.

20. Nubar Hovsepian, "Competing Identities in the Arab World," in *Islam and Globalisation: Critical Concepts in Islamic Studies*, Volume 1, ed. Shahram Akbarzadeh (London: Routledge, 2006), 104.

21. Al-Qur'ān 16:14.

22. Al-Qur'ān 16:13: And all the [beauty of] many hues which He has created for you on earth: in this, behold, there is a message for people who [are willing to] take it to heart!

23. Hovsepian, "Competing Identities in the Arab World," 105.

24. Hovsepian, "Competing Identities in the Arab World," 106.

25. R. Jacobson, "The "Austrian" School of Strategy," *Academy of Management Review* 17, no. 4 (1992): 782–807.

26. Al-Qur'ān 2:30.

27. Al-Qur'ān 2:265.

28. Al-Qur'ān 4:59.

29. Al-Qur'ān 96:1.

30. Al-Qur'ān 6:50, 2:44.

31. Ibrahim A. Shogar, "The Scientific Thinking in Islam: Factors of Flourishing and Decline," *Revelation and Science* 1, no. 2 (2011): 1–13.

32. Samih Mahmoud Al-Karasneh and Ali Mohammad Jubran Saleh, "Islamic Perspectives of Creativity: A Model for Teachers of Social Studies as Leaders," *Procedia Social and Behavioral Sciences* 2 (2010): 412–426.

33. Khairul Akmaliah Adhama, Mohd Fuaad Saidb, Nur Sa'adah Muhamadc, and Noor Inayah Yaakubd, "Technological Innovation and Entrepreneurship from the Western and Islamic Perspectives," *International Journal of Economics, Management and Accounting* 20, no. 2 (2012): 109–148.

34. Al-Karasneh and Saleh, "Islamic Perspectives of Creativity," 420.

35. Al-Qur'ān 2:164.

36. Al- Qur'ān 2:164–165.

37. Al-Qur'ān 2:259.

38. Al-Qur'ān 7:185.
39. Al-Qur'ān 88:21–26.
40. Khairul Akmaliah Adham, Mohd Fuaad Said, Nur Sa'adah Muhamad, and Noor Inayah Yaakub, "Technological Innovation and Entrepreneurship from the Western and Islamic Perspectives," *International Journal of Economics, Management and Accounting* 20, no. 2 (2012): 109–148.
41. Al-Qur'ān 7:204.
42. Al-Qur'ān 39:17–18.
43. Al-Qur'ān 2:285.
44. Al-Karasneh and Saleh, "Islamic Perspectives of Creativity," 414.
45. Al-Karasneh and Saleh, "Islamic Perspectives of Creativity," 415.
46. Al-Qur'ān 7:204.
47. Abdullaah Jalil, "The Significances of Maslahah Concept and Doctrine of Maqasid (Objectives) Al-Shari'ah in Project Evaluation," *The Journal of Muamalat and Islamic Finance Research* 3, no. 1 (2006): 171–202.
48. Abul Hasan Muhammad Sadeq, "Economic Development in Islam," *Journal of Islamic Economics* 1, no. 1 (1987): 35–45.
49. Al-Qur'ān 67:1–2.
50. Sayyid Qutb, *Tafsir Fi Zilal al-Qur'ān*, 2012. Accessed April 13, 2024. https://tafsirzilal.wordpress.com/2012/06/05/english-language/.
51. Adham, Said, Muhamad, and Yaakub, "Technological Innovation and Entrepreneurship from the Western and Islamic Perspectives, 110.
52. Adham, Said, Muhamad, and Yaakub, "Technological Innovation and Entrepreneurship from the Western and Islamic Perspectives, 112.
53. Paul Stevens, "The Role of Oil and Gas in the Economic Development of the Global Economy," in *Extractive Industries: The Management of Resources as a Driver of Sustainable Development*, ed. Tony Addison and Alan Roe (Oxford: Oxford University Press, 2018), 71–90.
54. Barry Buzan and Ole Wæver, *Regions and Powers: The Structure of International Security* (Cambridge: Cambridge University Press, 2003), 12.
55. William E. Shepard, "Sayyid Qutb's Doctrine of 'Jāhiliyya'," *International Journal of Middle East Studies* 35, no. 4 (2023): 521–545.
56. Mumtaz Hussain, "Asghar Shahmoradi and Rima Turk, An Overview of Islamic Finance," IMF Working Paper, 2015. Accessed April 13, 2024. https://www.imf.org/external/pubs/ft/wp/2015/wp15120.pdf.
57. MD Yousuf Ali, "Tawhid and its Effects on Man's Life," *Jurnal Usuluddin* 23–24 (2006): 1–34.
58. Yousuf Ali, "Tawhid and its Effects," 18.
59. Ahmad Dawamul Muthi and Khalid El-Awaisi, "The Contributions of Caliph Abu Bakr to The First Muslim Liberation of Islamic Jerusalem," *Journal of Islamic Jerusalem Studies* 22, no. 2 (2022): 133–152.
60. Muthi and El-Awaisi, "The Contributions of Caliph Abu Bakr," 139.
61. Khaliq Ahmad and Arif Hassan, "Distributive Justice: The Islamic Perspective," *Intellectual Discourse* 8, no. 2 (2000): 159–172.

62. Ahmad and Hassan, "Distributive Justice: The Islamic Perspective," 160.

63. Margherita Picchi, "Islam as the Third Way," *Oriente Moderno* 97, no. 1 (2017): 177–200.

64. Babayo Sule, Muhammad Aminu Yahaya, and Rashid Ating, "Globalisation and the Muslim Ummah: Issues, Challenges, and the Ways Out," *IIUM Journal of Religion and Civilisational Studies (IJECS)* 1, no. 1 (2018): 7–29.

65. Sule, Yahaya, and Ating, "Globalisation and the Muslim Ummah," 23.

66. Irfan Ahmed, Muhammad Akhtar, Ishaq Ahmed, and Saima Aziz, "Practices of Islamic Banking in The Light of Islamic Ethics: A Critical Review," *International Journal of Economics, Management and Accounting* 25, no. 3 (2017): 465–490.

67. Allioui Hanane and Youssef Mourdi, "Exploring the Full Potentials of IoT for Better Financial Growth and Stability: A Comprehensive Survey," *Sensors* 23, no. 19 (2023): 8015.

68. Muhammad Shahrul Ifwat Ishak and Nur Syahirah Mohammad Nasir, "Maqasid al-Shariah in Islamic Finance: Harmonizing Theory and Reality," *The Journal of Muamalat and Islamic Finance Research* 18, no. 1 (2021): 108–119.

69. Ishak and Nasir, "Maqasid al-Shariah in Islamic Finance," 116.

70. Yayan Satyakti, "The Effect of Applying Sustainability (Maqasid Shariah) and Competition on Islamic Bank Financing," *Sustainability* 15, no. 17 (2023): 12994.

71. Satyakti, "The Effect of Applying Sustainability (Maqasid Shariah)," 14.

72. Omprakash Ashtankar, "Islamic Perspectives on Environmental Protection," *International Journal of Applied Research* 2, no. 1 (2016): 438–441.

73. Odeh Rashed Al-Jayyousi, "Rethinking Sustainability: Islamic Perspectives," 2015. Accessed April 13, 2024. https://www.ecomena.org/sustainability-islamic-perspectives/.

74. Al-Jayyousi, "Rethinking Sustainability."

75. Adama Dieye, *An Islamic Model for Stabilization and Growth* (London: Palgrave Macmillan, 2020), 15.

76. Dieye, *An Islamic Model for Stabilization*, 17.

77. Osman Bakar, "Cultural Pluralism in a Globalised World: Challenges to Peaceful Coexistence," *ICR Journal* 1, no. 3 (2010): 528–531.

78. Bakar, "Cultural Pluralism," 531.

79. Peter Gan Chong Beng, "The Problem of Cultural Identity," in *Implications of Pluralism Essays on Culture, Identity and Values*, ed. Göran Collste (Bangi: Institute of Ethnic Studies Universiti Kebangsaan Malaysia, 2011), 7–31.

80. Bakar, "Cultural Pluralism," 529.

81. Mohammad Elius, Issa Khan, and Mohd Roslan Mohd Nor, "Interreligious Dialogue: An Islamic Approach," *Katha: The Official Journal of the Centre for Civilisational Dialogue* 15 (2019): 1–19.

82. Ahmad Husni Haji Hasan, "An Islamic Perspective of Interfaith Dialogue Amidst Current Interreligious Tensions Worldwide," *Global Journal Al-Thaqafah* 1, no. 1 (2011): 25–35.

83. Faatin Haque, "Countering Religious Militancy through Interfaith Cooperation: An Islamic Perspective," in World Universities Congress, Canakkale Onsekiz University, Canakkale, 20–24 October 2010.

84. Hilal Wani, Raihanah Abdullah, and Lee Wai Chang, "An Islamic Perspective in Managing Religious Diversity," *Religions* 6 (2015): 642–656.

85. Khairulnizam Mat Karim and Suzy Aziziyana Saili, "Inter-Faith Dialogue: The Qur'ānic and Prophetic Perspective," *Journal of Usuluddin* 29 (2009): 65–94.

86. Saleh Bin Humaid, "Islam and Dialogue with the Other," in *Interfaith Dialogue: Cross-Cultural Views*, ed. Saleh Bin Humaid (Riyadh: Ghainaa Publications, 2010), 24–48.

87. Mohd Roslan Mohd Nor, "Islamic Jerusalem under Muslim Rule: A Study of the Implementation of Inclusive Vision on the Region," *Journal of Al-tamaddun* 3, no. 1 (2008): 186–208.

88. Osman Bakar, *The Qur'ān on Interfaith and Inter-Civilizational Dialogue: Interpreting a Divine Message for Twentieth Century Humanity* (International Institute of Islamic Thought Malaysia (IIITM) and Institute for the Study of the Ummah and Global Understanding [ISUGO], 2006), 13 Publisher Location: Kuala Lumpur Malaysia.

89. Al-Qur'ān 10:99.

90. Ahmet Kurucan and Mustafa Kasım Erol, *Dialogue in Islam: Qur'ān-Sunnah-History* (London: Dialogue Society, 2012), 37.

91. Yahya ibn Sharaf an-Nawawi, *Riyad al-Salihin*, The Book of Greetings, Book 5, Hadith 1. Accessed April 13, 2024. https://sunnah.com/riyadussalihin/5#:~:text=with%20him)%20reported%3A-,The%20Messenger%20of%20Allah%20(%EF%B7%BA)%20said%20to%20me%2C%20%22,classified%20it%20as%20Hasan%20Sahih%5D.&text=Anas%20(May%20Allah%20be%20pleased,some%20children%20and%20greeted%20them.

92. Muhammad Zia-ul-Haq, "Muslims' Participation in Interfaith Dialogue: Challenges and Prospects," *Journal of Ecumenical Studies* 49, no. 4 (2014): 613–646.

93. Al-Qur'ān 22:67; 2:285.

94. Al-Qur'ān 4:136; 4:164.

95. Al-Qur'ān 4:150–151.

96. Al-Qur'ān 3:67.

97. Juan Cole, "Paradosis and Monotheism: A Late Antique Approach to the Meaning of Islām in the Qur'ān," *Bulletin of the School of Oriental and African Studies* 82, no. 3 (2019): 405–425.

98. Hasan, "An Islamic Perspective of Interfaith Dialogue," 29.

99. Halim Rane, "Cogent Religious Instruction: A Response to the Phenomenon of Radical Islamist Terrorism in Australia," *Religions* 10, no. 4 (2019): 1–22.

100. Ali Bin Muhammad Al-Jurjany, *Mujam al-Ta'rifat* [Glossary of Definitions]. Daru Al-Kutub Al-Ilmiyyah (Beirut: Scientific Books House, 1983), 13.

101. Badre-Eddine Ezziti, "The Historical Development of Constitutional Islamic Religious Text of the Legal Status of Non-Muslims in Islam," *International Journal of Innovation and Applied Studies* 23, no. 3 (2018): 290–298.

102. Wahbah Al-Zuhayli, *Mawsu'ah al-Fiqh al-Islami Wa al-Qadaya al-Mu'asara* [Encyclopedia of Islamic Jurisprudence and Contemporary] (Dar al-Fikr, 2010), 46, 14. Publisher Location: Damascus.

103. Kurucan and Erol, *Dialogue in Islam*, 34.

104. Khalid Duran, "The Drafting of a Global Ethic: A Muslim Perspective," 2020. Accessed April 13, 2024https://static1.squarespace.com/static/5464ade0e4b055bfb204446e/t/57211414ab48de3e8ab4eb73/1461785620458/The+Drafting+of+a+Global+Ethic+-+A+Muslim+Perspective.

105. Rane, "Cogent Religious Instruction," 17.

106. Ezziti, "The Historical Development," 290.

107. Ezziti, "The Historical Development," 291.

108. Fabio Petito, "Khatami' Dialogue among Civilizations as International Political Theory," *Journal of Humanities* 11, no. 3 (2004): 11–29.

109. Petito, "Khatami," 21.

110. Petito, "Khatami," 35.

111. OIC, Tehran Declaration 1997. Accessed April 13, 2024. https://www.oic-oci.org/archive/english/conf/is/8/8th-is-summits.htm.

112. OIC.

113. OIC.

114. OIC.

115. Turan Kayaoglu, "Constructing the Dialogue of Civilizations in World Politics: A Case of Global Islamic Activism," *Islam and Christian–Muslim Relations* 23, no. 2 (2012): 129–147.

116. Kayaoglu, "Constructing the Dialogue of Civilizations," 131.

117. Douglas Pratt, "The Vatican in Dialogue with Islam: Inclusion and Engagement," *Islam and Christian–Muslim Relations* 21, no. 3 (2010): 245–262.

118. Gerald O'Collins, S. J., *The Second Vatican Council on Other Religions* (Oxford: Oxford University Press, 2013), 86.

119. Edward Idris Cardinal Cassidy, *Ecumenism and Interreligious Dialogue* (New York: Paulist Press, 2005), 43.

120. Ataullah Siddiqui, *Christian–Muslim Dialogue in the Twentieth Century* (New York: Palgrave Macmillan, 1997), 19.

121. Kayaoglu, "Constructing the Dialogue of Civilizations in World Politics."

122. Md Golam Mohiuddin, "Decision Making Style in Islam: A Study of Superiority of Shura (Participative Management) and Examples from Early Era of Islam," *European Journal of Business and Management* 8, no. 4 (2016): 79–88.

123. Evren Tok and Abdurahman Jemal Yesuf, "Embedding Value-Based Principles in the Culture of Islamic Banks to Enhance Their Sustainability, Resilience, and Social Impact," *Sustainability* 14, no. 916 (2022): 1–23.

124. Tok and Jemal Yesuf, "Embedding Value-Based Principles," 12.

125. Labeeb Bsoul, Amani Omer, Lejla Kucukalic, and Ricardo H. Archbold, "Islam's Perspective on Environmental Sustainability: A Conceptual Analysis," *Social Sciences* 11, no. 228 (2022): 1–11.

CHAPTER 3

From Globalization to Global Islam
Tracing Intersections and Convergence

Introduction

The phenomenon of globalization has garnered significant attention from governments, scholars, global business communities, economists, educators, students, nongovernmental organizations (NGOs), and various stakeholders. The fervor and keen interest in the subject of globalization have prompted extensive research endeavors delving into its multifaceted intricacies. Seminars, dialogues, conferences, and similar forums convened at both governmental and academic echelons globally are primarily oriented toward a comprehensive exploration of the advantages and disadvantages inherent in the process of globalization. Furthermore, in international arenas, a recurring focal point of discussions and debates surrounding globalization revolves around the identification of genuine beneficiaries and the adversely affected entities.[1] Religion, as an institutional facet, has endured since the inception of humanity on Earth. The trajectory of globalization, spanning numerous centuries, is intricately interwoven with the historical evolution of religious paradigms. It is suggested that the initial impetus to forge a unified global community originated with the world's predominant religions—Buddhism, Judaism, Hinduism, Christianity, and Islam. These religious traditions undertook concerted initiatives to assert influence and garner followers across diverse regions, propelling a globalizing impulse that encompassed the dissemination of ideologies, cultural elements, trade practices, political frameworks, and economic dynamics on a worldwide scale. Within this narrative, Islam emerges as both an emissary and a catalyst for globalization. The convergence of these two concepts materialized notably during the period between 650 and 850 CE, marked by Islam's expansive diffusion from the Arabian Peninsula to the extensive regions of the Mediterranean, Africa, Asia, Europe, and the Balkans.[2]

This period witnessed the profound integration of Islamic principles with the globalizing forces of the time, solidifying Islam's role in shaping interconnected societies. The geographical expanse covered during this period underscores Islam's significant contribution to the global world, fostering cultural exchange, economic interactions, and the dissemination of knowledge across diverse regions. The dynamic interaction between Islam and globalization between the seventh and ninth centuries laid the groundwork for a complex interplay that continues to influence contemporary global dynamics. Islamic globalization manifested prominently during the Umayyad dynasty (661–750), marking a critical juncture in the historical continuum. The transition from the Umayyad era to the emergence of the Abbasid dynasty (750–1258) brought a notable shift in focus. Unlike their Umayyad predecessors, the Abbasid rulers demonstrated a heightened commitment to the pursuit of knowledge and scientific advancements. This era, often referred to as the Golden Age of the Muslims, witnessed a flourishing of intellectual endeavors supported by the rulers. Scholars and scientists thrived under this patronage, propelling progress in technology, natural sciences, and the social sciences.[3] Central to this intellectual renaissance were the Qur'ān and the traditions of the Prophet, serving as inspirational forces compelling Muslims not only to acquire knowledge but also to illuminate their souls through its pursuit. The Golden Age leaders, cognizant of the transformative power of knowledge, facilitated an environment conducive to the acquisition of new disciplines and technologies. In this pursuit, Muslims exhibited an open-minded approach, embracing positive and beneficial ideas from diverse sources, including Indian, Persian, and Greek contributions, thereby enriching their own civilization.

The Muslim leaders even engaged Jewish and Christian scholars to undertake translation works within academic circles. As Muslims delved into the realms of new knowledge, a profound interest in philosophy, particularly ancient Greek philosophy, emerged among scholars, further contributing to the intellectual vibrancy of the era. Considering the divergence between the Greek philosophers' ideas and the Islamic worldview, early Muslim scholars adopted a nuanced approach characterized by adoption, adaptation, assimilation, and integration. This approach epitomized the prevailing spirit and culture of learning during the nascent phase of Islamic knowledge expansion and exploration. Concurrently, in a reciprocal exchange, Western scholars also assimilated ideas from Muslim scholars, particularly during the Golden Age of the Muslims. An assessment of the Muslim era of globalization reveals that the expansion of Islam and its associated civilization into foreign territories can be attributed to the dynamic nature of Islam as a comprehensive way of life divinely revealed. The Qur'ān's message exerted a compelling appeal on new adherents, advocating a balanced lifestyle that equally prioritized the present and the afterlife. This Islamic scripture conveyed messages pertaining to faith while concurrently encouraging Muslims to actively pursue knowledge and scientific inquiry.

This phenomenon resulted in the dissemination of Islamic cultural, social, educational, and civilizational values on a global scale. The zenith of this expansionary dimension was witnessed during the Ottoman Empire's reign when the Islamic world asserted control over Europe, North Africa, and the Middle East.[4] In this context, Islam played a significant role in the context of globalization. The impetus to globalize the world originated in the competitive dynamics among the world's predominant monotheistic religions as they vied for followers. Islam, at certain junctures in history, emerged as the most universalized religion, boasting the highest followership and influence. Presently, it ranks second in terms of global population.[5] For over 1,400 years, Islam has propelled the advancement of cultural, political, social, and economic systems across the globe, predating the emergence of contemporary globalists. It is conceivable that the present proponents of globalization have drawn inspiration from Islam's historical exploration of the world in modern times.

This chapter attempts to explore the complex dynamics evolving from the intersections of Islam and the global landscape, progressing from the historical context of archaic globalization to the contemporary phenomenon of global Islam. The thematic journey spans various stages, examining the Islamic paradigm's engagement with early globalizing forces, the nuanced dynamics of cooperation and conflict during modern globalization, and the enduring manifestations of Muslim universalism in the postcolonial era. The exploration extends to the realm of postcolonial identity formation within the Islamic framework and delves into the complexities of the global Muslim diaspora, examining its formation, characteristics, and transnational connections. A focal point of the chapter is the multifaceted relationship between Islam and global governance, investigating the roles played by Muslim-majority states in international governance structures and their impact on the global order. The chapter concludes by synthesizing these diverse threads, offering insights into the convergences and intersections that define the complex relationship between Islam and the globalized world.

Islamic Paradigm and Archaic Globalization

As argued by Toynbee,

> a civilization may emerge through (1) the *spontaneous mutation* of a pre-civilizational society; (2) *stimulation* of a pre-civilizational society to develop into a civilization by the influence of an already existent civilization; or (3) *disintegration* of one or more civilizations of older generation and the transformation of some of their elements into a new configuration.[6]

In this categorization, Islam evolved into a civilization of the second type, affirming Prophet Muhammad PBUH's rightful succession within the Abrahamic monotheistic tradition. As the Prophet transitioned to Medina, solidifying his leadership and drafting a constitution, it became apparent that his vision extended beyond a conventional state. Islam, rooted in principles of equilibrium and fairness across human existence, emerged as a dynamic civilization, transcending borders. It emphasized a harmonious balance between worldly affairs and spiritual contemplation, acknowledging the significance of both the present life and the hereafter. Following the Formative period, the Islamic system transformed into a hereditary sultanate, replacing the caliphate with a heritage system. The initial Islamic empire (661–750 CE) under the Umayyads marked a phase of significant Islamic globalization, extending from Central Asia to Spain and France. This expansion was evident in administrative structures, military foundations, and the widespread use of Arabized currency and chancelleries.[7]

Geographically, Islam experienced significant expansion during the Umayyad period.[8] This era marked the establishment of robust institutional structures, forming the administrative backbone to tackle challenges across the empire. Centered in Damascus, the Umayyads implemented a potent and centralized governmental system, supported by a new bureaucracy mainly composed of Persians.[9] This period introduced a distinct Muslim identity, shaping new organizational, administrative, cultural, institutional, and social dynamics that set Muslims apart from Christians or Jews. As Fernand Braudel notes, Muslim civilization truly emerged with the widespread presence of Islamic schools throughout the *ummah*, the community of the faithful, spanning from the Atlantic to the Pamirs.[10]

During the dawning of the Axial Age, Islam underwent a transformation, transcending boundaries to embrace its universal nature, marking it as arguably the earliest exemplar of a globalized world religion. As such, Islam embodied both an integrative and dynamic force, weaving its influence across diverse realms. Within this context, Islam emerged as a pivotal catalyst in the processes of global interconnectedness, where developments in one region reverberated throughout the political, economic, and cultural landscapes of distant lands. Islam did not simply assume this role as a mere coincidence; rather, it became an inherent characteristic that shaped its very essence. A clearer illustration of this can be discerned by examining the expansion of Islam in Southeast Asia.[11] While some historians emphasize the part played in this growth by a global trade network that reached from North Africa to East Asia, others contend that the Indian Ocean became the hub of a new commercial network, as a result of which the South-East Asian islands obtained a major place within this new "global system" at a period when trade inside Europe and the Mediterranean's role as a bridge between Europe, Africa, and Asia declined. The ancient Silk Road and the spice route are well-known examples of the phenomenon of globalization. Through these trade routes, people moved from one region of Europe, Asia, and Africa to another, transforming goods and spreading knowledge and customs across the three well-known continents. Globalization was of a non-dominant kind when commerce was conducted via the silk trade route, with its broad and even worldwide purpose to establish a perfect society on Earth, replacing tyranny and injustice with justice and equality. The commerce caravans left China and traveled via China, India, Yemen after crossing the Indian Ocean, and the Eastern Roman Empire after passing through the Rub' al-Khali desert.[12]

The Silk Route, commencing around 1000 BC and extending for millennia, constituted an extensive network of intercultural trade spanning Eurasia from the Mediterranean to Japan and India, facilitating the exchange of spices, textiles, and religions. Islam held sway among traders from Western Eurasia for a substantial duration during this period, introducing a belief system and a culture steeped in history and achievements to millions. According to Amira Bennison, the dissemination of a comprehensive ideology impacting governance, cultural outlooks, and trade practices, along with the sacred language of Islam, Arabic, progressed in parallel with the success of Muslim politics and the economy.[13] While Arabic was not universally spoken among Muslims, its vocabulary and writing system left a profound imprint on the Islamic world, propelling the globalization of this ancient faith. The initial impetus for Muslims to aspire to universality originated from a Christian notion envisioning Islam as the eventual sole religion embraced by humanity. This unique endeavor was marked by the initial propagation efforts of an expanding empire, empowered to organize regional political, economic, and cultural domains in accordance with shared theological principles.[14]

The concept of *ummah*, the first prescriptive category, embodies Islamic universalism, offering a framework for religious unity while accommodating the cultural diversity among Muslims. The second category involves a binary division into the dominant *dār al-Islam* or the land of Islam, characterized by peace and brotherhood, and the periphery *dār al-harb* or the land of war, where disagreements on the sovereignty of God prevail. The third category, the caliphate (*khilafah*), serves as the political offshoot of the *dār al-Islam*, giving rise to unified Islamic notions of government and statehood. This tripartite conceptual framework circulated widely throughout Islamic lands, enabling Muslims to envision their place in the local context as part of a larger Islamic universal whole. The *ummah*, devoid of geographical or political boundaries, encompasses every Muslim globally, making it adaptable to trans-state migrations. It is not ethnically or politically defined but takes shape within the legal system. Between the ninth and twelfth centuries, five legal schools emerged based on principles of interpretation, analogy (*qiyās*), juristic preference (*istihsan*), presumption of continuity (*istishab*), and other forms of reasoning. The *sharī'ah* establishes broad guidelines through a legal framework and rules of interpretation, outlining religio-legal boundaries of human behavior in the Qur'ān. While not homogenizing Muslim societies, it provides a recognizable religio-cultural framework for social and business interactions within the community.[15]

Jurists from various law schools constantly expanded these traits by tailoring their judgments to specific situations. They focused more on consistent procedures rather than specific outcomes, addressing diverse regional needs. The Sunni (Hanafi, Maliki, Shafi'ī, and Hanbali) and Shi'ī schools held significant influence over vast areas, allowing their judgments to extend across different regions. While governments oversaw criminal trials, the academic formulation of the *sharī ah* allowed these schools to function together as a globally acknowledged legal system, operating beyond political boundaries. The *'ulamā* (religious scholars), businessmen, mystics, and travelers played pivotal roles in reshaping the sociocultural fabric established by the *sharī'ah* as they traversed the Muslim world, disseminating normative ideals, knowledge, and skills. Scholars, often engaged in trade alongside their religious pursuits, embarked on extensive journeys in pursuit of knowledge—both religious and secular. Mobility granted access to different regions within the Muslim world. Although travel was challenging and not always safe, possessing scholarship served as a de facto passport. Scholars, in addition to their quest for knowledge, shared wisdom through lectures in madrasas, mosques, and Sufi lodges, which had evolved into intricate religious networks across the Islamic realms by the twelfth century. Some scholars, seeking to supplement their income, took on roles in local legal systems or administrative offices, although those with higher moral standards often avoided such positions due to their corrupting influence. While travel experiences could evoke a sense of diversity, these sentiments were often tempered by a feeling of belonging to a larger cultural and religious collective.[16] The discussions about disparities among Muslim communities and lamentations about the lack of unity presupposed a common Islamic framework that served as a benchmark for comparison and critique.[17]

The similarities in legal procedures not only forged a novel form of global community that surpassed conventional notions of politics and society but also interlinked diverse Muslim state structures into a coherent entity, akin to modern state systems theoretically grounded in shared values. Admittedly, not all Muslim nations adhered to the ideals of their governing and religious elites, leading to the emergence of brilliant intellectuals, unique art and architecture, remarkable scientific and technological advancements, and a just social order. The term "medina," signifying the center of law, religion, and commerce, played a pivotal role as a central hub for networks involving learning, pilgrimage, and trade, serving as the overall seat of political authority.

On the flip side, penetrating rural and tribal communities, which maintained their universal Islamic essence while exhibiting distinctive local flavors, remained a challenging endeavor. Ibn Khaldun chronicled movements characterized by warrior tribes emanating from diverse cultural zones on the periphery, displacing their debilitated urban-based predecessors.[18] While occasionally unsettling the core of the Muslim world system, these warrior groups established connections bridging the Islamic heartlands and the periphery, effectively expanding the reach of the Muslim world order. Moreover, the aspiration of emerging leaders from tribal peripheries to emulate urban Muslim court styles enticed daring intellectuals to frontier regions, fortifying the Islamic infrastructure. Such migrations led to the replication of political systems across the Muslim world.[19]

Muslim Universalism and the Early Stages of Globalization

The classical era of Islamic civilization stands out as a notable exemplar of early globalization. It was marked by cosmopolitan and tolerant environments, fostering open discussions on religious matters between Muslims and non-Muslims without apprehension of reprisal.[20] As the empire expanded, this vision materialized into a cultural and economic reality, even though legal interpretations by Muslim religious scholars occasionally conflicted with policies imposed by rulers in response to governance needs after the empire's fragmentation into smaller political entities. The ongoing struggle for dominance, often favoring the ruling side at specific times and locations, retained the overarching notion of unity. Despite engaging in commercial relations, Muslim administrations refrained from initiating a global conquest that would seek to control or assimilate the northwestern part of Europe or the eastern part centered on China. This stance led to a clash between the mature Muslim commonwealth, shaped by the military absolutist gunpowder empires in the sixteenth century and the European proto-globalization ambitions between 1648 and 1850. During this period, archaic globalization persisted, with the civilizing process and proto-global systems like the Portuguese and Dutch overseas commercial empires adopting many of its forms in a parasitic manner. The era witnessed the expansion of European influence into the Muslim world, the annexation of new lands such as the Americas, southern Africa, and subsequently Australasia, and the emergence of a European concept of global centrality.

During the seventeenth and eighteenth centuries, the Muslim world underwent dynamic shifts that challenged the conventional order. While interactions were limited, the Muslim powers established a "proto-global" power structure, mirroring the European state system and fostering novel interconnections for trans-regional exchange. This Muslim proto-globalization, both dependent on and surpassing state institutions, led to diverse systems of government within the Western Muslim domain, particularly between the Ottoman and Moroccan "Alawi sultanates."[21] Muslim nations strategically portrayed interactions with Europeans at home, emphasizing Muslim superiority. The seventeenth-century surge in coffee consumption hinted at a growing cultural convergence between state ideological structures (Muslim and Christian). Gift-giving practices facilitated the circulation of aristocratic culture and goods, with European elites eagerly receiving exotic items.[22] Muslim networks, extending beyond state boundaries, adapted to economic changes and established a common proto-global system. Religious brotherhood-organized trans-Saharan trade networks, while not as cosmopolitan as Mediterranean networks, connected European and Muslim trading zones innovatively, playing a crucial universalizing role on the southern Islamic border in the eighteenth century.[23]

The active mindset of Muslims and their unifying concept of Muslim universalism signify a distinct phase in Muslim globalization concurrent with the transition from proto to modern globalization. While nineteenth-century academic discussions set the stage for subsequent pan-Islamist perspectives, the precise relationship among proto-globalization, Islamic renewal, and early modern globalization remains challenging to determine and has received limited scrutiny. Muslims, interpreting their territorial losses in various regions as divine retribution for perceived impiety, harbored a sense of impending catastrophe. This sentiment intensified with territorial setbacks in central Europe, the Caucasus, Central Asia, India, the Crimea, and Africa. However, before the 1830s, there were few explicit connections between these events in the Arabo-Islamic world. It was only in the North African context, around the 1830s, that locals attributed the French occupation of Algiers to divine retribution, advocating for the establishment of a just Islamic sociopolitical system to expel the French.[24]

Islamic Cooperation and Conflict in the Era of Modern Globalization

The period from 1648 to 1850 witnessed the observance of traditional relationships and the emergence of a system in the Mediterranean characterized by shared cultural and commercial practices, shifting away from religious conflicts. However, the cosmopolitanism of the eighteenth century gave way to violent European imperial expansions following increased interactions between the Islamic world and Europe in the late eighteenth century. In a bid to engage with and compete in the emerging international order, seen as a fundamental component of Islamic civilization, several Muslim nations endeavored to reform and Islamize political paradigms shaped by contemporary globalization. Despite these efforts, Muslim societies tended to revert to older notions of social and political unity promoted by Islamic movements advocating for the preservation of Islamic faith. Notably, these groups, not bound by the political constraints imposed by modern Muslim regimes and European imperial powers, were perceived as politically innovative and subversive.

European concepts of nation, nation-state, and nationalism permeated both state and cultural spheres in the Muslim world, undergoing reinterpretation in light of the global system in which Muslims participated. The shift in Christian–Muslim relations in the Mediterranean initiated with Napoleon's invasion of Egypt (1798–1801), though 1850 is often considered the onset of modern globalization. Beginning in 1798, Muslim states found it increasingly challenging to convince their populations that they could rely on support from European powers.[25] They faced restrictions on corsairing imposed by Europe, encountered protectionism in continental markets, and risked bombing if they resisted embracing new international ideas of territoriality and sovereignty. In response, Muslim states rationalized governance, adopted military technology and strategies from their European rivals, and reluctantly embraced geographical definitions of statehood to compete in the evolving global landscape.

The military restructuring initiative undertaken by Muslim governments was dubbed the New World Order, aptly reflecting its purpose. By introducing more streamlined central governance in specific districts, it ushered in innovative concepts of territorial sovereignty, replacing traditional sociopolitical frameworks with conscription, novel taxation systems, and redefined legal statuses. The New World Order received acclaim from European nations, which generously provided Muslim rulers with artillery and military advisors.[26] Their support was motivated by the recognition of the New World Order as a catalyst for imperial globalization, aligning with their aspirations to "civilize" and efficiently administer potential colonial regions.[27]

The acquisition of advanced technology, engagement with non-Muslim European educators, and the dispatch of educational delegations to Europe served as implicit endorsements and catalysts for the Fresh Global System. Simultaneously, however, these efforts were driven by a desire to counter Eurocentric globalization within the emerging global order. The imperative for increased interstate collaboration has reignited a yearning for the caliphate's symbolic representation of religious and political cohesion. Nonetheless, contemporary globalization has transcended national boundaries across historical epochs, leveraging the interconnectedness between the Muslim realm and Europe, fortified through imperial communication channels. Muslim scholars, traditional defenders of Islamic ethics, played a pivotal role in this dynamic. Traveling extensively, they now spent time in European cities and utilized the burgeoning Middle Eastern press to disseminate their beliefs. These Islamic modernists found significant benefits in these linkages, reaffirming the legitimacy of Muslim universalism and its compatibility with modernity. They argued that, for the welfare of the *ummah*, engagement with European advancements in science, politics, and culture was essential. Employing the techniques of Islamic renewal, they legitimized this process by equating European and Islamic institutions. One noteworthy comparison involved the concept of consultation, known as *shurā*, and parliamentary democracy.[28]

Islamic modernism held profound significance as it delineated the parameters for a novel Muslim global discourse, establishing a dialectical connection with European ideas rather than merely imitating them. This dynamic persisted throughout the era of postcolonial globalization, rendering the extensive debate over the authenticity of these links irrelevant in this context. The Islamic modernists contributed a framework for synthesizing these obligations through Pan-Islamism—a doctrine advocating global mass Muslim solidarity against European imperialism and corrupt domestic regimes. Additionally, they voiced criticism against Muslim dictatorships for their failure to uphold either traditional or modern political commitments.[29] In response to European imperialism, Islamic modernization, and pan-Islamism, the Ottoman Sultan Abdul Hamid II (1878–1909) revived the caliphate.[30] The objective of the Ottoman caliphate was to provide the *ummah* with a renewed focus in a world characterized by extensive commercial networks, along with a division between European metropolitan and non-European colonial regions. This period also witnessed the elimination of the freedom of movement once enjoyed by Muslims within Muslim countries. This goal was achieved, in part, by unsettling the British and French imperial administrations.

Starting in the mid-1700s, a wave of Muslim intellectuals and activists embarked on a comprehensive religious reform initiative to modernize Islam in response to European colonialism. Consequently, Muslim transnationalism has reacquired a distinctly political nature. A primary goal of this movement was to mitigate conflicts and animosities among various Muslim sects and factions. The initiative began with the contributions of Shah WaliAllah in India and reached its zenith with the influential figure of Jamal al-Din al-Afghani during the mid-1800s. al-Afghani serves as the embodiment of this progressive political drive for reform. His approach, rooted in a pan-Islamic worldview, aimed to modernize Islam to align it with Western scientific and technological values. Although Afghani was successful in influencing Ottoman Sultan Abdul-Hamid II, he eventually fell out of favor as the nationalist agenda of the Young Turks and later Mustapha Kemal took hold. It is worth noting, however, that key Islamic reformers and ideologues like Muhammad Abduh (Afghani's follower) and Syed Abul 'Ala Mawdudi in Pakistan were occasionally associated with pan-Islamic aspirations.[31]

Muslim Universalism in the Postcolonial World

Due to a universalizing religious impulse, Muslims engendered a systematic iteration of historical globalization, assimilating substantial regions of the world into a network of shared values, cultural norms, and trade. This Islamic sphere engaged with competing global systems, culminating in the emergence of burgeoning Christian and Muslim nations mirroring developments in both Europe and the Muslim world. While occasionally parasitic, European exploitation of non-European trade networks played a role in consolidating Muslim state structures in Africa. Simultaneously, in the Mediterranean, both European and Muslim kingdoms strategically employed intermediaries for economic gains. In essence, proto-globalization manifested as a multicentered process, strengthened by the active involvement of Muslim participants. The nations and peoples within the Muslim world found themselves subjugated within European-dominated imperial institutions during the transition from proto-globalization to modern globalization. This transition, ostensibly envisioned as a partnership of equals, marked a consequential shift in power dynamics. Nevertheless, even at this juncture, as the Ottomans grappled with the imperative to reconstruct and reimagine their empire in alignment with emerging European imperial principles, the Islamic world demonstrated a discernible agency. The innovative reinterpretation of the concept of the nation by Arab thinkers underscored a profound engagement with and reformulation of the global dissemination of European ideas.

Throughout the interwar years, the links between the Muslim world and the prevailing European world order reached their nadir. Numerous Muslim intellectuals asserted their entitlement to independence before the outbreak of the First World War, citing their adherence to the nationalism, secularism, and democratic principles intrinsic to the contemporary European system. It was anticipated, akin to the support rendered to Christian separatists in the nineteenth century, that the European powers would lend assistance to their pursuit of independence.[32] The evolution of contemporary globalization led to the disintegration of the Muslim world, marked by the compartmentalization of its constituent regions within enclosed colonial boundaries and the imposition of constraints on Muslim migrations, notably affecting the Hajj pilgrimage to Mecca. Ostensibly, the overarching objective of global economic integration seemed geared toward exploiting the wealth of the Muslim world to benefit Western corporations and colonial powers, frequently at the expense of indigenous populations.

Their ignorance was exposed by the Ottoman Empire's subsequent fall and split into British and French mandates. Subsequently, travel and migration routes were rerouted toward major European urban centers, where Muslims found themselves relegated to roles as both expendable military recruits and a source of inexpensive labor. The initial decades of the twentieth century bore witness to the widespread humiliation endured by many Muslims, a situation that appeared redeemable only through the pursuit and attainment of independence. In contrast to archaic and proto-globalization epochs, wherein the Muslim world maintained a sense of centrality and significance, contributing significantly to the flow of ideas, goods, and people, the era of modern imperial globalization emerges as atypical. For many decades, the emphasis placed by the governments of most postcolonial states on secular national categories of identity obscured the religious component of politics within the Muslim world. However, there existed a compelling need to reconstitute the Muslim world into a new form, enabling Muslim nations to assume their rightful place as equals within a genuinely global order. This transformation was deemed necessary for the restoration of Muslim self-confidence in the postcolonial milieu. Key milestones in this trajectory include the establishment of the Arab League in 1945, the prominence of Gamal 'Abd al-Nasir's influential pan-Arab ideology during the 1950s and 1960s, and the more recent inauguration of the Islamic Summit Conference, all indicative of progress along this path. Nevertheless, the effective integration of the Muslim world into the contemporary global framework remains uncertain.

The presence of agents and recipients has been a requisite feature in the majority of global systems, spanning both archaic and contemporary contexts, indicating an inherent bipolarity in global systems. The most pronounced critique of modern globalization posits it as synonymous with Western, particularly American, dominance. This criticism emanates not solely from Muslim perspectives but also resonates among Australians and other nations whose economies are intricately linked with the U.S. dollar. Upon Muslims adopting and utilizing novel forms of communication, a substantial number among them opted to interpret these developments as emblematic of subversion and the perceived threat posed by an international Islamic fundamentalist movement to democratic civilization.[33]

According to Ali Mazrui, the final phase of historical globalization witnessed an escalating dependence on information technology, resulting in heightened interconnectedness and exchange. During this period, the United States wielded unparalleled power and, through the enforcement of the Pax Americana, effectively harnessed three pivotal forces of globalization: technology, economy, and empire. While the Pax Americana refrained from explicitly endorsing any particular religion in the latter half of the twentieth century, it ardently upheld secularism and the principle of segregating religious affairs from the affairs of the state. This Americanization model propagated a novel cultural and economic paradigm.[34] Globalization, in this context, transcended mere economic dynamics, embodying an ideology that served to fortify this systemic framework. Consequently, the intertwining of Americanization and globalization was perceived as an intricately interconnected phenomenon.[35]

To emancipate themselves from colonial constraints, Muslim nations adopted the nation-state model; however, these entities grappled with challenges pertaining to legitimacy and historical significance. While genuine progress in the social, political, and economic spheres held the potential to address these ideological concerns, substantial advancements in these domains remain elusive. Concurrently, a significant segment of Muslim immigrants to Western nation-states has encountered difficulties integrating into their newfound communities. In response to these challenges, Muslims often turn to Islamic remedies, drawn by the values of purity and integration promised by modern globalization but not consistently realized for the majority of Muslims. Consequently, the current imperative appears to necessitate a reevaluation of globalization, necessitating the abandonment of entrenched notions of bipolarity and assumptions regarding the intrinsic supremacy of the nation-state. Instead, it urges an acknowledgment of the diversity of global perspectives and the various world civilizations that have given rise to them.

Islam and Postcolonial Identity Formation

Extending from the Atlas Mountains to the Malay Archipelago and from sub-Saharan Africa to Central Asia, there exist more than fifty-five Muslim states today. This group encompasses both heavily populated nations like Indonesia, Nigeria, Bangladesh, and Pakistan and more diminutive entities such as the Maldives and the Comoros. Despite the wide-ranging diversity among these states, a unifying factor in their political dynamics is Islam, functioning not only as a religious belief but also as a foundational element for identity and a substantial influencer in social relations and political affairs. Over the course of history, Islam has played a pivotal role in the efforts to gain independence from colonial powers in regions like sub-Saharan Africa, South and Southeast Asia, as well as the Middle East. Throughout various phases of the colonial era, Islamic forces, intellectuals, and political figures have consistently played a significant role in molding and impacting the political landscape. The pursuit of freedom from colonial rule has been framed within the context of Islamic movements, spanning various historical events and figures. Various other movements considered "Islamic" have emerged, such as *Hizbul Islam* (Islamic Party) in Malaya, *Jamiat-i Ulama-i Hind* (Party of Ulama) in India, Shiite *'ulamā* in 1920s Iran, Sanusiyyah in Libya (led by Umar Mukhtar, 1858–1931), and the Muslim Brotherhood in Egypt.[36]

In subsequent years, the tenets and objectives of politics have been significantly molded by the influence of Islam, as Islamist movements in recent times have not only reshaped the political landscape but have also asserted their claim to state control. The enduring political relevance of Islam, particularly in its role in resisting colonialism, has acted as a counterforce preventing the absolute dominance of secular nationalism in the politics of the Muslim world. Consequently, the process of state formation, intricately linked to both precolonial and colonial periods, has become a complex and sometimes problematic affair. A shared characteristic among Muslim states is their consistent categorization as developing entities. Predominantly arising during the twentieth century, these states have been closely aligned with the collective efforts of their societies to progress and industrialize. In this pursuit, they inherit a historical legacy, navigate a specific cultural milieu, and grapple with political and social challenges reminiscent of those encountered in the broader context of development in the Third World. The diverse responses of Muslim states to these challenges reflect distinct approaches influenced by factors such as size, geographical location, and economic resources, resulting in a spectrum of developmental patterns.

The legacy of colonialism plays a pivotal role in elucidating both the multiplicity and cohesion evident in diverse attempts at state formation within the Muslim world. Much like how Islam, ethnic identity, social attributes, and other native religious and cultural elements account for shared features among Muslim states—and conversely, economic factors, ideology, and leadership elucidate variations—colonialism too offers insights into both converging and diverging points in the trajectories of state formation across the Muslim world. Muslims have coexisted with nearly all colonial powers. In extensive regions of Africa, Asia, and the Arab world, the British and the French exercised dominion over expansive Muslim territories. The Dutch governed areas that eventually evolved into Indonesia, while the Germans, Spanish, Portuguese, and Russians held sway over Muslim territories in East Africa, the Philippines, Malaya (now known as Malaysia), the Caucasus, and Central Asia. The current Israeli control of the West Bank and Gaza Strip can be viewed as the last and lone persisting colonial relationship in Muslim lands.[37]

Although the defining characteristics of colonialism were at play in all these regions, disparities existed in how colonial powers approached their mandates, even varying approaches by the same colonial powers in different territories. Consequently, there exist fundamental parallels and specific nuances among diverse Muslim polities, rooted in historical legacies, and more significantly, shaped by the unique experiences of each colonial territory.

The commencement of the colonization of Muslim territories coincided with the ascendance of European empires, the subjugation of India, and the frenetic acquisition of African territories in the nineteenth century.

Its concluding phase involved the partitioning of the Arab domains of the Ottoman Empire following World War I. The epoch of colonization reached its conclusion post-World War II, with the successive withdrawals of Britain and France from the majority of their colonial holdings. The inception of Muslim states gained momentum from 1947 onward, even though some, like Iran or Afghanistan, had maintained nominal independence throughout. The formation of Muslim states unfolded through a combination of diplomatic handovers by colonial powers, exemplified in instances such as Malaya, India, and the Persian Gulf emirates, as well as through brutal and sanguinary struggles for independence, notably seen in Algeria. The process of decolonization manifested in fits and starts, driven by European powers striving to safeguard their economic interests subsequent to political and military disengagements in a shifting global landscape. Examples such as Iran in 1953 and Egypt in 1956 underscored instances of colonial reassertion, marking a gradual but decisive termination of direct European dominion over Muslim territories.[38]

The majority of Muslim lands had achieved independence from colonialism by the mid-1970s, and they either became separate Muslim nations or were components of independent non-Muslim republics. Nevertheless, their polities, economies, and communities were still being shaped and reshaped by the legacy of colonialism. The effects of colonialism extended much beyond the connections between political and economic imperialism that leftist thinkers have thoroughly discussed. State ideologies, political conceptions, and institutional frameworks of the newly formed states also retained elements of colonialism. Although the effects of colonialism were subtle, they were still widespread. It was an example of how history continued from an earlier era that the newly formed states tried to break away from and go on as separate entities.

The contemporary Muslim world is composed of nation-states. The OIC, designed as a global counterpart to the UN, possesses restricted authority. Nevertheless, the pursuit of Islamic unity remains a fundamental aspiration for Islamic movements, exerting a considerable influence on politics across the Muslim world. It is noteworthy that the concept of a territorial state is relatively recent in Muslim countries. During the premodern era, Muslims demonstrated an acute awareness of internal distinctions, encompassing ethnic, linguistic, and regional variances. Despite this diversity, a unifying political coherence prevailed within the ambit of the caliphate, subsequently extending into empires and sultanates. The transitory borders characterizing these political entities assumed a symbolic significance, representing the authoritative mandate exercised by rulers in the name of Islam. This stands in stark contrast to the contemporary comprehension of nation-states, typified by fixed territorial demarcations. In a parallel trajectory to the evolution of nationalism, the conception of a Muslim territorial state underwent an importation from the Western paradigm. The instantiation of delineated physical borders for Muslim nations and the assimilation of the territorial state concept into the discourse of Muslim politics both manifested as consequential byproducts of colonial influence.[39]

The proposition does not assert the absence of ethnic affiliations and national identities within the Muslim world antecedent to the onset of colonialism; rather, it underscores the enduring potency of such sentiments. Notably, Iranians have historically cultivated a distinct self-perception vis-à-vis Arabs and Turks, where Shiism has evolved as a seminal marker of their national identity, demarcating Iranians from the encompassing Sunni Turks, Arabs, and Türkmen. Analogously conspicuous distinctions manifest between Arabs and Berbers, Arabs and Turks, or Malays and Javanese. The phenomenon, however, of ethnic nationalism conjoined with the conceptualization of a nation-state constitutes a relatively nascent development within the Muslim world, with its roots tracing back to the colonial era. In this temporal juncture, nationalism assumes a pivotal role as a paramount form of political identity, transcending subjugation to Islamic identity and irrevocably intertwining itself as an autonomous entity correlated with a territorial state modeled upon Western prototypes. It is within the crucible of colonial influence that this instantiation of nationalism takes root, seamlessly integrating into the mosaic of Muslim political consciousness.[40]

Profound tensions have persistently marked the landscape of the Muslim world, emanating from the juxtaposition of the relatively recent nationalist political ideal, epitomized by the conception of the nation-state and the enduring Islamic principle of the *ummah*, denoting the sacred community that continues to serve as a foundational tenet in Muslim political philosophy. The paradigm of the *ummah* enjoins Muslims not merely to forge unity beyond national confines but, more fundamentally, to prioritize Islam above all other political affiliations in their quotidian lives. The intensity of these tensions has been contingent upon the degree of receptivity exhibited by the state toward accommodating Islamic consciousness. Nations such as Saudi Arabia, Pakistan, Bangladesh, and Malaysia have endeavored to harmonize the ideas of nationhood and the *ummah*, fostering a synthesis between the two. In contrast, Turkey, Pahlavi Iran, Tunisia, Algeria, and Indonesia purposefully sought to assert the superiority of the nation-state over the *ummah*, a conscious divergence in ideological orientation. A pivotal determinant in this context lies in the potency of nationalist sentiments within respective states. Nations characterized by robust national identities, exemplified by Turkey, Iran, and Egypt, have wielded state prerogatives with heightened assertiveness. This trend is further accentuated in regions harboring substantial non-Muslim minorities, as evident in Malaysia or Nigeria. Conversely, in locales like Pakistan, where national identity manifests in a comparatively attenuated form, the *ummah* assumes a more influential sway over political ideals.[41]

The operative mechanisms and resultant imprints of colonialism have profoundly influenced Muslims' constructions of their identities and political trajectories, discernibly diverging the trajectories of various Muslim states post-independence. In its initial phases, colonialism instituted a transformative dynamic through the cultivation of a nascent elite, meticulously groomed by colonial rulers in European languages and governance methodologies, thereby engendering the establishment of a governmental apparatus. This process of elite formation, in tandem with crystallizing perceptions regarding the domains under elite purview and the attendant possibilities and limitations, delineated the contours of Muslim territories. Embedded within these evolving perceptions were commitments to territorial demarcations, inextricably interwoven with extant ethnic identities. These commitments, in turn, engendered nascent visions of nationalism, endowing heightened significance to the delineated boundaries. Consequently, an administrative functionary in locales such as Kuala Lumpur or Damascus found it imperative to foster a distinct identity—be it "Malaysianness" or "Syrianness"—to safeguard against the prospect of relegation to the status of a provincial official within a larger, more encompassing Malay or Arab entity. It was precisely these sentiments that, in subsequent years, precipitated the dissolution of the Egyptian–Syrian unity pact of 1958–61. Bureaucrats in Iraq and Syria, once united under the Ottoman umbrella and immersed in a shared political, social, and literary milieu, underwent a transformation catalyzed by divergent ties to disparate European traditions and languages. This process significantly contributed to the crystallization of their distinct "separateness." The manifold administrative and political trajectories thus derived from the colonial experience coalesced to solidify parochial nationalisms, eclipsing more universalistic inclinations. In essence, the colonial milieu and its designated arenas for elite operation fundamentally laid the groundwork for the inception of states where none had previously existed.[42]

Within the Malay context, a parallel process induced a cleavage between Malaysian and Indonesian identities and, concomitantly, demarcated distinctions between Muslim Malay and non-Muslim Malay identities. Bureaucratic and political entities in British Malay and the Dutch Indies found their operative milieu in the variegated cultural, linguistic, and religious landscape specific to their respective British and Dutch domains. The envisagement of a Malay arena, encompassing segments of Indonesia and Malaysia, or a Muslim-Pattani region in Thailand and Mindanao in the Philippines, while excluding non-Muslim and non-Malay components, proved to be an impracticable notion. The demarcation of boundaries within the colonial paradigm, coupled with the divergent cultural and historical trajectories engendered therein, fundamentally dictated the contours of nascent states and political entities. The conceptualization of a unified Islamic Malaya was precluded by the disparate colonial authorities governing its constituent peoples. Conversely, the amalgamation of Borneo and, albeit briefly, Singapore into Malaysia was facilitated by their subjugation under a common British colonial administration. Thus, colonialism emerged as a determinant in delineating state borders and shaping the ensuing realities, standing in stark contradistinction to alternative conceptualizations of independence and statehood.[43]

Emergent states frequently engaged in the appropriation of extant ethnic identities, such as "Iraqiness" or "Syrianness," or contrived semblances thereof, exemplified in instances like Jordan or Malaysia. This strategic maneuver aimed to engender nationalist ideologies capable of buttressing the intricate process of state formation. Concurrently, this undertaking encompassed the subjugation of competing ethnic identities, forestalling their evolution into distinct nationalisms. Iran, Iraq, and Turkey, for instance, conscientiously endeavored to forestall the crystallization of Kurdish identity as a distinct nationalism. Iran pursued an assimilative approach, seeking to integrate Kurds into an overarching Iranian nationalist identity, while Turkey adopted the stance of portraying them as "Mountain Turks."[44]

The efficacy of these state formation experiments was contingent upon the adept cultivation of national consciousness, a variable predicated on the resilience of the ethnic identity serving as the foundational bedrock of the nascent nationalism. Subsequently, ethnic and territorial delineations emerged as salient parameters demarcating the boundaries of national identity formations. These delineations not only took root but also evolved as dominant and secular forms of political identity, superseding recollections of a historically united Islamic world. It is noteworthy that the enduring impact of colonial powers' territorial demarcations, ostensibly not intended for lasting consequences, became starkly evident as these boundaries became indelibly enshrined in the fabric of future states.

With each Muslim state claiming exclusive rights to its piece of the territory, territorial divisions have been a recurring cause of conflict.

Noteworthy instances include Jordan and Syria's post-independence aspirations to reconstitute a broader Syria, with Jordan concurrently maintaining territorial assertions over Palestine. Morocco similarly advanced territorial claims to Mauritania and segments of Algeria. Contentions between Syria and Turkey revolved around contested sovereignty over Alexandretta (Iskenderun), while Iran and Iraq found themselves embroiled in disputes over the Shatt al Arab channel. Egypt and Sudan grappled over Nile waters, Pakistan and Afghanistan over the Durand Line, and Pakistan and India over Kashmir. The contested territories extended to Saudi Arabia and Qatar, as well as Saudi Arabia and the United Arab Emirates, involving borderline oases and oil fields. Further, discord unfolded between Libya and Chad over their shared border regions, and Iran and the United Arab Emirates disputed sovereignty over the Tunbs and Abu Musa islands.

In certain instances, the very existence of Muslim states has been contested by neighboring entities, perceiving them as artificial constructs originating from colonial impositions. Illustrative examples include Syria's claims to Lebanon, Malaysia's erstwhile assertions over Brunei, Iraq's contentions over Kuwait, and Morocco's territorial claims to Western Sahara. The delineation of borders, while ostensibly shaping the contours of states, failed to assure their viability. Colonial authorities neglected the imperative of fostering a cohesive national culture among the diverse inhabitants within these demarcations. Paradoxically, colonial powers, at times, exacerbated divisions by fostering competition among ethnic, linguistic, religious, or tribal groups as a means of sustaining control. The territorial partitioning of Muslim lands, ostensibly undisputed, concurrently fostered national confusion and the fracturing of emergent national societies.[45]

Persistent tensions among diverse populations and regions, coalesced within the confines of a single state yet never coalesced into a unified nation, have engendered challenges to established state boundaries. Instances such as confessional tensions in Lebanon and ethnic and religious conflicts in Nigeria, Pakistan, and Malaysia, along with the protracted predicament of the Kurdish population across Iran, Iraq, and Turkey, underscore the multifarious issues intrinsic to state formation predicated upon colonial territorial delineation. Remarkably, none of these challenges have emanated from endeavors to reconstitute a cohesive "Islamdom." Paradoxically, the dominance of nationalist sentiments within Muslim political consciousness remains so pervasive that even Pakistan, conceived in the name of Islam, experienced an ethnic schism in 1971, ultimately fragmenting into Pakistan and Bangladesh. Despite its inherent complexities and challenges, the prevailing conception and materialization of Muslim states' territoriality persist in the colonial paradigm to this day.

Global Muslim Diaspora and Transnational Connections

The term "Muslim diaspora" is prevalent in colloquial usage, signifying Muslim populations in the Western sphere who are not indigenous to the region, predominantly tracing their origins to the Middle East, North Africa, or Asia. However, within the academic discourse of contemporary Islam in Europe, this terminology is sparingly invoked, emerging primarily when specific facets of the conventional diasporic experience, such as ethnonationalist sentiments or active political and economic mobilization linked to the country of origin, manifest conspicuously. Central tenets in widely accepted diaspora definitions encompass the dispersion of a particular ethnonational group and the community's enduring transnational linkages with its place of origin. The conceptual roots of the term diaspora find initial references in the Old Testament, delineating the experiences of Jewish communities in exile, later metaphorically appropriated to expound upon the role of Christians globally. Notably, present considerations would likely preclude characterizing Christians in the United States (excluding recent Middle Eastern refugees) as constituting a diaspora community. This prompts critical inquiry into the juxtaposition of "Islam" and "diaspora" concerning Muslim citizens and inhabitants of Europe, who could arguably be native or well-settled residents of the region, possessing, at most, attenuated connections with Muslim lands and ethnic groups.[46]

While the transnational and deterritorialized dimensions of religion constitute pivotal elements in the global articulations of Islam in the twenty-first century, as underscored by scholars such as Peter Mandaville and Olivier Roy, these elements, in isolation, are insufficient grounds to categorize Muslims as a diaspora. Rather, the determining factor lies in the enduring territorial affiliations with the origins of a community. Consequently, encounters within the United Kingdom may involve interactions with members of the Pakistani diaspora adhering to Islam, an Italian diaspora aligned with Catholicism, or a Moroccan diaspora associated with Islam. Simultaneously, one might also encounter the Pakistani Christian diaspora, the Italian evangelical diaspora, or Jewish constituents of the Moroccan diaspora, illustrating the nuanced diversity of diasporic experiences coexisting within a singular geographical entity.[47]

In recent years, a substantial influx of immigrants originating from Muslim-majority nations, notably Iraq and Syria, has been witnessed as a consequence of warfare and the imposition of Islamic religious norms through political selectivity. However, the nomenclature "Muslim diasporas" appears inadequate when considering that, in reality, immigrants and refugees encompass not only adherents of Islam but also Christian and Yazidi minorities, alongside individuals who profess no particular faith. Employing the overarching term "Muslim diasporas" fails to acknowledge the inherent pluralism and internal dissensions within Islam. The commonly acknowledged Sunni–Shia schism merely scratches the surface of these intricate dynamics. The practice, comprehension, and lived experiences of Islam exhibit a diverse spectrum, not confined solely to geographical distinctions but extending to different social, cultural, or ethnic milieus—even within the confines of the same family. Each subgroup within Islam exhibits distinctive inclinations and preferences across spiritual, intellectual, and political dimensions, grounded in unique theological reference points. The categorical label of "Muslim diaspora" proves unsuitable when applied to Muslims born and residing outside regions where Islam holds majority status.[48]

The conventional paradigm of diaspora, denoting the experience of exile and migration, whether coerced or voluntary, proves insufficient in encapsulating the multifaceted circumstances of all Muslims who have established residence in Europe, North America, or other global locales. Within this demographic, a considerable number may indeed trace their lineage to immigrant forebears; however, they themselves may lack direct personal experience in, or perhaps have never visited, the countries of origin of their parents or grandparents. A nuanced complexity arises when considering individuals born to unions between an indigenous European and an immigrant, prompting inquiry into whether they should be categorized as autochthonous or as constituents of a diaspora. The delineation of such classifications carries substantive implications, not only pertaining to legal rights but also within the frameworks of societal inclusion or exclusion. Furthermore, the evolving landscape encompasses a growing cohort of Western individuals who have embraced Islam through conversion. This demographic shift introduces additional dimensions to the discourse, necessitating a reevaluation of existing terminological and conceptual frameworks to more accurately capture the diverse narratives and affiliations within the Muslim population in these Western contexts.[49]

Should the generic categorization of diaspora be abruptly ascribed to this demographic solely on account of their professed faith? If such an attribution were made, would their emotional affiliations, political and ethnic identities, and inherent sense of belonging undergo immediate assimilation into a presumed, preemptive diasporic dimension? Subsequently, what ramifications would ensue from these intricate dynamics concerning our comprehension of citizenship and religious affiliations within democratic, secular nations characterized by varying degrees of separation between religion and public life? Within the contemporary milieu of globalization, transnational networks, and swift technological interconnectedness, the diasporic experience assumes an ostensibly universal character. Notably, the major religious traditions universally incorporate references to journeys and emigration experiences as metaphors emblematic of the human condition. Within this broader conceptual framework, the Islamic faith, from an anthropological standpoint, ceases to exhibit exceptionalism in its resonance with the overarching themes encapsulated within the notion of diaspora.

The burgeoning Muslim population in Europe, coupled with an increasing aspiration for the propagation of Islamic values within the host nations where they, or their forebears, have established residence, has elicited a notable shift in the approach of Western governments toward the Muslim presence since the 1990s.[50] Initially, various European nations attempted to regulate the integration of these labor migrant Muslims through the implementation of multicultural policies. The underlying objective of these policies was to cultivate a societal ethos transcending the confines of "national particularism," aspiring instead toward a harmonious coexistence of individuals from diverse ethnic backgrounds. This approach accentuated the significance of cultural diversity and acknowledged group distinctions.[51] However, according to Lebl, the outcomes of these policies led to a shift in perspective where advocating for the dominance or supremacy of the prevailing culture was deemed inappropriate. Such a stance, it was argued, would compromise the equality or standing of other equally valid minority perspectives. The intention was to uphold the legitimacy and mutual respect of each cultural manifestation, fostering an environment where diverse cultural perspectives coexist on equitable grounds.[52]

The mounting apprehensions surrounding the exponential growth of the Muslim populace in Western societies appear rooted in a perspective wherein the preservation of cultural values may be perceived as a potential rejection of host country values. In the case of Muslims, these concerns often center on the perceived incompatibility of their values with Western liberal ideals, particularly exemplified in practices such as the wearing of *hijab* and *niqab*. Various facets of cultural expression, ranging from festive observances and culinary preferences to dress codes, work schedules, prayer routines, and nuanced responses to leadership styles and gender dynamics, play a pivotal role in shaping the dynamics of international human resource management within organizations.[53]

Muslims in Western contexts navigate their identity negotiation by confronting stereotypes, visibly asserting their ethnic identity while concurrently veiling their religious identity. These dimensions dynamically coalesce and influence their interactions within organizational frameworks.[54] Some argue that there is no inherent conflict between the Islamic faith and contemporary workplaces. Consequently, any potential friction points between Islam and prevailing human resource management (HRM) practices can be effectively managed.[55] An illustrative example is the concept of Islamic piety (*taqwa*), which advocates for a harmonious equilibrium between spiritual and social responsibilities. Embracing Islam as a comprehensive way of life can foster positive organizational behavior and mitigate workplace deviance, including antisocial conduct, incivility, and aggression.[56]

Islamic worldviews are imbued with principles that advocate stewardship, support, and cooperative endeavors, exerting a profound influence on the interpersonal dynamics of Muslims within the workplace.[57] Islamic leadership aligns closely with ethical, transformational, and authentic leadership paradigms. Consequently, managers who subscribe to the Islamic faith often opt for leadership styles characterized by ethical considerations, transformative initiatives, and authenticity in organizational contexts. Leadership practices among Muslim organizational leaders lean toward collectivism, displaying a predilection for conflict avoidance and circumvention of disputes in organizational settings, particularly when such actions align with the communal good. Despite this, there exists a paradox wherein Muslim leaders, although more inclined toward autocratic leadership styles compared to their Christian counterparts, justify their approach by invoking strict adherence to Qur'ānic principles. The regulatory frameworks governing religious practices within institutions play a pivotal role in establishing robust systems for religious supervision. This ensures the harmonious practice of religion by adherents of various faiths within organizational and societal realms, fostering an environment of peaceful coexistence.[58]

The interplay of institutional actors, notably governmental entities and identity networks rooted in both source and host countries, assumes a critical role in determining success when religion becomes entwined with secularism, particularly in the context of Muslims in the West and international HRM.[59] A comprehensive examination of this phenomenon is essential, as underscored by Syed and Pio's (2010) multilevel study focusing on Muslim migrant women in Australia.[60] The authors caution against solely attributing accountability for diversity policies to organizations, advocating for a nuanced understanding that encompasses macro-societal and micro-individual factors influencing diversity management. Acquisti and Fong shed light on discriminatory hiring practices in certain Republican states in the United States, where job candidates with apparent Muslim affiliations on social networking profiles may face reduced interview prospects.[61] Nevertheless, an evolving organizational landscape increasingly recognizes the value of multicultural skills. Employees hailing from diverse faith and ethnic backgrounds are acknowledged as potential catalysts for positive transformations in the success of global projects and processes.[62] Human and social capital emerge as pivotal considerations for employers, a sentiment reinforced by Foroutan's statistical analysis, which suggests that employment differentials encountered by Muslim minorities in the labor market in Western contexts are primarily rooted in factors such as human capital and the duration of residence in the destination country.[63]

Scholarly discussions on individuals with ancestral ties extending beyond national borders often employ the term "mobilization of collective identities by immigrants." Koopmans, Statham, and Giugni have classified immigrant groups into four distinctive types of collective identity within this construct.[64] These types encompass groups affiliated with their homeland or place of ethnic descent, organizations focusing on broader racial groupings (e.g., Asians), cross-ethnic collectives including generic immigrants, minorities, or foreigners, and those centered around religious identification. The complexity of these categorizations is further heightened by the identification a group establishes with its place of settlement. In the realm of organized civil society groups, there is a considerable overlap in aims and objectives, creating a competitive environment for both membership and funding acquisition. Muslim organizations, in particular, exhibit significant fluidity, marked by fluctuations in activity levels, experiencing periods of ascent and descent in their trajectories.[65]

Religious Associations and Transnational Ties

In delving into the intricacies of diaspora religion, John Hinnells provides a definition that encapsulates the faith of communities perceiving themselves as living apart from their religious homeland or the "old country."[66] Gerrieter Haar further intertwines religion and diaspora by positing that migration inherently implies diaspora due to the religious practices of migrants.[67] However, Vertovec and Cohen challenge this interpretation, emphasizing the distinct nature of migration and minority status from the concept of diaspora.[68] This nuanced distinction also applies to the often-misused term transnationalism, which, while interconnected with diaspora, encompasses specific socioreligious transformative processes. Within this context, Islamic identity emerges as a pivotal link within the transnational networks of the Muslim diaspora.

This confluence of factors underscores a distinct evolution in the dynamics of socioreligious associations, mirroring the nuanced interplay between European political frameworks and the aspirations of Muslim communities. The limited emphasis on religion in European political initiatives and the exclusive channeling of resources toward social initiatives have catalyzed the geographical expansion of socioreligious networks from local domains to encompass national and transnational spheres. Navigating this landscape, these associations find themselves compelled to seek financial backing not only from international Islamic organizations but also from the countries of origin. Within this complex network, European institutions extend support primarily to cultural networks, while the religious dimension relies on external Islamic entities and nations. This strategic approach is oriented toward championing the interests of the diasporic Muslim population and fostering the extraterritorial reach of Islam. These organizations are driven by a collective ambition to solidify a shared identification with Islam within the European context.[69] The genesis of these associations and organizations can be traced back to a policy framework promoting "le droit à la difference" (the right to difference), notably prominent in France and subsequently adopted by other European nations. The resultant surge in voluntary associations serves as a nexus for a diverse array of cultural and religious activities. Within these community organizations, a symbiotic process unfolds as they function as sanctuaries for the interpretation, redefinition, and internalization of cultural, religious, ethnic, and national identities. Simultaneously, these entities strategically adapt their activities to align with the broader imperatives of families seeking to preserve a distinct Muslim identity while operating within the legitimate confines of the host state.[70]

Islam serves as a cohesive force among community leaders, even in the presence of apparent internal fragmentation exacerbated by national demarcations. In the context of the Netherlands, a pivotal facet of the ethnic minorities policy involved the subsidization of immigrant associations. These entities were allocated financial support to orchestrate cultural undertakings, thereby fortifying their affiliation with their respective ethnic cohorts. The underlying rationale posited that fostering group-specific facilities would propel the sociocultural emancipation of immigrant factions. The overarching policy objective, at that juncture, aimed at ameliorating the societal standing of ethnic minorities within the Dutch milieu. However, beyond the ostensibly benevolent impetus, subsidies played a dual role. They functioned not only as a means of enhancing social and cultural emancipation but also as a mechanism through which local and national authorities could maintain a symbiotic relationship with immigrant communities, thereby attributing responsibility for individual actions. Yet, amidst the contemporary discourse on immigration and Islam, a paradigm shift became evident. The state found itself compelled to redirect its focus toward augmenting the participation of minorities in educational and occupational spheres, relegating its involvement in religious–cultural activities. This paradigmatic transition, as elucidated by Bruquetas-Callejo et al., marked a departure from the preceding ethos, ushering in a more "assimilationist" policy milieu during the 1990s.[71] This paradigm cantered on individual considerations within the socioeconomic framework, eclipsing the hitherto emphasized cultural distinctions as a principal determinant in shaping prevailing conditions.

After significant changes in public and political discourse, exacerbated by perceived integration shortcomings, a noticeable response emerged among a significant proportion of immigrants—a clear propensity to strongly affiliate religiously and culturally with Islam. In the context of increasingly heated discussions, Dutch Liberal leader Frits Bolkestein began an investigation of whether Islam could coexist with Western cultural standards. According to Bolkestein, the cultural and theological principles of Islam were a significant barrier to the integration of the Muslim population in the Netherlands,[72] placing social issues in the perspective of a "Clash of Civilizations."[73] The idea that integration and identity preservation could coexist peacefully was categorically rejected by Scheffer in his seminal work, "The Multicultural Drama," calling it a "pious lie." He was an advocate of returning to the "brutal bargain" of integration and restoring "even-handedness."[74] Simultaneously, the horrific events of 2011 in Norway, highlighted by the abhorrent murder of seventy-seven children and teenagers connected to the Labour Party in Oslo and Utoeya by Anders Breivik, exposed a troubling viewpoint. In his manifesto, Breivik made the broad claim that "multicultural elites are waging total war against their populations" throughout Europe. Their objective is to continue the mass migration policy, which will lead to an Islamic Europe devoid of freedom, or "Eurabia."[75] This insightful speech captures a passionate and concerning viewpoint on the direction of European societal dynamics.

Diasporic Identity and the Dynamics of Cultural Reproduction

The discourse surrounding the perpetuation, adaptation, or abandonment of religious practices within post-migration generations engenders a complex inquiry into diasporic identity and cultural continuity. The engagement in religious and cultural activities, coupled with participation in formal places of worship, intricately sculpts the identities and pursuits of second and third generations.[76] This demarcates them from their parental generation, a distinction accentuated by exposure to Western education, the influence of secular and civil society norms, assimilation into Western popular culture, and a palpable discontentment with conservative community leaders who fail to grasp their unique position as post-migration youth.

An additional facet meriting consideration is the dynamic interplay of ethnic and religious pluralism within diasporic contexts. The immigrant experience and the concomitant minority status instigate a transformative trajectory in religious dynamics driven by self-awareness. Barbara Metcalf contends that "the sense of contrast—whether with a historical past or the broader societal milieu—lies at the core of a self-consciousness that profoundly shapes religious expression."[77] However, it is imperative to delineate that the construct of religious pluralism extends beyond the mere coexistence of diverse faith traditions. Migrants frequently encounter diverse traditions within their own religious framework. As posited by Eickelman and Piscatori, the interaction with the Muslim "other" assumes a significance comparable, if not superior, to the confrontation with the European "other" in the process of self-definition. The paradoxical outcome of voyaging, which enriches one's awareness of the spiritual unity inherent in the "*ummah*," also delineates boundaries between Muslims, potentially constricting their horizons.[78]

Emphasizing the paramount significance of cultural and religious adaptation and continuity within diasporic communities, Shaye and Frerichs underscore the nuanced interplay of preserving established practices and accommodating transformative influences.[79] Martin Sokefeld illuminates the intricate diasporic dynamic as a duality characterized by simultaneous continuity and change.[80] This conceptualization necessitates an understanding that parallel processes of change may be underway in the homeland, either catalyzed by the diaspora or influenced by non-diasporic factors. The manifestation of this "diasporic duality" extends across diverse socioreligious domains. Stephen Warner contends that religious identities assume heightened significance for individuals in their diaspora, undergoing various modifications over time.[81] A compelling rationale for this transformation lies in the establishment, adaptation, remodeling, and adoption of religious institutions within the diaspora. These institutions burgeon into self-contained realms, denoted as "congregations," where novel relationships among community members—be it between genders, generations, or varying degrees of settlement—are forged. Eickelman and Piscatori underscore the dynamic nature of identities, asserting that diasporic identification is fraught with intricacies and permutations.[82] The spectrum of identifications encompasses individuals who persist in considering their land of birth as the quintessential "home," while others gradually shift their primary allegiance to the land of settlement. Notably, certain cohorts, exemplified by Turkish workers in Germany or intellectuals like Salman Rushdie, find themselves in a liminal state of non-belonging, not entirely at ease in either their land of settlement or their land of origin. Such individuals grapple with a sense of displacement that transcends geographical borders. Moreover, the intricacies of diasporic identity extend to the coexistence of multiple and potentially conflicting identities. Teunissen introduces a nuanced categorization based on informants' attitudes toward religion. She distinguishes between those with a "conscious faith," adherents of a "personal faith," and those who outright "reject faith." The first group, characterized by their devout observance of Islamic precepts, prominently wear the headscarf and orient themselves toward educational pursuits and self-achievement in Dutch society.[83] For them, Islam serves as the linchpin of identity, a guiding framework through which they navigate and transcend traditional gender roles to integrate into Dutch society. Conversely, the second category acknowledges an inability to adhere strictly to all Islamic regulations and places a greater emphasis on the intuitive dimension of their faith, rooted in heartfelt conviction. This group exhibits flexibility and relishes independence from parental constraints, although educational pursuits are not a primary focus. Their faith is less prescriptive, allowing for a more personalized and adaptable interpretation. In contrast, those who outright "reject faith" grapple with extensive family issues. Parents voice concerns about their perceived abuse of freedom, which is deemed "too Dutch." This cohort, characterized as "recreation-minded" by Waardenburg, not only raises eyebrows within the community but also contributes to a tarnished communal reputation due to behaviors that sow doubt and defy prevailing norms.[84]

Transnationalism encapsulates the complex interplay of communication and interactions that transcend the confines of nation-states, forging extensive global connections between diverse individuals and institutions.[85] This phenomenon, intricately interwoven with the broader currents of globalization, denotes an elevated interconnectedness that permeates various domains, notably exerting a discernible influence on the multifaceted tapestry of religious dynamics.[86] Within the realm of diaspora and migration, Peggy Levitt discerns a conspicuous research lacuna concerning the intricate links between post-migration communities and their origins.[87] Levitt not only underscores the transformative impact of these connections on the globalization of everyday practices, discourses, and relations but also contends that existing scholarly endeavors, while rich in their exploration of immigrant incorporation, fall short of adequately illuminating the nuanced ways in which ongoing relationships between home and host-country institutions reshape religious practices. Levitt accentuates the overarching influence of these transformations, not only echoing within the host country but also reverberating back to the origin country, thereby delineating a reciprocal and multifaceted impact on religious practices.[88]

Eickelman delves into the ramifications of contemporary forms of travel and communication on organizational paradigms and strategies. He astutely observes a paradigm shift, elucidating the transformation of once-elite movements into mass movements, thereby effectively rendering obsolete prior conceptualizations of frontiers tethered predominantly to geographical boundaries.[89] In the current milieu, technologically mediated communication, particularly through computational platforms, assumes a pivotal role, significantly shaping transnational religious organization and activity at both collective and individual levels.[90] The integration of these technologies emerges as a transformative force, intricately molding the contours of the transnational religious landscape. This nuanced examination underscores the dynamic and evolving nature of transnationalism in contemporary globalized societies.

Islam and Global Governance

The predominant discourse on global governance within the existing literature accentuates the predominant roles assigned to Western nations, transnational corporations originating in the West, and international organizations such as the WTO and OECD. These entities conspicuously embody a Western neoliberal bias, wielding an overarching influence that extends to various corners of the world.[91] Despite recent scholarly endeavors redirecting attention to alternative geopolitical arenas, thus giving rise to the formation of transnational organizations representing regional interests and fostering opportunities for participation in the global governance landscape, it remains evident that the interpretative frameworks applied by non-Western countries often operate within confines limited by Western-centric paradigms. A salient illustration of this phenomenon is discernible in the context of the Muslim world—a geopolitical entity paradoxically foundational to modern disciplines in the West during the Renaissance and persisting as a formative intellectual force throughout the Enlightenment.[92]

From this rich intellectual heritage, the genesis of concepts concerning global governance can be traced within the annals of modern history, notably evidenced by its influence on Kant's seminal essay "Toward Perpetual Peace." However, the identification and elucidation of Islamic principles of governance in practical application prove intricate due to a tumultuous political history that witnessed the detachment of numerous Muslim states from their traditional foundations. This historical trajectory encompasses pivotal events such as the European colonization of the Middle East, the decline of the Ottoman Empire, and subsequent national independences coupled with political instabilities. Consequently, the governance structures and practices observable in contemporary Muslim countries emerge as a complex amalgamation shaped by the intricate interplay of multifarious factors. The majority find themselves ensconced in a postcolonial milieu characterized by the inheritance of colonial configurations within their national structures, political systems, legal frameworks, and institutional arrangements. This legacy emanates from complex interactions between colonial powers and the indigenous societies under their administration, thereby engendering a diverse spectrum of national regimes across the colonized expanse.[93] The landscape of governance encounters additional intricacies arising from adverse stereotypes associated with Islam. These stereotypes, notably expounded upon in Said's seminal work on Orientalism dating back to 1978, persist in contemporary discourse. Such prejudices are manifest in the notably polarized "Clash of Civilizations" theory, prominently advanced by scholars like Huntington.[94] The present political milieu, characterized by heightened polarization, does not favor the contemplation or endorsement of Islamic perspectives on global governance as complementary or contributory to ongoing discussions regarding the augmentation of current global governance paradigms.

Various dimensions of scholarship within Islamic studies are encapsulated in several presumptions concerning both Western theories and models, as well as those attributed to the Islamic world, ostensibly posited as antithetical. These encompass critiques of the secularized Western social sciences, characterized by overgeneralizations, distortions, negative stereotyping, and demonization perpetuated against Muslim societies. Furthermore, there exists a conflation of Islam with militant or fundamentalist Islamism, leading to the exclusion of diverse Islamic schools of thought from the scholarly purview.[95] Notably, figures such as Fukuyama and Huntington, while asserting the preeminence of the West in possessing the sole viable paradigm for development and democracy, are not singular in their erroneous assumptions, which pervade a significant portion of the discourse in the realm of global governance.[96] Nevertheless, Islamic conceptualizations of global governance exhibit a distinct yet not wholly disparate character in comparison to many

Western perspectives. Within an expanding cohort of scholars, Bilgin has castigated the empirical and ideological predicament embedded in adopting a "West versus the rest" paradigm. Such a dichotomy, she contends, lacks historical accuracy as it neglects the centuries of intellectual transmission between regions, adopting an inequitable dominant–passive framework that has historically been employed to rationalize colonization. Furthermore, this paradigm engenders a polarization of knowledge and values that, in reality, bear more resemblance than difference. The resultant assumptions stemming from such a construct tend to negate the acknowledgment of the substantial contributions from the "rest," attributing rationalism exclusively to the West while assigning a non-rational or spiritual character to other regions.

The prevailing paradigm, as posited by Grugel and Piper, is one characterized by a pro-Western orientation, wherein a "system based on pluralism and liberal inclusion" is orchestrated with the objective of ingraining "Western authority."[97] This orientation serves as the foundational ethos underpinning institutions such as the Commission on Global Governance, as explicated by Sabet (2008) and Sinclair (2012).[98] This pro-Western stance, as contended by Barkawi and Laffey (2006), permeates security studies, leading to the domination of Western powers within international organizations like the UN. Such dominance reflects a historical continuum of "civilizing missions," including the manifestations of the "white man's burden," the humanitarian interventions of the 1990s, and the post-9/11 invasions of Afghanistan and Iraq.[99] Consequently, a significant lacuna permeates the literature on global governance, resulting in an inadequate representation of genuine global perspectives and substantive contributions to the field. The Islamic framework of governance, inherently distinct from contemporary Western paradigms emphasizing attributes such as democracy, civil rights, transparency, the rule of law, and effective public services, nevertheless shares foundational elements. These shared tenets, manifesting across diverse societal and political contexts over time, contribute to the intricate fabric of Islamic governance—a nuanced and normative construct embracing various facets of government and leadership.

Crucially, the roots of conceptions regarding global and good governance within the Islamic milieu lie in the ideal and fundamental principles delineated in the Qur'ān, the *hadīth,* and the Sunnah (actions of the Prophet). A seminal period in the crystallization of these principles unfolded during the Prophet's tenure in Medina (622–632) and the subsequent era of the Rashidun, or the Rightly Guided Caliphs succeeding him. This foundational phase witnessed the establishment of pivotal governance institutions, encompassing a judicial system, administrative structures, economic frameworks, and diplomatic relations. Moreover, these early developments laid the groundwork for the subsequent evolution of social and cultural institutions within the broader framework of Islamic governance. During this historical juncture, widely regarded by most Muslims as an exemplary era of governance, the pristine principles that delineated political systems were yet to be overshadowed by subsequent influences and practices. Prominent figures from this epoch include Abu Bakr (632–634), Umar (634–644), Uthman (644–656), and Ali (656–661), with heightened emphasis placed on Abu Bakr and Umar. Their historical and personal proximity to the Prophet Muhammad PBUH positions them as figures closely aligned with the foundational principles, marking an epoch considered ideal in the collective consciousness of Muslim adherents.

Within the literature, two Arabic terms closely aligned with the English concept of "governance" have been discerned. The first, *al-hakimiya*, as delineated by Iqbal and Lewis, transcends a mere procedural definition, incorporating a heightened moral and social order.[100] For Muslims, it entails a submission to the authority of God, contrasting starkly with Western secular conceptions characterized by functionalist orientations. *Al-hakimiya* encompasses three primary dimensions: moral values, the conception of humanity as a brotherhood, and the pursuit of socioeconomic justice. These dimensions are intended to be actualized through the principles of fairness, equality, and honesty. Another term, *siyasa*, elucidated by Crone, manifests in three distinct forms: the governance of oneself through ethical considerations, the governance of the household, and the governance of the polity.[101] Additionally, *siyasa* broadly alludes to the diverse governance systems characterizing the caliphates, notably the Abbasid Caliphate (750–1258), a period marked by the evolution of numerous governmental structures. Empirically intricate are the contemporary governance traditions within Muslim states, marked by diverse histories, conditions, cultures, and societal configurations, yielding a rich mosaic of governance practices. Primarily, within the Islamic context, governance revolves around the selection of leaders and the delineation of qualities indicative of virtuous leadership that, in turn, beget commendable governance.

Islam directs its attention beyond state-level distinctions to foster the collective improvement of individuals and humanity. Sachedina characterizes the Islamic tradition as a "public project" founded on the core principle of coexistence, recognizing self-governing communities endowed with the autonomy to administer their internal affairs within a comprehensive religious, social, and political system.[102] These principles, as posited by Sachedina, possess universal applicability, regulating the dynamics of Muslim societies and shaping their interactions with the non-Islamic world, thus fostering a sense of communal interests among nations.[103]

While the participation of Muslim societies in the modern international order remains a subject of debate in Islamic discourse, advocates like Baderin argue that such engagement need not entail a departure from the normative principles of Islam. These principles, rooted in cooperation, amicable international relations, and peaceful coexistence, find endorsement in the political practices of the Prophet Muhammad PBUH, exemplified in the historic "Constitution of Medina." For many, this foundational document serves as a paradigm for pluralism and coexistence, reflecting the enduring essence of Islam through the exemplary actions of Prophet PBUH and the constitutional framework he established.

The Islamic framework of governance draws from principles rooted in its early historical development, prominently exemplified by the concept of *al-siyasah al-shar'iyyah*. This Arabic term encapsulates the complex interplay of arrangement, management, and political acumen employed to actualize the foundational objectives of human well-being and safeguarding, coupled with the pursuit of virtuous objectives or the notion commonly denoted as the "common good."[104] In a comprehensive examination of diverse sources on Islamic governance, Al-Qudsy and Ab Rahman articulate Islamic governance as a system steadfastly adhering to fundamental values and principles encompassing governance facets such as administration, constitutional law, individual rights, and the promotion of public interest and welfare.[105]

Al-Buraey introduces the concept of *yudabbiru*, signifying the orchestration, planning, management, and steering essential for cultivating constructive economic practices and guiding the populace—a notion that remarkably echoes elements found in contemporary democratic theory. This conceptual convergence underscores the nuanced synthesis of traditional Islamic governance principles with modern democratic ideals, accentuating the adaptability and enduring relevance of Islamic governance frameworks. The term *sharī'ah* is fraught with a spectrum of meanings, sparking debates and diverse interpretations. It concurrently embodies a set of religious values delineating "the way" and constitutes the foundational principles underpinning Islamic justice. These principles encompass civil transactions, the preservation of life, the protection of dignity or lineage, the safeguarding of intellect, the preservation of property, and the protection of *al-din* (religion). Inextricably linked with *sharī'ah* is *"fiqh,"* the comprehensive legal framework of the principal legal schools.[106] Hashem expounds on the dual nature of the term, elucidating a primary definition of *sharī'ah* as a value orientation, often conflated with a secondary historical understanding. The former, characterized by a value orientation, remains amenable to continual reinterpretation, ensuring the enduring stability of its unchanging foundational values and principles. This adaptability facilitates the dynamic application of these principles in response to evolving conditions.[107]

The concept of *al-shurā* not only encompasses the foundational principles of effective governance but also embraces a spectrum of values, including transparency, accountability, respect, empowerment, freedom of expression, and the preservation of the dignity of the individual.[108] These principles find complementarity in concepts such as *rida al awam* (popular consent), *ijtihād jama'i* (collective deliberation), and *mas'uliyah jama'iyyah* (collective responsibility). Furthermore, the Sunnah emerges as a prolific source of governance-related principles, elucidated through the practices of Prophet Muhammad PBUH. Notably, even before engaging in a battle, the Prophet convened the nearby Muslim community for consultation, exemplifying a dedication to collective decision-making. Additionally, when confronted with a dissenting majority position, the Prophet demonstrated a commitment to adhering to the consensus of the majority.[109]

Associated with the pursuit of good governance are three additional concepts: *'adl*, signifying justice and equity, and *ihsan*, representing benevolence. These principles extend beyond the Muslim community, encompassing nonbelievers, with the overarching objective of establishing a global order characterized by tolerance, justice, and equity.[110] Interconnected with these principles is the Qur'ānic concept of *amanah*, which denotes the entrusted responsibility bestowed upon humanity to establish justice in society. The term, rooted in its etymological origins, encompasses notions of peace, security, and safety, emphasizing the personal responsibility individuals bear in creating a moral order through interpersonal interactions and sociopolitical institutions. Amanah holds universal relevance, guided by an unwavering commitment to equality and social harmony, extending to relations between Muslims and non-Muslims.[111]

The primary objective of governance within an Islamic framework is to ensure that both state institutions and regulated entities in society align with the prescribed Islamic values, thereby fostering individual betterment and contributing to the establishment of a just, fair, and equitable society in accordance with the ideals of Islam. The scholarly discourse on global governance has witnessed substantial growth since the 1970s, a period marked by heightened globalization and increased international interconnectedness. This evolution has given rise to neoliberal global governance, characterized by the economic imperatives of neoliberalism. This phenomenon encompasses the expansion of the "market" into previously nonmarket sectors, the proliferation of commodification, the assimilation of formerly state-run enterprises, and the subordination of other spheres to economic considerations, thereby shaping the contours of the new global political economy.

Various conceptualizations of global governance exist, ranging from normative perspectives to critical analyses rooted in diverse ideological frameworks. The Commission on Global Governance (1995) defines it normatively as a process wherein different policy actors reconcile interests and engage in cooperative endeavors.[112] A liberal rights-based perspective, as articulated by Grugel and Piper (2007) and Sinclair (2012),[113] focuses on promoting human rights and individual equality.[114] Critical perspectives, exemplified by Barnett and Duvall, emphasize power dynamics,[115] while Marxist analyses, as presented by Overbeek, center on class hegemony at both national and international levels.[116] Weiss and Wilkinson offer a comprehensive definition, describing global governance as "the sum of the informal and formal ideas, values, norms, procedures, and institutions that help all actors—states, IGOs, civil society, and TNCs—identify, understand, and address trans-boundary problems."[117] It is noteworthy, however, that the prevailing discourse on global governance often overlooks references to Islamic sources and conceptions. Specifically, there is a notable absence of exploration into how Islamic principles align with contemporary notions of stewardship, peaceful coexistence, and assistance to developing nations.

Global governance is a multifaceted and complex concept that involves a myriad of actors operating at different levels. At its core are nation-states and supranational intergovernmental organizations, including prominent entities like the UN, EU, Gulf Cooperation Council (GCC), and others. Additionally, transnational and multinational corporations, NGOs, such as Médecins sans Frontières, citizen movements, think tanks, and private military forces contribute to this complex landscape. The legal underpinning of global governance encompasses a wide spectrum, from arms control agreements to intellectual property laws, laws of the sea, and environmental treaties. This legal framework provides the structure for interactions and collaborations among various actors on the global stage.[118]

Networks between state actors, both across borders and with supranational entities like the European Court of Justice, corporate bodies, NGOs, and individuals operating at elite levels, further contribute to the complexity of global governance.[119] The involvement of diverse entities and interaction levels in global governance can be advantageous for developing countries, including those with Muslim-majority populations. Engagement with global governance occurs through formal mechanisms such as treaties, accords, resolutions, and agreements, as well as through diplomatic negotiations, joint operations, information exchange, conferences, standards, laws, and regulations. This dynamic and interconnected system provides opportunities for countries to participate in global affairs, fostering collaboration based on shared values and interests.[120]

Global governance entails a complex array of challenges on the global stage, demanding collaborative endeavors among transnational and non-state actors. These challenges encompass a diverse range of issues, including the imperative for counterterrorism measures, addressing security threats like cybersecurity, effectively managing pandemics, mitigating the impacts of climate change, combating environmental degradation, dealing with water scarcity, navigating technological advancements, and contending with disruptions in global financial markets amid the processes of globalization. Concurrently, the phenomenon of globalization exacerbates existing inequalities and contributes to heightened instances of violence, resulting in substantial refugee migrations. Within the framework of global governance, critical issues also include the protection of human rights, with a specific focus on the rights of women and children, managing the arms trade, and effective pandemic response.[121]

In tandem, the discipline of development studies rigorously analyzes the mounting crises facing the developing world. This trajectory includes the repercussions of the economic and financial upheavals of the 1980s, the ensuing challenges related to debts and slowed growth in the 1990s, and subsequent financial upheavals intricately connected to the adverse effects of globalization. Migration emerges as a pivotal concern, particularly within the context of the Muslim world's significant role. Indonesia, as the largest Muslim state, assumes a prominent position as a primary exporter of labor, while the Arabian Gulf countries, integral within the Muslim world, stand out as one of the largest regions hosting foreign labor.[122]

In the current global context, the management of various activities requires an approach based on extensive global networks, prompting the proactive inclusion of Muslim states. This imperative gains prominence in light of the complex governance challenges that ensue within countries in the Middle East. Notably, certain nations in this region serve as pivotal global hubs for transportation and shipping while concurrently acting as sources of geopolitical conflict. For emerging countries and regions navigating the sphere of global governance, a critical litmus test revolves around their capacity to wield influence over the key structures of international institutions, notably the UN, including the Security Council, the Bretton Woods system, the IMF, and the WTO. The evolution of these institutions toward enhanced democratic, representative, and legitimate forms hinges on the intensified participation of the developing world. This transformative trajectory aligns with precedents set by entities such as the G-77, Non-Aligned Movement, and UN Conference on Trade and Development. However, it introduces the inherent challenge of heightened complexity in achieving consensus.[123]

In the current geopolitical landscape, numerous Muslim states actively participate in a diverse array of international governance-oriented organizations. These encompass a spectrum of entities, including the UN agencies such as UNESCO and WHO, peacekeeping initiatives, the IMF, the WTO, the G20, and regionally or economically focused institutions like OPEC, the League of Arab States, the GCC, and various environmental organizations. Through their engaged roles, these Muslim states have significantly contributed to shaping the complex structure of global governance.

Conclusion

In this chapter, we embarked on an intriguing exploration of the complex relationship between Islam and the ever-expanding realm of global interconnectedness. Our goal was to delve into the fascinating history of Muslim global engagement and its profound impact on the dynamics of Muslim societies. This relationship has ignited a profound discourse and sparked myriad interpretations. Some contend that Islam stands in opposition to globalization. However, it is crucial to discern that Islam does not harbor aversion toward progress or the sweeping tides of globalization. Rather, Islam perceives globalization through a prism that reveals distinct facets, diverging from the contemporary narrative. Unfortunately, since the tragic events of 9/11, the turbulent forces of globalization have stirred up a storm, causing a dangerous backlash orchestrated by a small group exploiting Islam for their political motives. These pernicious ideas have revitalized the "Clash of Civilizations" theory, casting an ominous shadow that fuels Islamophobia in certain parts of our world.[124]

The political, economic, cultural, and technological process of globalization is not particularly recent. Waves of globalization have occurred throughout history, with migration, commerce, and conquest serving as important vectors. The expansion, the extent, the pace, and eventually the structure that will combine the current trend toward global integration with liberalism, deregulation, privatization, and the hegemonistic characteristics of capitalism and American power are what are truly novel in our time. These elements work together to make modern globalization, in large part, a singular phenomenon. In this setting, the boundaries of time and space are being destroyed and the entire globe is indiscriminately becoming a a single global city.[125] The most important features of the modern era include the advancements in communication and transportation technology, notably the methods of fast information sharing. The whole web of international relations, including the flow of products, services, and financial flows, is being significantly impacted by quick global contacts and decision-making enabled by modern information technology. These advances have significant political, cultural, economic, intellectual, and moral repercussions.

America and Europe continue to play a significant role in the creation of this new international order because they represent the prevailing paradigm of power and civilization. Globalization now has a distinctly Euro-American character thanks to American military might, influence and economic might, as well as its mastery over technology and nearly absolute control over the media, verging on virtual thought control. The dominance of Western standards, value systems, socioeconomic institutions, and ultimately, political and economic interest is being created throughout the world in the guise of promoting liberalization, privatization, market economy, and modernization. Along with the governmental actors, there are three other significant participants on the scene: the media, multinational companies, and international NGOs.

They are jointly contributing significantly to what can be called the birth of a hyper-imperialism while giving it a kindly name: "globalization." Globalization itself is not problematic; nevertheless, when the fundamental facts that make up its backdrop are disregarded, severe issues start to appear. To provide some relief to the afflicted end of the world, the Muslim leadership needs to take a wise and sincere approach to dealing with these circumstances. Every religion has battled to be relevant in the world at some time in history. According to historical evidence, religion has really made a considerable contribution to the development of globalization, with Islam playing an especially notable role.[126] Furthermore, it is essential for Muslim leaders to actively participate in open dialogues with the global community, accentuating the positive aspects of Islamic teachings that promote peace, justice, and equality. Engaging in discussions on international platforms enables them to contribute to dispelling misconceptions and fostering a more inclusive and tolerant world. In essence, the considerate and genuine involvement of Muslim leadership in the current global landscape can play a crucial role not only in offering relief to the afflicted but also in shaping a more harmonious and interconnected world.

Notes

1. Abbas Mehdi Globalization, "Who Benefit Anyway?," in *Globalization and After*, ed. Samir Dasgupta and Ray Kiely (New Delhi: Sage Publications, 2006), 130–142.
2. Babayo Sule, Muhammad Aminu Yahay, and Rashid Ating, "Globalisation and the Muslim Ummah:
    Issues, Challenges, and the Ways Out," *IIUM Journal of Religion and Civilisational Studies (IJECS)* 1, no. 1 (2018): 7–29.
3. Mohd Abbas, "Globalization and the Muslim World," *Journal of Islam in Asia* 8, no. 3 (2011): 276–295.
4. Leonard A. Stone, "The Islamic Crescent: Islam, Culture and Globalization," *Innovation: The European Journal of Social Science Research* 15, no. 2 (2002): 121–131.
5. Radhakrishnan Puthenveetil, "Religion Under Globalisation," *Economic and Political Weekly* 39, no. 13 (2004): 1403–1411.
6. Arnold Toynbee, *A Study of History* (Oxford: Oxford University Press, 1995), 95.
7. Syed Hossain Nasr, *Islam: Religion, History and Civilisation* (San Francisco, CA: Harper San Francisco, 2003), 119.
8. Fred M. Donner, "Muhammad and the Caliphate," in *Oxford History of Islam*, ed. John L. Esposito (Oxford: Oxford University Press, 2000), 19.
9. Mehdi Mozaffari, "Islamic Civilization between Medina and Athena," in *Globalization and Civilizations*, ed. Mehdi Mozaffari (London: Routledge, 2002), 199.
10. Fernand Braudel, *A History of Civilizations* (New York: Penguin Books, 1995), 73.
11. Duane Swank, "Taxation, Institutions, and Control of the Macroeconomy," in *The Global Transformations Reader: An Introduction to the Globalization Debate*, ed. David Held and Anthony Mcgrew (Cambridge: Polity Press, 2000), 415.
12. Myra Shackley, *Atlas of Travel and Tourism Development* (Burlington, VT: Elsevier, 2006), 7.
13. Amira K. Bennison, "Muslim Universalism and Western Globalisation," in *Globalisation in World History*, ed. Antony Gerald Hopkins (London: Pimlico, 2002), 75.
14. Bennison, "Muslim Universalism and Western Globalisation," 79.
15. Bennison, "Muslim Universalism and Western Globalisation," 80.
16. Dale Eickelman and James Piscatori, "Introduction," in *Muslim Travellers: Pilgrimage, Migration and Religious Imagination*, ed. Dale Eickelman and James Piscatori (London: Routledge, 2013), 11.
17. Bennison, "Muslim Universalism and Western Globalisation," 76.
18. Ibn Khaldun, *The Muqaddimah: An Introduction to History*, transl. Franz Rosenthal (Princeton, NJ: Princeton University Press, 1969), 45.
19. Ross E. Dunn, "International Migrations of Literate Muslims in the Later Middle Period," in *Golden Roads: Migration, Pilgrimage and Travel in Modern and Medieval Islam*, ed. Ian Richard Netton (London: Routledge, 1993), 77–80.

20. Dunn, "International Migrations of Literate Muslims," 76.
21. Bennison, "Muslim Universalism and Western Globalisation," 81
22. Bennison, "Muslim Universalism and Western Globalisation," 84.
23. Bennison, "Muslim Universalism and Western Globalisation," 86.
24. Aḥmad Ibn Ṭuwayr al-Jannah, *The Pilgrimage of Ahmad, Son of the Little Bird of Paradise: An Account of a 19th Century Pilgrimage from Mauritania to Mecca*, transl. H. Norris (Warminster: Aris & Phillips, 1977), 83–93.
25. Bennison, "Muslim Universalism and Western Globalisation," 89.
26. Bennison, "Muslim Universalism and Western Globalisation," 90.
27. Bennison, "Muslim Universalism and Western Globalisation," 90.
28. Bennison, "Muslim Universalism and Western Globalisation," 91.
29. Nikki Keddie, *An Islamic Response to Imperialism: Political and Religious Writings of Jamal al-Din al-Afghani* (Berkeley, CA: University of California Press, 1983), 34.
30. Kemal H. Karpat, "The Hijra from Russia and the Balkans: The Process of Self-Definition in the Late Ottoman State," in *Muslim Travellers: Pilgrimage, Migration and the Religious Imagination*, ed. Dale F. Eickelman and James Piscatori (London: Routledge, 2013), 131–152.
31. Peter Mandaville, "From Medina to the Ummah: Muslim Globalization in Historical and Contemporary Perspective," in *World Religions and Multiculturalism: A Dialectic Relation*, ed. Eliezer Ben-Rafael and Yitzhak Sternberg (Leiden: Brill, 2010), 195.
32. Bennison, "Muslim Universalism and Western Globalisation," 93.
33. Martin Kramer, *Arab Awakening and Islamic Revival* (London: Transaction Publishers, 1996), 265–278.
34. Mazrui, "Globalisation, Islam and the West," 2.
35. Muhammad 'Ābid al-Jābirī, "Al-Awlamah, Niẓam wa Aydyolojjiyah," *Al-Majlis al Qawmī al Thaqafah al 'Arabīyah, al 'Arab Watahadiyāt al 'Awlamah* (Rabāt: al Majlis al Qawmī li al- Thaqāfah al 'Arabīyah, 1997), 15. See also Muhammas Ibrāhīm Mabrūk, *Amerika wa al Islām al-Nafi ī* [America and Pragmatic Islam] (Cairo: Dār al Tawzī' wa al-Nashr al Islāmīyah, 1989), 191–211. 'Ādil Husayn, *al Iqtiṣād al Misrī: Min al Istiqlālilā al Taba īyah* [The Egyptian Economy: From Autonomy to Dependency] (Cairo: Dār al Mustaqbal al 'Arabi), 23.
36. Sayed Vali Reza Nasr, "European Colonialism and the Emergence of Modern Muslim States," in *The Oxford History of Islam*, ed. John L. Espoito (Oxford: Oxford University Press, 1999), 549–600.
37. Jamil Hilal, "Rethinking Palestine," *Contemporary Arab Affairs* 8, no. 3 (2015): 351–362.
38. Arlo Kempf, "Contemporary Anticolonialism: A Transhistorical Perspective," in *Breaching the Colonial Contract Anti-Colonialism in the US and Canada*, ed. Arlo Kempf (New York: Springer, 2009), 13–35.
39. Nasr, "European Colonialism," 583.
40. Nasr, "European Colonialism," 584.
41. Norshahril Saat and Afra Alatas, "Islamisation in Malaysia Beyond UMNO and PAS," Last Modified October 11, 2022. Accessed April 13, 2024. https://fulcrum.sg/islamisation-in-malaysia-beyond-umno-and-pas/.

42. Nasr, "European Colonialism," 557.

43. Victor Lieberman, "Local Integration and Eurasian Analogies: Structuring Southeast Asian History, c. 1350-c. 1830," *Modern Asian Studies* 27, no. 3 (1993): 475–572.

44. Merve KAVAKÇI, "Türkiye'nin Milli Kimliğinin Yapı Sökümü: Öncesi ve Şimdi (Postkolonyal Bir Eleştiri) Deconstruction of Turkey's National Identity: Then and Now (A Postcolonial Critique)," *Üniversitesi Sosyal Bilimler Dergisi* 1, no. 1 (2016): 49–86.

45. Nasr, "European Colonialism," 559.

46. Sara Silvestri, "Misperceptions of the 'Muslim Diaspora'," *Current History* 115, no. 784 (2016): 319–321.

47. Silvestri, "Misperceptions of the 'Muslim Diaspora'," 320.

48. Silvestri, "Misperceptions of the 'Muslim Diaspora'," 320.

49. Steven Vertovec, *Superdiversity: Migration and Social Complexity* (London: Routledge, 2023), 13.

50. Patrick Loobuyck, Jonathan Debeer, and Petra Meier, "Church–State Regimes and their Impact on the Institutionalization of Islamic Organizations in Western Europe: A Comparative Analysis," *Journal of Muslim Minority Affairs* 33, no. 1 (2013): 61–76.

51. Marta Bolognani and Paul Statham, "The Changing Public Face of Muslim Associations in Britain: Coming
   Together for Common "Social' Goals?," *Ethnicities* 13 (2013): 229–249.

52. Leslie Lebl, "The EU, the Muslim Brotherhood and the Organization of Muslim Cooperation," *Orbis* 57 (2013): 101–119.

53. Edwina Pio, *Longing and Belonging: Asians, Middle Eastern, Latin American and African Peoples in New Zealand* (Wellington: Dunmore, 2010), 23.

54. Tahseen Shams, "Bangladeshi Muslims in Mississippi: Impression Management Based on the Intersectionality of Religion, Ethnicity and Gender," *Cultural Dynamics* 27, no. 3 (2015): 379–397.

55. Gary Bouma, Ali Haidar, Chris Nyland, and Wendy Smith, "Work, Religious Diversity and Islam," *Asia Pacific Journal of Human Resources* 41 (2003): 51–61.

56. Gillian Forster and John Fenwick, "The Influence of Islamic Values on Management Practice in Morocco," *European Management Journal* 33 (2014): 143–156.

57. Aikaterini Galanou and Dalia Farrag, "Towards the Distinctive Islamic Mode of Leadership in Business," *Journal of Management Development* 34 (2015): 882–900.

58. Sebastian Elischer, "Autocratic Legacies and State Management of Islamic Activism in Niger," *African Affairs* 114 (2015): 577–597.

59. Sibel Yamak, Ali Ergur, Artun Ünsal, Selcuk Uygur, and Mustafa F. Ozbilgin, "Between a Rock and a Hard Place: Corporate Elites in the Context of Religion and Secularism in Turkey," *The International Journal of Human Resource Management* 26 (2015): 1474–1497.

60. Jawad Syed and Edwina Pio, "Veiled Diversity? Workplace Experiences of Muslim Women in Australia," *Asia Pacific Journal of Management* 27 (2010): 115–137.

61. Alessandro Acquisti and Christina M. Fong, "An Experiment in Hiring Discrimination Via Online Social Networks," *Management Science* 66, no. 3 (2020): 1005–1024.

62. Yves L. Doz, "The Rise of Multicultural Managers." Accessed April 13, 2024. https://www.forbes.com/sites/insead/2013/08/01/the-rise-of-multicultural-managers/?sh=51f012fd3445.

63. Yaghoob Foroutan, "Ethnic and Religious Discrimination? A Multicultural Analysis of Muslim Minorities in the West," *Journal of Muslim Minority Affairs* 31 (2011): 327–338.

64. Ruud Koopmans, Paul Statham, Marco Giugni, and Florence Passy, *Contested Citizenship: Immigration and Cultural Diversity in Europe* (Minneapolis, MN: University of Minnesota Press, 2005), 24.

65. Bolognani and Statham, "The Changing Public Face of Muslim Associations in Britain."

66. John R. Hinnells, "The Study of Diaspora Religion," in *A New Handbook of Living Religions*, ed. John R. Hinnells (Oxford: Blackwell, 2008), 682–690b.

67. Gerrie ter Haar, "Strangers and Sojourners: An introduction," in Gerrie ter Haar (ed.) *Strangers and Sojourners: Religious Communities in the Diaspora* (Leuven: Peeters, 1998), 1–11.

68. Steven Vertovec and Robin Cohen, "Introduction," in *Migration, Diasporas and Transnationalism*, ed. Steven Vertovec and Robin Cohen (Cheltenham: Edward Elgar, 1999), pp. xiii–xxviii.

69. Riva Kastoryano Riva, "Muslim Diaspora(s) in Western Europe," *South Atlantic Quarterly* 98, no. 1–2 (1999): 191–202.

70. Riva, "Muslim Diaspora(s) in Western Europe," 198.

71. Maria Bruquetas-Callejo, Bianca Garcés-Mascarenas, Rinus Penninx, and Peter W. A. Scholten, "Policymaking Related to Immigration and Integration: The Dutch case," IMISCOE Working Paper: Country Report, No. 15, Amsterdam, 2007.

72. Dutch News, "Bolkestein: West Threat to Islam." Accessed April 13, 2024. https https://www.dutchnews.nl/2011/09/bolkestein_west_threat_to_isla/.

73. Erik Snel, *De Yermeende Kloof Tussen Culturen* [The Perceived Gap Between Cultures] (Enschede: Universiteit Twente, 2003), 57.

74. Ron Eyerman, *The Assassination of Theo van Gogh: From Social Drama to Cultural Trauma* (Durham, NC: Duke University Press, 2008), 12.

75. Johan Leman, Erkan Toğuşlu, and İsmail Mesut Sezgin, "The Manifestation of Identities in a Plural Post-Secular Europe," in *New Multicultural Identities in Europe: Religion and Ethnicity in Secular Societies*, ed. Erkan Toğuşlu, Johan Leman, and İsmail Mesut Sezgin (Leuven: Leuven University Press, 2014), 9–34.

76. Robert Jackson and Eleanor M. Nesbitt, *Hindu Children in Britain*. Stroke-on-Trent (Stoke on Trent: Trentham Books, 1993), 45.

77. Metcalf Barbara, "Introduction: Sacred Words, Sanctioned Practice, New Communities," in *Making Muslim Space in North America and Europe* Metcalf (Berkeley, CA: University of California Press, 1996), 1–27.

78. Dale F. Eickelman and James Piscatori, "Preface," in *Muslim Travellers: Pilgrimage, Migration and the Religious Imagination* (London: Routledge, 1990), xii–xxii.

79. Ernest S. Frerichs, "Preface," in *Diasporas in Antiquity*, ed. Shaye J. D. Cohen and Ernest S. Frerichs (Atlanta, GA: Scholars Press, 1993), i–iii.

80. Martin Sokefeld, "Religion or Culture? Concepts of Identity in the Alevi Diaspora," in *Diaspora, Identity and Religion: New Directions in Theory and Research*, ed. Waltraud Kokot, Khachig Tölölyan, and Carolin Alfonso (London: Routledge, 2004), 133–155.

81. Stephen R. Warner, "Religion, Boundaries, and Bridges," *Sociology of Religion* 58, no. 3 (1997): 217–238.

82. Eickelman and Piscatori, *Muslim Travellers*, xiii.

83. Stefano Allievi and Jorgen Nielsen, *Muslim Networks and Transnational Communities in and across Europe* (Leiden: Brill, 2003), 23.

84. Jacques Waardenburg, "The Institutionalisation of Islam in the Netherlands," in *The New Islamic Presence in Europe*, ed. Tomas Gerholm and Yngve Georg Lithman (London: Mansell, 1988), 8–31.

85. Michael P. Smith and Luis Eduardo Guarnizo, *Transnationalism from Below* (New Brunswick, NJ: Transaction Publishers, 1998), 9.

86. James Beckford, "Religious Movements and Globalisation," in *Global Social Movements*, ed. Robin Cohen and Shireen S. Rai (London: Athlone, 2000), 161–183.

87. Levitt Peggy, "Local-level Global Religion: The Case of US-Dominican Migration," *Journal for the Scientific Study of Religion* 37, no. 1 (1998): 74–89.

88. Driss Habti, "The Religious Aspects of Diasporic Experience of Muslims in Europe within the Crisis of Multiculturalism," *Policy Futures in Education* 12, no. 1 (2014): 149–162.

89. Dale F. Eickelman, "Trans-State Islam and Security," in *Transnational Religion and Fading States*, ed. Susanee Hoeber Rudolph and James Piscatori (Boulder, CO: Westview Press, 1997), 27–46.

90. Driss Habti, "The Religious Aspects of Diasporic Experience of Muslims in Europe within the Crisis of Multiculturalism," *Policy Futures in Education* 12, no. 1 (2014): 149–162.

91. Jonathan Michie, "Introduction," in *The Handbook of Globalisation*, ed. Jonathan Michie (Cheltenham: Edward Elgar, 2011), 1–13.

92. Leen Spruit, "Intellectual Beatitude in the Averroist Tradition: The Case of Agostino," in *Renaissance Averroism and Its Aftermath*, ed. Anna Akasoy and Guido Giglioni (Dordrecht: Springer, 2012), 125–144.

93. Marcel Maussen and Veit Bader, "Introduction," In *Colonial and Post-Colonial Governance of Islam*, ed. Marcel Maussen, Veit Bader, and Annelies Moors (Amsterdam: Amsterdam University Press, 2011), 9–26.

94. Samuel P. Huntington, *Clash of Civilisations* (London: Simon & Schuster, 1997), 23.

95. Margot Badran, "Understanding Islam, Islamism and Islamic Feminism," *Journal of Women's History* 13, no. 1 (2001): 47–52.

96. Mojtaba Mahdavi and W. Andy Knight, "Introduction," in *Towards the Dignity of Difference?* ed. Mojtaba Mahdavi and W. Andy Knight (Farnham: Ashgate, 2012), 24.

97. Jean Grugel and Nicola Piper, *Critical Perspectives on Global Governance* (London: Routledge, 2007), 98.

98. Amr G. Sabet, *Islam and the Political: Theory, Governance and International Relations* (London: Pluto Press, 2008), 24.

99. Barkawi Tarak and Laffey Mark, "The Postcolonial Moment in Security Studies," *Review of International Studies* 32, no. 2 (2006): 329–352.

100. Zafar Iqbal and Mervyn K. Lewis, *An Islamic Perspective on Governance* (Cheltenham: Edward Elgar), 1–5.

101. Patricia Crone, *God's Rule: Government and Islam* (Edinburgh: Edinburgh University Press, 2004), 34.

102. Abdel Aziz Sachedina, *The Role of Islam in the Public Square* (Leiden: Amsterdam University Press, 2006), 87.

103. Mashoud Baderin, "The Evolution of Islamic Law of Nations and the Modern International Order," *American Journal of Islamic Social Sciences* 17, no. 2 (2000): 57–80.

104. Sachedina, *The Role of Islam in the Public Square*, 34.

105. Sharifah Hayaati Syed Ismail al-Qudsy and Asmak Ab Rahman, "Effective Governance in the Era of Caliphate Umar Ibn Al-Khattab (634–644)," *European Journal of Social Sciences* 18, no. 4 (2011): 612–624.

106. Mohammad Hashim Kamali, *Shari'ah Law: An Introduction* (Oxford: Oneworld, 2008), 12.

107. M. A. Muqtedar Khan, *Islam and Good Governance: A Political Philosophy of Ihsan* (New York: Palgrave Macmillan, 2019), 27.

108. al-Qudsy and Rahman, "Effective Governance in the Era."

109. Ibnomer Mohamed Sharfuddin, "Toward an Islamic Administrative Theory," *American Journal of Islamic Social Sciences* 4, no. 2 (1987): 229–244.

110. Iqbal and Lewis, *An Islamic Perspective*, 56.

111. Stephen B. Young, "Qur'ānic Guidance on Good Governance," in *Guidance for Good Governance*, ed. Abdullah al-Ahsan and Stephen B. Young (New York: Palgrave Macmillan, 2017), 83–116.

112. "The Commission on Global Governance," *Medicine and War* 9, no. 4 (1993): 344–349.

113. Timothy Sinclair, *Global Governance* (London: Polity Press, 2012), 13.

114. Grugel and Piper, *Critical Perspectives*, 45.

115. Michael Barnett and Raymond Duvall, "Power in International Politics," *International Organisation* 59, no. 1 (2005): 39–75.

116. Henk Overbeek, "Global Governance, Class, Hegemony," in *Contending Perspectives on Global Governance*, ed. Alice D. Ba and Matthew J. Hoffmann (London: Routledge, 2004), 39–56.

117. Thomas G. Weiss and Rorden Wilkinson, "Continuity and Change in Global Governance," in *Rising Powers, Global Governance and Global Ethics*, ed. Jamie Gaskarth (London: Routledge, 2015), 41–45.

118. Sinclair, *Global Governance*, 34.

119. Eugenie A. Samier, "Philosophical and Historical Origins and Genesis of Islamic Global Governance," in *Global Governance and Muslim Organizations*, ed. Leslie A. Pal and M. Evren Tok (New York: Palgrave Macmillan, 2019), 83–104.

120. Samier, "Philosophical and Historical Origins," 85.

121. Samier, "Philosophical and Historical Origins," 87.

122. Grugel and Piper, *Critical Perspectives*, 11.

123. Alan S. Alexandroff and Andrew F. Cooper, "Introduction," in *Rising States, Rising Institutions: Challenges for Global Governance*, ed. Alan S. Alexandroff and Andrew Cooper (Waterloo: Centre for International Governance Education, 2010), 1–16.

124. Samuel P. Huntington, *The Clash of Civilisations and the Remaking of World Order* (New York: Simon & Schuster, 2011), 23.

125. Khurshid Ahmad, "Globalization: Challenges and Prospects for Muslims," *Policy Perspectives* 3, no. 1 (2006): 1–11.

126. Muhammad Adil Iqbal, "Islam, Globalism and Globalisation." Accessed April 13, 2024. https://islamicgovernance.org/tp12/n.

CHAPTER 4

Islamic Revivalism in the Era of Globalization

Unraveling the Dynamics of Religion, Culture, and Resistance

Introduction

As elucidated in chapter 1, contemporary conceptualizations of globalization in the social sciences place considerable emphasis on the economic, political, and technological domains. In addition to these aspects, a range of cultural interpretations has emerged, rectifying an exclusive focus on economics and fortifying the assertion that globalization is inherently a cultural phenomenon. Culturalist perspectives elucidate the crucial role of social (revivalist) movements, including "fundamentalisms," in the dynamics of globalization. One of these theories posits that concerns regarding cultural dilution or foreign cultural dominance trigger reactions and resistance at local and national levels, propelled by the potentially unifying yet homogenizing expansion of global capitalism. The paradoxical outcome of globalization, as articulated by Philip Sutton and Stephen Vertigans, manifests as an intensification of local diversity.[1]

For businesses to achieve success, a crucial imperative is the integration of their goods and services into preexisting cultural frameworks of meaning. Robertson introduced the term "glocalization" to encapsulate this nuanced shift in our perception of the anticipated effects of globalizing processes. As noted in chapter 1, glocalization, by definition, entails the simultaneous adaptation of cultural goods into diverse localities through the incorporation of local customs and practices. The questionable commercialization of indigenous cultures can still be interpreted as part of this adaptive process, fostering the utilization of traditional, religious, or community ideas as forms of resistance. Despite the growing literature on modern globalization, the role of Islamic movements with a religious focus remains under-theorized.

Frequently characterized as simple reactionary movements, Islamic movements deserve a more nuanced examination.[2] Wallerstein's world-systems theory, which perceives religious and ethnic movements primarily as defensive reactions to the expanding worldwide spread of the capitalist world-system, is a limiting stance. This perspective fails to enhance our understanding of Islam's diversity, vitality, and the dedication demonstrated by practitioners.

Similarly, culturalist theories of globalization frequently underscore religious "counter-movements" as instances of opposition to capitalist growth, thereby emphasizing the limitations of political-economy approaches to globalization. For example, comprehending the Islamic renaissance necessitates a deeper understanding of Islamic cultures. This understanding is crucial to decipher why resistance is robust in specific regions but not in others, or why some groups embrace Western, modernist behavioral norms while others resist them. Although Islamic revivalism aims to avoid Eurocentrism, it presents analytical challenges for cultural theories of globalization. The challenge persists as the argument relies on a broad concept of fundamentalism, lacking sufficient empirical research findings on "fundamentalisms." This chapter aims to distinguish Islamic revivalism from fundamentalism, thereby offering a more nuanced understanding. In light of this, the analysis in this chapter centers on whether Islamic revivalism constitutes a response to globalization or a mere endeavor to reinvigorate religion. By delving into the perspectives of Muslim scholars, we can elucidate some of the reciprocal mistrust and hostility between Western and Islamic interpretations of globalization and provide a more analytical assessment of the current global state.

Islamic Revivalism: A Global Perspective

The term "Islamic revival" (*ihyā*) denotes the advocacy for a more pronounced influence of Islamic ideals in the contemporary world. It posits that the optimal approach to address issues within Islamic cultures and broader contemporary society is a return to Islam. Despite the diverse expressions encompassed by Islamic resurgence, it is not a monolithic movement and should not be solely equated with the militant fundamentalism often prevalent in media narratives.[3] Analogous challenges that propel revival in other religious and community contexts are also instrumental in driving the resurgence observed in the Islamic world. There exists a pervasive latent discontent with what consumerist, materialist society offers, coupled with dissatisfaction with national governments' shortcomings in delivering more than a medley of technological "fixes." These fixes often amount to inadequate resolutions within political, social, and economic institutions. To devise effective and original solutions to this discontent, it becomes imperative to set aside certain thinking and perception patterns. Empathy with the historical and cultural struggles of Muslims and other communities is essential, fostering an imaginative exploration of more equitable and beneficial forms of intercultural collaboration.

Islamic Fundamentalism and Revivalism

Fundamentalism primarily entails the elevation of restrictive and finite elements to absolute status, achieved by equating substance with specific delimited forms. Religious fundamentalism, on the one hand, strives for existential security by reinforcing boundaries between its own group and outsiders, often adopting a hostile or defensive stance against the latter. On the other hand, political fundamentalism extols certain institutions while disparaging others, arguing that only specific forms of human organization genuinely embody fundamental principles such as democracy, freedom, and truth. Both modalities constrict alternative strategies by reducing idealized objectives to idealized methods, maintaining the conviction that there is only one path to the truth.[4]

Islamic fundamentalism must be differentiated from Islamic revivalism—a movement aimed at revitalizing the community from within—and recognized as a forceful, exclusivist response to a perceived foreign threat. Islamic revivalism involves an endeavor to address human needs for religious meaning, community, identity, and participation in political and developmental spheres. In times of cultural, economic, and political marginalization, individuals often turn to deeply ingrained religious discourses, seeking authentic values and alternative solutions to their challenges.[5] Amid a backdrop where many perceive Western ideals as failed and traditions as historically insignificant, Muslims find themselves grappling with the dichotomy of either emulating or rejecting the West. As asserted by Asghar Ali Engineer, Islamic fundamentalism is not merely a theological concept but primarily a political one, signifying political enmity rather than religious rigidity, militancy, conservatism, or orthodoxy.[6] The characterization of Saudi Islam, which is conservative and rigorous yet aligned with the United States, illustrates that fundamentalism is essentially a political designation. In his book "Islam: Challenges in the Twenty-first Century," Asghar Ali Engineer argues that fundamentalism involves theological rigidity and the utilization of Islam for political objectives rather than the promotion of spirituality and morals. It is crucial to recognize that fundamentalism should not be narrowly applied to describe a dogmatic approach solely focused on moral and religious issues. Therefore, the term "Islamic fundamentalism" should be used judiciously and contextually.

Does globalization contribute to the rise of religious fundamentalism? Engineer argues that while there is some evidence in the present, such a correlation did not exist in the past. Thus, globalization itself may not inherently lead to the spread of fundamentalism; rather, specific variables must be present for this outcome. It becomes imperative to discuss these factors to comprehend the relationship between globalization and fundamentalism. As highlighted by Engineer, it is crucial to acknowledge that contemporary globalization exhibits qualitative distinctions from historical globalizations.[7] This shift in quality is attributed to the widespread adoption of communication and education technologies. In developing nations, enhanced knowledge acquisition, facilitated by broad education, is now prevalent, and information technology simplifies the dissemination of this understanding.

No phenomenon remains confined to a specific place or nation; a significant event holds international influence. This was not feasible in the past. Democracy, a crucial component, empowers individuals, albeit in an unequal manner. In societies, especially in emerging nations marked by poverty and backwardness, different collectivities are disparately empowered.[8] One group, caste, or tribe often secures a disproportionate share of political authority or economic growth, maintaining their advantages, while others utilize their religious, caste, or tribal identity for similar ends. Depending on the prevailing political and social climate, mobilization based on religious, caste, or tribal identities can lead to extremism.

Engineer contends that in India, caste and community identities have contributed to the rise of religious fanaticism and extremism. Globalization, causing community members to relocate overseas and fostering relative economic prosperity among financial leaders of these groups, has further fueled this fundamentalism. This partially explains the emergence of Hindu hardline groups in India and Islamic fundamentalism in Pakistan. It is noteworthy that the educated middle class is a breeding ground for fundamentalism. This class not only inspires but also exhibits religious fanaticism to organize the less fortunate members of their community.[9] A similar role is played by Islamist extremism in Pakistan, where the political objectives of extremists are apparent. The most sectarian, radical form of Islam is embraced by Muslims engaged in power struggles and those who perceive Islam as a significant avenue to approach centers of power. The rise of fundamentalist Islam in Pakistan is, in part, attributed to America's involvement.

He contends that the phenomenon of fundamentalism present in the Islamic world is a product of globalization. However, it is inaccurate to assert, as the American media often does, that Islam is solely to blame. Firstly, fundamentalism is not exclusive to the Islamic world; Christian fundamentalism remains a significant concern in America today. Right-wing Christians, commonly referred to as born-again Christians, played a pivotal role in George Bush Jr.'s election to the presidency. These conservative Christians advise President Bush and exert influence over his national security decisions, posing a serious threat to Iran and Syria and playing crucial roles in conflicts involving Afghanistan and Iraq. These groups have their influential think tanks and television networks, shaping policies and offering pertinent guidance to the President.

Furthermore, the prevalent consumerism in the United States has subjugated Asian and African cultures, commodifying them to such an extent that little room is left for their genuine expressions. Consequently, marginalized cultural communities find themselves in a state of significant turmoil, witnessing the gradual erosion of their distinct ethnic and cultural identities. The proliferation of neoorthodox ideologies is gaining prominence as a response to this phenomenon. The rise of Islam in numerous Asian nations can be largely attributed to the neo-imperialistic hegemony on one hand and the complete commercialization of culture on the other. Ongoing American hostilities in the Middle East have contributed to the surge in Islamist extremism and militancy.[10] Islamic revivalism is not solely a religious movement, nor is it as extensive as some portray. The objective of Islamic revivalists is not to construct a new empire but rather to rejuvenate an ancient civilization. It is crucial to contextualize Islamic revivalism comparatively, viewing it as a regional iteration of a global religious revivalism that advocates a normative stance against liberal democratic reforms.[11] The various regional and local expressions of revivalism undoubtedly exhibit distinct trends and perspectives, each warranting further scholarly examination.[12]

Revivalism in the Early Period

Islamic revivalism is a purposeful effort to challenge the existing status quo, perceived to have deviated from the fundamental principles of authentic Islamic heritage. Its aim is to reinstate a social framework that mirrors the ideals of the time when the Prophet lived. This perspective arises in response to the widely acknowledged societal decline and the looming threats posed by external influences. In the contemporary era, Islamic revivalist movements have gained traction in Muslim countries as a reaction to the dismantling of Islamic institutions caused by the impact of colonialism and Western modernization. It can be seen as a strategic approach to navigate the complexities of societal transformation. Aligned with the classical concept of Islam, Islamic revivalism functions as a transitional movement, guiding society away from a deteriorating social system and toward the establishment of a new, rejuvenated order. Following the Islamic calendar, the early period corresponds to the Islamic civilizations that immediately followed the four rightly guided Caliphs.

The realization of a departure from the tenets of the societal belief system within the framework of Medinan civilization sparked social disputes among different social groupings on multiple occasions, leading to social transformation within Muslim communities. This deviation manifested in blatant social injustice, egregious immorality, political dictatorship, corruption, a crisis of the mind, sectarianism, and, notably, the invention and introduction of peculiar socioreligious and cultural activities into the Islamic belief system. The belief system played a role in the divergence of cultures from one another through a process of rise and collapse.

During various periods of the Umayyad era, the social movements led by 'Umar Ibn 'Abdul al-'Aziz (d.720), Imam Abu Hanifah (699–767), Imam Malik (718–798), and the Shiite/Abbasid movement (750) elucidate the processes of defiance and resurrection. The groups guided by Ibn Hanbal (780–855) and al-Shafi'ī (767–854) exemplify those that restructured the social order during the Abbasid era in response to the apparent socioeconomic degradation of that period. This societal evolution continues through the times of the social movements of Ibn Taymiyyah, Ibn al-Qayyim, and Ibn Kathir. In certain instances, Ibn Taymiyyah expressed that his objective was to instigate societal transformation in three crucial areas amid the prevalent heresy in the society's belief system. First and foremost, a set of guiding principles must be established that recognize how to authentically adhere to the Qur'ān and the Sunnah concerning God's names, attributes, and oneness in both expression and belief; to establish that the Sunnah and the Qur'ān are the exclusive sources of guidance and that deviating from them leads to heretical divisions and misguidance; and, lastly, to caution that all developments, whether positive or negative, stem from excess and have their roots in ambiguous language. Consequently, societal transformation and change oscillate within the belief-driven dialectic dynamic of decline and resurgence.[13] A new system, aligned with Islamic principles, emerges when an old one is overthrown. As the newly formed system begins to deteriorate, a social movement arises to regenerate the social fabric, opposing the system and advocating for its overthrow.

Eighteenth- and Nineteenth-Century Revivalism

This period serves as a bridge between the aforementioned early historical era and the modern era in the history of Muslim societies, predating the time when Muslim cultures began evolving into contemporary nation-states. The social framework established during this era not only defines the society but also forms the foundation of its structure. The belief system, which drove violent attempts seeking restoration after a deviation from it, also plays a crucial role in shaping social issues. Imperialism and capitalism gained prominence due to the West's dominance in the global economy, significantly influencing the contamination of Islamic rituals in Muslim cultures. Consequently, this has added to the list of issues and ignited social awareness among the people in the Muslim world. Muhammad ibn 'Abd al-Wahab (1703–1792), residing in Saudi Arabia, expressed concern about the state of religion amid the increasing popularity of spiritual and social activities incompatible with Islam. In the Indian subcontinent, influential figures driving the Islamic resurgence include Shah Wali Allah (1703–1762), Shah 'Abd al-'Aziz (d. 1824), Sayyid Ahmad Shahid (1786–1831), and Isma'īl Shahid (1779–1831).[14] Shah Wali Allah directed his focus toward the profound societal division stemming from escalating disagreements on Islamic law, Sufism, and *hadīth* studies, among other subjects.[15] Due to this ideological perspective, Sayyid Ahmad Shahid and Isma'īl Shahid mobilized against Hindu and Sikh elements prevalent among Muslim Indians in society. In certain regions, Sayyid Ahmad later succeeded in establishing a social order aligned with the widely recognized traditional religious system. In addition to al-Sanusi's revivalist movement in Libya, which aimed to counter religious fanaticism and provide rationale for defending society's fundamental values, countries like Algeria experienced various social movements striving to protect Islam, particularly in the aftermath of colonial powers' intrusion. Notable among them are those led by Mustafa Ibn 'Azzuz between 1844 and 1866, as well as al-Murqani and Shaykh al-Haddad in 1871.[16] In Sudan, a societal conflict emerged regarding the integration of indigenous customs into Islamic rituals and resistance against external influences and the aggressive actions of Western colonial powers, which posed a threat to the existence of Islam in the community.[17]

Tajdīd: Islamic Renaissance in the Eighteenth and Nineteenth Centuries

During the eighteenth and nineteenth centuries, movements akin to those emblematic of the middle and end of the twentieth century, or even earlier, emerged. This period witnessed a global upsurge of Islamic reform and revival movements known as *tajdīd* or renewal. Rooted in the backdrop of global political and economic developments, these movements shared fundamental theological and ideological beliefs with modern Islamic revivalist groups.[18] They served as a reaffirmation of the Sunni–Sharī'ah–Sufi synthesis, which harmonizes mysticism with Islamic legal doctrine, forming the core of Sunni Islam. This synthesis encompasses the four schools of Islamic law, the mystical teachings in the lineage of al-Ghazali that emphasize correct ritual and legal practice combined with an ethical and pious inner life, and the theological schools that strike a balance between reason and faith. Institutionally, this religious stance found representation in various "conservative" Sufi brotherhoods and law schools. The reformers, while giving great prominence to the Qur'ān and the earliest *hadīth* sources as accurate representations of the Prophet's teachings, often favored autonomous legal judgment, or *ijtihād*, over the uncritical acceptance of the four prestigious schools of law.

The substantial expansion of "alternative" expressions of Islamic society, worship, and religious practices from the thirteenth to the eighteenth centuries served as the catalyst for the *tajdīd* movements. The Safavids declared Shi'ism as Iran's official religion during this protracted era, and its influence expanded throughout the Indian Ocean basin. Concurrently, the acceptability of Sufism among Muslims experienced a steady rise. As Sufism evolved, synthesizing beliefs, practices, and identities with non-Muslim or recently converted but unassimilated communities, the conversion of new populations to Islam fostered increased trust in saints as miracle workers and led to the veneration of shrines. Sufi theosophy and Gnosticism functioned as a bridge among intellectuals, connecting general religious beliefs with specific Muslim commitments.[19]

The internal struggle within Muslim cultures to establish proper beliefs and practices was intricately connected to the era's processes of modernization and global political and economic changes. Globally, Islamic regimes faced decline or collapse during the eighteenth century. The Safavid monarchy, which had held control over Iran since 1500, was overthrown by forces from Afghanistan and other tribal groups. The Ottoman Empire experienced fragmentation as local authorities, warlords, tribal chiefs, landlords, and other notable figures established local governments. In the eighteenth century, Sikh, Maratha, and the expanding British authority in Bengal posed threats to Mughal sovereignty. British paramountcy eventually replaced it, leading to its complete abolition after the Mutiny of 1857.

What made *tajdid* resonate across various social and political contexts? Firstly, the *tajdidi* ideology proved adaptable for network building, facilitating the fusion of diverse groups and political mobilization.[20] While many Islamic societies were traditionally structured around familial, tribal regional and ethnic communities, *tajdīd* presented a more universalistic and international form of Islam grounded in the Qur'ān and Sunnah, rather than regional, particularistic expressions of saint devotion and specific religious laws. *Tajdīd* provided a foundation for shared dedication in fragmented communities, promoting unity over divisions in favor of religious and intellectual cohesion. Reform movements played several roles in the commercialization of societies. One such role was the establishment of new communities comprising dispersed individuals based on Islamic brotherhood principles. These communities aimed to adopt a more conventional, universal, and less sectarian form of Islam to foster trust in business, ensure political unity, and uphold the universal ethos essential in mobile commercial communities. Additionally, reform served as a source of inspiration and justification for conflicts involving Muslim and non-Muslim adversaries in politics and the economy. Islam played a crucial role in guiding and morally grounding individuals engaged in economic and political development, providing them with direction, a distinct intellectual identity, and political inspiration.[21]

Modern Revivalism

Islamophobic traditions rooted in European colonialism, imperialism, and capitalism have deeply permeated Muslim nations. The onset of colonialism in Egypt marked the Arab world's first encounter with this phenomenon in 1798, as the French invasion unfolded, only to be quelled by Ottoman forces in 1801.[22] Subsequently, British invasion and control persisted from 1882 to 1952. Post-World War I, the Arab East, encompassing societies in Syria, Palestine, Jordan, Lebanon, Iraq, and the Hijaz, faced disintegration due to the delineation of British and French boundaries. Algeria fell under French control in 1830, enduring until 1962. Integration into the global economic system has given rise to distinct social classes within Muslim societies. Notably, a Westernized elite emerged, deeply engrossed in modernity and Western sciences due to exposure to Western education. Influential figures such as Jamal al-Din Al-Afghani (1838–1897), Sayyid Ahmad Khan (1817–1898),

Muhammad Abduh (1849–1905), Rashid Rida (1869–1935), and Muhammad Iqbal (1877–1938), among others, belonged to this social group.

The imperative to reassess Islamic intellectual and traditional currents arose due to the alleged backwardness of Muslim communities, notwithstanding the considerable damage inflicted by external forces on the unique structures of these cultures.[23] Consequently, advocates for change championed several reforms, notably the embrace of a rational interpretation of Islamic texts in lieu of uncritical adherence to traditional Islamic schools. In response to these developments, Isma'īl Raji al-Faruqi (1921–1986) asserted that the philosophical foundations of the Western educational system, coupled with its associated contents and institutional framework in Muslim societies, were detrimental to all facets of Muslim life and, therefore, the primary cause of the *ummah*'s challenges.[24] Akbar Ahmad contends that Faruqi embarked on the arduous and monumental task of reevaluating the core ideas of contemporary social sciences within an Islamic context, a process he termed the "Islamization of Knowledge." His dedication materialized in the establishment of the Islamic Institute of Advanced Studies and the International Institute of Islamic Thought, both in the United States. To further advance this cause, he orchestrated numerous global conferences.[25]

The unanimous consensus prevailed that the foundation of the society needed reinvigoration, particularly in light of the evident erosion of its fundamental values. Pioneering this awareness, Hassan al-Banna (1906–1949) laid the groundwork for the social movement, the Muslim Brotherhood, in Egypt. Previously recognized for a tradition of unwavering commitment to the religious and political authority of Islam, the Muslim Brotherhood, under Al-Banna's vision, gained influence over the entire Muslim world by conceiving the *ummah* as a unified entity with the socioreligious environment shaping the belief system at large. The mantle of revitalizing Islam was subsequently taken up by Sayyid Qutb, who contended that the imperialist onslaught against Muslim nations sought to undermine Islam and its teachings. According to Qutb, following the end of the illustrious Islamic era, the world once again plunged into widespread ignorance due to the dominance of Western civilization. Consequently, he vehemently opposed contemporary Western-influenced notions and theories, including democracy, nationalism, capitalism, socialism, and communism.[26] His staunch opposition extended to Gamal 'Abd Nasser's socialist government. Despite facing aggressive crackdowns on his social activism, leading to his detention and eventual execution, the movement for the restoration of traditional Islam proliferated extensively throughout Egypt.

Ibrahim Abu Rabi' argues that the West's historical engagement with the Muslim world, dating back to at least the early nineteenth century, has engendered a state of perplexity in modern Islamic thought. He posits that since the advent of colonialism, Muslim scholars have grappled with defining the essence of the West. This has posed a substantial intellectual challenge for contemporary Muslims and Arabs. In response to this challenge, modern Islamic thought has felt compelled to scrutinize historical perspectives and endeavor to assimilate the scientific paradigm inherent in the contemporary Western worldview. Despite the nebulous nature of the term "West" in modern Islamic thought, it has persistently presented itself as a formidable scientific and sociocultural entity, continuously influencing the Muslim world.[27]

The myriad possibilities intrinsic to the Western mindset and scientific advancements captivated the philosophers of the Nahdah movement in the Arab world and the liberal thinkers of Muslim India during the nineteenth century. Recognizing stagnation within their communities and deeming it detrimental to the common welfare (*al-maslahah al-'āmah*), a fundamental tenet of Islam, they sought to revitalize the concept of "the common interest" by intertwining it with the imperative of embracing Western science. In their perspective, Western science and the Muslim doctrine of common interest were not inherently incompatible; rather, the adoption of the logic of modernity (i.e., science) was deemed essential for the proper realization of the Muslim doctrine.[28]

Another influential figure in Islamic revivalism during this period is Sayyid Abul A'la Mawdūdī (1903–1979). The socioreligious upheaval observed in his local context and beyond captured his attention. According to him, the challenges facing the *ummah* are multifaceted, permeating every facet of Muslim life. The erosion of Islamic ideals, he argued, manifests intellectually, morally, technically, socially, economically, and politically. This, he contended, is primarily due to the prevalence of materialist and godless leadership plaguing Muslim nations. His concern for Muslim society is encapsulated in his assertion: "When tyranny or oppression exist, when injustice is committed, when human culture and politics are poisoned, anytime there is a misuse of resources, there is terrible leadership."[29] Despite the presence of numerous virtuous individuals in society, the predicament lies in the dominance of those who espouse materialism and godlessness holding positions of power.[30] In light of the aforementioned concerns, he initiated a social movement to facilitate transformative change in Muslim societies, particularly in Pakistan, his local milieu.[31] The Jama'at-I-Islami movement, established in 1941, was conceived with the primary objectives of reforming the power structure across all societal levels and realigning human life in accordance with Islamic principles. Despite acknowledging that far-reaching changes should not be rushed, as the swifter the change, the more ephemeral its impact tends to be, he maintained that *jihād* (the social struggle) is a process aiming to restore human existence to divine principles.[32]

One of the most significant and successful transformations in recent history, extending beyond the Muslim world, is exemplified by the Iranian case. Before the 1979 revolution, Reza Shah's liberal government faced widespread discontent due to its close ties with Western nations. Apart from nurturing social inequality and corruption, the Shah's regime banned the traditional Islamic code, linking modernization solely with Westernization. Despite continuous pleas from the people for the restoration of traditional Islamic institutions as the societal foundation and the preservation of their culture, the stubborn Shah, influenced by the United States, disregarded these appeals. This led to prolonged conflicts between the regime and the general populace, including local clerics inspired by Ali Shari'ati's radical ideas of removing corrupt leaders and rebuilding an authentically Islamic society grounded in justice, equality, and fairness. Eventually, a successful uprising in 1979 resulted in the Shah's exile and the overthrow of his government. The establishment of an Islamic theocracy followed by Ayatollah Khomeini's ascendancy (1902–1989), guided by their interpretation of the traditional Islamic model centered on principles of social justice and equality across all aspects of human life.[33]

The ideological perspective of practitioners appears to be grounded in a theological foundation that gives them a conviction that globalization can be directed, contrasting with other views emphasizing its unintended nature and consequences. While organizations linked to al-Qaida attract attention due to their violent methods, less extreme groups like Jamat-I-Islami and the Muslim Brotherhood are also active globally. Amid the significant impact of modernization, industrialization, and globalization on Muslim life, these groups aim to restore the *ummah* as the basis for collective identity, transcending nationalist differences. Muslim scholars assert that Islamic revivalism is propelled not by economic interests but by shared religious beliefs, rooted in social consciousness influenced by socioreligious conditions rather than socioeconomic circumstances. Islamic revivalism is inherent in Islamic communities, responding to any decadence or degeneration by seeking to reinstate fundamental elements. Given that the belief system permeates all facets of society, observable differences in politics, education, the economy, the judiciary, and international relations signify a departure from fundamental principles. Therefore, the current surge of global conflicts should not be surprising, as it reflects the dialectic process inherent in the evolution of Islamic communities.[34]

Technology and Islamic Revivalism

A compelling dynamic exists between the influences of globalization and the revival of Islamic ideals. Notably, the technological tools employed by Muslim revivalists for increased interconnectedness have transformed into powerful catalysts for global integration in the contemporary era. These transformative technologies, including the vast realm of cyberspace comprising the internet and the World Wide Web, have led to two inseparable outcomes in the pursuit of creating a global village: the diminishing of national sovereignty and the breakdown of geographical barriers. In this intricate interplay, Islam and globalization are interlinked—their fates woven together in a network of interconnectedness. At the heart of Muslim identity is a profound anchor—the concept of a universal *ummah* that surpasses the constraints of nationality, race, ethnicity, and gender, particularly within the theological domain.[35] While the written word has historically played a crucial role in shaping national identity and fostering collective awareness, the swift advancement of communication technologies presents a dual-faced opportunity. On one side, these transformative instruments possess the potential to encourage the development of trans-ethnic communities, blurring the lines of conventional nationhood. Conversely, they pose a challenge to the very fundamentals of national identity. Islam, inherently resistant to the constraints of nationalism, aspires to break down the barriers of competing sovereign nations, aligning with the forces of globalization and the surge of new technologies. Contemporary advancements present Islam with a renewed opportunity to realize its vision—a unified global community of devoted believers. A compelling illustration etched into the history of American television features Osama bin Laden, standing alone in the remote expanses of Afghanistan, holding a cellphone—an evocative portrayal of the intricate interplay between pan-Islamic connections and cutting-edge communication tools in the contemporary era.[36]

According to Mazrui, the Muslim awareness is intricately connected with the idea of a shrinking world. As a religion, Islam has consistently aimed to uphold both progress and guidance. While Prophet Muhammad PBUH's birth occurred in 570 CE, the Islamic calendar did not commence at that moment, nor did it initiate with his passing in June of 632 CE. Instead, it began in 622 CE, marking the establishment of the Islamic era or calendar when Prophet Muhammad PBUH undertook the migration known as the

Hijra. The Hijra, in many aspects, signifies a celebration of purposeful movement. The Prophet not only transformed and reconciled pre-Islamic and Islamic religious concepts but also physically moved from Mecca to Medina. Movement marked the commencement of Islamic time.[37] Mazrui suggests that the elements of awareness, such as the shrinking of distance facilitated by religion, have drawn certain Muslim fundamentalists toward modern information and communication technologies, potentially leading to a significant Islamic Reformation. In the twentieth century, Western scholars have debated whether the Christian Reformation was a direct outcome of earlier stages of the capitalist revolution or if the Protestant Reformation served as the origin of capitalism in Europe. Conversely, some theorists argue that technological advancements predating the Reformation laid the groundwork for both capitalism and Protestantism. Similar inquiries are now arising about what impact the internet, Cyberspace, and the third Industrial Revolution of information technology might have on Islam, analogous to the effects of printing and the first Industrial Revolution on Christianity.

The winds of revolution stirred once again, this time propelled by international trade and exploration. The conventional fabric of Christian beliefs was unraveled by the ingenious invention of the printing press. Now, as the internet and the World Wide Web take center stage, one contemplates whether Islamic traditions will undergo a similar seismic shift at their core. Will this technological marvel prompt the doors of *ijtihād*, Islamic legal reasoning, to swing open once more? While Islam grapples with internal transformations, the Muslim world is witnessing the rise of diverse quasi-reformist movements aiming to infuse scientific knowledge with the essence of Islam, aspiring to Islamize the very fabric of modernity itself. At the heart of this pursuit lies the remarkable endeavor to Islamicize the realm of computer technology. As Nasim Butt keenly observes, mastery and influence over information technologies have become the central pivot around which power and manipulation revolve.[38] In this complex network, adapting technology to align with the needs and ambitions of Muslim society becomes the sensible path forward. In this context, the growing influence of expertise and skill gains compelling momentum, driving the pursuit of a seamless integration of faith and technological progress.[39] In spite of the digital divide, Muslim revivalists have effectively utilized the internet and the World Wide Web for networking and advocacy, both within and beyond Africa.[40]

Critique of Islamic Revivalist Movements in the Arab World

Recent studies on Islamist movements reveal that some Muslim thinkers strive for engagement in discourse and maintain openness to diverse societal viewpoints, all while rejecting the necessity of an exclusively Islamic resolution to the challenges faced by Muslim communities.[41] They also critique the violent conduct exhibited by more extremist organizations, particularly those that attract the youth. For instance, Al-Ghannoushi has acknowledged the right of non-Islamic organizations to fully partake in the political affairs of an Islamic state in Tunis. Nevertheless, it is essential to note that this acknowledgment does not imply any disdain or rejection of the legitimacy of extremist groups by these intellectuals.

Furthermore, it is crucial to view this not as a uniform opposition against the state but as a reassertion of their steadfast commitment to restoring the essence of the Islamic paradigm, emphasizing that such restoration does not necessarily have to involve resorting to violence. Alongside this internal critique, a varied range of perspectives has contributed to the ongoing intellectual discourse on the intricate relationship between Islam and the modern societal framework. Despite differing opinions, there exists a group of critics who paradoxically embrace these Islamist groups, sincerely seeking to comprehend their struggle and resistance against contemporary society. Others, adopting a less judgmental stance, consider Islamist movements—including the extreme and extremist factions—as essential and legitimate instruments for instigating social and political transformation. Others align primarily in rejecting Western ideology, ethics, and influence in the Arab world with these groups.[42] This perspective is also shared by certain journalists who have served as advocates for specific Islamic organizations. However, despite their endeavors, these individuals are seldom recognized or embraced as members of the Islamist movements.

Islamist movements have garnered both supporters and critics who stand outside their organizational structures. In the late 1980s, a novel trend emerged, where individuals not only scrutinized the ideologies and practices of various Islamist groups but also expressed their opposition to the imposition of Islamic law as the predominant legal system in society. For example, Faraj Foudah advocated for a secular perspective and resisted the implementation of *sharī'ah* legislation. He asserted that Islamist movements were tainted by corruption, supported vested interests, and worked to undermine civil society. Another figure, Hussein Amin, critiqued the acceptability of allowing Islamist movements, especially those with violent and extreme tendencies, to dictate the portrayal of Islam. Instead, he challenged the notion of implementing *sharī'ah* regulations and proposed his vision of a liberal, Westernized Islam. He strongly condemns the conduct of some Islamist organizations, denouncing it as bloodthirsty, violent, barbaric, and inconsistent with Islamic principles.[43] Foudah and Amin exemplify this movement, though they are not solitary in their stance. A quandary or an inherent impossibility confronts Islamist groups in the contemporary Arab world. The dilemma arises from the Islamist movements' ambition to institute an Islamic political order. Despite the incapacity to establish an Islamic political government, the modern Arab elite has effectively vied for the support of religious masses, leading to sustained or heightened divisions in the Arab and Muslim world.[44] Nevertheless, the current conditions in the Arab world still offer favorable circumstances for revivalist groups to rejuvenate themselves and once again assume a significant role in the region's religious and political landscape.

In the midst of the prevailing emphasis on Islamist movements, various Arab thinkers appear to have sought to articulate their distinct interpretations of the Islamic cosmology. Among these intellectual figures, Hassan Hanafi stands out, skillfully integrating elements of philosophy, religious discourse, and revolutionary literature to revive and refine the concepts introduced by Sayyid Qutb. While Hanafi's perspectives may not find unanimous acceptance among followers of various Islamic sects, his writings have earned substantial acclaim in intellectual circles for presenting a fresh and invigorating Islamic perspective. Hanafi has endeavored to establish a form of Muslim liberation theology. Although he aimed to elucidate the theological experience of Latin American Catholics to Arab readers and advocate for similar efforts in Islam, his ideas encountered limited acceptance in conventional circles but found resonance among former Marxist and leftist intellectuals. These viewpoints remain relatively uncommon and less recognized.[45] The contemporary Islamic revival in Turkey is perceived as the initiation of a substantial reevaluation of the Kemalist revolution, which established Turkish secularism. Despite the military's attempts to hinder it, there is a growing electoral support for revivalist organizations in Turkey.

The Qur'ān has sparked intellectual exploration from various perspectives, and Hanafi's efforts to formulate a theology of liberation serve as a noteworthy example of this scholarly inquiry. This intellectual endeavor presents a distinctive and formidable challenge to established knowledge, diverging significantly from the insightful contributions of Muhammad Shahrour in the realm of Qur'ānic scholarship. A particularly revolutionary aspect of this exploration is the treatment of traditional Qur'ānic exegesis, employing innovative methodologies and literary criticism theories for analyzing the Qur'ānic text. This approach stands in direct contrast to conventional methods and directly challenges Shahrour's ideas. These unconventional interpretations not only clash with traditional views of the Qur'ān but also signify a profound departure in the field of Qur'ānic studies as traditionally taught in the Arab world. Moreover, these authors have questioned the stances of Islamist movements on issues such as women, banking, and economics. The viewpoints advocated in these writings are so extreme that they may be seen as not only opposing Islamic movements but also challenging Islam itself. Despite being highly unconventional and introducing brand-new interpretations in the Muslim world, such beliefs are gaining popularity, particularly in Egypt and Tunisia.

Islamic Revivalist Movements and the Global Perception of Islam

Irrespective of its form, Islam emerges before the West as a political ideology encompassing thinking, imagination, behavior, and policy that challenges prevailing political dominance. The notion of political Islam raises concerns within liberal, predominantly secular democracies. Apprehensions about an intolerant, oppressive, and potentially "totalitarian" Islamism are fueled by recent events in countries like Iran, Afghanistan, Pakistan, and Saudi Arabia. However, Islamic principles do not necessitate Muslims to perceive democratic and pluralistic perspectives as incompatible with their faith. In reality, the inclination to restrict or control such perspectives in the name of Islam has coexisted with plurality and syncretism. Islam's role on the global stage does not hinge on the simplistic assumption that it might advocate a new form of order; rather, it can contribute to expanding spaces for critical thinking that challenge prevailing organizing ideas and normative values worldwide. Ironically, this crucial role is becoming more apparent with the rise of modern Islamic revivalist movements. Despite their concerns about the historical portrayal or misinterpretation of Islam, these groups heavily rely on tightly controlled knowledge of Islamic history.[46]

Due to various political factors, the more fundamentalists attempt to sanitize Islamic history, the more Muslims concerned about this issue fight back and highlight Islam's pluralist, progressive, and syncretic past. The Indonesian Liberal Islam Network serves as an example of this dynamic. Despite being slow to emerge, these histories are still under attack, having been previously neglected in Muslim communities and either concealed or rejected in the Western imagination. However, they persistently come to light.[47] Conversely, fundamentalist groups filter all the diverse social and cultural experiences that shape Islam through an obsession with appearances rather than content. They exhibit unwavering dedication to a homogeneous ideological image of Islam, where normative or moral possibilities are constrained by signs and symbols that are mistaken for substantive content. The majority of fundamentalist movements, despite claiming to challenge intellectual modernity, paradoxically find themselves entangled within the prevailing late-modern political paradigm. In essence, for these groups, a few regulations regarding dress code in the Qur'ān are elevated to represent the epitome of Islam. In the capitalist moral economy, where the right and ability to embrace the latest fashion in clothing or technology are touted as essential freedoms, politics becomes fixated on matters such as men's or women's facial hair, overshadowing all other conventional political and economic conflicts. This fixation diminishes the significance of other crucial aspects, including the Prophet's consistent emphasis on seeking knowledge from various sources and the Qur'ānic emphasis on social and economic fairness throughout society.[48]

The suppression of historical Islamic diversity in ideas has been the prevailing outcome of the form of Islamic politics witnessed in the last fifty years, largely unchallenged within the Islamic community. Nevertheless, with careful consideration, the prospect of the pluralist and progressive histories—of which the current Islamisms only have a truncated understanding—becomes more imminent as this type of Islamism is scrutinized and questioned. This holds true even when these histories are marginalized and downplayed rather than comprehensively summarized. In essence, these fundamentalist Islamisms are increasingly appearing as histories steeped in negative narratives. When examined in a broader context, Islamic histories take on a fresh perspective, revealing that the lifeworlds shaped by Islam are fundamentally more about openings, interactions, translations, and innovations than about exclusions, terminations, halts, and prohibitions in human existence. Islam's early history, known as *fatun* in Arabic, originally meant "opening," but in Orientalist narratives, it has come to signify "conquest" as capture and absolute dominion.

In reality, the impact of the Islamic conquests on the conquered lands was complex and interconnected. Understanding the development of pluralist politics—an Islamic humanism—that influenced early Islamic ideas and garnered significant followers provides insight into Islam's remarkable transition from a tribal movement to a global religion within a century of its establishment.[49] Through this humanist perspective, Muslims not only revered the civilizations of the Hellenic, Roman, Persian, and Indian but also assimilated them into their own initiatives, contributing to the formation of an Islamic civilization. Therefore, in this historical context, the endeavor to "preserve" Islam necessitates embracing the openness that Islam has long advocated. Consequently, any concern about the fundamentals of Islam should recognize the dynamic orientations and attitudes that shaped Islamic law and behavior for a substantial period before Islam emerged as a global religion. Modern-day Islamic extremism, with its restrictions and prohibitions, contradicts Islamic history and inadequately represents all aspects of Islamic history, especially the diverse forms of humanism that have characterized it throughout its historical development.

Regardless of the motivations, obscurantism proves detrimental to Islam and Muslims in today's increasingly globalized world. While contemporary political and economic pressures may contribute to the rise of conservative views in Islamic cultures, these pressures should not serve as an excuse for embracing authoritarian dogmatism. Many present-day Islamic cultures offer fertile ground for community organization, shaped by the logic of endless or irreconcilable civilizational differences due to their marginalized position in modernity and submission to the West. It is important to note that certain Orientalists and fundamentalists may desire the realization of such a prophecy to discuss eventual confrontations between vastly different civilizations. However, this rationale places reactionary tendencies at the center of Islamic experiences and conflicts. Moreover, it assumes that Muslims will be limited to the Islamist norm—whether moderate or fundamentalist—as their system of government. Consequently, ongoing processes in the contemporary landscape, including the resurgence of the Islamic element in shaping national and international collective identities, do not imply either the "end of history" in the sense of ceasing ideological confrontations between various cultural programs of modernity (Fukuyama) or a "Clash of Civilizations," which challenges the fundamental tenets of modernity (Huntington).

The influence of distinct civilizations, particularly Islam and historical experiences on the development of contemporary civilizations, does not imply the creation of closed entities continuing their unique historical patterns. Instead, these diverse experiences act as reference points for ongoing exchanges and interactions across various modernities, transcending any specific community or civilization. While this diversity has undermined old hegemonies, it has paradoxically contributed to the emergence of common reference points, networks, and a globalization of cultural connections beyond previous limits. Additionally, the political dynamics of these societies are intricately connected to geopolitical realities, influenced by both historical experiences and contemporary developments and conflicts, making it challenging to establish "closed" organizations. It is important to note that these processes do not remotely represent a "return" to the challenges of ancient Axial civilizations, as achieving such a scenario is practically impossible.[50]

Based on the preceding discussion, it can be deduced that Muslim scholars acknowledge the role of globalization processes in the resurgence of Islam. However, the revitalization of Islam is not solely attributed to economic globalization, awareness of global phenomena, postmodernism, or any singular source. Instead, contemporary socialization processes are undergoing transformation, primarily due to advancements in global communication, increased transnational connections facilitating the exchange of information and ideas and shifts in the economic, political, cultural, social, and legal systems of national societies within the global context. As the construction of Muslim identity differs significantly from previous generations, there is a heightened emphasis on religion in personal, social, political, and other spheres of activity. By amalgamating these components, it becomes more convenient to draw parallels between contemporary Western and capitalist forms of globalization, along with the challenges they pose, and the historical Islamic expansion, which many moderates and practitioners now perceive as a successful manifestation of globalization. This interpretation plays a crucial role in establishing the legitimacy of Islam in the present day. The increased comparisons within Islam also stem from the impact of globalization. The transformation of the *ummah* has been influenced by globalization's role in uniting diverse populations, enhancing information accessibility and emphasizing significant cultural distinctions. The realization of such substantial variations is leading to further divisions within Islam. While practitioners strongly oppose the lack of consistency and aim to preserve what they consider authentic Islam, moderates from various nations are engaging in the exchange of ideas and practices. Both moderates and practitioners seek validation for their discourses in international relations and communications, contributing to their further divergence.[51]

Conclusion

Islamic revivalist groups emerged in the public sphere, offering a resurgence of Islamic glory and dispelling the hopelessness and pessimism that afflicted Muslim communities throughout the twentieth century. This crisis impacted various facets of Muslim nations, encompassing cultural, political, social economic, psychological, and spiritual dimensions. By the late 1960s, the failure of secular ideologies and development models became evident in the inability to construct prosperous societies that could rival the dominant influence of the West. It is evident that the driving force behind Muslim revivalists is the perceived threat to the fundamental integrity of Islamic culture and way of life posed by non-Islamic forces of secularism and modernism, often endorsed by Muslim governments.[52] A significant challenge they face is attributing blame not only to external actors like the West or globalization but also to their own governments, which have failed to address underlying issues within their societies.

The increase in religious activity over the same decades as the acceleration of globalization has two significant consequences. Firstly, the Christian renaissance manifests as a rebellion against the allure of cosmopolitanism in politics and culture. Various groups worldwide, such as Latin American Catholic liberation theologies and Muslim "*jamaats*" (brotherhoods), have redefined religion as a source of power. This shift persists despite the affirmation of traditional practices and institutions by postcolonial peoples who believe in the uniqueness and greater value of such traditions compared to contemporary, artificial structures. This argument is grounded in the right to locality and the primary rights of place, culture, and community, which these groups seek to uphold against what they perceive as the dual threats of the global juggernaut: the hegemony of neo-intellectual liberalism and the legal dismantling of national sovereignty.[53]

The struggle for identity, authenticity, and community in the face of globalization is a pivotal challenge.[54] Whether the perceived dangers are real or imagined, religion embodies, as expressed by Michel Foucault, "a diversity of resistances," representing a deliberate assertion of one's identity linked to a performative worldview and a strategy for improvement in this life or the next.[55] Paradoxically, the religious resurgence gains vitality from the global information exchange networks established by globalization. The discovery of videos from extremist groups like Al-Qaeda and Islamic State of Iraq and the Levant (ISIL or ISIS) in Afghanistan in late October 2001 serves as stark evidence of how modern communications and technological advancements are utilized to spread their sociopolitical message globally. Copies of these videos were distributed via the internet and international airmail to thousands of seminaries and schools across Africa, the Middle East, Southeast Asia, and Europe. Ironically, despite efforts to resist globalization, religious revival depends on it for its vitality.

Notes

1. Philip W. Sutton and Stephen Vertigans, *Resurgent Islam: A Sociological Approach* (Cambridge: Polity Press, 2005), 91–92.
2. Ulreck Beck, *What is Globalization?* (Cambridge: Polity Press, 2000), 33.
3. Anwar Ibrahim, "Islamic Renaissance and the Reconstruction of Civilization," *Islamic Horizons* 25, no. 5 (1996): 14–15.
4. Abdul Aziz Said and Nathan C. Funk, "Islamic Revivalism: A Global Perspective," in *Toward a Global Civilization: The Contribution of Religions*, ed. Patricia M. Miche and Melissa Merking (New York: Peter Lang, 1997), 312–330.
5. Yuonne Yazbeck Haddad, "The Revivalist Literature and the Literature on Revival: An Introduction," in *The Contemporary Islamic Revival: A Critical Survey and Bibliography*, ed. Yuonne Yazbeck Haddad, John Obert Voll, and John L. Esposito (New York: Greenwood Press, 1991), 4–8.
6. Asghar Ali Engineer, *Islam in the Contemporary World* (New Delhi, India: New Dawn Press, 2007), 117
7. Engineer, *Islam in the Contemporary World*, 117
8. Engineer, *Islam in the Contemporary World*, 118.
9. Engineer, *Islam in the Contemporary World*, 119.
10. Asghar Ali Engineer, "Islam, Globalization and Challenges." Accessed April 14, 2024.http://www.theamericanmuslim.org/tam.php/features/articles/islam_globalization_and_challenges/0016134.
11. Haddad, "The Revivalist Literature," 312.
12. Haddad, "The Revivalist Literature," 313.
13. Hakeem Onapajo, "Islamic Revivalism and Social Change in Muslim Societies: A Rethink of Marxist Historical Materialism," *World Journal of Islamic History and Civilization* 2, no. 4 (2012): 200.
14. Ahmad Dallal, "The Origins and Objectives of Islamic Revivalist Thought, 1750–1850," *Journal of the American Oriental Studies* 113, no. 3 (1993): 341–359.
15. Dallal, "The Origins and Objectives of Islamic Revivalist Thought," 347.
16. Julia Clansy-Smith, "Saints, Mahdis and Arms: Religion and Resistance in Nineteenth-Century North Africa," in *Islam, Politics and Social Movements*, ed. Edmund Burke III and Ira M. Lapidus (Berkeley, CA: University of California Press, 1988), 60–80.
17. Clansy-Smith, "Saints, Mahdis and Arms," 64.
18. Ira M. Lapidus, *A History of Islamic Societies* (Cambridge: Cambridge University Press, 1988), 192–224.
19. Lapidus, *A History of Islamic Societies*, 208–218.
20. Ira M. Lapidus, "Islamic Revival and Modernity: The Contemporary Movements and the Historical Paradigms," *Journal of the Economic and Social History of the Orient* 40, no. 4 (1997): 444–460.
21. Lapidus, "Islamic Revival and Modernity," 453.

22. Onapajo, "Islamic Revivalism and Social Change," 198.
23. Carole Collins, "Colonialism and Class Struggle in Sudan," *MERIP Reports* 46 (1976): 3–20.
24. Abdul Aziz Abu Sulayman, "The Islamisation of Knowledge: A New Approach towards Reform of Contemporary Knowledge," in *Islam: Source and Purpose of Knowledge: Proceedings and Selected Papers of Second Conference on Islamisation of Knowledge 1402 AH/1982 AC* (Herndon, VA: IIIT, 1988), 91–118.
25. Akbar Ahmad, *Discovering Islam: Making Sense of Muslim History* (London: Routledge, 2002), 205–207.
26. Ahmad, *Discovering Islam*, 210.
27. Rabi, "Globalization: A Contemporary Islamic Response?," 21.
28. Abu al-"Ala Madi, *Jama at al- Unf al-Misriyyah al-Murtabitah Bi'l islam: al-Judhur al-Tarikhiyyah wa'l Usus alfikriyyah Wa'l Mustaqbal* (Cairo: Al-Markaz al-Duwali li'l Dirasat, 1997), 56; Muhammad Salah, "Kharitat Harakat al-'Unf fi Misr," *Wijhat Nadhar* 1, no. 4 (1999): 20–25. John Cooley, *Unholy Wars: Afghanistan, America and International Terrorism* (London: Pluto Press, 2000), 247.
29. Abdul Rashid Moten, "Islamic Thought in Contemporary Pakistan: The Legacy of 'Allama Mawdūdī," in *Contemporary Islamic Thought*, ed. Ibrahim Abu-Rabi (Oxford: Blackwell Publishing Limited, 2006), 175–194.
30. Moten, "Islamic Thought in Contemporary Pakistan," 177.
31. Moten, "Islamic Thought in Contemporary Pakistan," 178.
32. Moten, "Islamic Thought in Contemporary Pakistan," 180.
33. Onapajo, "Islamic Revivalism and Social Change," 203.
34. Onapajo, "Islamic Revivalism and Social Change," 204.
35. Ali A. Mazrui, "Religion and Political Culture in Africa," *Journal of the American Academy of Religion* LIII, no. 4 (1985): 817–839.
36. Mazrui, "Religion and Political Culture," 820.
37. Mazrui, "Religion and Political Culture," 820.
38. Nasim Butt, *Science and Muslim Societies* (London: Grey Seal, 1991), 62.
39. Ali Mazrui and Alamin M. Mazrui, "The Digital Revolution and the New Reformation: Doctrine and Gender in Islam," *Harvard International Review* 23, no. 1 (2001): 52–55.
40. Lansine Kaba, "Islam in West Africa: Radicalism and the New Ethic of Disagreement, 1960–1990," in *The History of Islam in Africa*, ed. Nehemia Levtzion and Randall L. Pouwels (Athens, OH: Ohio University Press, 2000), 189–208.
41. Abubaker A. Bagader, "Contemporary Islamic Movements in the Arab World," in *Islam, Globalization and Postmodernity*, ed. Akbar Ahmad and Hastings Donnan (London: Routledge, 1994), 117.
42. Bagader, "Contemporary Islamic Movements," 118.
43. Hussain Amin, *Al-Islam fi Alam Mutaghir* [Islam in a Changing World] (Cairo: Madbooli Bookshop, 1987), 287–307.

44. Mohamed El-Tahir El-Mesawi, "Religion, Society and Culture in Malik Bennabi's Thought," in *The Blackwell Companion to Contemporary Islamic Thought*, ed. Ibrahim Abu Rabi (Oxford: Blackwell Publishing Limited, 2006), 254.

45. Bagader, "Contemporary Islamic Movements in the Arab World," 119.

46. Bagader, "Contemporary Islamic Movements in the Arab World," 123.

47. Navzat Soguk, *Globalization and Islamism: Beyond Fundamentalism* (New York: Rowmann and Littlefield, Navzat Soguk, 2011), 22–23.

48. Soguk, *Globalization and Islamism*, 24.

49. Soguk, *Globalization and Islamism*, 25.

50. Shmuel N. Eisenstadt, "The Resurgence of Religious Movements in Processes of Globalization," *International Journal on Multicultural Societies*," IJMS 2, no. 1 (2000): 13–14.

51. Sutton and Vertigans, *Resurgent Islam: A Sociological Approach*, 112–114.

52. Abdulaziz Sachedina, "Islamic Religion and Political Order," *SAIS Review* 18, no. 2 (1998): 59–64.

53. Sean L. Yom, "Islam and Globalization: Secularism, Religion, and Radicalism." Accessed April 14, 2024. https://www.fes.de/ipg/IPG4_2002/ARTYOM.HTM.

54. Paul Marshall, "Disregarding Religion," *SAIS Review* 18, no. 2 (1998): 13–18.

55. Michel Foucault, *The History of Sexuality, Volume I: An Introduction*, trans. Robert Hurley (New York: Vintage Books, 1990), 96.

PART II

ADAPTIVE ISLAM

UNRAVELING NARRATIVES OF RESILIENCE IN THE GLOBAL CONTEXT

CHAPTER 5

Embracing or Resisting Globalization? Ali Mazrui's Exploration of Interdependence and the Muslim World's Dilemma

Introduction

Ali Mazrui (d. 2014), renowned for his intellectual leadership at Makerere University, sparked global discourse and controversy during his tenures as the head of the Department of Political Science and Dean of Social Sciences. His profound exploration of globalization, centered on the African context, utilizing Makerere as a focal point for dissecting its intricacies. Proposing avant-garde strategies, Mazrui aimed to empower non-Western cultures to navigate and leverage the pervasive force of globalization for their own agendas. This chapter delves into Mazrui's scholarly exploration of the process of globalization, examining its complex interactions with non-Western cultures. The analysis aims to unveil Mazrui's nuanced insights regarding the impacts, challenges, and innovative strategies he advocated for non-Western cultures within the globalizing landscape. The exploration attempts to elucidate the layers of Mazrui's scholarly discourse, contributing to a comprehensive understanding of his views on globalization and its implications for diverse societies.

As Mazrui explores the intricacies of global changes, he identifies four key factors—religion, technology, economy, and empire—playing crucial roles in shaping its patterns. Mazrui emphasizes that, although the term "globalization" is relatively new, the roots of interconnectedness and international exchanges were planted centuries ago, fostering ongoing interactions. Mazrui describes how people from all over the world come together despite distance, creating a unified blend of humanity. However, he uncovers a stark truth within this unified fabric—a concerning concentration of power held by a select few nations. Coined as "hegemonization" by Mazrui, this phenomenon carries both risks and opportunities, revealing a narrative of inequalities and aspirations as the world stands at the brink of a global transformation.[1]

Whether for better or worse, the Muslim world is poised to emerge as a pivotal arena in the global battleground of the twenty-first century as a result of the forces of globalization. This phenomenon, characterized by both victors and losers, has already inflicted losses upon Africa and substantial portions of the Muslim world in its initial stages, a trend supported by a growing body of evidence. At its core, globalization manifests as a set of activities engendering interdependence among nations and accelerating trade across vast distances. The confluence of these multifaceted elements is engendering a world that is progressively contracting, evolving into a cohesive and interconnected global community wherein traditional boundaries diminish in significance and mobility experiences a heightened pace. Globalization has emerged as an incremental process gradually transforming the entire planet into a unified global village. These compelling forces, with a historical lineage deeply embedded in the annals of time, have long been operative on the world stage, permeating every corner of the Muslim world.[2] At present, the Muslim world faces challenges from both homogeneity and hegemonization, with the realization of potential benefits from homogeneity contingent upon the widespread permeation of Islamic principles globally. The mere assimilation of Muslims and Islam into Western culture is insufficient to dismantle Western hegemony. However, a substantial Muslim population within the Western sphere holds the potential to hinder the encroachment of cultural uniformity, introducing a refreshing divergence in values, tastes, and perspectives. In the evolving global arena, characterized by moral calculations, clashes of values, and convergences of viewpoints, the increasing tide of homogenization fosters a growing semblance among cultures.

Ali Mazrui: Brief Biography and Works

Born on February 24, 1933, in the dynamic coastal city of Mombasa, Kenya, Ali Al'Amin Mazrui, a distinguished philosopher, pan-Africanist, and visionary, has left an enduring imprint on the intellectual landscape. His commitment to popularizing African concepts has played a pivotal role in enhancing the continent's prominence on the global stage, revealing its complex interplay of knowledge and wisdom. Descending from a lineage imbued with profound respect for Islam, Mazrui belonged to the Mazrui dynasty, a family with a historical legacy marked by erudite scholarship, exerting its influence over Mombasa for over a century until 1837. Ali Mazrui was fortunate to inherit a legacy steeped in eminence, as his father, the Grand Qadi, graced the corridors of justice with his wisdom. From a young age, Mazrui accompanied his father to halls of the courtroom, serving as a witness to captivating dialogues on matters of politics and morality.[3] Immersed in the richness of his Islamic heritage, it was inevitable that Mazrui's education would deeply connect with Qur'ānic institutions, where young Muslim minds delved into the sciences and theological intricacies of their faith. Mazrui's father had high hopes for his son to embark on a scholarly journey to Al-Azhar University in the heart of Cairo, known for its profound Islamic scholarship. Due to the demise of his father at the tender age of fourteen, this plan was thwarted. Mazrui found himself nurtured and employed at the Mombasa Institute of Muslim Education, where encounters with British educators facilitated his acquisition of a scholarship for studies in the United Kingdom. Despite Mazrui's engagement in Western education, he remained steadfast in his commitment to Islam, concurrently honing his proficiency in the Arabic language through coursework at the University of Manchester.[4]

Commencing his academic journey at the University of Makerere in Uganda fulfilled Mazrui's longstanding aspiration. Assuming the role of John Wayne, professor of political science at Makerere, Mazrui garnered international acclaim.[5] Reflecting on his tenure at Makerere, Mazrui regarded those years as particularly pivotal and fruitful. In 1974, Mazrui assumed the position of a political science professor at the University of Michigan. Concurrently, he held a professorship at the University of Jos in Nigeria during his Michigan student days. Mazrui underscored the importance of dedicating time to teaching in Africa, emphasizing the necessity of staying attuned to the African perspective. Leading the Center for Afro-American and African Studies at the University of Michigan from 1978 to 1981 added another dimension to Mazrui's multifaceted academic journey. He assumed the role of director at the Institute of Global Cultural Studies at the University of Binghamton, New York, and concurrently held the directorship of the Center for Afro-American and African Studies at the University of Michigan. Cornell University benefited from his academic presence as the Andrew D. White Professor-at-Large Emeritus and Senior Scholar in African Studies.[6] Furthermore, Mazrui received the honor of being appointed as Chancellor of the Jomo Kenyatta University of Agriculture and Technology by Kenya's Head of State. During the period spanning from 1997 to 2000, Mazrui contributed his erudition as the Ibn Khaldun Professor-at-Large at the Graduate School of Islamic and Social Sciences in Leesburg, Virginia. In Georgetown, Guyana, he assumed the mantle of the Walter Rodney Professor at the University of Guyana from 1997 to 1998. Mazrui's academic journey commenced with distinction at Manchester University in England, followed by the acquisition of an MA from Columbia University in New York and culminating in a PhD from Oxford University in England.[7] In addition to his academic pursuits, Mazrui lent his expertise as a special advisor to the World Bank. Moreover, he assumed leadership roles on the boards of the American Muslim Council in Washington D.C. and the Center for the Study of Islam and Democracy. Unfortunately, Mazrui passed away on October 12, 2014, leaving behind a legacy of profound contributions to academia and international affairs.

Mazrui was interested in various subjects, including African politics, global political culture, political Islam, and North–South connections. He contributed to over thirty books as an author or co-author and his writings extended to numerous articles in both the news media and prominent academic publications. Moreover, he played editorial roles in more than twenty academic publications worldwide. Leaders, global media, and research organizations often sought Mazrui's political advice and alternative perspectives. He contributed more than thirty publications that greatly influenced our understanding of various topics. Notable works, such as "Towards a Pax Africana" (1967) and "The Political Sociology of the English Language" (1975), showcased his brilliance. His novel "The Trial of Christopher Okigbo" (1971) displayed his storytelling talent. Two significant publications, "Cultural Forces in World Politics" and "A World Federation of Cultures: An African Perspective," published in 1976, were key parts of his intellectual legacy.[8] His fascination with the power of language led to collaboration on "The Power of Babel: Language and Governance in Africa's Experience" in 1998. Before his passing, he and Alamin M. Mazrui were jointly exploring Black Reparations in the Age of Globalization. Some of his earlier works include "A Tale of Two Africas: Nigeria and South Africa as Contrasting Visions" (2006), "Islam between Globalization and Counterterrorism" (2006), and "The Politics of War and the Culture of Violence" (2008).[9] His impact on diverse fields continues to be felt through these insightful contributions.

The Driving Forces of Globalization

Globalization is the result of mechanisms that facilitate worldwide interconnectedness and the swift exchange of goods and ideas across vast distances. Although the term "globalization" is relatively recent, the foundational processes behind global interdependence and interaction have roots spanning many centuries. As noted before, Mazrui identifies religion, technology, economy, and empire as the primary drivers of globalization throughout history. He argues that these factors often synergize, reinforcing each other rather than operating in isolation. A case in point is the global spread of Christianity, which commenced with the conversion of Roman Emperor Constantine I in 313 AD, initiating a process that extended its influence beyond Europe to various nations governed or inhabited by Europeans. In contrast, Islam's globalization process involved the creation of an empire from scratch, rather than transforming an existing one. Blending elements from once-mighty civilizations such as Byzantine Egypt and ancient Persia, the Umayyad and Abbasid dynasties constructed an entirely fresh society. In this expansive narrative, Islam and Christianity have occasionally collided, each striving to be the primary spiritual force in Africa. Amid this fierce contest, Mazrui explores Africa's role in the global amalgamation of religions—does it play an active role or merely experience the consequences? In the shifting currents of intellectual trends, a prominent concept emerges in religious history: monotheism, the belief in a single divine entity. Many historians concur that the earliest recorded monotheist was Pharaoh Akhenaton, an African ruler of Egypt's eighteenth Dynasty, reigning from 1379 to 1362 BCE. His courageous embrace of a sole deity has left a profound impact, emerging as a potent influence in the broader narrative of religious globalization.[10]

Mazrui emphasizes that exploration voyages represent another pivotal phase in the process of globalization. Vasco da Gama, assisted by East African navigators, initiated a new chapter in the global interaction's history. The primary driving forces behind this were economic interests and imperial ambitions. Subsequently, human movements continued to unfold. The Portuguese played a role in constructing Fort Jesus in Mombasa. Theological and economic pressures in Europe prompted the Pilgrim Fathers' journey to America. The influx of millions from different hemispheres marked the zenith of demographic globalization in the Americas. The United States, with its diverse immigrant population from nearly every civilization, eventually became a microcosm of the world. Mazrui also points to the industrial revolution as a crucial era in global development. He argues that during this period, production surged and Europe's prosperity fueled its ambitions to colonize new territories. Consequently, the Atlantic slave trade gained momentum, leading to the widespread movement of millions of people across the globe.

Mazrui posits that the final stage of historical globalization unfolded when the industrial revolution intersected with the burgeoning information revolution. The British accomplished an extraordinary feat by establishing the most expansive and geographically extensive empire ever witnessed by humanity, a venture that persisted until the aftermath of World War II. In contrast, the era of Pax Americana, which harnessed the primary forces of globalization—economy, empire, and technology—deviated from actively promoting any religious doctrine. Instead, the focus shifted to championing the concept of a clear division between religious institutions and governmental entities. Consequently, the deepening interconnection and the proliferation of reciprocal transactions became profoundly reliant on the emergence and widespread adoption of information communication technology.

Unveiling the Paradoxes of Globalization: Homogenization vs. Hegemonization

Despite apparent cultural differences or distinctions among civilizations, globalization results in a striking outcome where individuals display a heightened resemblance to one another, surpassing any previous similarities. Simultaneously, Mazrui characterizes hegemonization as the apex of globalization, where authority becomes entirely consolidated within a single nation or civilization. This ongoing phase of globalization has fostered increased similarity among nations, transcending boundaries, yet it has also concentrated an excessive amount of power within the hands of a select few influential individuals. As people gravitate toward adopting a lingua franca spanning multiple continents, propelled by specific catalysts and holding the status of a national language in no fewer than ten nations, a sense of homogenization emerges. However, a closer examination of the origins of these languages reveals a prevailing hegemonization, as English, French, and Spanish predominantly trace their roots back to European origins.[11] Despite the ever-growing interconnectivity of the global economy, the dominant forces wielding paramount influence overwhelmingly originate from the Western sphere. In terms of economic prowess, the United States, Germany, Japan, Britain, Canada, France, and Italy emerge as the dominant powers, underscoring the contours of hegemonization.

The emergence of the internet has granted humanity a dual-natured gift: swift access to extensive knowledge repositories and the capability to connect across great distances. Yet, beneath the seemingly boundless realm of connectivity, a subtle process of homogenization is at play. Although the operational roots of the internet are still embedded within the United States, closely linked with the power corridors in Washington, its central hub assumes a commanding position, influencing the intricate network of global human integration. This phenomenon serves as an illustration of the covert currents of hegemonization. Nonetheless, Mazrui keenly observes that the United States and Europe, acting as pioneers in academia, have been instrumental in shaping this educational integration. As these institutions disseminate their scholarly ideals, a concerning pattern emerges: the proliferation of notable similarities in the structures of professorial hierarchies.[12] This undeniable convergence stands as a poignant indication of the growing uniformity permeating academic institutions worldwide, a tangible expression of the hegemonization phenomenon in action.

The Three Abodes: Islam's Influence and the West's Appropriation

Mazrui posits that upon the conclusion of World War II, a noteworthy development transpired wherein the Western world, perhaps inadvertently, embraced an Islamic conceptual framework delineating the world into three principal domains: *dar al-Islam* (the Abode of Islam), *dar al-harb* (the Abode of War), and *dar al-sulh* (the Abode of Peace). The latter constituted an unofficial empire of Islam. In *dar al-Islam*, the ascendancy of Par Islamica was envisioned, fostering harmony and collaboration grounded in Islamic ideals. This domain encompassed both Muslim and non-Muslim entities within the safeguarded groups (*ahl al-kitab*, or "People of the Book," and *dhimmis*, or "non-Muslims under Islamic protection"), shielded by the state against internal discord and external intrusion.[13] *Dar al-harb* did not uniformly denote a site of overt armed hostilities; rather, it frequently comprised non-Muslim nations displaying hostility toward Islam, embodying a circumstance that aligns with Thomas Hobbes' characterization of a state lacking a common sovereign.[14]

The concept of *dar al-harb*, denoting a state of conflict, was developed by Muslim jurists to acknowledge the authority of rulers in nations with differing perspectives on the supremacy of God. According to Khadduri, Islam's recognition of non-Islamic sovereignties implied the inherent necessity of some form of governance for human survival, even in regions beyond the Islamic societal structure, existing in a natural state.[15] Mazrui noted that non-Muslim nations engaged in a neo-imperial pact with Muslim rulers, obtaining increased autonomy and peace in exchange for a tax remitted to the Muslim treasury; these were referred to as the realms of *dar al-sulh* (alternatively known as *dar al-'ahd*). Some Muslim jurists did not distinguish *dar al-sulh* separately, arguing that if the inhabitants of a land negotiated a peace treaty and paid tribute, it constituted part of *dar al-Islam*. Post-World War II, the Western world effectively replaced Islam by adopting Islam's fundamental threefold worldview. During the Cold War era, the global landscape was categorized into *dar al-maghrib* (the Domain of the West), *dar al-harb*, also known as the communist world and the Domain of War, and *dar al-ahd* or *al-sulh* (the Third World).[16]

In a modern adaptation reminiscent of the tribute exacted by medieval Muslim rulers in *the dar al-sulh*, the Third World—encompassing Islamic nations—has been making payments to the West, manifesting as onerous debt and various forms of economic exploitation. It is crucial to highlight a pivotal aspect: despite the Western philosophy labeling the communist world as the Abode of War, the nations of the Third World, including Islamic states, have found themselves entangled in nearly all conflicts of the latter half of the twentieth century. This reality persists even in the face of the Western perspective designating the communist world as the Abode of War. The belligerent inclinations of the Western world, marked by its impulsive deployment of weaponry, have led to the loss of no fewer than 500,000 lives among Muslim populations in Iraq, Palestine, Iran, and Libya since 1980.[17] During the Gulf War in 1991, the West utilized the UN flag to impart a universalistic appeal and legitimacy to its militarism.[18]

As Mazrui points out, the ongoing deprivation resulting from British–American financial sanctions, universally validated by the UN Security Council, led to an increasing death toll in Iraq during the war.[19] Since the conclusion of the war, the infant mortality rate in Iraq has quadrupled, and the number of common Iraqis succumbing to preventable diseases has risen.[20] Due to the geographic and military weakness of the nation, there is growing concern about its ability to withstand potential challenges and threats in the foreseeable future.[21] The purported reason behind the restrictions was to prevent Iraq from reassembling its weapons of mass destruction. However, every permanent member of the Security Council had its own stockpile of WMD. Historically, Iraq refrained from testing nuclear bombs thousands of kilometers away from its core population due to the lack of arrogance necessary, thereby avoiding endangering the lives of people in neighboring countries. Pacific nations, with limited military strength, expressed their objection to these tests through public demonstrations, diplomatic deterioration of relations, and boycotts of French products such as wine. Furthermore, Iraq faced a challenge in finding a negotiating partner for a nuclear deal.[22]

International Law, the United Nations, and Western Hegemony

With regard to the UN, Mazrui claims that in spite of being a worldwide organization, the UN only tries to represent governments and regions.[23] Even though Christians make up only about one-fifth of the world's population,

Embracing or Resisting Globalization ~ 199

six out of the last seven UN secretaries-general have come from Christian backgrounds. Despite the fact that when other major religious communities are combined, they outnumber Christians by more than a two-to-one ratio, there has never been a secretary-general who is Hindu, Muslim, or Confucian. U Thant is the sole Buddhist who has served as secretary-general, and despite the global population of Buddhists likely being on par with Christians, the UN has had only one Buddhist and five Christians in this position. The question arises: should the UN system place more emphasis on achieving a balanced representation of cultures within its organization?

The origin of the UN can be traced back to a coalition of nations, the victorious powers that emerged triumphant from the devastation of World War II. Among them, Britain, the United States, France, and the European faction of the Soviet Union assumed joint responsibility for guiding Western civilization, while the Asian expanse of the Soviet Union added its distinctive contributions to this captivating panorama. Yet, as these robust nations secured lasting positions within the UN Security Council, they demonstrated a rare generosity by offering an unprecedented concession to another culture. They graciously admitted pre-Communist China as a member, showcasing an inclusive spirit that transcended boundaries and embraced diverse global perspectives.

It is interesting to note that most of the official languages of the UN— English, French, Spanish, and Russian—originated in Europe. However, in a beautiful celebration of cultures, the international community also chose to honor the Chinese language. This move brought China's linguistic heritage to life on the global stage, highlighting its importance and reviving its unique sounds that define its culture. It is like a rebirth, where European languages, which have historically dominated, share the spotlight with China's celestial script. As we move through time, we are witnessing a remarkable rise in the significance of Arabic, gaining newfound popularity. This versatile language, filled with ancient wisdom and adorned with the elegant arabesque of its script, is taking a prominent place in various fields. It is a vivid example of how languages can change and influence the world, with Arabic making its mark on people's hearts and minds as they delve into the complex fabric of human expression. In the complex world of international communication, change is in the air. The winds of change carry the melodies of diverse cultures and a call for harmony among civilizations. The UN functions as a harmonious collaboration of nations, languages, and ideals, echoing common themes that promote mutual understanding and transcending borders. It also embraces the diverse hues of our shared cultural heritage. A form of bicameral legislature began to emerge, consisting of a lower house, sometimes referred to as the General Assembly and a more powerful but less representative upper chamber known as the Security Council. This structure was heavily influenced by Western ideas and developed through practical experience rather than intentional planning. The main responsibility of the UN was to help maintain peace based on international law norms.[24] The Law of Nations originated from European statecraft and diplomatic history. Initially, it was the law of Christian countries, later transforming into the law of civilized nations and eventually evolving into the law of developed countries. This outdated international law played a role in justifying Western colonization of other nations.

According to Mazrui, the proud Eurocentrism of the early thinkers in Western political philosophy was noticeable.[25] John Mill distinguished between cultures he believed deserved recognition under the Law of Nations and those he considered barbaric. What is even more surprising is that early socialists showed support for colonialism: Karl Marx praised Britain's control over India and Engels admired France's control over Algeria. The majority of the white world viewed these actions as "civilizational standards." Following that, the UN began to welcome new nations and cultures. For instance, Pakistan was admitted in 1947, followed by Myanmar (previously called Burma) and Sri Lanka (also known as Ceylon) in 1948 and later Malaysia and Singapore. Soon after, newly independent Arab nations (except Egypt, which was already a member) like Morocco, Tunisia, Sudan, and Algeria, as well as newly independent African nations, starting with Ghana in 1957, were also included.

Efforts were underway to establish communication within a Eurocentric framework. Eventually, additional nations and civilizations began advocating for changes to international law through the UN. Krishna Menon challenged the legitimacy of colonialism by declaring it as permanent aggression when India intervened in Goa, liberating it from Portuguese rule. The concept of domestic jurisdiction in relation to South Africa's apartheid policy diminished due to African resistance, and apartheid eventually became recognized as a global security threat.[26] Consequently, the UN became more actively involved in combating apartheid. Mazrui raises a question: Could the dominant culture, namely the West, use the UN against other nations in the post-Cold War era? Did this happen during the Gulf War? Was the UN employed by the West to justify actions that protected its oil interests? Is the West utilizing the UN in Bosnia to prevent the emergence of a strong Muslim state in the heart of Europe?

In the aftermath of the Cold War, contemporary Western theories on international relations grapple with a unique set of challenges. The present stark disparities result from historical forces, shaping three distinct paradigms: the current unipolar world, the former bipolar world of the Cold War, and the emerging multipolar world, where influential players like China and potentially India assert their power. Unfortunately, despite the diverse populations within these superpowers, none explicitly identify with a Muslim identity. This realization prompts a critical examination of the nature of a unipolar world—is it akin to the embodiment of *dar al-harb*, a domain characterized by perpetual conflict? Moreover, does the shadow of the Cold War, with its past bipolar dynamics, persist as a manifestation of *dar al-harb*? In a global landscape where non-Muslims dominate governance, does it then transform into a *dar al-harb* scenario?

These inquiries delve into the complex fabric of international relations, challenging existing paradigms. The concept of a unipolar world, where a single superpower dominates, prompts exploration into the dynamics of power and its potential implications. Does the concentration of power in one entity inherently lead to conflict and disharmony, aligning with the idea of *dar al-harb*? On the other hand, the lingering effects of the Cold War, characterized by a bipolar structure, compel a reassessment of its lasting impact. Does it endure as a persistent manifestation of *dar al-harb*, where two opposing spheres vied for supremacy, fostering an environment of perpetual tension and hostility? As we navigate the complexities of our global village, where non-Muslims predominantly govern, the inquiry expands. Does this cosmopolitan order, shaped by diverse ideologies and perspectives, fit into the concept of *dar al-harb*—a realm of perpetual conflict between Muslims and non-Muslims? Such introspection delves into the core of international relations, challenging preconceived notions and demanding a nuanced understanding of the intricate interplay among power, identity, and the pursuit of peace. In this mosaic of diverse paradigms, answers remain elusive, urging scholars and theorists to engage in a dialogue that transcends boundaries. Bridging the gap between cultures and ideologies becomes imperative, with the ultimate goal of fostering a more equitable and harmonious global order.

Acts of War, Globalization, and American Military Engagements

Mazrui points out a crucial aspect of economic globalization, emphasizing how more powerful governments consistently wield economic power to weaken the economies of less robust countries over the long term.[27] Examples such as the prevalence of Western multinational corporations and the dominance of the U.S. currency in global economic relations illustrate just a couple of the many established mechanisms contributing to this unequal relationship. Unfairly pursued financial benefits include market access, opportunities for private investment, access to raw resources, and the utilization of low-cost labor. Overall, economic globalization has exacerbated the marginalization of Africa and other nations, often pushing local economies to the edge of collapse and jeopardizing essential social services like education and healthcare.

Faced with these challenges, many Muslims turn to the Islamic moral code for guidance and comfort amid the hardships of deprivation. This spiritual and identity-driven journey within Islam has, at times, led Muslims to reorganize themselves to address their fundamental needs for survival. In Muslim-majority regions across sub-Saharan Africa, community-based groups composed of men, women, and both genders have emerged as platforms for organized action to improve the quality of life for local residents. Following the tumultuous civil war in Somalia, an intriguing phenomenon has surfaced. Islamicist networks have taken on an extraordinary role, presenting themselves as an alternative administration intricately woven into the societal fabric. Notably, there is a growing curiosity among community members who ardently embark on a quest to explore the profound teachings of Islam. Their fervent intellectual endeavors mirror the essence of these grassroots initiatives. The indomitable spirit of community reconstruction and religious revitalization converges within the confluence of these parallel streams. These paths are seamlessly intertwined, moving toward a shared destiny.[28]

Mazrui identifies one of the potentially positive outcomes of the upheaval caused by economic globalization: the reorganization of Muslims in novel ways to alleviate suffering in their communities and promote communal development. In this context, Muslims have complemented the efforts of existing developmental programs and have even collaborated with NGOs operated by Christians, all for the collective welfare.[29] However, on the flip side, fierce competition for diminishing resources has occasionally sparked major religious conflicts in some African cultures. While globalization has elevated Africa's diplomatic standing, it has also exposed the continent to risks when diplomatic efforts turn violent. The events of September 11, 2001, and August 7, 1998, underscored this shift toward violence.

The responsibility of Osama bin Laden for the atrocities on September 11, 2001, within the United States and the acts committed in East Africa on August 7, 1998, remains uncertain. Nevertheless, his name has become synonymous with infamy. Mazrui introduces the idea of distinguishing between two distinct sentiments: Osamaphobia, marked by a dislike or fear of Osama and the ideals he represents, and Osamaphilia, a concealed admiration prevalent among marginalized individuals burdened by the consequences of Israeli policies or the pervasive influence and global dominance of the United States. This differentiation prompts an exploration of the intricate nuances of human perception, political dynamics, and the pursuit of justice as we navigate the complex landscape where emotions, ideologies, and power converge.

On the ominous day of August 7, 1998, an explosion violently shook the American embassy in Nairobi, resulting in a tragic toll of over 200 Kenyan lives and 12 American lives extinguished abruptly. As perceptively noted by Mazrui, it was the resilient Kenyan people who bore the weight of this vicious assault, experiencing the dire consequences firsthand. Interestingly, the events in Nairobi and the parallel attack in Dar es Salaam served as foreboding dress rehearsals, anticipating the catastrophic events that would echo through New York and Washington D.C. a mere three years later. The heart-wrenching reality emphasizes that among the victims of the 2001 World Trade Center attack, a multitude hailed from the African continent, representing diverse nationalities. The Muslim community mourned the loss of lives belonging to Bangladeshi waiters, Nigerian investors, and individuals from the Arab world. Nevertheless, certain issues have transcended borders, permeating the collective consciousness of nations globally, and terrorism stands prominently as a testament to this global affliction. It is crucial to recognize that the roots of anger and despair experienced by those impacted by actions originating from power centers such as Washington, New York, Paris, London, and Moscow are intimately interwoven with the very causes that fuel acts of terror. This fosters a complex web of interconnectedness across nations and continents.[30]

Mazrui argues that addressing the root causes of terrorism is crucial for an effective global alliance against terrorism. The perception of a United States–Israel alliance, which disregards significant Muslim concerns, is the primary factor contributing to anti-American terrorism.[31] The Arab–Israeli conflict, at the heart of the Middle Eastern crisis, requires a comprehensive international coalition to achieve a lasting resolution. Israelis and Palestinians lack the ability to resolve their issues independently. The United States' pro-Israel stance prevents it from being an unbiased mediator. To aid both Palestinians and Israelis in finding a lasting solution, a coalition comprising members from the EU, the United States, the OIC, the League of Arab States, and Russia is necessary. Without such a collective effort, there is a risk of forgetting these critical issues.[32]

The Zionist movement once discussed founding an independent Jewish state in East Africa. As noted by Mazrui, parts of what are now Kenya and

Uganda were promised to Theodor Herzel by Joseph Chamberlain, Britain's colonial secretary, around the start of the twentieth century. The later-named White Highlands of Kenya were among the properties made available to Jews. Thankfully for East Africa, the Zionist movement was unable to come to an agreement. Jews rejected Britain's offer after receiving it. Africans in Kenya had to engage in guerilla warfare to reclaim the White Highlands, which the British labeled as terrorism. The Kenyan Jewish Highlands were almost the target of the Mau Mau conflict.[33] Despite the global prevalence of terrorism, there has not been a widespread acceptance of an act of war as a universal norm. Mazrui prompts us to reflect on whether many Americans would recognize the ongoing act of war illustrated by the Anglo-American no-fly zones over Iraq spanning the past decade. These zones effectively restrict Iraqis from operating their own aircraft within their sovereign airspace, lacking legal legitimacy or approval from the UN. If Iraqis express opposition to American or British aircraft above their territory, they face the risk of being subjected to attacks. Furthermore, Mazrui highlights instances where President Bill Clinton ordered bombings in Sudan and President Ronald Reagan initiated strikes against Libya. He also challenges the perspective of Bush administration officials on Israel's occupation of the West Bank and Gaza, a situation once characterized as "permanent aggression" by the Indian Foreign Minister. Mazrui questions whether it is both unlawful and belligerent for Israel to establish settlements on occupied land, suggesting that former President George W. Bush came close to labeling these settlements as such.

Mazrui contends that every American president since Franklin D. Roosevelt has played a role in some type of conflict. Roosevelt found himself compelled to participate in World War II. The initiation of the Korean War was influenced by Harry Truman.[34] Subsequent to the conclusion of the Korean War, Dwight Eisenhower initiated preparations for the Bay of Pigs invasion in Cuba. Both the Bay of Pigs invasion and the onset of the Vietnam War were facilitated by John F. Kennedy. Lyndon Johnson heightened the Vietnam conflict, while Richard Nixon initiated an attack on Cambodia. In a dispute with Cambodia involving a U.S. cargo ship, the Mayaguez, Gerald Ford deployed the Marines. Jimmy Carter faced severe repercussions for his attempt to quell the Iranian revolution. On the contrary, Ronald Reagan was accused of committing war crimes in Lebanon, the Caribbean, and Libya and through the destruction of a passenger plane over the Persian Gulf.[35]

During the execution of Desert Storm in the Persian Gulf, George Bush Senior initiated an attack on Panama. Subsequently, Bill Clinton, overseeing the military campaign, directed attacks on Sudan and Afghanistan, in addition to their involvement in Yugoslavia over Kosovo. According to Mazrui, the decade-long bombardment of Baghdad and the support for Israeli aggression against Palestinians over fifty years were left to George W. Bush. The younger Bush was on the brink of launching what he termed a crusade against terrorism, commencing with an attack on Afghanistan. All victims of American militarism, except for the former Yugoslavia, have emerged from the Third World. Since Franklin Roosevelt, every U.S. president has viewed going to war as a rite of passage, where acting as the Chief Executive leads to a surge in popularity among Americans. Curiously, these actions, although often involving warfare, are seldom officially labeled as acts of war by the United States, even in the case of the Vietnam War, which claimed numerous lives. A more compassionate approach to leadership rites of passage is needed in America.[36]

The phenomenon of a spike in popularity for presidents when leading a conflict prompts the question of why this occurs. Even as the concept of an act of war has not been universally embraced globally, terrorism has proliferated. However, the definition of terrorism remains restrictive, contingent on the strength of the offender or the status of the victim. It is essential to prevent the transformation of Osamaphobia into Islamophobia in the future. The call for a coalition is evident, seeking genuine peace while combating terrorism and acknowledging the innocent lives lost. Globalization, as per Mazrui, has facilitated the emergence of global moral leadership among Black and African people. The foundation of this development can be traced back to Nobel laureates in peace, including F.W. de Klerk (1994), Anwar Sadat (1978), Desmond Tutu (1984), Nelson Mandela (1994), Albert Luthuli (1960), Ralph Bunche (1950), and others throughout the years. It is noteworthy that Black Nobel laureates in economics or literature do not consistently serve as moral authorities. Globalization has led to Africans assuming leadership positions in international organizations, marking a significant shift.[37] However, Mazrui suggests the importance of distinguishing between "Africans of the land" and "Africans of the blood" in this context. Boutros Boutros-Ghali, the first African Secretary-General of the UN and a native of the continent, exemplifies this distinction. Kofi Annan, the second African Secretary-General and also a native of Africa, follows suit. It is emphasized that North Africans, like Boutros-Ghali, are not categorized as Black people but are integral parts of the African continent, connected to it through the soil rather than the blood. On the other hand, African Americans, constituting members of the Black race, are connected to Africa through the blood rather than the soil, symbolizing the African continent.[38]

Globalization has opened up new avenues for leadership on a global scale for both Africans of the soil and Africans of the blood. Prior to the appointment of the two African Secretaries-General of the UN, Africans had already given birth to a Black Director-General of UNESCO in Paris—Amadou Mahtar M'Bow, a Senegalese-born African. His overtly pro-Third World policies led to the withdrawal of the United States from UNESCO in 1985, followed by the United Kingdom, a compliant ally. The United Kingdom, however, rejoined UNESCO in 1997 after the Labour Party's resounding victory in the 1996 elections. In a momentous chapter in history, the African continent made a significant choice in 1994 by appointing Mohammed Medjauni, a distinguished Algerian, as the president of the esteemed International Court of Justice in The Hague. The vibrant 1990s witnessed visionary leadership at the World Bank from two remarkable individuals: Callisto Madivo, a Zimbabwean-born African deeply connected to the African tapestry, and Ismail Serageldin, an Egyptian-born African whose unyielding pride in his African heritage was evident. Notably, Ismail Serageldin, catching the attention and admiration of Mazrui, emerged as a significant contender in 1999, poised to assume the groundbreaking role of the first Director-General of UNESCO, marking the onset of a new era filled with possibilities for the world.[39]

Mazrui argues that for two decades, Guyana's Ramphal and Nigeria's Emeka Anyouku served as Secretaries General of the Commonwealth, formerly the British Commonwealth, representing the Third World.[40] In our interpretation, Ralph Bunche and Martin Luther King Jr. were Africans of the blood but not of the land, yet they were recognized as African American Peace Laureates. Anwar Sadat and F. W. de Klerk, as Peace Laureates, were Africans of the land but not of the blood. In contrast, Desmond Tutu, Nelson Mandela, and Albert Luthuli were authentic Africans, hailing from South Africa, while F. W. de Klerk's connection to Africa was through adoption rather than birthright. Mandela's recognition of shared ethical values marked a significant step in humanity's pursuit of moral principles, having endured a grueling twenty-seven-year imprisonment for supposed acts of terrorism before being awarded the Nobel Peace Prize.[41]

The likelihood of Osama bin Laden receiving such a prestigious accolade is highly improbable, but the prospect of his conviction by an international tribunal, similar to Slobodan Milosevic's trial from Yugoslavia, rather than by his adversaries, akin to Mandela's experience, remains a possibility.[42] During the Cold War, Africa had a brief opportunity to step into the global spotlight and temporarily escape marginalization. The intense power struggle between superpowers elevated Africa's importance in international arenas like the UN, UNESCO, and the Commonwealth. However, as the echoes of the Cold War faded, Africa found itself marginalized again, as if the world collectively pressed the pause button on globalization. In this bittersweet symphony of deglobalization, some harmonies of hope emerged. The second act of French decolonization unfolded gracefully as the Cold War's curtain fell, systematically dismantling the French informal empire in Africa with emancipatory strokes.

In the midst of shifting military dynamics in Africa and the rise of French economic ambitions toward recently liberated nations that were once part of the Warsaw Pact, a noteworthy reversal of French neocolonialism in Africa unfolds. Mazrui keenly points out that there is cause for celebration. While the path to complete independence for any part of Africa remains lengthy, the conclusion of the Cold War has sparked the commencement of a compelling second phase of decolonization in Francophone Africa. Despite the ongoing journey toward genuine liberation, the positive development lies in the transformative impact of the Cold War's conclusion, breathing vitality into the dawn of a new era in Francophone Africa's pursuit of autonomy.[43] The unfolding Phase II of French decolonization in Africa is like a story painted with contrasting hues. It presents a brighter picture of African liberation, while concurrently casting a shadow due to the Cold War's demise, leading to further marginalization of the continent within the global community. It is in this paradox that the most severe consequence of the Cold War's end for Africa surfaces—the deepening sidelining of the continent. Africa, once a stage of strategic significance that garnered earnest attention from powerful nations, now finds itself diminished in importance, with its vibrant voice muffled in the corridors of global affairs. The loss of this strategic allure stands as a poignant testament to the impact of the Cold War's conclusion. As Africa navigates this new reality, the echoes of its past significance resonate with a touch of melancholy.[44]

In the realm of international relations and the UN, former Warsaw Pact nations, once aligned with socialist principles, now exhibit a greater inclination to appease the West than to champion causes of the Third World. Africa, with its significant one-third representation in the UN, faces a transformed landscape since 1990, witnessing the addition of almost twenty new members, of which only two are African (Namibia and Eritrea). Within this intricate transformation, entities such as Czechoslovakia, the former Soviet Republics, and the dissolved Yugoslavia have splintered into new trajectories. Former Cold War adversaries of the West have evolved into competitors, actively seeking Western resources within the African context. Africa, however, experiences unequal treatment, as former Warsaw Pact countries receive more significant assistance and investment. The advent of "market Marxism" in China and Vietnam, as underscored by Mazrui, has turned these nations into flourishing hubs for Western resources, diverting attention and resources away from longstanding Western allies in Africa. Additionally, the collapse of the USSR and the conclusion of the Cold War have paved the way for India's increased liberalization, attracting heightened Western investment and aid, inevitably impacting Africa's own prospects. In this context of global shifts, Africa grapples with the challenging consequences of evolving dynamics in resource allocation and investment patterns.

The end of the Cold War has dealt a blow to the traditional Western rationale of "enlightened self-interest," resulting in a gradual reduction of financial commitments by Western governments to international aid initiatives. The diminished incentive for providing assistance abroad, in the absence of competition from the USSR, has led to a decline in the globalization of African education since the end of the Cold War. The once-vibrant era of offering numerous scholarships for African students to pursue studies in cities like Moscow, Prague, Warsaw, Budapest, and Belgrade is now fading. Funding for such opportunities in Western nations has been significantly slashed, leaving aspiring African scholars with limited alternatives. The consequential shift in global education dynamics has profound implications within the African academic landscape.[45]

Financial support for Western visiting professors has been substantially curtailed, signaling the conclusion of an era where Czech, Hungarian, and Polish academics lectured in African colleges. Africa now lacks a cornerstone of its foreign orientation, just as the West has lost one of its main pillars of foreign policy with the end of the Cold War. While the nonaligned movement remains robust in the post-Cold War era, questions arise about the applicability of the term "nonalignment" to African policy today. Former Cold War adversaries of the West have transformed into rivals for Western resources in Africa, with former Warsaw Pact nations receiving more aid and investment than Africa itself. The emergence of market Marxism has turned China and Vietnam into new hubs for Western resources, diverting attention and resources away from longstanding Western allies in Africa.[46]

Western Culture, Islam, and Censorship

Mazrui devotes significant attention to civil liberties in his exploration of globalization, with censorship being a compelling focal point. He highlights that a book can be prohibited for various reasons, one being the morally objectionable nature of its content. For instance, Salman Rushdie's

The Satanic Verses faced bans in numerous Muslim nations due to its perceived blasphemy and moral offensiveness. Another reason for prohibiting a book may stem from the perceived moral repugnance of its author.[47] The case of the book titled *Goebbels, Mastermind of the Third Reich*, slated for release by St. Martin's Press in 1996, exemplifies this. Intense global pressure was exerted on St. Martin's Press to ban the book, with the criticism directed at the author, David Irving, for being an anti-Semitic revisionist historian of the Holocaust. Despite the likelihood that those pressuring the publisher had not read the book's draft, it was ultimately David Irving's reputation that played a pivotal role in convincing St. Martin's Press to reconsider and withdraw the publication. Mazrui introduces the concept of the opposite of a "clear and present danger," where a book is restricted or prohibited based on potential implications. He points out that the West was unsympathetic when India cited this justification for preventing the publication of Rushdie's Satanic Verses, claiming that it could incite religious fervor. Despite prior warnings from India about the provocative nature of the book, Rushdie's publishers did not heed them. The release of the book in 1989 led to civic unrest and fatalities in Bombay, Islamabad, and Karachi.[48]

In contrast, there are instances where prestigious Western publishers have rejected submissions due to concerns for the well-being of their own workers. For example, Cambridge University Press rejected Anastasia Karakasidou's book *Fields of Wheat, Rivers of Blood*, which delved into ethnicity in Macedonia, a Greek region. In Mazrui's perspective, the rejection by Cambridge and the human cost associated with *The Satanic Verses* could have been minimized if the publisher of Rushdie's book had exhibited the same level of concern for Asian lives as Cambridge University Press demonstrated for its employees in Greece. Censorship in Muslim nations often takes on a crude form, orchestrated by various entities such as governments, clerics, religious scholars, and more recently, militant Islamist organizations. In contrast, censorship in the West adopts a more sophisticated and decentralized approach. Multiple actors, including viewers of the Public Broadcasting System, advertisers for commercial television, ethnic pressure groups, interest organizations, editors, publishers, and other custodians of communication channels, contribute to this nuanced system. Additionally, European governments occasionally engage in censorship practices.

The critique of Mazrui oversimplifying the diversity within Western nations stems from the observation that his exploration lacks a comprehensive analysis of the full spectrum of censorship practices across these countries. Mazrui uses the rejection of Salman Rushdie's *The Satanic Verses* to illustrate censorship in the West; however, this specific instance does not provide a comprehensive representation of the diverse array of censorship policies and practices prevalent in Western nations. Western countries display significant variations in their approaches to censorship, shaped by a range of legal, cultural, and societal norms. Some nations prioritize freedom of expression with liberal stances, while others enact more restrictive policies, considering factors such as public morality or national security. By focusing predominantly on a singular example, Mazrui's discussion may fail to capture the intricate complexity inherent in the various censorship approaches within Western democracies.

For example, in the United States, the preservation of freedom of speech stands as a core principle of the country's democratic values, explicitly detailed in the initial amendment of the U.S. Constitution. This constitutional emphasis is reflected in a legal framework generally more accommodating toward freedom of expression compared to certain other Western nations.[49] The First Amendment provides robust safeguards for a variety of expressions, spanning verbal communication, written text, symbolic gestures, and artistic creations, even those that might be considered controversial or provocative. The U.S. legal system staunchly opposes prior restraint, discouraging the government from intervening to prevent the publication or dissemination of speech before it occurs, preferring to address potential issues through legal channels after the expression has taken place. It is worth noting the clear distinction between private and government censorship; while the First Amendment limits government censorship, private entities like organizations or platforms may enforce their content guidelines, sparking discussions about the role of private censorship, especially in the digital age. Despite the extensive protection, specific speech categories remain beyond the shield of the First Amendment, including obscenity, incitement to violence, and "fighting words" capable of immediately provoking a violent response. Legal challenges may arise within this permissive framework, and the courts play a crucial role in balancing the right to unrestricted expression with societal considerations, including public safety and individual privacy.[50]

In the EU, there is a diverse array of approaches to censorship laws and practices among member states, underscoring the intricacies of the issue. For instance, Germany has implemented stringent laws against hate speech, demonstrating a dedication to combating discriminatory content. These laws are designed to foster social harmony and prevent the incitement of hatred based on protected characteristics.[51] In contrast, Nordic countries within the EU, including Sweden, Denmark, and Finland, often prioritize freedom of information. This emphasis reflects a commitment to ensuring open access to knowledge and adopting a more permissive stance on the dissemination of information. The varying approaches within EU nations highlight the nuanced and multifaceted nature of censorship policies in the union. The EU's framework allows for flexibility, recognizing the diverse cultural, legal, and historical contexts that shape the individual member states' approaches to the regulation of expression.

The United Kingdom adheres to a longstanding tradition of reconciling the principle of freedom of expression with constraints on specific content, as exemplified by legislation against hate speech. This nuanced approach to censorship is ingrained in the country's regulatory landscape. The United Kingdom's legal framework aims to delicately balance the imperative of fostering diverse viewpoints with the necessity of curbing the dissemination of harmful or discriminatory content. Hate speech laws are crafted to address expressions targeting individuals or groups based on protected characteristics, fostering an environment that promotes societal cohesion and inclusivity. The United Kingdom's approach underscores an ongoing commitment to navigating the complexities of free expression while concurrently safeguarding individuals and communities from potential harms associated with certain forms of speech. In this historical and legal context, the United Kingdom demonstrates its dedication to a nuanced and equitable approach to censorship, situated within the broader framework of democratic values and societal well-being.[52]

France upholds a unique approach to censorship, placing a significant emphasis on the protection of freedom of expression as a fundamental value. However, this dedication to free speech is not absolute, and there are instances where legal measures are applied to restrict content deemed offensive or harmful. Notably, the country has instituted laws against hate speech, with the aim of curbing the dissemination of discriminatory content based on factors such as race, religion, ethnicity, or other protected characteristics. These legal provisions are crafted to maintain social harmony and prevent the incitement of hatred. Additionally, France criminalizes Holocaust denial, demonstrating a commitment to preserving historical truth and preventing the propagation of revisionist narratives.[53] The nation has also enacted anti-terrorism legislation, providing authorities with the means to swiftly address content associated with extremist ideologies. While France leans toward favoring freedom of expression, its legal framework allows for restrictions when deemed necessary to protect public order, such as by prohibiting public demonstrations or speeches that may pose a threat to safety. Legal actions against offensive or blasphemous art further underscore the delicate balance sought between artistic freedom and respect for societal values. France's nuanced approach to censorship manifests a commitment to striking a balance between individual liberties and the prevention of harm or offense, thereby navigating the complexities inherent in managing the tensions between free speech and societal well-being.

A comprehensive evaluation of how censorship is managed across various Western nations provides a nuanced understanding of the complex interplay involving legal frameworks, cultural values, and societal expectations. This analytical approach significantly contributes to a more in-depth comprehension of the varied methods employed in approaching censorship within the Western context. Examining how different countries navigate the delicate balance between the freedom of expression and the prevention of harm or offense offers valuable insights into the complex dynamics that influence the regulation of speech and content in democratic societies. This multifaceted analysis facilitates a deeper exploration of the factors that shape censorship practices, encompassing historical legacies, legal traditions, and the evolving cultural landscapes of individual nations. Ultimately, it results in a comprehensive understanding of censorship within the Western context, emphasizing the diverse approaches and the ongoing dialogue regarding the boundaries of free expression in democratic societies.

Intersections of Violence, Globalization, and Islam

Within the discussion of violence and Islam, Mazrui explores a realm often neglected in conversations about Islamic fundamentalism and Arab terrorism. A notable paradox emerges from the shadows of the twentieth century—the potential clash between Islam's inclination toward political violence and Western culture's prevalence of street crime. While Western civilization contends with an excess of street crime, Islam appears to give rise to a disproportionate number of *mujahidin*. These contradictions raise profound questions about the trade-offs between the liberal state's excesses and those of the Islamic state and how they influence the quality of life for ordinary citizens.[54] In his thought-provoking exploration, Mazrui examines the evolving dynamics within the Western liberal state, revealing a perplexing reality—citizens are increasingly shielded from their governments yet progressively vulnerable to each other. As life in the West adopts a harsher edge, societal transformations give rise to growing social unrest, even amid political contention in certain corners of the Muslim world. Mazrui invites us to contemplate alternative paths, drawing inspiration from indigenous traditions and pre-modern ideals that have found resonance, as seen in places like the Islamic Republic of Iran. Can these solutions be applicable beyond the confines of a single civilization? Tehran, the vibrant capital of

Iran, teeming with a population exceeding ten million, presents a compelling paradox. Despite its history tainted by political violence during periods of war and revolution, it stands relatively less affected than the power hubs of Washington, D.C., or the bustling streets of New York City. Mazrui suggests that the Iranian government may pose fewer threats to its citizens compared to the United States, yet Iranians find a unique form of protection within their society—a morality deeply rooted in anti-modernist values. Mazrui raises a probing question: Can the Muslim world navigate its challenges through the lens of postmodernist ideas? Is it plausible to embrace the benefits of Westernization while skillfully sidestepping its pitfalls? In contrast, Cairo, a thriving metropolis symbolizing Westernization in Africa, stands in stark comparison to Johannesburg. Despite its larger size, Cairo experiences notably lower levels of street violence, inviting contemplation on the role of Islam in upholding the city's peace. How far back in history does this tranquility extend? Perhaps, the complexity inherent in these intricate measurements has been underestimated. Mazrui leads us on an intellectual journey, confronting these paradoxes directly, unraveling the mysteries that lie at the crossroads of violence, globalization, and Islam.[55]

Cultural Globalization: Struggles, Contradictions, and Muslim Responses

The economic and political structures molded by the currents of globalization carry their unique set of values and beliefs, constituting an aspect of what can be labeled as cultural globalization.[56] Despite facing widespread criticism for its role in environmental degradation, the United States consistently opts out of international environmental protection pacts, driven by the neoliberal ideology prioritizing business concerns over societal well-being. This stance has elicited escalating disapproval from the global civil society. Similarly, there is a pervasive global censure for the Machiavellian principles guiding American foreign policy. Mazrui cites the example of how the United States approaches the promotion of democracy in the "Third World." While advocating for liberal democracy on a global scale, the United States has been known to leverage its influence to impede the democratic election of Islamic parties, exemplified in the case of Algeria. When discussing the impact of globalization on the Muslim world, Mazrui underscores the persistent presence of American forces in nations like Saudi Arabia since the Gulf War in 1990.[57] Recent developments, such as granting foreign businesses, including those from the United States, the ability to acquire land, sponsor their personnel, and enjoy privileges previously exclusive to Saudi corporations, may stem from the Saudi royal family's desire to strengthen ties with the United States in response to criticism from a burgeoning capitalist faction within its own class. However, this move could also incite internal dissent under the guise of Islam. The amalgamation of the survivalist objectives of the Saudi family and global American neoliberal interests is fostering tumultuous conditions in the core of Islam, contributing to a more diverse face of terrorism as American (and Western) economic, political, and military engagements persist in their global expansion.

The unsettling repercussions of cultural globalization have deeply affected the morals, customs, traditions, and identity of "other" societies. This impact is a result of the overwhelming sway of assimilating cultures, propelled either by proselytizing agendas or as an unintended outcome of various forms of dominance, be it economic, military, or political forces. With the progression of cultural globalization, it has essentially become synonymous with the dissemination of Western values and practices. Mazrui observes that the Muslim response to the ramifications of economic and political globalization tends to be primarily rooted within national boundaries, molded by the internal dynamics of each nation. Nevertheless, even when articulated within a national context, Muslim reactions to cultural globalization exhibit a noteworthy inclination to transcend borders, adopting an inter-national and, at times, a global perspective. This underscores the authentic emergence of an international wave of Islamic consciousness, instigated by the influences of cultural globalization.[58]

In the contemporary era, advancements in technology offer the potential for increased interaction among Muslims worldwide, especially those in the middle and upper echelons of society. This facilitates the establishment of new connections geared toward enhancing welfare, trade, and commercial activities. With leadership predominantly emerging from the middle class, this interconnected network breathes fresh vitality into the transnational nationalism of the Muslim *ummah*. Its primary objective revolves around resisting Western cultural imperialism and purging perceived Western capitalist principles from the global Muslim community. However, this pan-Muslim nationalism grapples with internal conflicts and tensions, echoing the challenges faced by other nationalistic movements. A notable inconsistency lies in the treatment of women, where various interpretations of Islamic texts across the Muslim world exhibit unmistakable patriarchal tendencies, mirroring patterns in other religions. The most extreme form of Islamic fundamentalism, marked by absolutism, constructs systems purportedly in the name of "true Islam," simultaneously subjugating Muslim women while vehemently striving to "liberate" the Muslim world from Western imperialism.

Mazrui emphasizes that within the backdrop of globalization, it is frequently overlooked that Islamic reformers themselves fell victim to the absolutism of Islamic fundamentalism. Presently, some Muslim philosophers seek a renewed understanding of Islamic teachings in light of the contemporary world's realities and challenges.[59] They contend that the Islamic message is inherently dual—partly specific to historical contexts and partly universal. According to this viewpoint, the relativist aspects of Islam, including stringent penalties, were intended exclusively for seventh-century Arabs. In contrast, the other facet of Islam is believed to convey timeless and universal principles. The challenge of Islamic scholarship lies in distinguishing the relativistic from the universal within Islamic ideas through the practice of *ijtihād*. It is asserted that the full revelation of what is global can only unfold with the passage of historical time. Some reformers have taken an unconventional stance, asserting that modern capital punishment is no longer in alignment with Islamic principles. They argue that society is no longer permitted to play God and take a human life, citing the illumination of root causes of crime and violence by history. These reformers also strive to provide fresh interpretations of Islamic teachings, challenging the more traditional and patriarchal views that still keep Muslim women in servitude. As pointed out by Mazrui, fundamentalist Islamist groups have reportedly completely withdrawn from local politics and ongoing struggles for new national constitutions, and, in some cases, more democratic systems.[60] They firmly believe that engaging in these political activities is incompatible with Islam, asserting that the Qur'ān serves as the primary source of Muslim law and that the only legitimate political order is one grounded in the concepts of *tawhīd* (God's unity), *risalat* (Prophethood), and *khilafah* (Vicegerency of man). Additionally, the traditions of *shurā* (consultation), *ijmā'* (consensus), and *ijtihād* (independent interpretative judgment) are considered as endorsed by democracy.

The Intersection of Islam and Western Culture

The current ramifications of hegemonization and homogeneity present a negative outlook for the Muslim world. However, Mazrui raises the intriguing question of whether homogeneity could ever be advantageous for Islam, suggesting that it might be beneficial only if Islamic principles were to spread globally. He poses a critical query: Can Muslims effectively communicate their ideals without strictly adhering to their religion? Mazrui contends that one can share Islamic principles without necessarily adopting the Muslim faith. As an illustration, after World War I, the United States briefly aligned with Muslim opposition to alcohol and endorsed the eighteenth Constitutional Amendment, prohibiting it in 1919. However, this stance was not widely embraced, and it took over a decade for the twenty-first Constitutional Amendment, legalizing alcohol, to be ratified after Al Capone's exploits. Mazrui ponders whether American attitudes toward Islamic principles will undergo another shift in the twenty-first century. In a historical context, the Muslim presence had a profound impact on the Western world, imprinting its influence on intellectual and scientific domains. This epoch saw the infusion of Arabic eloquence into Western scientific lexicons, introducing terms like algebra and cipher, sparking an era of enlightenment. The initial half of the twentieth century played a pivotal role in shaping the cultural Westernization of the Muslim world, laying the groundwork for its destiny. As the tapestry of time unfolded into the latter half of the twentieth century, a captivating transformation occurred— the mosaic of Islam gradually interwove with the fabric of the West, giving rise to a demographic Islamization. This journey explores two distinct stages in the intricate interplay between Europe and Islam, spanning from the ancient city of Kano to the bustling streets of Karachi, from majestic Cairo to vibrant Kuala Lumpur, and from charismatic Dakar to enchanting Jakarta. The West assumed an imperial role, colonizing over two-thirds of the Muslim world and leaving an indomitable legacy in the first half of the twentieth century.[61]

The disintegration of the Ottoman Empire unfolded in the first half of the twentieth century, marking a more comprehensive de-Islamization of the European state structure. This period witnessed the abolition of the Caliphate, a symbolic seat of Islamic power. The resulting fragmentation of the *ummah* rendered it more susceptible to Western cultural infiltration. Various factors fueled the cultural Westernization of the Muslim world, encompassing the transformation of Islamic and Qur'ānic schools into Western-style institutions, the adoption of European languages in certain Muslim countries, and the pervasive influence of Western media on news and information, spanning magazines, movies, television, and the modern computer age. Homogenization emerged in response to the pressures of hegemonization. A significant impact was also attributed to Western technology, introducing not just new skills but also new ideals. This globalization of cultural facets, however, predominantly took on an American and Eurocentric character.

Mazrui argues that other civilizations gradually assimilate a feature of Western culture presented as universal, leading to the triumph of hegemony and the emergence of an unofficial cultural empire. Examples such as the Gregorian calendar and the global clothing code for males illustrate Eurocentric world culture that has attained global prominence, offering glimpses into potential future trends. The Western Christian calendar has been widely adopted by nations in Africa and Asia, shaping their Independence Day celebrations and historical records. Even in Muslim nations, Sunday is often observed as the day of rest instead of Friday.[62] Some societies have replaced the Hijra with the Christian calendar, reperiodizing the entirety of Islamic historiography. The second half of the twentieth century witnessed the construction of a new human Islamic presence through Muslim immigration to the West and Western conversions to Islam. Currently, there are 30 million Muslims residing in Europe, with 10 million in Western Europe, excluding the approximately 84 million Muslims in the Republic of Turkey. New mosques have emerged from Marseille to Munich. Paradoxically, the cultural Westernization of the Muslim world has contributed to the demographic Islamization of the West.

The cultural Westernization of Muslims has paved the way for a brain drain of professionals and specialists from Muslim nations to North America and Europe, facilitated by the ancient Western formal empires. Some of the world's top Muslim professionals have been drawn to careers in Europe or North America, marking the first half of the twentieth century as a period of cultural Westernization in the Muslim world. This, in turn, set the stage for the demographic Islamization of the West in the second half of the century. However, not all Muslim immigrants to the West hold advanced degrees. In a postcolonial demographic interplay, the echoes of Western colonialism provided opportunities for less qualified Muslims from countries like Pakistan, India, Bangladesh, and Algeria to embark on journeys to Britain and France. There were instances when the West intentionally beckoned less qualified Muslim immigrants to meet its economic ambitions, seeking an affordable labor reservoir. One notable example is the influx of Turkish laborers into the Federal Republic of Germany during the transformative decades of the 1960s and 1970s, where destiny intertwined with opportunity, borders blurred, and cultures intertwined in the timeless dance of human migration.[63]

In the United States alone, there are already more than a thousand mosques and Qur'ānic centers, along with professional organizations for Muslim scientists and educators—an illustration of the ongoing demographic Islamization of the West. The Muslim population in the United States has surpassed 6 million and continues to grow impressively. Since the turn of the century, Muslims have outnumbered Jews in the United States, positioning Islam as the fastest growing religion in North America. In France, Islam holds the second-highest number of adherents, with Catholicism ranking first. Muslims in Britain advocate for public funding for Muslim-only schools, and some explore options for their Islamic parliament. Germany, which invited Turkish workers in the 1970s, now finds itself hosting the muezzin and the minaret. Australia, bordering the most populous Muslim country, Indonesia, has also discovered the presence of Islam within its political system. Historically labeled as part of the Judeo-Christian civilization in the twentieth century, the Western world may see a shift, with Islam potentially surpassing Judaism as the second most significant Abrahamic religion after Christianity. Despite future immigration laws, Islam may eventually outnumber Judaism in much of the West.[64]

The portrayal of Islam in Western classrooms, textbooks, and media has become a crucial issue as Islam increasingly integrates into Western culture. The education system in the Muslim world has predominantly embraced Westernization, prompting the question of whether it is time for Western education to incorporate certain Islamic practices. The ongoing interpenetration between Islam and Europe raises the question of whether this marks a new threshold in globalization or is merely another manifestation of the postcolonial predicament that has shaped world history. In reality, it could be a combination of both. While the counter-infiltration of Muslims and Islam into Western culture alone may not bring an end to Western hegemony, a robust Islamic presence in the West has the potential to impede the process of cultural homogeneity. As a new moral calculus takes shape on the global stage, conflicting values, competing appetites, and converging viewpoints are expected to unfold.

Conclusion

In his scholarly exploration of the interplay between globalization and Islam, Mazrui offers a comprehensive and nuanced understanding of the complex dynamics where these phenomena intersect. Delving into the economic, political, and cultural dimensions of globalization, Mazrui provides insight into the challenges and opportunities that arise within Muslim communities globally. In the realm of economic globalization, Mazrui draws attention to the nuanced power dynamics between dominant and weaker nations, shedding light on how more powerful governments exploit their economic prowess. This exploitation occurs through various channels, such as the influence wielded by Western multinational corporations and the supremacy of the U.S. currency, perpetuating an imbalanced relationship marked by systemic inequalities. These imbalances confer undue advantages upon economically powerful nations, including preferential market access, increased opportunities for private investment, unimpeded access to vital raw resources, and the exploitative utilization of cheap labor. In contrast, weaker economies bear the brunt of this asymmetry, enduring prolonged economic instability and marginalization within the global economic framework. Mazrui's scholarly analysis emphasizes the imperative of critically examining these exploitative mechanisms and the urgent need to rectify the inherent imbalances within the prevailing global economic order.[65]

Nevertheless, in the face of these formidable challenges, Mazrui's scholarly investigation reveals the resilience and ingenuity displayed by Muslim communities as they navigate the complex landscapes of globalization. He underscores the emergence of grassroots associations in predominantly Muslim regions of sub-Saharan Africa, serving as vibrant and inclusive platforms for collective action aimed at improving the well-being of individuals and society at large. These associations, known for their inclusivity across gender lines, act as catalysts for community-driven initiatives that transcend the constraints imposed by economic globalization. In adversity, Muslim communities showcase remarkable adaptability and resourcefulness by forming strategic alliances, confronting societal hardships, and fostering a tapestry of communal progress. Mazrui's scholarly insights inspire acknowledgment and celebration of the inherent capacity for resilience within Muslim communities, instilling hope for a future where innovative solutions and collective solidarity counteract the adversities imposed by dominant global forces.

Expanding the analysis to include the political and cultural dimensions of globalization, Mazrui sheds light on the guiding principles shaping interactions among nations benefiting from this global phenomenon. Specifically, he critically examines the United States' approach to environmental protection policies and foreign affairs. The bold refusal of the United States to engage in international environmental accords, driven by a neoliberal ideology prioritizing economic interests over social and environmental welfare, has prompted widespread international consternation and generated increasing indignation within global civil society. Additionally, the United States' selective endorsement of liberal democratic values, juxtaposed with its inclination to manipulate democratic processes to hinder the rise of Islamic parties, as seen in the case of Algeria, illustrates the intricate web of American hypocrisy and inconsistent standards permeating its interactions with other nations. Mazrui's scholarly analysis calls for introspection and remedial action, advocating for a principled approach to global politics that upholds moral standards and equitable practices.[66]

Mazrui emphasizes the urgent necessity to confront entrenched power imbalances within the global economic system, champion the resilience of Muslim communities amid adversity, and advocate for a more equitable and inclusive approach to globalization. In recognizing the myriad challenges and opportunities stemming from economic, political, and cultural globalization, concerted endeavors can be undertaken to construct a global framework that embraces cultural diversity, rectifies social and economic disparities, and nurtures a world characterized by justice and sustainability. Mazrui's analytical insights prompt critical reflection on the impact of globalization, compelling collective action toward a future marked by enhanced justice and sustainability.

Addressing the structural inequalities perpetuated by globalization requires a holistic and collaborative approach, involving active participation from governments, international organizations, civil society, and individuals. Collective efforts are imperative to formulate policies and practices prioritizing economic fairness, social inclusivity, and cultural diversity. This entails establishing a global economic order emphasizing equitable trade, encouraging investment in weaker economies, and safeguarding workers' rights across borders. Additionally, supporting and acknowledging initiatives undertaken by Muslim communities to address societal challenges holds paramount importance. Grassroots associations and community-driven projects play a pivotal role in promoting individual and societal well-being, necessitating governments and international organizations to provide requisite resources, support, and platforms for these initiatives to flourish. Empowering communities, facilitating knowledge exchange, and fostering collaboration can harness the positive potential of globalization to advance communal progress.[67]

In the political sphere, a commitment to transparency, accountability, and ethical decision-making stands as a crucial imperative. Addressing issues such as the manipulation of democratic processes, selective endorsement of liberal democracy, and the disregard for human rights by influential nations is essential and requires proactive rectification. It is imperative to advocate for a values-based approach to international relations—one rooted in principles of justice, equality, and respect for sovereignty. Such an approach is crucial for fostering constructive interactions among nations and promoting global stability. Moreover, the era of cultural globalization demands a nuanced understanding that appreciates the diversity and vitality of different civilizations. While the widespread dissemination of Western culture has undoubtedly left a significant imprint, it is equally important to safeguard and celebrate the distinct identities, values, and traditions of non-Western societies. Encouraging cultural exchange, nurturing dialogue, and supporting initiatives aimed at preserving cultural heritage play vital roles in fostering mutual understanding, appreciation, and coexistence. The realization of true inclusivity and a harmonious global society hinges upon the acknowledgment and celebration of cultural diversity.

Mazrui's exploration of globalization and Islam unveils the complex dynamics among economic, political, and cultural forces, shedding light on the myriad challenges and opportunities encountered by Muslims globally. Proposing a shift toward a fairer and more holistic approach to globalization, one that prioritizes economic equity, empowers communities, adheres to ethical principles, and embraces cultural diversity, presents a pathway toward a more just, inclusive, and sustainable global order. The chapter's findings resonate as a call to action, imploring stakeholders at every level to collaborate toward a future where the advantages of globalization are equitably distributed and where the values of justice, equality, and respect shape our interactions and mold our world.

Notes

1. Bwesigye bwa Mwesigire, "5 Strategies for De-Westernising Globalization, by Ali Mazrui." Accessed April 14, 2024. https://thisisafrica.me/politics-and-society/5-strategies-de-westernising-globalization-ali-mazrui/.

2. Ali Mazrui, "From Slave Ship to Space Ship: Africa between Marginalization and Globalization," *African Studies Quarterly* 2, no. 4 (1999): 6–9.

3. IAN, "Who was Professor Ali Mazrui?" Accessed April 14, 2024. https://web.archive.org/web/20141016004156/http://www.independent.co.ug/ugandatalks/2014/10/who-was-professor-ali-mazrui/.

4. Winifred E. Akoda, "The Contributions of Ali Mazrui to African Historical Scholarship," *International Journal of Humanities Social Sciences and Education (IJHSSE)* 2, no. 6 (2015): 65

5. Akoda, "The Contributions of Ali Mazrui," 67.

6. Ali Mazrui, "Top Kenyan Academic, Dies in the U.S.," *BBC News*. Accessed April 14, 2024. https://www.bbc.com/news/world-africa-29595175.

7. Melinda C. Shepherd, "Ali Al Amin Mazrui: Kenyan-American Political Scientist," *Encyclopedia Britannica*. Accessed April 14, 2024. https://www.britannica.com/biography/Ali-Al-Amin-Mazrui.

8. Shepherd, "Ali Al Amin Mazrui."

9. Shepherd, "Ali Al Amin Mazrui."

10. Ali A. Mazrui, *Globalization: Origins and Scope*, University of Georgia Series on Globalization and Global Understanding (Athens, GA: The Center for Humanities and Arts and The Center for International Trade and Security, Georgia, 2001), 2.

11. Mazrui, *Globalization: Origins and Scope*, 3.

12. Salahudin Kafrawi, Alamin M. Mazrui, and Ruzima Sebuharra, "Globalization, Islam and the West: Between Homogenisation and Hegemonisation," in *Islam between Globalization and Counterterrorism*, ed. Salahudin Kafrawi, Alamin M. Mazrui, and Ruzima Sebuharra (Oxford: James Currey, 2006), 268.

13. Majid Khadduri, *The Islamic Law of Nations: Shaybani's Siyur* (Baltimore, MD: Johns Hopkins Press, 1966), 11–13.

14. Khadduri, *The Islamic Law of Nations*, 11–12.

15. Khadduri, *The Islamic Law of Nations*, 13.

16. Khadduri, *The Islamic Law of Nations*, 14.

17. Charles W. Mayncs, "America's Third World Hang-ups," *Foreign Policy* 71 (1988): 117.

18. Burns H. Weston, "Security Council Resolution 678 and Persian Gulf Decision Making: Precarious Legitimacy," *American Journal of International Law* 85, no. 3 (1991): 516–535.

19. Eric Rouleau, "America's Unyielding Policy Toward Iraq," *Foreign Affairs* 74, no. 1 (1995): 59–72.

20. Rouleau, "America's Unyielding Policy," 63.

21. Steve Platt, "Sanctions Don't Harm Saddam," *New Statesman and Society* 7 (1994): 10.

22. Ali Mazrui, "Globalization, Islam, and the West: Between Homogenization and Hegemonization," *American Journal of Islamic Social Sciences* 15, no. 3 (1998): 7.

23. Mazrui, "Globalization, Islam, and the West," 8.

24. Mazrui, "Globalization, Islam, and the West," 8.

25. Mazrui, "Globalization, Islam, and the West," 8.

26. Mazrui, "Globalization, Islam, and the West," 9.

27. Ali A. Mazrui, "Globalization Between the Market and the Military: A Third World Perspective," *Journal of Third World Studies* 19, no. 1 (2002): 13–24.

28. Mazrui, "Globalization Between the Market," 15.

29. Mazrui, "Globalization Between the Market," 17.

30. US Department of State, "24th Anniversary of the 1998 Embassy Bombings." Accessed April 14, 2024. https://www.state.gov/24th-anniversary-of-the-1998-embassy-bombings/.

31. Mazrui, "Globalization Between the Market," 17.

32. Aaron David Miller, "Arab-Israeli Progress Seemed Impossible. That's Because of Old Assumptions," Carnegie Endowment for Peace. Accessed April 14, 2024. https://carnegieendowment.org/2020/09/23/arab-israeli-progress-seemed-impossible.-that-s-because-of-old-assumptions-pub-82798.

33. Asher Naim, "Perspectives—Jomo Kenyatta and Israel," *Jewish Political Studies Review* 17, no. 3/4 (2005): 75–80.

34. Mazrui, "Globalization Between the Market," 17.

35. Lou Cannon, "Ronald Reagan: Foreign Affairs." Accessed April 14, 2024. https://millercenter.org/president/reagan/foreign-affairs.

36. Ali A. Mazrui, "Globalization and Cross-Cultural Values: The Politics of Identity and Judgment," *Arab Studies Quarterly* 21, no. 3 (1999): 103.
37. Mazrui, *Globalization: Origins and Scope*, 4.
38. Mazrui, *Globalization: Origins and Scope*, 5.
39. Kelechi Johnmary Ani, "Globalization and Its Impact on African Political Culture," *World Affairs: The Journal of International Issues* 17, no. 2 (2013): 44–61.
40. Mazrui, *Globalization: Origins and Scope*, 6.
41. Mazrui, *Globalization: Origins and Scope*, 7.
42. Mazrui, "Globalization Between the Market," 18.
43. Mazrui, "Globalization Between the Market," 19.
44. Mazrui, "From Slave Ship to Space Ship," 7.
45. Mazrui, "From Slave Ship to Space Ship," 8.
46. Mazrui, "From Slave Ship to Space Ship," 9.
47. Ali A. Mazrui, "Wole Soyinka as a Television Critic: A Parable of Deception," *Transition* 54 (1991): 165–177.
48. Mazrui, "Globalization and Cross-Cultural Values," 103.
49. Emily Howie, "Protecting the Human Right to Freedom of Expression in International Law," *International Journal of Speech-Language Pathology* 20, no. 1 (2018): 12–15.
50. Andrew Jensen Kerr, "Art Threats and First Amendment Disruption," *Duke Journal of Constitutional Law and Public Policy* 16 (2021): 173–212.
51. David Little, *Essays on Religion and Human Rights: Ground to Stand On* (Cambridge: Cambridge University Press, 2015), 81–198.
52. Marcel Maussen and Ralph Grillo, "Regulation of Speech in Multicultural Societies: Introduction," *Journal of Ethnic and Migration Studies* 40, no. 2 (2014): 174–193.
53. Yucheng Xue, "French Content Moderation and Platform Liability Policies." Accessed April 14, 2024. https://jsis.washington.edu/news/french-content-moderation-and-platform-liability-policies/.
54. Mazrui, "Globalization and Cross-Cultural Values," 103.
55. Mazrui, "Globalization and Cross-Cultural Values," 104.
56. Mazrui, "Globalization and Cross-Cultural Values," 105.
57. Bahgat Gawdat, "Managing Dependence: America-Saudi Oil Relations," *Arab Studies Quarterly* 23, no. 1 (2001): 1–14.
58. Mazrui, "Globalization Between the Market," 20.
59. Mazrui, "Globalization Between the Market," 21.
60. Mazrui, "Globalization Between the Market," 22.
61. Mazrui, "Globalization, Islam, and the West," 10.
62. Mazrui, "Globalization, Islam, and the West," 11.
63. Mazrui, "Globalization and Cross-Cultural Values," 99.
64. Mazrui, "Globalization, Islam, and the West," 14.

65. Ali Mazrui, "Globalizing Africa and The Commonwealth: Four Ethical Revolutions," in *Globalizing Africa*, ed. Malinda S. Smith (Trenton, NJ and Asmara: Africa World Press), 27–45.
66. Mazrui, "Globalizing Africa," 29.
67. Mazrui, "Globalizing Africa," 29.

CHAPTER 6

~

Islam and the Globalization Paradox

Akbar Ahmad's Reflections on Crisis and Resilience

Introduction

This chapter offers a thorough and in-depth examination of Akbar S. Ahmad's distinctive perspectives on the multifaceted phenomenon of globalization, providing detailed analysis of his insights and observations. Ahmad posits that the manifestations of globalization in developing countries elicit a dual response of fascination and repulsion. The desire for improved economic growth, enhanced transportation networks, and access to diverse commodities coexists with exposure to foreign nations and cultures through global media, generating feelings of anger and alienation when perceived as unfamiliar or potentially dangerous. Ahmad's seminal work, *Journey into Islam: The Crisis of Globalization*, focuses on how the Muslim world responds to globalization. Within this context, individuals in the Muslim world often experience fear as they contrast the poverty in their nations with the wealth of Western CEOs or the idealized images of peace projected by Western societies through television. These stark disparities create dangerous divides between the affluent few and the majority struggling for basic survival. Ahmad argues that while globalization can bring people together and offer benefits, it also creates divisions among those excluded from its advantages or perceive it as a threat. Consequently, conflicts and violence may arise as individuals opposing facets of globalization seek to preserve their cultural integrity in the face of perceived external threats. Therefore, Ahmad dedicates his scholarly efforts to promoting effective communication and fostering mutual respect among diverse civilizations, faiths, and cultures globally. He sees these efforts as crucial for averting conflicts in the era of globalization. Ahmad challenges the dangerous notion that a perpetual Clash of Civilizations is inherent to this age, aiming to dismantle its widespread acceptance and promote a more inclusive and harmonious global future.[1]

Ahmad asserts that prior to the terrorist attacks on September 11, 2001, globalization was widely regarded as an inexorable force, with the prevailing belief that small groups, tribal cultures, and traditional civilizations were all succumbing to its overarching influence. However, the events of September 11 shattered this theoretical foundation. The aftermath of the attacks and subsequent years were profoundly influenced by notions of ethnicity, ethnic retaliation, and honor. The destruction of the World Trade Center and the Pentagon collision can be interpreted as a significant reversal of the globalization process, with far-reaching consequences that may still be underestimated. In the aftermath of 9/11, numerous Western commentators propagated the idea of a Clash of Civilizations between the West and the Muslim world. They contended that the attacks were merely the latest chapter in a historical struggle originating with the founding of Islam. These critics drew on the ideas of scholars such as Samuel Huntington and Bernard Lewis, who popularized the concept of a Clash of Civilizations. However, this thesis is flawed, as historical evidence contradicts it, showcasing instances of peaceful coexistence and remarkable cultural achievements among Muslims, Christians, and Jews. One notable example is Muslim Spain, which does not align with the Clash of Civilizations theory.[2]

It is crucial to note that before the events of 9/11, the United States had been involved in instances where it demonstrated support for Muslim populations. Particularly noteworthy are the interventions during the 1980s Soviet invasion of Afghanistan and the 1990s Balkans conflict, where the United States actively aided Muslims facing dire circumstances, including ethnic cleansing. However, in the aftermath of 9/11, there was a swift and decisive shift in U.S. policy toward Muslim cultures, driven by the objective of combating "terrorists." This approach was guided by officials subscribing to the Clash of Civilizations theory but lacking a comprehensive understanding of both the perpetrators behind the attacks and the intricate nuances of Muslim culture and history. Consequently, the United States collaborated with central governments determined to suppress peripheral populations perceived as problematic, resulting in unintended consequences. Thus, even for those who reject the notion of a historical Clash of Civilizations between the West and Islam, it remains an unquestionably naive yet pervasive concept that warrants refutation. For Ahmad, it is imperative to advocate an opposing viewpoint, that of a "dialogue of civilisations," initially proposed by Iranian President Mohammad Khatami. This perspective calls for fostering understanding, education, and collaboration across racial, ethnic, and cultural divides.[3]

Brief Biography and Works

Possessing an illustrious career marked by scholarly excellence, Akbar S. Ahmed, the former Pakistani High Commissioner to the United Kingdom and Ireland, currently occupies the Ibn Khaldun Chair of Islamic Studies at American University in Washington D.C.[4] Widely acknowledged as the foremost authority on modern Islam, his erudition has earned acclaim from the BBC. Ahmed's intellectual acumen is complemented by a wealth of experience in international relations, reflected in his role as a Nonresident Senior Fellow at the esteemed Brookings Institution.[5] Beyond his academic pursuits, Ahmed has made substantial contributions to anthropology, showcasing a multidisciplinary approach to comprehending global Islam and its nuanced impact on contemporary society. His profound insights into interreligious dialogue and cultural dynamics have captured the attention of influential figures, including President George W. Bush and Prince Charles, engaging in substantive discussions on Islam and its broader implications. Ahmed's professional trajectory encompasses noteworthy positions in the civil services of Pakistan and Bangladesh, concurrently holding visiting professorships at prestigious institutions like Harvard University, Cambridge University, and the Institute of Advanced Studies at Princeton.[6] Motivated by a profound commitment to fostering intercultural understanding, Ahmed seamlessly merges his scholarly and diplomatic pursuits to facilitate dialogue and bridge gaps between diverse societies. His rich background, combining academia and public service, endows him with a comprehensive perspective on the intricacies of our interconnected world. Through his unwavering pursuit of knowledge and dedication to promoting cultural harmony, Ahmed continues to shape discourse and make significant contributions to the realms of Islamic studies and global relations.[7]

Ahmed has significantly enriched the academic landscape with an extensive body of work. One of his noteworthy publications, "Discovering Islam: Making Sense of Muslim History and Society," not only serves as a seminal work but also laid the foundation for the acclaimed BBC television series "Living Islam." This comprehensive exploration of Muslim history and society reflects Ahmed's profound knowledge and insightful analysis. Beyond his groundbreaking research on Islam, Dr. Ahmed has gained international acclaim for his four-part project, the "Jinnah Quartet," which meticulously examines the life and legacy of Pakistan's founding father, M. A. Jinnah.

This ambitious project has earned him numerous prestigious honors, attesting to the scholarly rigor and significance of his contributions.

Additionally, Ahmed's thought-provoking book, *Postmodernism and Islam: Predicament and Promise*, received a nomination for the esteemed Amalfi Award, highlighting its intellectual and academic impact. His ability to distill complex concepts into a concise format is evident in *Islam Today: A Short Introduction to the Muslim World*, recognized by the Los Angeles Times as one of the finest nonfiction works of the year. Ahmed's insights into contemporary Muslim experiences and challenges resonate globally, with his writings translated into languages such as Chinese and Indonesian. Renowned as an influential intellectual, he has shared his expertise with major media outlets, including CNN, MSNBC, NBC Nightly News, and the BBC, offering invaluable insights through interviews and analysis. Furthermore, his syndicated contributions to Religion News Service underscore his ongoing commitment to fostering a deeper understanding of Islam among diverse audiences.[8]

Ahmed's scholarly eminence extends to delivering keynote lectures at prestigious academic institutions. Notable engagements include addressing legislators during the joint congressional retreat at Greenbrier and serving as Chief Moderator for the Society of Fellows Seminar and the Socrates Society, both hosted by the Aspen Institute and the World Bank. Particularly significant was his captivating keynote address at the Aspen Institute's Summer Speakers Series in 2003, showcasing his talent for captivating oratory and providing profound insights. His ability to enthrall audiences and offer profound insights solidifies his reputation as an eminent thought leader, evidenced by honors such as the Star of Excellence in Pakistan and the Sir Percy Sykes Memorial Medal from the Royal Society of Asian Affairs in London. These accolades reflect the high regard for his scholarly achievements, firmly establishing him as a preeminent scholar in the field of modern Islam.[9]

Islam, Migration, and the Forces of Globalization

Ahmad discusses how globalization unfolds as a complex network driven by rapid advancements in technology, travel, and information sharing.[10] This phenomenon breaks down geographical barriers, making even the most remote corners of the world easily reachable. An illustration of this interconnectedness is found in Salman Rushdie's controversial novel, *The Satanic Verses*. In today's digital age, events in New York can swiftly echo across Cairo or Karachi due to instant information transmission. The Rushdie controversy spread rapidly across continents, triggering responses in cities like Bradford, London, Islamabad, and Mumbai, resulting in significant fatalities.

This unprecedented pace of global events unfolded through various channels like official statements, media discussions, editorials, vigils, and protests, marking a remarkable speed in historical terms.

Ahmad and Donnan further explore the ramifications of globalization, emphasizing the need to view Islamic studies not as an exclusive academic pursuit but as an integral force shaping the global landscape. They argue that this shift calls for recognizing the tangible influence of Muslims in diverse parts of the world on the lives of non-Muslims in their immediate spheres, moving beyond specialized academic domains. Additionally, the substantial global Muslim population, exceeding 1.6 billion across about fifty-seven nations, notably concentrated in the United States and Europe with ten to fifteen million, brings forth multifaceted migration-related issues. Muslim immigrants often face significant challenges, including various forms of discrimination. These evolving dynamics within the Islamic faith and its surrounding environment have introduced terms like fatwa (a public proclamation), *jihad* (encompassing armed struggle), and ayatollah (a learned religious scholar) into Western discourse, signifying the changing interactions between Islam and the West.[11] Ahmad emphasizes the substantial impact of Western media in shaping language and influencing perceptions, citing examples from popular tabloids that have significantly contributed to the widespread adoption of specific terms in the English language. This process elucidates how these terms are initially introduced or misappropriated in Western media and eventually become deeply embedded in local vernacular through processes of adoption and adaptation. The dynamic interaction between Islam and the West stands as a noteworthy illustration of the continuous exchange of ideas and influences.[12] A precedent for linguistic assimilation can be discerned in the term "mughal," originally linked to the renowned Mughal emperors and dynasty of India, which has undergone an evolution to now denote any influential individual, particularly in the realm of business tycoons. Similarly, the term *"harem,"* originating from Arabic to signify a sanctuary for women accessible solely to close male relatives, has, upon translation into English, acquired associations with licentious and exploitative treatment of women. This evolution underscores the intricate interplay between cultures and the dynamic transformation of language over time.[13]

Economic and Cultural Dimensions in Global Interconnections

Ahmad posits that Muslims and the West have shared a historical connection within the framework of the "economic global order," a relationship forged through extensive international commerce and commercial interactions, often marked by elements of both exchange and exploitation.[14] This interplay between agents of colonial authority and the local elites aligned with them in governance could be considered an early manifestation of globalization, particularly in the late twentieth century. Some argue that this era might be viewed as one stage, albeit not necessarily the initial one, in the unfolding evolution now recognized as globalization. Ahmad contends that the early fourteenth century might signify the commencement of five distinct phases leading to the contemporary intricacies of the global landscape. Thus, globalization is not merely a recent phenomenon but is deeply rooted in historical processes, encompassing the notions of a "system" and "stages of growth" that distinguish it from its predecessor, world-systems theory. Despite this historical continuity, critics acknowledge notable distinctions between late twentieth-century globalization and its predecessors. Historically, international relations were predominantly viewed through the lens of an economic global system, sidelining the cultural exchanges that coincided with material transactions. Debates have arisen regarding the role of "culture" in analyses such as world-systems theory, with claims that it has been overshadowed. Nevertheless, instances of collaborations between colonial powers and local entities extended beyond mere political and economic cooperation. For example, the introduction of values like gentlemanly conduct and fair play from England to India, as a cultural export, was embraced by groups such as the Parsis seeking to align with their former colonial rulers. While cultural processes existed in the past, they often seemed ancillary to practical realities, with researchers primarily focusing on the pragmatic underpinnings that gave rise to these cultural phenomena.[15]

Cultural Currents and Contested Homogenization

Contemporary perceptions of globalization center around the exchange of cultural elements transcending national borders. It is imperative to acknowledge that these cultural flows are intricately interwoven with political and economic dynamics. Notably, certain flows, predominantly emanating from the West, wield greater influence due to their origins, thereby reaching a broader audience. This has sparked extensive debates regarding the potential homogenization of cultures, envisioning a shift toward a global culture characterized by uniform consumption patterns, such as the preference for specific soft beverages, Marlboro cigarettes, or the emulation of JR-like behavior.

Multiple perspectives have contested the notion of cultural homogenization, emphasizing the nuanced complexities that extend beyond conventional assumptions.[16] Ahmad contends that there is a tendency to assume rather than accurately describe the existence of a hegemonic global cultural center disseminating its products to peripheral regions worldwide.[17] Even if such a center exists, uncertainties persist regarding whether its cultural exports hold greater significance for recipients compared to those exported by the same center a generation or two ago. The rapidity, breadth, and volume of these interactions, facilitated by modern technology, have captivated public attention, contributing to the prevalent depiction of globalization. These technologies effectively detach culture from its geographic moorings, enabling its dissemination through airwaves to anyone with access, irrespective of spatial constraints. While the current stage of globalization has connected more individuals to multiple cultures than ever before, the ultimate impact of this phenomenon remains uncertain, encapsulating Ahmad's use of the term in this specific context.[18] As Ahmad notes, one significant consequence of globalization is the way that technology, images from the worldwide media, and international networks are used to promote violence between religious groups.[19] The erosion of central state structures, their disproportionately harsh responses to perceived dissent within minority communities, and the hastened resort to lethal weapons by both majority and minority communities contribute to the impact of globalization on societies influenced by Indic religions. Hence, ethnic and religious conflicts emerge as both a cause and a symptom of the animosity prevailing in this era of globalization.

Ahmad contends that globalization yields both moral and physical effects, with unbridled materialism and industrialization exacerbating global warming as a grave consequence. Indicators of this issue include heightened occurrences of cyclones and tornadoes, record-breaking temperatures, intense rainfall, severe droughts, and accelerated glacier melting.[20] Despite these manifestations, nations, including major industrial players like China, prioritize integration into the global economy over environmental conservation.[21] Another economic consequence of globalization is the stark increase in asymmetrical living conditions. Approximately a billion people endure poverty, earning less than $1 per day, resulting in thousands of deaths annually. Irony underscores these disparities, exemplified by the fact that 358 individuals possess more wealth than the entire global population combined. This economic inequality is another facet of globalization's multifaceted impact on societies worldwide.[22]

Clash of Civilizations and the Sense of Siege among Muslims

Contrary to the perspective held by many experts that Islam is inherently antagonistic to the modern era and on a collision course with the West, Islamic communities, much like other traditionally influenced cultures, are grappling with a complex response to the current global changes.[23] This response encompasses a mixture of rage, confusion, and intense animosity, alongside a simultaneous intrigue with Western modernism. Ahmad challenges the oversimplified notion of a Clash of Civilizations, wherein Muslims are depicted as the primary adversaries of the West.[24] He contends that this narrative perpetuates historical views of Islam as a predatory culture posing a threat to the West.[25] In contrast, Ahmad advocates for the dialogue of civilizations, a perspective endorsed by the former UN Secretary-General Kofi Annan and initially proposed by the former Iranian President Muhammad Khatami. While the concept of a dialogue of civilizations is not entirely new, Khatami's endorsement carried significant weight, especially considering the association of his nation with terrorism and extremism in the eyes of Westerners.[26] The events of September 11 intensified personal ideologies, with some individuals, like Dr. George Carey, the Archbishop of Canterbury, redoubling efforts to promote discussion. However, President Bush's rejection of dialogue left others, including President Khatami, demoralized. In the aftermath of September 11, as Muslims began to feel under assault, the complexities of engaging in dialogue became more challenging.[27] Ahmad acknowledges that it is not just Muslims but also people in traditional civilizations who have felt unease due to the rapid and extensive political, cultural, and technological changes emanating from the West. The shared sentiment is one of apprehension toward the rapid pace and magnitude of these transformations.

Globalization is characterized by a complex interplay of interconnected features, including global communication systems, media, transnational corporations' efficiency, travel, tourism, and a shared awareness of free trade and capital movement. These elements presuppose a framework of law and order, underpinned by the anticipation of progressing toward a period of justice and fairness.[28] Globalization's fundamental tenet is the interconnectedness of these aspects, with the failure of one potentially impacting the others. The September 11 attacks have inflicted a negative impact on all these facets, despite media and communication continuing to function normally. Globalization, wounded in the rubble of the Pentagon and World Trade

Center, faces a critical juncture that depends on how international leaders respond—whether the wound is lethal or not.[29]

Ahmad notes that for the majority in developing societies, globalization is perceived as equivalent to Armageddon, despite its benefits in certain regions like China and India.[30] Citing Malaysia's former Prime Minister, Dr. Mahathir Mohamad, a prominent Muslim public intellectual, Ahmad explores the perspective that globalization, in its current form, poses a threat to faith and society. Dr. Mahathir expresses confusion and hopelessness, acknowledging the challenges brought about by globalization. Kofi Annan, the former UN secretary-general, highlights that millions globally view globalization not as a force for growth but as a disruptive power capable of ruining lives, jobs, and traditions. The 9/11 attacks exacerbated tensions and distortions within the ongoing globalization processes.[31] Ahmad points out that Muslims have historical experience with globalization, both conceptually and practically. Islam's inherently universal worldview, as seen throughout its history, reveals periods akin to what we now call globalization.[32] Despite residing within different ethnic, geographic, and political boundaries, these societies shared a common language, cultural sensibility, and overarching ethos. Notably, figures like Ibn Khaldun in the fourteenth century exemplify individuals who traversed multiple continents while remaining within a familiar cultural setting, illustrating the interconnectedness inherent in Islamic history.

Global Media, Culture, and Identity

After delving into the intricacies of Asian societies, Ahmed shifts his focus to the dynamics of identity. He argues that the foundational elements of identity, prevalent in most people's lives, are facing challenges from the forces of globalization. The concept of family undergoes strain as individuals move in search of work or respond to political and cultural shifts, leading to fragmented family units. Tribes experience a loss of identity as they relocate to densely populated urban areas, where the fundamental idea of shared ancestry diminishes. The state, influenced by political and economic transformations, witnesses changes in its core elements, particularly the concept of well-defined boundaries, impacting society as a whole.[33] Globalization's emphasis on materialism and commercialization poses a threat to the spiritual foundations of religion. Ahmed posits that enduring concepts of morality and justice, representing divine command, become paramount for individuals when their multifaceted identities erode due to globalization. Consequently, religion not only serves as a means of interpreting justice—often construed as honor and retribution—but also functions as a source of identity.

Ahmad observes certain prevailing beliefs about globalization, acknowledging some truths among them.[34] There is a perception that globalization is designed and sustained to benefit American politics and the economy, characterized by moral corruption and a focus on personal gain.[35] The materialistic portrayal in media, including television commercials and documentaries depicting affluent lifestyles, is seen as the norm. Western media images are perceived as intrusive. Despite glimpses of global progress, one commentator laments that empirically, globalization is not inherently beneficial. Television content, such as reruns of shows like Dallas and Dynasty, project scenes from American life onto individuals in countries like Brazil, Indonesia, or Nigeria. Modern TV images promoting various products further fuel a preoccupation with the physical and superficial aspects of life. These images, seductive yet simultaneously infuriating and depressing, epitomize consumerism. The world's reaction to the United States is a blend of horror and fascination, viewing it as the small, wealthy ruling class in the global village.

McDonald's emerges as a symbol deeply intertwined with American society and globalization. The golden arches, ubiquitous in America, signify ritual, symbol, and myth.[36] McDonald's global presence is illustrated by its locations overlooking significant landmarks worldwide. From Casablanca's majestic mosque to Moscow's Pushkin monument, Rome's Trevi Fountain, London's Big Ben, and Cambridge's Trinity College, McDonalds serves as a tangible connection to the globalized world, tying together diverse cultures and histories.[37] McDonald's became a prime target for deadly attacks post-September, notably in Indonesia and India, underscoring its status as an instantly recognizable American symbol. Paradoxically, if you were to inquire with children in these regions about their preference between a Big Mac and a traditional indigenous meal, they would overwhelmingly opt for the latter. Similar to the McDonald's situation, globalization is perceived as an unyielding force with no apparent exit. However, there is a possibility of reversing globalization. The mechanisms of globalization—media, Western technology, foreign recruitment, cash flow, and the portrayal of the United States as the primary adversary—were effectively employed by Khomeini in the 1970s and later by bin Laden.[38] However, for Muslims, the repercussions of globalization were overturned due to Bin Laden's actions. They suddenly faced insurmountable challenges at borders, underwent routine airport searches, had their financial and commercial affairs scrutinized, saw their beliefs and practices questioned and often ridiculed, and were left feeling unwelcome in the global community of cultures.

Risk Society and a Post-Honor World

Some scholars characterize the present era as "a moment of mild apocalypse" and "a perplexing and disturbing postmodernity."[39] The impact of global changes on local communities is now recognized as neither gentle nor merely troubling, especially in the aftermath of the attacks in New York and Washington. Over the last decade, the juxtaposition of the global and the local, the significant and the trivial, the past and the present, the sacred and the profane, and the serious and the frivolous has been striking and readily accessible, evoking a range of emotions from inspiration to confusion and rage.[40] Violence seems almost inevitable, with ethnic victims often in close proximity. Those disillusioned by modernity's legacy inhabit an uncertain world marked by global consciousness. Even institutions like Buckingham Palace and St. James's Palace have been violated, emphasizing the vulnerability of individuals and places. This has led sociologists to label our current reality as a risk society.[41] According to Ahmad, globalization intensifies individuals' feelings of vulnerability, fostering defensiveness and apprehension as conventional institutions and values shift while new ones are yet to solidify. Such individuals experience a state of anomie, akin to Durkheim's description.[42] Ahmad suggests that responding to this requires an excessive focus on group loyalty, setting the stage for a post-honor society. It is not only individuals who feel endangered; the honor of families, groups, countries, and even religions seems to be at risk in various contexts and unexpected ways. This sense of insecurity extends even to residents of the leading global hegemon, the United States and the unrecognized Palestinian state. Accusations of lacking dignity and being dishonorable are exchanged between both parties.[43]

Mass media further invades the most private spaces in people's homes worldwide with its ominous and menacing images. The constant replaying of news feeds amplifies emotions of shock and wrath, reinforcing atavistic preconceptions. In response, individuals rally to defend the honor of their culture, religion, or cult. In some instances, this response takes the form of vengeance or martyrdom. Many believe in their own righteousness while denouncing others. Historical incidents or the reprehensible actions of others are often cited to justify these claims. The concept of honor is applied to acts of violence through warped and distorted reasoning, with innocent bystanders frequently becoming victims. The defense of honor sometimes involves the humiliation and even rape of women. Thus, a distinction can be drawn between honor as a lofty, humanistic ideal and honor as an extreme manifestation of group loyalty defined by violence against others.

As argued by Ahmad, the endangered ideals of honor continue to hold significant sway in political rhetoric and actions across much of the Muslim world today. This is evident in the resonance of the Satanic Verses debate, drawing Muslims from places like Bradford to Bombay.[44] The belief that the wives of the Prophet of Islam had been dishonored fueled this engagement. While the sensation of losing honor is not new, what is novel is the sense of catastrophic upheaval that compels people to reassess their understanding of honor, often leading to a focus on vengeance as its purest expression. The narrative transitions from figures like Dr. Mahathir to bin Laden. In his attempts to galvanize the Islamic world, bin Laden seized upon the idea of honor. He argued that corrupt Muslim leaders, supported by the West and particularly the United States, were robbing Muslims of their respect and dignity. bin Laden believed that launching ferocious attacks against targets involving people was the solution. Ahmad acknowledges the accuracy of Bin Laden's first assumption—Muslims globally felt degraded and robbed of their honor. The second assumption was partially correct, as there were indeed corrupt and shortsighted rulers contributing to Muslims' predicament. However, bin Laden's third presumption was entirely incorrect. The Qur'ān unequivocally states that Islam cannot condone the killing of even one innocent person.[45] Muslims emphasize a valid argument made by figures like Osama bin Laden: Islam encompasses not only mercy and compassion but also the fight for justice and against oppression, whether in Palestine, Kashmir, Kosovo, or Chechnya. Those who solely emphasize the former are seen as dishonorable apologists hiding a significant aspect of their faith. As a result, bin Laden's words and actions have an impact on the common people in the Muslim world, a dynamic that is not well-understood in the West.

Culture, Territory, and Power: Dynamics of the Muslim Diaspora

Individuals seamlessly transport culture and technologies across borders, and over the last few decades, we are witnessing major changes in how simple it is for people to move from one state to another.[46] These changes have given rise to various diasporas, including those of migrant workers and refugees. Islam both promotes and forbids certain types of travel, a fact that has been frequently emphasized and the migration of Muslims across the world, for whatever reason, reflects this.[47] Globalization seems to have given a new dimension to and substantially promoted this readiness to shift, though, in this case as well. Ahmad argues that the globalization of markets and labor during the late capitalist era, sometimes known as "disorganised capitalism," has transformed the international economy and caused massive migrations of people in pursuit of employment. A sizable component of this population migration is made up by Muslims, leading to the seamless integration of Muslim civilizations with Western nations today.[48]

Since the majority of Muslim migrant workers have made long-term residence abroad, it is critical to view these civilizations as local and indigenous rather than exotic or Oriental. Sensitive and cutting-edge research is especially important for comprehending the Muslim diaspora. The diaspora has given rise to the frequently mentioned search for identity and authenticity, for those who live outside their countries of origin or those who work at home and find that their culture is now being defined and practiced in novel and occasionally upsetting ways in new settings.[49] Thus, identity-related concerns and the susceptibility of having to remake oneself in a world that seems to be continually changing are the main empirical challenges addressed by diaspora. To use Fischer and Abedi's terminology, the hyphen of hyphenated identities such as British-Muslim or American-Muslim, for instance, both reflects and obscures the required combination of diverse cultural traces brought together in the act of "re-membering" and "re-creating."[50] However, the diaspora also raises questions about identity and direction at "home" for those who must choose between the fantasy of moving and the reality of doing so, as well as for those who now perceive their "local cultures" as being less pervasive, less obvious, and less clearly bounded toward the outside than they once may have been. In addition to bringing new perspectives that differ from those of those who remained behind, migrants occasionally bring outdated versions of the things they left behind, including customs regarding dressing, acting, and believing that have evolved and changed while they were gone but that they had lovingly and carefully preserved intact while abroad.[51]

With the emergence of cultures seemingly detached from any specific location, the diaspora's disassociation of culture from territory has unleashed powerful forces that impact everyone, extending beyond those immediately affected. According to Ahmad, various global fundamentalisms, including Islamic and Hindu fundamentalism, are increasingly focused on this deterritorialization. He notes that the challenges faced by the Hindu diaspora in replicating culture overseas are linked to the politics of Hindu extremism at home.[52] The Muslim diaspora faces similar complexities, with the added challenge that Muslims abroad lack a common motherland, making Ahmad emphasize the importance of considering the Muslim diaspora in analyzing emerging Islamic movements in the Arab world. In this postmodern era, Ahmad asserts that the politics of all Muslim nations must be understood within a global context.[53]

Even before September 11, bin Laden had been issuing warnings of his intention to strike America from his caves in Afghanistan, often using the term "honor" to justify his call for violence. President Bush, in his impassioned addresses following the attacks, explicitly linked honor to the need for redemption through revenge. Bush, perceived by the majority of his people as embodying the man of honor, pursued his vision of redeeming honor through the foreign policy of the United States, sidelining economic, geopolitical, and humanistic considerations for primal ideas of revenge. Ahmad acknowledges the widespread nature and intensity of religious clashes but clarifies that he does not intend to imply that it is characteristic of, or exclusive to, our age.

While honor may be uplifting and noble in the abstract, in practice, it is often intertwined with death and violence. Societies delve into the past, reinterpreting events such as Masada for Jews, Kosovo for Serbs, and Ayodhya for Hindus, which symbolize communal tragedy and loss, invoking deep passions and ideas of honor and revenge. Ahmad points out that group loyalty is heightened, and group exclusivity becomes a dogma, leading to a perceived loss of honor centuries ago being avenged on the putative descendants of supposed antagonists. Ahmad emphasizes the importance of understanding in a post-honor world where different codes clash, particularly considering the economic, political, and cultural power of the United States, which now directly links the rest of the world to Washington in a way inconceivable only a decade or two ago. He underscores the need for Americans to contemplate their responsibility in shaping the emerging post-honor world.

Faith in Flux: Unearthing Layers of American Muslim Identity

While African Americans and Muslim immigrants share a common religious affiliation, their approaches to practicing Islam differ significantly. For African American Muslims, Islam involves addressing concerns related to health, education, violence, drugs, and poverty, embodying a straightforward and practical way of life influenced by the social reformer role of Prophet Muhammad PBUH. Conversely, immigrant Muslims, often more affluent and educated, perceive Islam as a complex and all-encompassing historical experience, serving as a model for grand empires and dynasties initiated by the Prophet.[54] In Ahmad's view, African American Muslim role models are contemporary Americans like Muhammad Ali, Malcolm X, Martin Luther King Jr., and Imam W. D. Mohammed.[55] In contrast, immigrant Muslims typically look up to historical figures from the Arab world, including the Prophet of Islam, Umar, Ali, and Saladin. While African Americans embrace their chosen brand of Islam voluntarily, developed through trial and error and valued for its unique reasons, immigrant Muslims view their practice as a legacy transmitted through generations, fostering a possessive ownership of Islam and projecting a superiority complex over other Muslims—an attitude perceived as conceited and irritating by African American Muslims.[56]

The historical interaction between African Americans and Muslim immigrants in the American context carries both burdens and ambitions. Immigrants have a vivid memory of their history, having conquered North America while enslaving African Americans. This disparate recollection of the past contributes to divergent perspectives on the future. African American Muslims aspire to forge a future based on a fictional civilization, while immigrants seek to build a future grounded in traditions and culture preserved from the Middle East and South Asia. Ahmad highlights that after 9/11, the U.S. government's response to perceived Muslim-related threats was an overreaction, exaggerating all aspects of Muslim identity, fueling American anger and terror. The rhetoric of a "war on terror" was often interpreted as a war on Islam, exacerbated by President Bush's use of the term "crusade." Even Christian evangelists prepared to send missionaries to Iraq with millions of Bibles before the invasion, combining conversion efforts with humanitarian aid.[57]

In his exploration of global conflict dynamics, Ahmad extensively examines the role of the American private military company Blackwater in perpetuating anti-Muslim prejudice. Erik Prince, the CEO of Blackwater, is noted for engaging in more hostile and aggressive eye contact with Muslims. A former Blackwater employee, in an affidavit presented to a Virginia court, alleged that Prince viewed himself as a Christian crusader tasked with eradicating Muslims and Islam worldwide. Additionally, the employee claimed that many Blackwater staff had call signs inspired by those of the Knights of the Templar, warriors in the Crusades. This kind of American behavior overseas contributed to hostility toward American Muslims domestically, resulting in verbal and physical abuse.[58]

The animosity toward American Muslims manifested in derogatory terms such as "Arabs," "ragheads," "towelheads," and "sand niggers," despite only around 20 percent of Muslims worldwide being from Arab countries. Reports included instances of burning crosses outside mosques and attacks on Islamic institutions. Muslims faced suspicion and scrutiny in various aspects of life, from foreign accents and front-row seats on flights to charities for the poor and gatherings to celebrate Muslim holidays. Some Muslims expressed a sincere hope for America to embrace Islam, believing that it would bring compassion and wisdom. However, such statements were often misinterpreted, leading to heightened tensions. The Founding Fathers emphasized the freedom for any American to express religious opinions, as long as it did not violate the law. Immigration itself profoundly and unexpectedly reshapes identity and this complexity heightened for Muslim immigrants in America post-9/11. Muslim social structures brought by immigrants from their home countries responded differently to expressions of American identity in Buffalo and nationwide. The mystics embraced the entirety of American identity, even its predatory elements, promoting principles of love. Pluralism appealed to modernists, while literalists, considering themselves the true defenders of Islam, dismissed American identity as irrelevant to their way of life.[59]

Backlash and Responses

The dispersal of Muslim immigrants across diverse global regions, encompassing varied racial contexts, carries significant implications for both traditional communities and industrialized societies. In their actions, Muslim immigrants illuminate the intricacies of traditional communities, fostering enhanced communication and interaction with their more industrialized counterparts. The primary advantage arising from this dispersion lies in its potential to facilitate a comprehensive understanding of Islam, a religion that has gained global relevance in recent times.

The challenges giving rise to the global crisis of globalization are being addressed by different religious and communal groups, with some choosing to disregard these concerns altogether. Ahmad argues that backlashes against globalization are not confined to Muslim communities alone but are observable in other parts of the world as well. Instances of Leftist regimes coming to power in Latin America and the eruption of numerous demonstrations, riots, and related incidents in China, attributed to economic disparities and privatization policies, underscore the widespread ramifications of these issues. Notably, China's estimated Muslim population ranges from 20 million to as high as 100 million, further exemplifying the global repercussions of such developments.

Ahmad contends that within the sphere of Islam, characterized by its predominantly conventional context, lies an opportune environment for exploring the multifaceted effects of and responses to global pressures. This religious framework serves as a crucible for understanding and analyzing the consequences stemming from these pressures, providing valuable insights into the intricate interplay between tradition and globalization. Scholars and observers can delve into the complexities of contemporary global dynamics and the resulting societal transformations through the lens of Islam. Ahmad further emphasizes that major global faiths share a common quest to perceive the divine for leading happy lives on Earth. Individuals approach this quest in various ways, seeking similarities and parallels outside their own traditions, utilizing lessons from the external world to support their convictions, or focusing on conserving their own tradition. Similar to other global religions, Islam attempts to navigate between numerous viewpoints or methods, categorized as "accepting," "preserving," and "synthesising."

Believers in preservation opt for simple orthodoxy or a literal interpretation of the faith, while believers in acceptance approach the divine through universal mysticism. Synthesizers aim to engage with modernism and its upheld ideals, such as democracy, women's rights, and human rights. Each viewpoint is considered the most authentic expression of the religion, serving as a means to combat societal toxins. Consequently, each perspective impacts globalization and contributes to internal conflicts in Islamic society. Islam's response to the pressures of globalization manifests in at least three different ways: mystics engage with other religions, traditionalists seek to maintain Islam's purity, and modernists aim to synthesize society with non-Muslim systems. People in the West often oversimplify their comprehension of U.S. interactions with the Muslim world, categorizing Muslims as moderates and extremists. Ahmad argues that this oversimplification occurs due to a lack of appreciation for the complexity of Muslim culture through models like ours.[60]

Ahmad argues that three Indian towns—Ajmer, Deoband, and Aligarh—serve as analogies for different worldviews within Islam.[61] He asserts that these titles represent various perceptions of Islam held by locals identifying with specific Muslim worldviews and their locations in South Asia, particularly India, are coincidental geography and history-related happenstance. Despite occasionally appearing under other titles and forms, the models bearing their names are universally recognizable in Muslim countries, shedding light on how Muslims generally react to one another. Simplifying vast populations into models and categories provides the benefit of clarity. According to Ahmad, adherents of Ajmer perceive Deobandis as overly critical of other religions and excessively focused on mysticism, while Aligarh adherents are seen as overly involved with the physical world. In turn, Deoband adherents may hold Ajmer accountable for innovation and heresy, while those from Aligarh might view them as too secular and Western-influenced. Ahmad highlights that the Aligarh group would consider Ajmer outdated and reject Deoband as a gathering of dimwitted clergy, rural bumpkins, and hapless rustics. However, these models are "ideal kinds" that loosely represent the situation and do not serve as a direct replacement for reality.[62]

Contrary to appearances, all three designs are inspired by the Prophet of Islam, providing a sense of oneness to different Muslim communities worldwide. Traditional Muslims express high regard for the Prophet by saying "Peace be upon him." These models aid in understanding how the majority of Muslims perceive themselves. The Ajmer model stands in opposition to materialist and consumerist ideals underlying globalization, emphasizing diversity and acceptance of others. Sufi philosophy within this model encourages reflection on the hereafter and prioritizes shared humanity, poverty, and compassion. While less visible in the era of globalization, the Ajmer model provides a meaningful and long-term answer to global issues.[63] Deoband, on the other hand, effectively counters the tides of globalization by preserving its "purity" through self-imposed limits. It exposes and combats the hollowness of global consumerism and immoral portrayals on television. Deoband emphasizes Islam's moral superiority and seeks to instill a sense of Muslim pride. According to the Deoband theory, the West is perceived as not only aggressive and cruel but also morally bankrupt, especially post-9/11. The incidents at Abu Ghraib support the idea, endorsed by Muslim sages, that Islam will eventually triumph. While the Deoband model may manifest through various means, such as involvement in local politics and religious ceremonies, it is on the ascent in the Muslim world and shows no signs of apology. Surprisingly, the Deoband model seems to be energized more by globalization compared to the other two models, prompting it to take on a more active role in shaping Muslim culture. Conversely, the Aligarh model aligns more closely with contemporary Western concepts, incorporating terms such as democracy, reason, development, and science. Leaders in this tradition, such as Sir Sayed Ahmad Khan in South Asia and Muhammad Abduh in the Middle East, define Islam as a balance between religion and reason. They foresaw the successful integration of Western modernity with Islamic culture in the evolution of Muslim civilization.[64]

Promoting Dialogue in the Age of Uncertainty

The 9/11 attacks underscored the urgent need for a comprehensive understanding of Islam, given its vast size and the scope of Muslim society, comprising 1.6 billion adherents and fifty-seven Muslim states.[65] This imperative necessitates a reciprocal exchange, wherein Muslims educate non-Muslims about Islam, and non-Muslims strive to comprehend Western thought. However, Muslims often exhibit reluctance, associating globalization with

Westernization and perceiving certain cultural and intellectual aspects as threatening. This sentiment aligns with Western scholars, such as Anthony Giddens, who posit modernity as a "Western project"[66] and Thomas Friedman, who characterizes globalization as "Americanisation."[67]

Contrary to contemporary reservations, Ahmad argues that Islam, by its inherent nature, possesses a global perspective on the world.[68] Historical instances of early forms of globalization within the Islamic world are cited, wherein communities, despite residing within distinct borders, shared a common language, cultural sensibility, and overarching ethos. Notable figures like Ibn Khaldun exemplify extensive travels across continents while remaining within a singular civilizational framework. Historical examples, such as the coexistence of Jews, Christians, and Muslims in Spain under Muslim rule until 1492, further illustrate the potential for complex cultural confluences and intellectual exchanges.[69] The lack of awareness about Islam's historical influence on European culture and thought is critiqued by Ahmad.[70] Moreover, Ahmad sheds light on the perception of a deliberate West-led effort to dehumanize and potentially subjugate Muslims, citing instances like the Salman Rushdie controversy, BCCI failure, Gulf War, and conflicts in Bosnia, Kosovo, Chechnya, Palestine, and Kashmir. Academic writings by Francis Fukuyama and Samuel Huntington, particularly "The End of History" and "The Clash of Civilisations," are regarded by many as integral components of a global conspiracy to undermine Islam.[71] While these writings introduce an unexpected dimension to the study of Islam by emphasizing the role of religion in contemporary culture, they also give rise to ingrained historical biases, occasionally affording them a semblance of respectability.

In light of these dynamics, Ahmad underscores the strategic importance of Muslim countries as vital allies, intimately linked to the West's global strategic and security objectives. Five of the nine "pivotal states" shaping U.S. foreign policy are Muslim nations, and the approximately 20 million Muslims permanently residing in the West serve as crucial bridges between Islamic and Western civilizations.[72] The events of 9/11 accentuate their potential to dispel opposition between Islam and the West. The critique of perceived biases and the call for nuanced understanding resonate with the overarching goal of fostering meaningful dialogue and mutual comprehension between Islam and the West. Ahmad identifies genuine initiatives promoting global understanding. Illustratively, the Pope's statements and the Prince of Wales' effort to bridge Islam and Western culture through his 1993 talk at Oxford garner attention.[73] Ahmad asserts that fostering dialogue necessitates a sincere effort to comprehend the evolving world. Despite a dim outlook for peaceful coexistence in the near future, Ahmad underscores the profound impact of those championing communication and understanding. Identifying universal issues affecting all, regardless of race, nationality, or religion, is crucial.[74] Ahmad suggests drawing encouragement from Islamic teachings to address topics such as drug abuse, violence, and environmental depletion. The authentic Islamic concept of jihad, if properly understood, could infuse positive energy into addressing these challenges. Ahmad urges Muslims to move beyond simplistic solutions and rediscover the foundational pillars of Islamic civilization, emphasizing justice, tolerance, and knowledge pursuit.[75] Despite reservations about postmodernism and globalization, Ahmad advocates inclusive scholarship to address the adverse consequences of globalization.[76] This approach becomes essential to mitigate conflicts among major faiths in regions like the Balkans, South Asia, and the Middle East. Ahmad underscores the urgent need for a globally engaged effort, emphasizing active participation in creative dialogues among civilizations, the pursuit of a just and peaceful global order, and comprehensive solutions to global challenges.[77]

Conclusion

Ahmad provides a nuanced analysis of the diverse responses within the Muslim world during the nineteenth century and their enduring relevance in the contemporary era. Three distinct patterns of Muslim response—modernists, literalists, and mystics—emerged during this period, shaping subsequent developments. The modernists, epitomized by influential figures like Mustafa Kemal Ataturk and Muhammad Abduh, embarked on reformist agendas in the late nineteenth century. Their objective was to reconcile Islam with Western modernity, embracing scientific knowledge and advocating for reform. This inclination toward modernization was evident in the efforts of individuals like Sir Syed Ahmed Khan, Allama Iqbal, and Muhammad Ali Jinnah in South Asia.

In contrast, the literalists, also originating in the nineteenth century, sought to demarcate and preserve boundaries around Islam. Responding to perceived Western attacks on their faith, literalists, inspired by scholars like Ibn Taymiyyah, emphasized a literal interpretation of sacred texts and a return to the foundational principles of Islam. Prominent examples of literalist thought include Syed Abul Aʻla Mawdūdī's Jamaat-I-Islami and the Deoband Islamic school in South Asia, reflecting a commitment to safeguarding the purity of Islam.[78] The third group, Sufi mystics, transcends national and religious boundaries through spiritual and intellectual endeavors. Advocating peace with all, Sufi mystics, guided by luminaries like Rumi, employ music and poetry to establish a profound connection with the divine. The widespread influence of Rumi's teachings, even in the modern United States, attests to the enduring impact of Sufi thought.

Ahmad contends that in the post-9/11 landscape, the perception of Islam being under attack by the West has elevated the status of literalists over mystics and modernists. Literalists advocate stringent adherence to Islamic law and tradition, resisting external influences to preserve the purity of Islam—a stance reminiscent of the nineteenth-century Deobandis. This ideological conflict has contributed to unrest within the Muslim world, emphasizing the continued significance of these historical patterns.[79] Ahmad's emphasis on fostering effective and nuanced communication within the Muslim world is indeed a cornerstone for addressing the conflicts and tensions that characterize it. By promoting dialogue and understanding among individuals with diverse ideological backgrounds, Ahmad advocates for a bridge between modernity and Islamic tradition. This approach is crucial for overcoming perceived gaps and fostering substantive conversations. The open-minded and receptive approach advocated by Ahmad recognizes the dynamic nature of society while respecting the foundational principles of the Islamic faith. This balance is essential in navigating the complex contemporary global landscape, where the interplay between Islam and modernity becomes a significant and delicate issue. The plea for a harmonious equilibrium between Islam and modernity underscores the recognition that Islam is a living faith capable of adaptation. This acknowledgment of its vibrancy and capacity to evolve over time while maintaining essential tenets is vital for addressing the challenges of the present era. To strike this delicate balance, Ahmad suggests meticulous deliberation and contemplation of Islamic teachings, including a thorough examination of historical contexts.[80] An astute evaluation of the applicability of these teachings to contemporary challenges is also emphasized. This approach requires a willingness to engage in critical analysis and contextualization of religious texts and principles, acknowledging that interpretations may naturally diverge and evolve over time.

The emphasis on initiating dialogues that foster appreciation for diverse perspectives and a commitment to seeking common ground is crucial in addressing longstanding tensions within Muslim societies. Creating inclusive and constructive platforms for engagement allows individuals to move beyond rigid ideological boundaries, overcoming limitations and finding shared areas of understanding. This process cultivates a sense of unity, laying the foundation for collective progress and advancement. However, the success of this transformative process depends on establishing an environment characterized by mutual respect. Active listening, perpetual learning, and a dedication to personal growth are essential components for individuals engaging in these dialogues. Ahmad's examination of how Muslims responded in the nineteenth century serves as a timeless reminder of the ongoing significance of these patterns in today's world. It encourages individuals to commit themselves to promoting understanding, unity, and dialogue, recognizing that comprehensive solutions are required to address the complex challenges faced by Muslims today. An inclusive and scholarly approach that values diverse voices and perspectives is essential for gaining a deep understanding of the intricate relationship between Islam and modernity. Armed with this knowledge, individuals can actively devise and implement strategies that align with principles such as mutual respect, peaceful coexistence, and collective advancement. Ahmad's insights serve as a guide for navigating the complexities of the contemporary world and building bridges toward a more harmonious and united future within Muslim societies.

Ahmad highlights the importance of fostering effective communication, recognizing shared humanity, and achieving a harmonious balance between Islam and modernity. His message encourages Muslims to actively participate in dialogue, appreciate diverse perspectives, and earnestly seek common ground, all with the overarching goal of mitigating deep-seated tensions and cultivating a future marked by harmony and inclusivity. By embracing the transformative potential inherent in inclusive scholarship and by acknowledging the intricate interplay between Islam and modernity, individuals can collectively contribute to the creation of an environment characterized by mutual respect, peaceful coexistence, and abundant opportunities for collective progress. Ahmad's guidance serves as a call to action for Muslims to engage in constructive conversations, appreciate the richness of diversity, and work toward a future where understanding and unity prevail over divisive forces. Through these efforts, a path can be forged toward a more inclusive and harmonious coexistence within the diverse tapestry of Muslim societies.

Notes

1. Kourosh Ziabari and Akbar Ahmed, "The Dialogue of Civilizations, Not the Clash of Civilizations," *Fair Observer*. Accessed April 14, 2024. https://www.fairobserver.com/region/europe/the-dialogue-of-civilizations-not-the-clash-of-civilizations-02158/#.

2. The Globalist, "Akbar Ahmed: When Honor is Threatened." Accessed April 14, 2024. https://www.theglobalist.com/akbar-ahmed-when-honor-is-threatened/.

3. Akbar Ahmed and Brian Forst, "Toward a More Civil Twenty-first Century," in *After Terror: Promoting Dialogue Among Civilizations*, ed. Akbar Ahmed and Brian Forst (London: Polity Press, 2005), 3–13.

4. Professor Akbar Ahmad, *The Muslim 500: The World's Most Influential 500 Muslims* (Dabuq: Royal Islamic Strategies Centre, 2023), 104.

5. Ahmad, *The Muslim 500*, 104.

6. American University, Washington, DC, School of International Service, Faculty, Akbar Ahmad. Accessed April 14, 2024. https://www.american.edu/sis/faculty/akbar.cfm.

7. American University, Washington, DC.

8. Brookings, Akbar Ahmed, Former Brookings Expert. Accessed April 14, 2024. https://www.brookings.edu/people/akbar-ahmed/.

9. Brookings, Akbar Ahmed.

10. Giddens, *The Consequences of Modernity*, 64.

11. Akbar S. Ahmad and Hastings Donnan, "Islam in the Age of Postmodernity," in *Islam, Globalization and Postmodernity*, ed. Akbar S. Ahmad and Hastings Donnan (London: Routledge, 1994), 1–20.

12. Ahmad and Donnan, "Islam in the Age of Postmodernity," 3.

13. Akbar Ahmad, *Islam Today: A Short Introduction to the Muslim World* (London: I. B. Tauris, 2002), 19.

14. Ahmad and Donnan, "Islam in the Age of Postmodernity," 6.

15. Arjun Appadurai, "Disjuncture and Difference in the Global Cultural Economy," *Public Culture* 2, no. 2 (1990): 1–5.

16. Akbar Ahmad, *Journey into Islam: The Crisis of Globalization* (Washington, DC: Brookings Institution Press, 2007), 29.

17. Ahmad, *Journey into Islam*, 31.

18. Jonathan Sacks, *The Dignity of Difference: How to Avoid the Clash of Civilisations* (London: Continuum, 2002), 106–107.

19. Ahmad, *Journey into Islam*.

20. Ahmad, *Journey into Islam*, 30.

21. Ahmad, *Journey into Islam*, 32

22. Hastings Donnan and Pnina Werbner, "Introduction," in *Economy and Culture in Pakistan: Migrants and Cities in a Muslim Society*, ed. Hastings Donnan and Pnina Werbner (London: Macmillan, 1991), 9–10.

23. Bernard Lewis, *What Went Wrong? Western Impact and Middle Eastern Response* (New York: Oxford University Press, 2002), 23.

24. Akbar S. Ahmad, *Islam under Seige: Living Dangerously in a Post-Honour World* (Cambridge: Polity Press, 2003), 46.

25. Fred Halliday, *Islam and the Myth of Confrontation* (London: I.B. Tauris, 1996), 56.

26. Muhammad Khatami, "Dialogue of Civilisations," Speech to United Nations General Assembly, New York, September 24, 1998. Accessed April 14, 2024. https://www.un.org/en/chronicle/article/dialogue-among-civilizations-contexts-and-perspectives.

27. Ahmad, *Islam under Seige*, 47.
28. Akbar Ahmed, *Discovering Islam: Making Sense of Muslim History and Society* (London: Routledge, 1988), 200.
29. Ahmed, *Discovering Islam*, 201.
30. Ahmad, *Islam under Seige*, 51.
31. Mahathir Mohamad, *Islam and the Muslim Ummah: Selected Speeches of Dr. Mahathir Mohamad* (Putrajaya: Pelanduk Publications, 2001), 24.
32. Kofi Annan, "Problems Without Passports," *Foreign Policy*. Accessed April 14, 2024.https://foreignpolicy.com/2009/11/09/problems-without-passports/.
33. Mohamad, *Islam and the Muslim Ummah*, 44.
34. Ahmad, *Islam under Seige*, 50.
35. Roland Robertson, *Globalization: Social Theory and Global Culture* (London: Sage Publications, 1992), 6.
36. Conrad Phillip Kottak, *Cultural Anthropology* (Boston, MA and New York: McGraw-Hill, Higher Education, 2000), 466–468.
37. Ahmad, *Islam under Seige*, 52.
38. Ahmad, *Islam under Seige*, 53.
39. Ahmad, *Islam under Seige*, 54.
40. Ahmad, *Islam under Seige*, 54.
41. Akbar S. Ahmad, *Postmodernism and Islam: Predicament and Promise* (London: Routledge, 1992), 45.
42. Ahmad, *Postmodernism and Islam*, 46.
43. Kathleen Christison, *Perceptions of Palestine: Their Influence on U.S. Middle East Policy* (Berkeley, CA: University of California Press, 1999), 34.
44. Christison, *Perceptions of Palestine*, 35.
45. Ahmad, *Islam under Seige*, 52.
46. Ahmad, *Journey into Islam*, 29.
47. Ahmad and Donnan, "Islam in the Age of Postmodernity," 4.
48. Ahmad and Donnan, "Islam in the Age of Postmodernity," 5.
49. Ahmad and Donnan, "Islam in the Age of Postmodernity," 6.
50. Ulf Hannerz, "Cosmopolitans and Locals in World Culture," in *Global Culture: Nationalism, Globalization and Modernity*, ed. Mike Featherstone (London: Sage, 1990), 249.
51. Ahmad and Donnan, "Islam in the Age of Postmodernity," 6.
52. Ahmad and Donnan, "Islam in the Age of Postmodernity," 7.
53. Ahmad and Donnan, "Islam in the Age of Postmodernity," 9.
54. Steven Waldman, "Jesus in Baghdad: Why We Should Keep Franklin Graham Out of Iraq," *Slate*. Accessed April 14, 2024. www.slate.com/id/2081432/.
55. Akbar Ahmed, *Journey into America: The Challenge of Islam* (Washington, DC: Brookings Institution Press, 2010), 214.
56. Ahmed, *Journey into America*, 215.
57. Ahmed, *Journey into America*, 216.

58. "Erik Prince and the Last Crusade," *The Economist*. Accessed April 14, 2024. https://www.economist.com/democracy-in-america/2009/08/06/erik-prince-and-the-last-crusade.

59. Ahmed, *Journey into America*, 215.

60. Ahmed, *Journey into America*, 217.

61. Ahmad, *Journey into Islam: The Crisis of Globalization*, 29

62. Ahmad, *Journey into Islam: The Crisis of Globalization*, 41.

63. Ahmad, *Journey into Islam: The Crisis of Globalization*, 41.

64. Ahmad, *Journey into Islam: The Crisis of Globalization*, 41.

65. Ahmad, *Journey into Islam: The Crisis of Globalization*, 43.

66. Giddens, *The Consequences of Modernity*, 174.

67. Thomas Friedman, *The Lexus and the Olive Tree* (New York: Picador, 2000), xix.

68. Akbar S. Ahmed, "Islam and the West: Clash or Dialogue of Civilisations?," in *Islam and Global Dialogue Religious Pluralism and the Pursuit of Peace*, ed. Roger Boase (Aldershot: Ashgate, 2005), 106.

69. Ahmed, "Islam and the West," 107.

70. Ahmed, "Islam and the West," 108.

71. Ahmed, "Islam and the West," 109.

72. Ahmed, "Islam and the West," 109.

73. Akbar S. Ahmed, *Jinnah, Pakistan and Islamic Identity: The Search for Saladin* (London: Routledge, 1997), 23.

74. Ahmed, *Jinnah, Pakistan and Islamic Identity*, 24.

75. Ahmed, "Islam and the West: Clash or Dialogue of Civilisations?," 110.

76. Ahmed, "Islam and the West: Clash or Dialogue of Civilisations?," 111.

77. Muhsin Mahdi, "'Ibn Khaldun," in *International Encyclopaedia of the Social Sciences*, ed. David L. Sills (New York: Macmillan, 1968), Vol. 7, 56.

78. Akbar Ahmed, *Journey into Europe: Islam, Immigration and Identity* (New York: Brookings Institution Press, 2018), 9.

79. Akbar Ahmed, *The Thistle and the Drone: How America's War on Terror Became a Global War on Tribal Islam* (New York: Brookings Institution Press, 2013), 13.

80. Akbar S. Ahmed, *Religion and Politics in Muslim society: Order and Conflict in Pakistan* (Cambridge: Cambridge University Press, 1983), 18.

CHAPTER 7

Toward a Moral Dimension in Globalization

Umar Chapra's Exploration of Islam's Response to Economic Challenges

Introduction

In recent decades, the phenomenon of globalization has swept across the world, influencing various interconnected processes in economics, politics, society, culture, and ideology. Economic globalization, particularly since the establishment of the General Agreement on Tariffs and Trade in the early 1990s, has emerged as a dominant force shaping this global transformation. However, the underpinning ideologies of globalization, notably capitalism and liberalism, find themselves under the scrutiny of critical discourse, facing accusations of inherent biases and systemic limitations.[1] While capitalism has ostensibly triumphed over socialist–communist ideologies, its status as an incomplete economic theory is underscored by its potential exacerbation of socioeconomic disparities. Critics posit that the system tends to privilege select individuals, thereby leaving others vulnerable to exploitation and depriving them of equitable access to resources and opportunities. This chapter examines Umar Chapra's critique of the phenomenon of globalization, focusing particularly on its economic dimensions. Chapra contends that economic integration stands as the linchpin of globalization, cautioning against its reduction to a mere imposition of principles by affluent nations upon their less-developed counterparts. Instead, he advocates for a vision of globalization that transcends conventional paradigms, one that fosters uneven yet shared global progress and wealth, catering to the needs of both economically deprived and prosperous nations. However, he laments that the prevailing state of globalization falls short of realizing this transformative vision. Chapra introduces the imperative of social and political integration as concomitant pillars to economic globalization. He sheds light on the adverse consequences of consumer behavior transcending budgetary constraints and posits the inclusion of a moral dimension as a corrective measure for the prevailing issue of unjust wealth distribution. At this pivotal juncture, Islam, anchored in the principles of *sharī'ah*, emerges as a salient alternative.

Islamic economics, guided by the *maqasid al-sharī'ah*, prioritizes the preservation of religion, the soul, the mind, lineage, and human property. It offers a paradigm that accentuates mutually beneficial relationships over individual desires, positioning it as a viable counterpoint within the discourse on globalization. Implementation of Islamic economics necessitates a multifaceted approach, encompassing the revitalization of variables linked to human welfare, the mitigation of wealth concentration, structural reforms within the existing economic framework, and comprehensive financial restructuring. Chapra accentuates the importance of according due weight to these multifarious facets to facilitate judicious economic growth and development. In essence, Umar Chapra's work positions Islamic economics as a substantive alternative, offering valuable insights for achieving judicious economic growth and development in a globalized world.

Umer Chapra: Brief Biography and Works

Umer Chapra was born in India in 1933. He completed his undergraduate and postgraduate studies at Karachi University, ultimately obtaining his doctoral degree from the University of Minnesota in 1961.[2] Prior to his extensive thirty-four-year tenure as a consultant with the Saudi Arabian Monetary Organisation, during which he was granted Saudi citizenship, Chapra held positions at the Institute of Development Economics and the Islamic Research Institute in Pakistan. Later, he worked as a research assistant at the University of Minnesota and reached the position of associate professor of economics at both the University of Wisconsin and the University of Kentucky. Chapra, acknowledged as an authority in Islamic economics, has made significant contributions to the realms of Islamic finance and economics throughout his distinguished career.[3] He authored over ninety articles and reviews, along with approximately fifteen volumes and monographs. One of his pioneering works is the book *Towards a Fair Monetary System* (1985). He initially published *The Future of Economics: An Islamic Perspective* in 2002, followed by the equally well-received *Objectives of Islamic Economic Order: An Introduction in Economics and Islamic Financing* in 2005. In 2008, he released a book addressing the decline of Islamic civilization and the imperative for change. Chapra actively participated in numerous events and delivered countless invited speeches.[4] At present, Chapra holds the position of research advisor at the Islamic Research and Training Institute within the Islamic Development Bank in Jeddah. He is highly regarded within scholarly circles and is a member of esteemed intellectual societies, including the Islamic Economic Association, the Saudi Economic Association, the American Economic Association, and the revered Royal Economic Society in London. Beyond these affiliations, his sagacity and erudition shine through his role as a valued contributor to the editorial boards of various prestigious international economics journals.

Chapra's illustrious career, marked by a spectrum of intellectual accomplishments, has garnered him numerous coveted prizes and awards. His academic journey is adorned with a multitude of medals and prizes, each serving as a testament to his intellectual prowess. The distinguished King Faisal International Prize for Islamic Studies stands as the pinnacle of his achievements, symbolizing the recognition he has earned for his profound scholarship and enduring impact on the field. In academia, Chapra is a significant figure with a rich history of intellectual accomplishments. His journey inspires aspiring scholars, guiding them toward excellence in Islamic economics and making a lasting impact in the field. His works have transcended language barriers, with translations in Arabic, Bangla, French, Indonesian, Japanese, Malay, Persian, Polish, Spanish, Turkish, and Urdu.

Chapra's influence extends globally, as evidenced by his lectures at esteemed institutions such as Harvard Law School and Kyoto Universities in Tokyo and Kyoto, Japan. He has shared his expertise at various universities and professional institutions worldwide, participating in international and regional gatherings hosted by entities like the IMF, International Bank for Reconstruction and Development (IBRD), OPEC, Islamic Development Bank (IDB), OIC, and GCC.[5] Throughout his career, Dr. Chapra has imparted economic knowledge at the University of Minnesota (1957–1960), the University of Wisconsin–Platteville (1960–1961), the University of Kentucky–Lexington (1964–1955), and the Saudi Arabian Monetary Agency (July 1965–October 1999). Serving as an economic advisor and later as a senior economist at the Saudi Arabian Monetary Agency, he has significantly contributed to the field. Some of his well-known works and monographs include *The Future of Economics: An Islamic Perspective* (1993), *Islam and the Economic Challenge* (1992), and *Towards a Just Monetary System* (1985). His notable publications also include *Muslim Civilization: The Causes of the Decline and the Need for Reform* (2008), *The Islamic Welfare State and Its Role in the Economy, Objectives of the Islamic Economic Order*, and *Islam and Economic Development*, among others.[6]

Islam's Vision of Equality and Solidarity

Chapra contends that Islam maintains a continuum in the principles and values inherent in all revealed faiths.[7] This continuity is coupled with an inner harmony and a distinct sense of purpose that perseveres through various historical circumstances. According to Chapra, God sent Messengers to every corner of the world at different intervals, reiterating the same message.[8] This is explicitly stated in the Qur'ān: "Nothing is being said to you [Muhammad] that was not said to Messengers before you."[9] A new Messenger would only emerge when the preceding one's message was distorted or lost. Notably, these messengers, especially in Islam, aimed to unite people rather than divide them, emphasizing the shared responsibility of all individuals as vicegerents of God or khalifahs. This universal brotherhood mandates peaceful coexistence to ensure everyone's *falāh*.[10] The Qur'ān asserts that, due to disagreements among people, Mankind, despite being created as one nation, became divided. This division is attributed to their transgressions against each other, even after knowledge had reached them.[11] The worldview, encompassing beliefs and moral standards in religious perspectives and institutional economics, is referred to as knowledge. Chapra emphasizes that the Messengers' primary goal was to impart essential moral principles to humanity.[12] These guidelines dictate how individuals should interact to foster justice, fairness, collaboration, and solidarity among nations, social groups, and family members. However, the Qur'ān acknowledges that justice, collaboration, and unity do not always prevail, attributing this to interpersonal violations. Entrenched interests, unfairness, bias, exploitation, breach of contracts and duties, and abuse of authority are identified as root causes of transgression, hindering peaceful integration. Messengers were sent by God to address these issues, with the Qur'ān describing the Prophet of Islam as a blessing to mankind.[13]

To comprehend Chapra's perspective on contemporary globalization, it is instructive to examine how he situates Qur'ānic concepts of social justice and solidarity in the modern world. He argues that injustice, exploitation, and division are incompatible with blessings.[14] True blessings, in his view, come when everyone's needs are met, families are integrated, society is robust, and there is peace and harmony.[15] Islam, according to Chapra, seeks to unite people rather than divide them, and the Qur'ān upholds the oneness of humanity. Human failure to provide the necessary moral environment is identified as the obstacle to achieving this unity.[16] Chapra underscores the significance of treating one's family well, emphasizing that this virtue holds special favor in God's eyes, irrespective of individuals' religious, racial, economic, or gender differences. He makes reference to the final sermon of the Prophet, highlighting the importance of character in determining one's superiority in the eyes of the creator.[17] The Prophet's call for mercy toward those on Earth further reinforces the idea that all people, regardless of their background, are equal members of the same divine family. Islam teaches a profound message about the unity of humanity and globalization. Actions such as killing people, destroying property, and employing weapons of mass destruction, as exemplified in events like the U.S. intervention in Iraq, are deemed incompatible with Islamic teachings and, more broadly, with the principles of any revealed religion.[18]

Justice as the Key

As mentioned earlier, the Qur'ān attributes the current turmoil and conflict, dividing people along religious, secular, sectarian, theological, and ethnic lines, to transgressions against each other. Rectifying this transgression among Muslims necessitates the establishment of justice and collaboration.[19] Chapra contends that with these two elements, the possibility of globalization in economic integration, as well as social and political harmony, emerges.[20] The Qur'ān asserts that God sent Messengers to Earth with clear signs, the Book and the Balance to facilitate the creation of justice. Consequently, establishing justice was a primary objective of all God's messengers. Chapra interprets the term "Book" in this context as referring to the Qur'ān, providing a worldview and moral guidelines. Additionally, he suggests that "Balance" extends beyond the standards of good and evil outlined in the Qur'ān and the Sunnah. Chapra posits that adherence to these guidelines fosters globalization and human unity. Without implementing these norms of conduct, he argues, justice, harmony, and peace become unattainable. The Qur'ān explicitly states, "Those who believe and do not impair their belief with injustice, for them there is peace and they are the rightly guided ones."[21] Chapra contends that achieving global peace and harmony is contingent on treating people justly, emphasizing that faith alone is insufficient. The elimination of injustice is imperative to strengthen belief.[22] Fairness is highlighted as a fundamental tenet of Islam, with the Prophet underscoring that injustice results in darkness on the Day of Judgment. The Arabic term "Zulmat," denoting pitch blackness or complete darkness, is used to emphasize that those who engage in injustice will experience profound darkness in the Hereafter.[23] Chapra argues that without justice, conflicts, lack of collaboration, and challenges in globalization and integration will persist. To be just, equals must be treated equally and non-equals unfairly.[24]

Economic Integration: A Path to Peace and Prosperity

Chapra contends that economic integration is crucial as it fosters mutual dependency and reduced mutual dependence decreases the likelihood of conflict and war. He draws on Ibn Khaldun's rationale, asserting that economic activities, labor division, and specialization hinge on market size. Globalization facilitates market expansion, leading to increased demand for products and services, employment, faster growth, and an improved standard of living. This underscores the significance of trade expansion, as people become accustomed to a higher quality of life and resist any threats to it, even resorting to violence. Chapra emphasizes the urgent need to accelerate growth in the global North, particularly in European countries, suggesting that market growth is a means to propel development, boost incomes, and advance research and education.[25] Chapra highlights that Muslim thought aligns with the notion of integrating the world's economies. The core Islamic concept of the Unity of God correlates with the necessity of human unity (*tawhīd*).[26] According to him, a religion promoting human brotherhood rejects artificial divisions based on race, color, and nationality. Although the Qur'ān indicates that humans were initially formed as one nation (*ummah*), divisions arose due to differences stemming from prejudice, conflicts of interest, exploitation, and abuse of authority.[27] Islam's ultimate goal is to unite humanity.[28] Achieving this integration involves developing better understanding among people through increased engagement and collaboration. Since economics dominates human existence, the integration process can be accelerated by intertwining the economies of many nations, fostering more interdependence.[29] However, economic integration may face challenges without the removal of artificial obstacles through liberalization, enabling the free flow of commodities, money, labor, technology, and information.

Justice in Islamic Economics: Implications for Global Integration

Attempts to achieve integration will likely falter without justice and fairness in interpersonal relationships. The Qur'ān highlights that one of the primary reasons God sent prophets was to establish justice. The Prophet of Islam likened injustice to "total darkness," asserting that it disrupts unity, heightens tensions, and exacerbates human issues.[30] During the zenith of Muslim civilization, efforts were made to integrate many economies under Islamic influence with a commitment to justice and fairness. This contrasted with the tribal warfare in pre-Islamic Arabia, marked by levies and customs hindering commerce. Under Muslim rule, the region transformed into an expansive single market with low taxes, facilitating economic monetization and unrestricted movement of people and products. This facilitated trade growth from Morocco and Spain to India, China, and Africa. Archaeological findings of Muslim coins and existing historical documents from regions like Russia, Finland, Sweden, Norway, the British Isles, and Scotland indicate this extensive trade expansion.[31]

Chapra notes that the growth of industrial skill during this period reached unparalleled heights, contributing to overall development in agriculture, crafts, and trade. This inclusive development led to a substantial rise in incomes, ensuring that the benefits of progress were equitably shared among all countries rather than monopolized by a few.[32] Ibn Khaldun and his predecessors recognized that specialization and division of labor could not be sustained without justice and fairness in interpersonal interactions. Chapra argues that justice plays a crucial role in the equitable distribution of growth benefits, fostering solidarity.[33] The absence of fairness hampers mutual dependency and reduces motivation for increased work, investment, and development, thwarting the intended outcomes of increased output and specialization.[34] Without fairness, markets would not expand and progress will be sluggish. Throughout Muslim history, eminent jurists, including Caliph Harun al-Rashid and Abu Yusuf, asserted that fairness is a vital component of growth, with the removal of injustice expediting progress.[35]

Chapra contends that Al-Mawardi (d. 450H/1058G) asserted that comprehensive justice is essential for fostering cooperation, maintaining law and order, promoting national progress, accumulating economic wealth, increasing population, and ensuring national security.[36] Ibn Taymiyyah (d. 728H/1328G) viewed justice as a necessary byproduct of *tawhīd*, or faith in one God.[37] In his perspective, justice is imperative for everyone and injustice is universally prohibited, regardless of whether it is inflicted upon a Muslim, non-Muslim, or an unjust person.[38] Ibn Khaldun emphasized that progress is unattainable without justice, stating that oppression halts development and a decline in prosperity is the inevitable outcome of injustice and transgression.[39] However, Chapra adds that for justice to prevail and markets to function efficiently in an environment conducive to growth with justice, there must be a restraining force or political authority.[40] This role is crucial on a global scale to prevent powerful nations from oppressing weaker ones. Chapra suggests that the WTO is a potential candidate for this role, but laments that the WTO, dominated by strong industrial nations, has become a tool serving their interests and lacks the capacity to ensure fairness and justice in global commerce.[41] This perspective encapsulates the essence of

Islamic economic theory regarding global economic integration. Human existence is seen as a unity, and one of the primary objectives is the fusion of various cultures. Increased interdependence and unrestricted trade in commodities, people, money, and information are deemed crucial for achieving this objective. Artificial boundaries are viewed as hindrances to realizing human oneness and advancing the well-being of all. Chapra emphasizes that lasting integration is contingent on justice. Without justice, integration may initially progress but will eventually face disappointment as nations realize that the benefits are not equitably distributed.[42]

Challenges in Global Economic Integration and the Role of Developing Nations

The global economy, despite its strong emphasis on economic integration, falls short in giving justice the significant status it holds in Islamic thinking.[43] Justice implies the need to treat equals equally and unequals unequally. This suggests that not only should exports of developing countries grow, but ideally, the exports of industrial countries should grow faster. This would increase the share of developing nations in global commerce and narrow the gap between wealthy and poor nations. However, unless barriers to their exports to industrial nations are eliminated, the percentage of developing countries in global exports cannot increase. Without faster development, which enhances their capacity to manufacture for export at competitive rates, the growth of exports from developing nations is inconceivable. Unfortunately, liberalization, in this context, might increase developing nations' imports and stifle any manufacturing capacity they have previously established. Emphasizing a few successful nations as examples of how liberalization promotes growth overlooks the fact that many successful nations initially used protection. It is impractical to advise developing nations to take actions that even developed nations did not take in the past or do not take today.[44]

Chapra emphasizes the necessity of establishing an atmosphere that promotes growth, acknowledging that different nations have varying stages of development and different environments conducive to growth and export increase. To benefit from integration, these nations must be able to compete in the export market, requiring an educated and healthy workforce, along with appropriate social and physical infrastructure. However, these essentials are beyond the budgets of most developing nations. They also lack the funds required for safety nets, administration oversight, and retraining and re-employing workers displaced by globalization.[45] Under these circumstances, the intricate interplay of political instability and societal unrest becomes increasingly probable. Chapra argues that the full realization of the benefits of globalization for developing nations depends on support from affluent nations, which unfortunately remains elusive.[46] Jeffrey Sachs echoes this sentiment, highlighting the meager annual aid from the United States to the poorest nations, which fails to sufficiently address their needs and dilutes collective responsibility.[47] Amid grand rhetoric from international institutions like the G-7, the World Bank, and the IMF, access to developed nations' marketplaces, crucial for economic growth, remains shielded, protecting industries in which emerging nations have a competitive advantage. Addressing challenges like labor migration and technology transfer becomes imperative for expediting the developmental trajectory of impoverished nations.

The twin pillars of financial aid and liberalized markets are heralded as catalysts for development in underdeveloped nations, holding the promise of economic transformation. This symbiotic relationship envisions a mutually beneficial exchange, conveying progress to industrialized nations through facilitated exports to emerging nations. However, a cautionary note is sounded, warning that if the growth momentum of emerging nations falters, industrialized nations might temporarily boost their exports, potentially at the expense of development and employment in the developing world. The looming threat of heightened unemployment, already a significant challenge in many emerging nations, could trigger political and social upheaval.[48] This sets the stage for a narrative of global economic integration, where justice, fairness, and equitable prosperity are interwoven threads. Only through concerted and harmonious collective efforts can the dividends of globalization be bestowed upon all, transcending geographical boundaries and societal divisions.

Chapra, however, argues that industrialized nations overlook empirical findings, indicating a modest impact of exports from developing nations on wages and employment in their countries, with a few exceptions.[49] He suggests that emerging nations, facing socially unstable problems, should be treated differently and given the option of using protection until they gain the capacity to compete with industrialized nations. This temporary break should not be limitless and should allow emerging nations to establish favorable conditions for competition. They should not be pressured to prematurely liberalize their foreign currency markets, lacking the required conditions and reserves. The global economic paradigm lacks fairness, placing undue pressure on negotiators. Wealthy and powerful nations tend to dominate negotiations, while poorer nations are compelled to make concessions. The process of joining the WTO is depicted as complicated and time-consuming, with industrialized nations using their economic might to extract concessions from developing countries, as described by Dr. Ahmad Mohamed Ali, president of the Islamic Development Bank.[50]

The imbalance in skilled representation during WTO discussions is exemplified by the fact that, in 1997, industrialized nations dispatched an average of 6.8 highly skilled personnel, while developing nations could only muster around half of that total, on average.[51] Chapra argues that these authorities from developing nations may not have been as skilled and educated as their counterparts from industrialized nations. The average for developing nations is misleading, as some of these poorer nations have even less competent workers than the average suggests, making them less able to conduct successful negotiations. Consequently, developing nations struggle to secure favorable trading conditions. The unfairness becomes apparent as major industrialized nations pressure oil-producing nations to increase oil production, disregarding the impact on these nations' revenues and their ability to finance growth. This approach goes against the demands of fairness, which should entail a reduction in the oil taxes of industrialized nations, accounting for around 75 percent of the pump price in some countries. Additionally, trade restrictions apply to petrochemicals, a significant export of oil-producing nations, as well as textiles and agricultural goods, the primary exports of developing nations. Particularly detrimental are the subsidies given to agriculture by industrialized nations, artificially lowering the price of their agricultural products globally and rendering exports from developing nations uncompetitive.[52]

The critical point not grasped is that developing nations have a comparative advantage in agriculture. If subsidies from industrialized nations impede the increase in exports of agricultural products from developing nations, they cannot achieve the export surplus necessary to finance the development of their industries and agriculture. This compels these nations to take on substantial debt, increasing the burden of debt service and limiting resources for development. The type of economic integration advocated by Islam and emphasized by Muslim scholars is deemed impossible in such an unfair climate.

Redefining Globalization through Islamic Economic Principles

Islamic economics provides a strong rationale for promoting economic unity, as it decreases the likelihood of conflict and enhances the prospect of achieving the Islamic objective of human unity and globalization.[53] However, Chapra is skeptical about the current economic globalization trend, asserting that it is unlikely to lead to the realization of these ideals. The existing globalization model prioritizes market development through deregulation but often neglects the crucial element of justice. For poverty and unemployment to decrease in developing nations, justice necessitates that as exports from industrialized nations increase, those from developing nations should ideally grow at a faster pace. Therefore, globalization should not solely focus on boosting commerce in industrialized nations but also on expanding trade in developing nations. However, the current form of globalization fails to lift all export restrictions and enhance production capabilities in developing nations, hindering their participation in the global market. Certain products, such as petrochemicals, oil, textiles, and agriculture, have been excluded or only recently included, impeding the comprehensive integration of these nations into the global economy. Agricultural subsidies in industrialized nations, including Europe, America, and Japan, further obstruct the development of agriculture in the developing world. Despite their comparative advantage in agriculture, these nations struggle to compete globally, leading to a decline in their agricultural output. Chapra emphasizes the historical significance of agricultural development in the industrialization of all nations, including during the early centuries of Islam. Agricultural growth is essential for the development of emerging nations, and the elimination of subsidies is crucial for fostering their progress.[54]

The Qur'ān's Message of Social Integration

Chapra emphasizes the significance of social integration as a key factor in determining whether globalization is a positive force or a deception. He contends that fostering social integration is essential for the development of a global village, characterized by diverse cultures rather than a single, imposed cultural identity. Attempts by a dominant nation to enforce its culture globally would be offensive to other nations. Instead, Chapra advocates for a world enriched by cultural diversity, asserting that a perfect, homogeneous civilization is nonexistent, and the world benefits from embracing various cultures. Chapra encourages the pursuit of understanding and respect for others' cultures and religions.[55] Examining this perspective through classical Islamic literature, Chapra underscores the Qur'ānic stance on social integration. He points out that the Qur'ān explicitly prohibits Muslims from disparaging the religious symbols or deities of others, emphasizing the importance of avoiding ridicule or mockery that could lead to conflicts. Chapra argues against such a negative approach to globalization, stating that it is counterproductive and harmful.[56] Furthermore, Chapra references the Qur'ān's guidance to Muslims to refrain from arguing with followers of the book (*People of the Scriptures*) unless they have committed injustice. The Qur'ān emphasizes the shared belief in revelations and surrender to the one God, promoting a sense of commonality rather than discord.[57] In essence, Chapra advocates for a form of globalization that values and respects diverse cultures, fostering harmony and mutual understanding.

Building Alliances for Peace: Political Integration and Global Cooperation

Chapra asserts that political integration does not involve the establishment of a single country under the dominance of a superpower. Instead, he argues that true political integration can only occur under a government committed to justice, conflict reduction, and the promotion of peace and prosperity for all nations.[58] The UN was supposed to play a pivotal role in this regard, but it has fallen short of its intended purpose. Chapra points out instances of the United States and Israel violating UN resolutions and he criticizes the U.S. invasion of Iraq, which he believes was aimed at serving the interests of Israel and establishing dominance in the Middle East. He notes the undesirable consequences of having a single superpower controlling the oil-rich Middle East, citing the potential for manipulating oil flow to influence other nations' policies. Chapra underscores that political unification is a global necessity, but he emphasizes that force cannot be employed to achieve it. Instead, effective communication, mutual respect for beliefs and cultures, collaborative efforts, increased economic interdependence, and the avoidance of societal disputes are the key elements for achieving political integration. He contends that these principles, grounded in fairness, understanding, and unity, are essential components of the broader process of globalization, which he views as crucial for global prosperity.[59] In essence, Chapra advocates for a form of globalization that embraces economic, social, and political integration, guided by principles of justice and collaboration among nations.

Islam's Moral Foundation for Societal Transformation and Economic Justice

Muslim nations currently face challenges in serving as role models due to decades of decline, sharing similar issues with the West but varying in severity.[60] This prompts consideration of whether the ongoing Islamic renaissance in Muslim cultures will lead to meaningful improvement. While acknowledging the difficulties, many Muslims believe in the potential for positive change. Islam stands out as the only force capable of drawing people together, transcending diversity and inspiring moral behavior despite moral and material deterioration. In confronting challenges, the Islamic worldview, rooted in various beliefs, rejects secularism, value neutrality, materialism, and social Darwinism. Unlike systems reliant solely on the state or the market, Islam places a high priority on moral principles, human brotherhood, socioeconomic fairness, and family unity. Adopting a holistic perspective, it emphasizes the complementary roles played by the market, families, society, and the state to achieve socioeconomic justice and universal well-being.[61]

Chapra underscores the necessity for personal and societal transformation to address existing inequalities perpetuated by market and government systems. According to him, social change through these two avenues is crucial.[62] Central to the Islamic faith is the belief in a one, all-encompassing God responsible for creating the entire universe, including humanity. Individuals, as appointed representatives of God, possess inherent dignity and respect.[63] This fundamental principle establishes a sense of equality, rejecting notions of superiority based on race, gender, nationality, wealth, or social status. In the Islamic perspective, individuals are considered brothers and sisters, united through their shared membership in the universal family of God. It is crucial to recognize that their time on Earth is temporary, as their ultimate destination lies in the Hereafter, where they will be held accountable before God. The measure of their happiness in the eternal realm depends on the extent to which they have fulfilled their responsibilities toward others, working toward the well-being of all.[64] Chapra thus emphasizes the moral and spiritual dimensions inherent in the Islamic worldview, advocating for a holistic approach to personal and societal change that aligns with these fundamental beliefs.

Chapra contends that the manner in which limited resources are utilized has a significant impact on the well-being of everyone.[65] Throughout history, the Creator and Owner of these resources, through a succession of His messengers, has imparted certain values, standards of behavior, or institutions to guide people in making effective and equitable use of these resources. This continuity and resemblance in the value systems of various revealed faiths highlight the enduring importance of these messages. Humans are obligated to use and interact with the resources provided by God in accordance with the moral standards He has established to ensure the well-being of everyone.[66] However, the messengers not only brought principles but also engaged in efforts to transform individuals and the institutions influencing them. The central focus of the Islamic message is social, economic, and political transformation. It is argued that achieving the well-being of everyone may not be feasible without such comprehensive reform.⁶⁷ Therefore, Chapra emphasizes the transformative potential of adhering to the moral standards and principles outlined in the Islamic worldview for the equitable and responsible utilization of resources.

In the context of Islam, accepting the status quo and relinquishing the pursuit of an envisioned ideal are considered unacceptable. Such a mindset is viewed as a passive endorsement of existing injustices, and Islam insists on active engagement in the transformation of society to align with its values. This transformation is seen as crucial for realizing the *maqasid al-sharī'ah*, the overarching aims of Islamic law, which include socioeconomic fairness and the well-being of all of God's creations, encompassing animals, birds, and insects.⁶⁸ The acknowledgment of injustice hinders genuine well-being, exacerbates societal conflicts, diminishes people's motivation to contribute their best efforts, and consequently impedes progress. In contrast to traditional economics, which assumes the dominance of self-interested behavior, Islam does not presuppose the prevalence of ideal conduct. While recognizing that some individuals may exhibit ideal behavior, Islam acknowledges that most people's actions may fall between selfishness and altruism. Consequently, Islam emphasizes the continuous individual and collective striving (*jihād*) for moral elevation and improvement.

Due to a sense of moral obligation, individuals are inclined to act in the best interests of others and may even make sacrifices on their behalf. Chapra emphasizes that despite having the freedom to preserve inherent goodness, individuals also have the option to act contrary to it.⁶⁹ Such actions can be beneficial for both the individual and society. In order to motivate people to work diligently for their own well-being and the welfare of others, as well as to deter them from causing harm, it is crucial to provide both worldly and spiritual incentives and deterrents. While market discipline serves as a vital tool for creating incentives and barriers by promoting efficiency, Chapra argues that it alone cannot safeguard societal interests. Although competition is essential for ensuring efficiency, it cannot be solely relied upon to protect societal interests, as there are covert methods to suppress competition and exploit others for personal gain. In this context, governments play a crucial role by creating and enforcing rules. However, the effectiveness of rules depends on a shared sense of moral goodness within society, serving as the foundational principle for regulation.

Chapra argues that relying solely on rules might not be practical because there are numerous ways to deceive and exploit others without being detected. Governments may face challenges in succeeding unless there is an internal desire among people to do what is right, honor contracts and commitments faithfully, and refrain from unfair competition or unethical means of earning.[70] The belief in reward and punishment in the hereafter, ingrained in individuals, becomes crucial. People's conditions in the hereafter are believed to be better if they avoid wrongdoing and prioritize the interests of others over their own. This concept extends self-interest beyond the individual's lifespan in this world, providing a long-term perspective. Chapra contends that protecting societal interests requires the support of all institutions, including proper upbringing, the preservation of human nature's goodness, adherence to moral ideals, market discipline, effective governmental roles, and faith in accountability in the Hereafter. By combining all these elements, human welfare can be more fully realized compared to relying solely on government or market forces.[71] This perspective illustrates that Islam recognizes the importance of market discipline and effective government in achieving human welfare. To enhance the market system's ability to achieve equality and efficiency, three methods are introduced: filtering, incentive, and socioeconomic and political transformation.[72]

Chapra asserts that Islam considers it crucial to screen out all demands on resources that jeopardize the attainment of complete human well-being.[73] While socialism and central planning were not effective tools for this objective, market mechanisms assist in balancing supply and demand, although they may fail to protect social interests. The moral filter is essential in altering people's preferences to sift out earning and spending behaviors that hinder overall well-being. This moral filter becomes even more crucial when avoiding the use of force. To achieve an equilibrium between supply and demand for resources that supports the realization of society's humanitarian aims, two layers of filter—the moral filter and the pricing filter—are employed. However, the moral filter may be ineffective without a system in place to encourage people to uphold its principles, as individuals must sacrifice their own interests to faithfully adhere to moral principles. Therefore, the moral filter can function effectively when belief in the afterlife is included.[74]

Chapra argues that the utilization of limited resources and human behavior, influenced by physical, social, and political contexts, requires supplementation with socioeconomic and political reform in the Islamic worldview. This reform, a primary goal of all God's Messengers, aims to encourage individuals, families, society, and the government to utilize resources and collaborate in ways that promote overall well-being. In a community of human brotherhood, each person is individually and communally accountable for their own and others' well-being. Cooperation is essential to encourage positive behavior and curb negative actions that hinder overall well-being.[75] Without an effective mechanism to identify and penalize offenders, dishonesty, bribery, and unfair practices may go unchecked, leading to embedded behaviors through route dependency and self-reinforcing processes. In such cases, thorough transformation through socioeconomic and political restructuring becomes necessary. Islam seeks to provide a moral dimension to economics, emphasizing the positive effects of good governance, aiming to enable all facets of society to contribute positively to the realization of human well-being.[76]

Islamic Economic Thought and *Maqasid al-Sharī'ah*

Islam envisions a fundamentally distinct economic structure from the ones currently in place, drawing its ideology, objectives, and tactics from the *sharī'ah*, serving as its foundation.[77] In contrast to the predominantly secular systems of the modern world, Islam's purposes, known as *maqasid al-sharī'ah*, are not exclusively materialistic. Instead, they are based on conceptions of human welfare and the good life that prioritize brotherhood and socioeconomic justice, addressing both the physical and spiritual needs of all people. This perspective arises from the belief in the equality of all individuals as God's vicegerents on Earth and His dependents, emphasizing that true inner contentment requires the fulfillment of both material and spiritual needs.[78] The *maqasid al-sharī'ah* contains all the necessary information for human welfare and a good life within the framework of the *sharī'ah*, including aspects important for preserving and enhancing religion, life, intellect, posterity, and riches, as articulated by Al-Ghazali.[79]

From an Islamic standpoint, faith is considered the most crucial component for human well-being. Placing faith at the forefront establishes a solid foundation for human connections, fostering fair and compassionate communication, and promoting the well-being of everyone. Faith also serves as a moral filter for resource allocation and distribution, aligned with the principles of brotherhood and socioeconomic justice and a motivational mechanism supporting the objectives of meeting needs and distributing wealth and income fairly. Chapra argues that without incorporating the element of faith into human decisions across various spheres, achieving efficiency and equality in resource distribution and allocation, reducing macroeconomic imbalances and economic instability, and addressing issues like crime and unrest become challenging.[80] The concept of efficiency, defined in physical science as the ratio of usable output to total output or input, is explored within the Islamic perspective. Efficiency, particularly when considering the well-being of everyone, requires a metric of usefulness that goes beyond individual preferences and prices. Moral standards accepted by society supplement these economic metrics. Chapra emphasizes that defining efficiency and equality without moral standards is challenging, highlighting the importance of a moral filter in assessing economic outcomes.[81] Al-Ghazali ranks wealth last among the *maqasid* since it is not considered a goal in itself.

The main purpose of the *sharī'ah* is to promote the welfare of humankind, with the three goals—life, intellect, and posterity—all linked to the wellbeing of individuals. In a secularist context, relying solely on pricing and markets cannot ensure the allocation and distribution of resources with the strong moral commitment needed to enrich these three aspects for everyone. Chapra argues that the definition of a need should encompass all that is essential to enhance these three goals for everybody, emphasizing that reasonable measures must be employed to guarantee its fulfillment.[82] This includes access to sufficient food, clothing, suitable environments for raising children, and an education fostering spiritual and intellectual growth. Other needs consist of housing, a peaceful environment free from violence and pollution, medical services, convenient transportation, adequate spare time for family and societal responsibilities, and the opportunity to earn a decent income. Any distribution and allocation of resources that do not contribute to the realization of human welfare cannot be considered efficient or equitable.[83]

However, there exists a significant gap between the ideals of the *sharī'ah* and the actual practice in Muslim nations due to historical circumstances such as the decline of Muslims and subsequent enslavement by imperialist powers, both capitalist and communist. Muslim societies often do not exhibit the spiritual radiance of Islam, and a significant portion of the population may lack awareness of the essential qualities characterizing a Muslim or an Islamic civilization. Secularism, blended with feudalism, capitalism, and socialism, prevails in many Muslim-majority nations. There is no dominant Islamic economic system in any region of the Muslim world. Attempts to address economic issues have been made using policies derived from the secularist viewpoint of existing systems, leading to worsening problems. Despite an increase in gross domestic product, poverty has risen and the basic necessities of the population remain unmet. Income and wealth disparities have exacerbated, and public sector budgetary deficits, balance of payments issues, and the threat of inflation persist.[84]

Chapra highlights the observation made by Mahathir Muhammad, the former prime minister of Malaysia, who noted a lack of new solutions to address poverty in the Third World.[85] The search for answers in conversations with developed economies seemed to have ceased, and officials from the Third World faced a challenging task in finding fresh solutions to help poor countries escape rising debt.[86] Chapra proposes that Islamization—the rebuilding of Muslim nations' economics in the context of Islamic teachings—could be beneficial. He suggests an Islamic economic system with a worldview and strategy aligned with the maqasid, providing a just and equitable resolution for Islamic countries.[87] Islam offers a realistic perspective, presenting a comprehensive and interconnected system that is aware of the challenges involved in problem-solving. Islam provides various solutions consistent with its *maqasid* and worldview. Implementing the Islamic economic strategy based on the *sharī'ah* involves a thorough understanding of the Islamic worldview's efficiency and equity, aiming to benefit all people globally and help them succeed. Chapra defines the purpose of the Islamic worldview as serving as a normative principle based on the Qur'ān and sunnah, while the Islamic economic methodology (*maqasid*) supports the normative justification framework in the form of *mu'amalah* jurisprudence for factors related to public economy.[88]

Overcoming Challenges

Chapra argues against Muslim countries obstructing liberalization despite the challenges posed by industrialized nations, emphasizing that justice is not achieved by isolating themselves. He asserts that justice can only be accomplished through concerted effort. The solidarity of Muslim countries, supported by organizations like the IDB and the OIC, is deemed crucial in facing these challenges. Chapra acknowledges that industrial nations' trade prohibitions are not the sole obstacle to the rapid growth of Muslim countries; they face various difficulties. He highlights the significant issue of poor technical and educational levels among their people, which, according to Ibn Khaldun, are both the goal and the method of advancement.[89] Chapra contends that Muslim nations cannot fully benefit from globalization without the capacity and willingness to exert the effort required for increased output and exports.[90] He identifies key variables in growth, including political authority, the economic system, and the presence of domestic justice. While Islam provides ideals beneficial to growth, Chapra emphasizes the need to educate those who do not already uphold these ideals.[91]

Muslim-majority nations have not yet established the necessary educational infrastructure to effectively support their economic goals. The prevalence of corruption in these economies disrupts the optimal allocation of resources, leading to inefficiencies. Additionally, the presence of restrictive economic systems conflicting with Islamic principles acts as a deterrent to investment and innovation, exacerbating socioeconomic disparities in these nations. A significant obstacle to progress is the dominance of influential land-owning families manipulating the political and economic landscape to protect their interests, neglecting broader growth and development. While some degree of protectionism may be justified in early growth stages, an excessive focus on such policies can lead to complacency. Lack of international competition reduces the incentive for the agricultural and industrial sectors to improve efficiency and productivity. This absence impedes necessary transformative changes in social, political, and economic realms to prepare adequately for global competitiveness challenges. Chapra contends that protectionism results in higher costs for consumers importing goods and services, further burdening the economy.[92]

Islamic values perceive such injustices as unacceptable. Any temporary allowance of injustice in the public interest should be strictly necessary and limited; no one has the authority to impose ongoing injustice on the populace. Often, trade restrictions are implemented to serve specific interests rather than the broader public good. Ibn Khaldun argues that justice is crucial for progress, and liberalization would enhance efficiency and development. Chapra recognizes the common economic challenges faced by countries worldwide. He contends that the root of these problems lies in the ineffective and unfair distribution of the resources bestowed upon humans, a flaw the current system cannot rectify.[93] Chapra proposes an Islamic economic framework aligned with the *maqasid al-sharī'ah*, offering a practical and reasonable solution for Muslim nations to achieve efficiency and fairness as an alternative. The primary goal in controlling allocation and distribution is to ensure adherence to the *maqasid al-sharī'ah*, ultimately promoting the welfare of the population.[94]

Chapra's interpretation of Islamic economics revolves around the concept of *tawhid*. A comprehensive strategy for organizing the economic system should encompass four essential elements: a filter mechanism, a correct motivation, socioeconomic and financial restructuring, and the role of the state. Mere harmony between *sharī'ah* and the worldview is insufficient to bring about efficiency and justice for the well-being of the people.[95] Chapra contends that there is no need to be overly apprehensive about globalization, considering it as both a challenge and an opportunity. He points out that Muslims have historically been pioneers of globalization, transforming the regions under Muslim dominion into an expansive common market, and fostering overall growth and a significant increase in everyone's incomes. Chapra emphasizes that instead of fearing globalization, efforts should be directed toward fighting for justice and implementing appropriate political, legal, economic, and social changes to effectively utilize resources and address the challenges posed by globalization.[96]

Conclusion

In this chapter, we have explored Umar Chapra's analysis of globalization and its implications for Muslim-majority nations. Chapra argues that globalization, fundamentally, involves economic integration, connecting nations through various channels such as trade, investment, and capital flow. Crucially, he rejects the idea that this integration should be a tool to impose the principles and values of affluent nations onto their less developed counterparts. Instead, he advocates for a vision of globalization that prioritizes justice and recognizes the necessity for an asymmetrical distribution of progress and wealth, benefiting both affluent and impoverished nations. Despite these ideals, Chapra contends that the current state of globalization falls short of achieving the noble objective of justice and egalitarian growth. He emphasizes that focusing solely on economic integration neglects essential aspects of social and political integration. Chapra highlights the negative repercussions of consumer behavior, especially when it extends beyond financial boundaries, leading to excessive debt and causing detrimental effects on individuals and societies. This underscores the importance of addressing not only economic determinants but also the social and behavioral dimensions when assessing the impact of globalization.[97]

Furthermore, Chapra underscores the critical importance of addressing the issue of wealth distribution. He argues that the current global economic structure often leads to an unjust concentration of wealth in the hands of a privileged few, exacerbating socioeconomic inequalities. To remedy this situation, he advocates for the infusion of a moral dimension into economic systems. Drawing inspiration from the principles of Sharia-based economic theory, which emphasize concepts of fairness, equity, and social welfare, Chapra proposes an alternative path to navigate economic challenges and ensure the fair distribution of wealth. Aligned with the tenets of Islamic economics, which resonate with *the maqasid al-sharī'ah*, Chapra outlines five fundamental concerns that warrant attention: the preservation of religion, the soul, the mind, lineage, and human property. These profound objectives create a comprehensive framework, guiding economic policies and practices that prioritize holistic well-being and address the diverse needs of individuals and society at large. To realize these aspirations, Chapra suggests revitalizing elements associated with human dignity, reducing the concentration of wealth, reforming existing economic paradigms to align with Islamic principles, and restructuring financial circumstances to promote ethical conduct and prudent behavior.[98]

The chapter further explored the diverse challenges faced by Muslim-majority nations in fully harnessing the benefits of globalization. Chapra highlights significant impediments, including insufficient educational infrastructure, corruption, and restrictive economic systems. These multifaceted challenges obstruct the smooth integration of these nations into the global economy, preventing them from capitalizing on the numerous opportunities presented by globalization. Moreover, the dominance of land-owning families wielding influence over political and economic systems emerges as a formidable barrier to inclusive growth and development. This situation underscores the need for concerted efforts to promote equitable policies, redistribute wealth, and ensure broader access to economic opportunities for the entire population.

Chapra acknowledges the potential advantages of protectionism in specific contexts but advises against an excessive emphasis on this approach. He argues that international competition acts as a catalyst for efficiency and innovation, prompting essential transformations in social, political, and economic realms. Maintaining a delicate balance between protecting domestic industries and actively participating in global trade and collaboration is crucial for sustainable growth and development. The potential role of Islam in fostering economic growth and justice is thoroughly examined by Chapra. While Islam promotes ideals and principles conducive to economic progress, Chapra emphasizes the need to disseminate these principles among individuals who are not already familiar with them. He underscores the crucial role of a moral dimension in influencing resource allocation and distribution, ensuring fairness and contributing to societal harmony and familial tranquility. Through embracing Islamic principles and adopting a comprehensive approach to development, Muslim-majority nations can strive to achieve genuine human well-being in alignment with the noble vision outlined in the Qur'an.

Chapra advocates for the integration of economic, social, and moral dimensions to chart a course for sustainable and equitable growth in Muslim-majority nations amid the challenges of globalization. By embracing Islamic values, implementing policies rooted in Islamic economics, and addressing the multifaceted aspects of globalization, these nations can navigate the complexities of the global economy. Chapra's vision underscores the importance of a comprehensive understanding of globalization that encompasses economic, social, and behavioral dimensions, alongside the crucial goals of equitable wealth distribution and adherence to moral principles. Through these efforts, Muslim-majority nations can strive for holistic development and the creation of just and prosperous societies.

Notes

1. Mohammad Abo Gazleh, "Globalization and Politics: The Effects of Globalization on Human Life Aspects," Paper Presented in the International Conference on Malaysia and Globalization, University of Malaya, Kuala Lumpur, 2001.
2. Arikha Dahlia, "Monetary Policy in Perspective of Umer Chapra." Accessed April 14, 2024. https://mpra.ub.uni-muenchen.de/87022/.
3. Dr. Umer Chapra, Research Centre for Islamic Legislation and Ethics. Accessed April 14, 2024. https://www.cilecenter.org/about-us/our-team/dr-umer-chapra.
4. Dr. Umer Chapra, Research Centre for Islamic Legislation and Ethics.
5. Dr. M Umer Chapra, "A Brief Biography." Accessed April 14, 2024.https://web.archive.org/web/20121102020952/http://www.muchapra.com/about.html.
6. Islamic Economics, "Biography: Dr. Muhammad Umar Chapra: The Pioneer of Modern Islamic Economics." Accessed April 14, 2024. http://islamiceconomicsbd.blogspot.in/2011/09/biographydr-muhammad-umar-chapra.html.
7. Umer Chapra, "Global Economic Challenges and Islam," *Policy Perspectives* 3, no. 2 (2006): 19–41.
8. Al-Qur'ān, 41:43.
9. M. Umar Chapra, *Islam and Economic Development: A Strategy for Development with Justice and Stability* (Islamabad: Islamic Research Institute Press), 7.
10. M. Umar Chapra, *The Islamic Vision of Development in the Light of Maqasid Al-Sharī'ah* (Herndon, VA: The International Institute of Islamic thought, 2007), 1.
11. Al-Qur'ān, 19:10.
12. Al-Qur'ān, 24:14.
13. Chapra, "Global Economic Challenges and Islam," 31.
14. Al-Qur'ān; 21:107.
15. Chapra, "Global Economic Challenges and Islam," 40.
16. Chapra, "Global Economic Challenges and Islam," 40.
17. Qur'ān; 49:13.
18. Qur'ān; 49:13.
19. Chapra, "Global Economic Challenges and Islam," 25.
20. Chapra, "Global Economic Challenges and Islam," 27.
21. Al-Qur'ān: 57:25.
22. Chapra, Global Economic Challenges and Islam," 29.
23. Al-Qur'ān, 6:82.
24. Umer M. Chapra, "Islamic Economic Thought and The New Global Economy," *Islamic Economic Studies* 9 (2001): 1–16.
25. Abd al-Rahman Ibn Khaldun, *Muqaddimah* (Cairo: Al-Maktabah al-Tijariyyah al-Kubra, n.d.), 360–370.
26. Chapra, "Global Economic Challenges and Islam," 28.
27. Chapra, "Global Economic Challenges and Islam," 28.
28. Al-Qur'ān, 10:19.
29. Al-Qur'ān, 10:19.

30. Al-Qur'ān, 57:25.

31. Umer Chapra, *The Future of Economics: An Islamic Perspective* (Leicester: The Islamic Foundation, 2000), 173–252.

32. Howard Kramer, "Geography and Commerce," in *Legacy of Islam*, ed. Thomas Arnold and Alfred Gindllaume (Oxford: Oxford University Press, 1952), 104.

33. Abraham Udovitch, *Partnership and Profit in Medieval Islam* (Princeton, NJ: Princeton University Press, 1970), 104.

34. Chapra, *The Future of Economics*, 176.

35. Abu Yusuf, *Kitab al-Kharaj*, 2nd edition (Cairo: al-Matba[ah al Salafiyyah, 1933), 111.

36. Abu al-Hasan Mawardi, *Adab al-Dunya wa al-Din*, ed. Mustafa al-Saqqa (Cairo: Mustafa al-Babi al-Halabi, 1955), 125.

37. Ibn Taymiyyah, *Majmu al- Fatawa Shaykh al-Islam Ahmad Ibn Taymiyyah*, ed. Abd al-Rahman al-Asimi, 1st edition (Riyadh: Matabah al-Riyadh, 1961–1963), Vol. 18, 165.

38. Taymiyyah, *Majmu al- Fatawa*, 166.

39. Khaldun, *Muqaddimah*, 287.

40. Khaldun, *Muqaddimah*, 288.

41. Chapra, "Islamic Economic Thought and the New Global Economy," 8.

42. Chapra, "Islamic Economic Thought and the New Global Economy," 11.

43. Timur Kuran, "Islam and Economic Performance: Historical and Contemporary Links," *Journal of Economic Literature* 56, no. 4 (2018): 1292–1359.

44. Sebastian Edwards, "Openness, Trade Liberalization, and Growth in Developing Countries," *Journal of Economic Literature* 31, no. 3 (1993): 1358–1393.

45. Chapra, "Islamic Economic Thought and the New Global Economy," 9.

46. Chapra, "Islamic Economic Thought and the New Global Economy," 9.

47. Chapra, "Islamic Economic Thought and the New Global Economy," 11.

48. Chapra, "Islamic Economic Thought and the New Global Economy," 13.

49. Bob Anderson and Paul Brenton, "The Dollar, Trade and Technology, and Inequality in the USA" *National Institute Economic Review* 166 (1998): 78–86.

50. Islamic Development Bank, *Proceedings of the Seminar on Accession to the WTO and Implementation of the Uruguay Round Agreements* (Jeddah: IDB, 1997).

51. Chapra, "Islamic Economic Thought and the New Global Economy," 10.

52. Chapra, *Islam and Economic Development*, 11.

53. Chapra, *The Future of Economics*, 179.

54. Chapra, *Islam and Economic Development*, 11.

55. Chapra, *The Future of Economics*, 181.

56. Al-Qur'ān, 6:108.

57. Al-Qur'ān, 29:46.

58. Chapra, "Global Economic Challenges and Islam," 21.

59. Chapra, "Global Economic Challenges and Islam," 22.

60. Chapra, "Global Economic Challenges and Islam," 23.

61. Umer Chapra, "Ethics and Economics: An Islamic Perspective," *Islamic Economic Studies* 16, no. 1 and 2 (2008–2009): 14.
62. Chapra, "Ethics and Economics: An Islamic Perspective," 15.
63. Chapra, *Islam and the Economic Challenge*, 426.
64. Mansoor Alam, "The Qur'ān and Muslim Unity." Accessed April 14, 2024. https://www.islamicity.org/20730/the-quran-and-muslim-unity/.
65. M. Umer Chapra, "The Economic Problem: Can Islam Play an Effective Role in Solving it Efficiently as well as Equitably?," IRTI Working Paper Series, Islamic Research and Training Institute, 2011, 5. Accessed April 14, 2024. https://www.researchgate.net/publication/303498620_The_Economic_Problem_Can_Islam_Play_an_Effective_Role_in_Solving_it_Efficiently_as_well_as_Equitably.
66. Chapra, "The Economic Problem," 6.
67. Chapra, "Ethics and Economics: An Islamic Perspective," 19.
68. Chapra, "Ethics and Economics: An Islamic Perspective," 20.
69. M. Umar Chapra, "The Islamic Welfare State and its Role in the Economy," in *Development Issues in Islam*, ed. Abul Hasan M. Sadeq (Kuala Lumpur: IIUM Research Center, 1995), 355–388.
70. Chapra, "The Islamic Welfare State and its Role in the Economy," 356.
71. Chapra, "The Islamic Welfare State and its Role in the Economy," 357.
72. Chapra, *The Future of Economics*, 26.
73. Chapra, *Islam and the Economic Challenge*, 427.
74. Chapra, *Islam and the Economic Challenge*, 428.
75. Chapra, *The Future of Economics*, 29.
76. Chapra, *Ethics and Economics*, 24.
77. Chapra, *Ethics and Economics*, 26.
78. Chapra, *Islam and the Economic Challenge*, 429.
79. Chapra, *Islam and the Economic Challenge*, 430.
80. Umer Chapra, "Islamic Economics: An Approach to Human Welfare," in *Studies in Islamic Economics*, ed. Khurshid Ahmad (Leicester: The Islamic Foundation, 1980), 3–18.
81. Chapra, *Islam and the Economic Challenge*, 7.
82. Chapra, "Islamic Economics: An Approach to Human Welfare," 8.
83. Chapra, "Islamic Economics: An Approach to Human Welfare," 10.
84. Chapra, "The Islamic Welfare State and its Role in the Economy," 357.
85. Chapra, "Ethics and Economics: An Islamic Perspective," 21.
86. Chapra, "The Economic Problem," 7.
87. Chapra, "Islam and the Economic Challenge," 7.
88. Chapra, "The Economic Problem," 9.
89. Franz Rosenthal, *The Muqaddimah: An Introduction to History*, Vol. I (London: Routledge, 1967), lxxi.
90. Umer Chapra, *Towards a Just Monetary System* (Leicester: The Islamic Foundation, 1985), 122–125.
91. Chapra, *Towards a Just Monetary System*, 124.
92. Chapra, *Towards a Just Monetary System*, 123.

93. Chapra, "The Economic Problem," 8.
94. Chapra, *Towards a Just Monetary System*, 124.
95. Khusniati Rofiah and Mohammad Ghozali, "Construction of M. Umer Chapra's Economic Thoughts in Realizing Efficiency and Justice," *Al-Iktisab: Journal of Islamic Economic Law* 4, no. 1 (2020): 15–31.
96. Chapra, "Islamic Economic Thought and The New Global Economy," 14.
97. Chapra, *The Future of Economics*, 145.
98. Al-Qur'ān, 21:107.

CHAPTER 8

Islamic Thought in the Age of Globalization
Ibrahim Abu Rabi's Perspective on Epistemological, Ethical, and Socioeconomic Changes

Introduction

The notion of progress has been central to the Western worldview, significantly influencing global socioeconomic and intellectual trajectories since the Industrial Revolution.[1] This perspective, rooted in the belief in continual human advancement, has historically driven endeavors to conquer and dominate the so-called Third World.[2] The contemporary worldview places economic expansion and technological innovation at the forefront, framing development as a salvational concept. Traditional civilizations, along with their socioeconomic structures and ethical frameworks, have faced profound challenges due to the relentless pursuit of progress. Globalization, a modern manifestation of this pursuit, has introduced new forms of colonialism, raising concerns reminiscent of late nineteenth-century imperialism, as noted by Hannah Arendt.[3] The current wave of globalization, however, represents a more sophisticated and potentially more devastating form of colonialism.

Moreover, globalization has obscured essential aspects of life, reshaping prevailing notions of success, belonging, community-building, and philanthropy. The contemporary worldview tends to prioritize aggressive ideals aligned with the bottom line, sidelining traditional values. The Muslim religious elite, until the early twentieth century, perceived European development as lacking a moral foundation. However, some argue that Western thought has been constructing ethical frameworks distinct from monotheistic revelations for centuries. To comprehend and address the adverse effects of globalization, there is a pressing need for heightened awareness, particularly within the Muslim community. Efforts must be concentrated on revitalizing the social, financial, and economic ethics embedded in Islam as a monotheistic phenomenon. This rejuvenation is imperative to withstand the onslaught of individualism prevalent in sophisticated industrial countries and their satellite cultures in the Third World. The revival of a sense of community is crucial to counteract the widening disparities between regions, both globally and within South American countries, as well as the increasing numbers of disadvantaged individuals in urban areas.[4]

In facing the competitive and individualistic nature of contemporary society shaped by globalization, it is essential to utilize traditional worldviews and philosophies as the foundational framework for viable solutions.[5] This chapter primarily aims to present Ibrahim Abu Rabi's critique of Western-dominated globalization, offering critical insights into the state of modern Arab and Islamic thought. It also provides recommendations for navigating the profound changes in epistemology, ethics, science, economics, and politics induced by recent global transformations. Importantly, the lack of a comprehensive Islamic analysis of globalization has led to a limited consideration of the Islamic perspective on the economy and community, even among those supportive of globalization. While there has been a political reaction against Western modernity in some Muslim nations, a robust intellectual response to the challenges posed by globalization within an Islamic framework is long overdue.

Ibrahim Abu Rabi': Brief Biography and Works

Ibrahim Abu Rabi was born in the year 1956 in Nazareth.[6] Abu-Rabi commenced his intellectual journey in 1980, completing his undergraduate studies at Birzeit University in Palestine, marking the inception of his scholarly pursuits. Driven by an insatiable quest for knowledge, he continued his academic exploration in political science, earning a master's degree from the University of Cincinnati in 1982. Undeterred in his pursuit of intellectual advancement, he pursued a PhD in Islamic studies at Temple University in 1987, with his dissertation focusing on "Islam and the Search for Social Order in Modern Egypt: An Intellectual Biography of Shaykh 'Abd al-Halim Mahmud." Concurrently, he broadened his academic scope by obtaining a master's degree in religious studies in 1984. Abu-Rabi, leveraging his considerable expertise, contributed to prestigious American institutions, including Virginia Commonwealth University and the University of Texas at Austin.

Immersed in contemporary Islamic thought, he explored the intricate interplay of religion and society and delved into the profound realms of mysticism. In 1991, he assumed the distinguished position of professorship at Hartford Seminary in Connecticut, coupled with the significant role of director at the esteemed Macdonald Center for the Study of Islam and Christian–Muslim Relations. In this academic institution, he cultivated his intellectual reflections, engaging deeply in interfaith dialogue and nurturing an environment of understanding and respect for diverse religious perspectives. In 2006, he took on the role of Senior Fulbright Scholar at Singapore's Nanyang Technological University, leaving a lasting impression. His work delved into the relationship between Islam and contemporary societies, showcasing a commitment to advancing knowledge in Islamic studies. Abu-Rabi's journey is a testament to his unwavering dedication, making a significant impact on the scholarly landscape.[7]

He also served as the senior editor for The Muslim World. In 2008, Abu-Rabi assumed the inaugural Edmonton Council of Muslim Communities Chair in Islamic Studies at the University of Alberta, making history as the first occupant of this teaching and research chair in Canada. Known for his extensive publications, he was a dedicated researcher and prolific writer. His work includes the book *The Contemporary Arab Reader on Political Islam* (University of Alberta Press, 2010), an anthology featuring writings by influential figures in the field of Islamism, aimed at dispelling misconceptions about modern Islam.

Abu-Rabi believed that education, often referred to as "soft power," played a crucial role in enhancing communication between the West and the Muslim world. He emphasized the importance of the West understanding the diverse cultural and linguistic traditions within modern Muslim societies and their pursuit of democracy. Abu-Rabi held a particular interest in exploring the connections between Muslims and Christians in the Muslim world, as well as examining modern Islamic ideas and movements. His extensive travels throughout the Muslim world reinforced his belief in the necessity of building bridges across different religious communities in today's globalized society. During his time as a student at Hartford Seminary, Dr. Abu-Rabi significantly contributed to the institution's prominence in global Muslim–Christian relations. The seminary attracted students from various nations, including Turkey, Syria, Egypt, Indonesia, Singapore, and Pakistan.[8] Throughout his illustrious career, Professor Abu-Rabi held prestigious positions that underscored his prominence in Islamic studies. Taking on the role of program chairman for the well-regarded annual conference of the American Council for the Study of Islamic Societies, he played a crucial part in shaping scholarly discourse. Additionally, he served as the esteemed co-director of the Macdonald Center for the Study of Islam and Christian–Muslim Relations at Hartford Seminary, reflecting his deep commitment to promoting interfaith dialogue and understanding.

Beyond his academic appointments, Abu-Rabi leveraged his scholarly acumen as the senior editor of the distinguished academic journal The Muslim World. He extended his intellectual influence by taking on the role of editor for various academic publications, skillfully guiding and enhancing the scholarly work of his peers. Demonstrating his global impact, Abu-Rabi was appointed as the distinguished Senior Fulbright Scholar for Singapore and Indonesia in 2006. In these roles, he made invaluable contributions to the intellectual landscape at Nanyang Technological University within the renowned Institute of Defense and Strategic Studies. Going beyond editorial responsibilities, he assumed the editorship of significant works such as the "Blackwell Companion to Contemporary Islamic Thought" and "Challenges and Responses of Contemporary Islamic Thought: The Contributions of M. Fethullah Gülen," solidifying his legacy as a preeminent scholar and intellectual figure. Unfortunately, Abu-Rabi passed away on July 2, 2011, in Amman, Jordan. Despite this untimely end, his profound insights and intellectual contributions continue to resonate within the scholarly community, leaving an enduring impact on the field of Islamic studies and interfaith dialogue.[9]

Contemporary Islamic Thought in the Face of Globalization

Defining the term globalization in a singular, concise manner proves nearly impossible due to its extensive implications across various domains such as the economy, society, politics, ideologies, education, and the psyche.[10] In his essay, Abu Rabi' emphasizes that the absence of a comprehensive Islamic perspective on and critique of globalization is the fundamental reason why advocates of globalization have not taken the Islamic stance on economics and community seriously.[11] While some Muslim nations, notably Iran, Sudan, and Egypt, have exhibited a political backlash against Western modernism, there remains a significant need for a thoughtful Muslim intellectual response to the challenges posed by globalization. Abu Rabi' contends that understanding the issue of globalization requires a deep awareness of recent trends in literary criticism, economic and social thought, their impact on religious thought in both the Muslim world and the West, and the ensuing moral response. Modern Islamic thought must integrate critical tools, alongside those derived from revelation, to propose practical solutions to the contemporary problems faced by the Muslim world. In this context, Abu Rabi' presents three principles outlining how contemporary Islamic philosophy can rejuvenate itself amid globalization's impacts on the economy and human psyche.

First, he suggests a reassessment of the core theological and normative principles of Islam to combat the totalitarianism propagated by dominant educational and political institutions in the modern Muslim world, which receive support from the onslaught of globalization. Emphasizing egalitarianism as Islam's cornerstone, Abu Rabi' argues that adhering to Islamic ideals entails opposing all forms of oppression prevalent in the Muslim world, encompassing political, economic, social, and intellectual oppression. In essence, he advocates for the promotion of a liberationist understanding of Islam.[12] The second foundational premise revolves partly around historical aspects and primarily addresses the profound social and economic transformations unfolding in the contemporary capitalist West. These changes exert a significant influence on the modern Muslim world and general ideas. It would be naive to assume that contemporary Islamic thought operates within an internal dynamic completely detached from the intricate evolutions of contemporary Western thought or that it steadfastly refuses to draw inspiration from other sources.[13] The worldview of the West has undergone considerable shifts over time, particularly in American and European history, with globalization standing out as the most recent manifestation. Islamic or Arabic philosophy cannot remain apathetic to the pervasive changes shaping the global political and economic landscape.

The majority of Muslim and Arab intellectuals, spanning from the most radical to the most traditional, view globalization as an inevitable reality.[14] In a sense, it is accurate to assert that the destiny of the Muslim world is intricately linked to the triumph of Western capitalism, owing to the fundamental historical, political, and economic transformations in the modern West. However, Abu Rabi' raises several important questions. What does globalization signify within the context of an assertive/hegemonic Western capitalism, particularly American capitalism, and in a postmodern, post-Soviet, and post-Cold War world?[15] How do nation-states constructed during the Cold War era adapt to globalization? What transformations have transpired in Muslim civil society over the past decade? Is the economic and societal collapse in Indonesia a direct consequence of globalization's intrusion? What role do Muslim thinkers play in navigating this transition? In this scenario, how can one uphold the essential components of Muslim identity, especially if they were formulated before the onset of globalization? What conceptual tools must be developed to interpret preservation as a defensive strategy in revitalizing contemporary Islamic thought regarding globalization? Lastly, who advocates for the common interests of the people, considering that the basis for manufacturing consent in modern society lies in the power of ideas and dominant (capitalist) perspectives are propagated in private schools and universities across the Muslim world?

The third proposition is derived from the preceding one, highlighting a profound transformation in the educational landscape of the Muslim world. A significant shift is occurring, where the best education is becoming privatized, catering primarily to affluent students. Over the past few decades, the elite has clandestinely orchestrated an exceptionally subtle intellectual revolution against the general populace.[16] The rise of for-profit schools and the expansion of distance learning facilities in countries like Turkey, Egypt, Jordan, Malaysia, Morocco, and Saudi Arabia provide additional evidence that education has become a highly prized commodity, available to the highest bidder. The concerns of a mass uprising and a liberal integration of education are deemed unnecessary. Due to the escalating privatization, elitism, Westernization, and Americanization of education in numerous Muslim nations, the common people have relinquished their connection to traditional values, giving way to a new consciousness rooted in social and economic segregation.

Poverty, Wealth Concentration, and State Repression

The emergence of the capitalist mode of production in eighteenth-century England, following centuries dominated by tributary and feudal modes of production, as well as extensive long-distance commerce, marked the inception of globalization.[17] Recently, the term globalization has acquired new and profound implications, accurately representing one of the most dominant concepts for understanding the political economy of international capitalism.[18] Its scope extends far beyond business and encompasses issues in politics, culture, national identity, and more.[19] For example, long-distance trade played a significant role in Muslim economic history, contributing to the advancement of their superior civilization, with Egypt as a possible exception. Numerous economists have underscored the relentless expansion of the capitalist mode of production and the concurrent pursuit of new markets and raw materials. Europe served as the epicenter of globalization throughout the nineteenth century and persisted as such until World War II, shifting to North America with American involvement in the conflict.[20] This historical context is crucial because, understandably, many intellectuals in the Arab and Third Worlds associate globalization with Americanization. Moreover, the intellectual stance in France transitioned to one of wariness against the Americanization of other civilizations, leading to a hostility toward American ideas and concepts.

As stated by Abu Rabi', globalization exerts formidable pressures on the nation-state, compelling a reconfiguration to accommodate and facilitate the unfolding of a novel, unbridled competitive terrain.[21] The presumption that political elites within the nation-state would unreservedly endorse proposed business ventures undergoes scrutiny, particularly in the nuanced context of numerous Third World nation-states ensnared by burdensome debt obligations to the developed world or the IMF. This financial encumbrance frequently renders the realization of national capital an impracticable pursuit, thereby fundamentally reshaping the dynamics. Foreign capital accumulation emerges as a potent impediment to national development and growth in the Third World, thereby introducing a significant alteration to the operational landscape.

The historical legacy of the Soviet socialist economy, the Bandung project of the nonaligned world, and the involvement of the capitalist state in the process of capital accumulation during the 1950s and 1960s resonate profoundly within the unfolding paradigm of globalization.[22] The aspirational vision of self-sufficiency and empowerment for the marginalized, anchored in nationalism and socialism, undergoes a palpable stagnation with the rise of privatization in nations espousing these sociopolitical ideals. A case in point is evident in the Arab world, where the Gulf region finds itself coercively isolated from the broader regional milieu by the Center. This strategic maneuver, precipitated by heightened economic and military potency following Iraq's military defeat in the second Gulf war, transfigures the Gulf states into de facto protectorates, deprived of the latitude to maneuver both economically and politically. The analytical prism, drawing insights from Immanuel Wallerstein, accentuates this geopolitical transformation.[23] While the Third World effectively clinched a political victory for decolonization during the 1950s and 1960s—a triumph achieved virtually universally—the ensuing phase of this sociopolitical struggle, namely national development, grappled with a multitude of challenges and, in many instances, remained unrealized.[24] The complex task of fostering autonomous functionality within local economies assumes acute complexity amid the sweeping forces of liberalization and integration that globalization unfurls.[25]

Rabi' critically engages in a nuanced examination of the paradigm of a "global village economy," propounded by advocates of globalization, positing its potential to catalyze the diffusion of modernization and technical rationalization throughout the global landscape. They contend that the integration of hitherto marginalized societies into the global economic fabric stands as a consequential outcome of the globalization process. According to this perspective, the impact of globalization extends beyond the mere creation of new employment opportunities and amelioration of socioeconomic conditions for the underprivileged; it concurrently engenders a perceptible schism in the cultural and cognitive fabric of less developed countries.

Rabi' astutely notes that even within the acceptance of the aforementioned viewpoints advocated by globalization proponents—a phenomenon that has become inexorable within numerous Third World nations—one is compelled to discern and deliberate upon other concomitant processes of equal import. Most notably, the ascendancy of globalitarian regimes has surpassed the grip exercised by totalitarian regimes of historical precedence.[26] The global subjugation of the nation-state, as expounded by Rabi', manifests deleterious consequences, precipitating the erosion of social cohesion within the Third World. This, in turn, begets novel modalities for already oppressed nation-states to curtail civil society and systematically constrict the democratic space within society. The transformative shifts in social power structures, as delineated by Rabi', function as formidable impediments to the flourishing of civil society, thereby relegating the occurrence of freedom of speech to a lamentably infrequent phenomenon.

The democratic space in the emerging nation-state of the 1980s and 1990s has been severely contested. Contrary to the expectation that the developed Center, long espousing the democratic ethos, would actively endorse genuine democracy in the Southern Hemisphere, this anticipation remains unfulfilled. The advent of globalization engenders a novel nexus between the political elite and economic forces, notably multinational corporations. In the context of the Muslim world, the tribal and ad hoc state structures, typically governed by a single family or tribe, witness an augmentation in oppressive authority. The curtailment of freedom permeates civil society comprehensively, leading to a diminished agency for both working individuals and women. Instead of mitigating poverty and alleviating the suffering of urban and rural underprivileged populations, the incremental integration of multinational corporations into economies of the Third World gives rise to three interconnected phenomena: a surge in the ranks of the impoverished and unemployed; an accumulation of wealth within the purview of the political elite; and an escalation in state-sanctioned repression.[27] An illustrative example of this phenomenon is discernible in the case of Indonesia. The historical objective of the West, epitomized by the mission civilisatrice, experiences a contemporary reaffirmation in the burgeoning deification of money, technology, investment, and prosperity under the guise of globalization. This unfolds through the impact of contemporary technologies, ostensibly advancing in the name of globalization.[28]

Neocolonialism and Cultural Hegemony

To grasp Abu Rabi's perspective on the phenomenon, it is imperative to promptly delve into his insights regarding the post-colonial phase of globalization and its repercussions on the Muslim world. The Arab and Muslim states, post-independence, find themselves grappling with a myriad of inherited incongruities. In swift succession to the colonial era, neocolonialism emerges, establishing fresh economic and political affiliations that confer a decisive advantage to the Center in global and economic spheres over its erstwhile dependents. Concurrently, an earnest pursuit of cultural and political decolonization unfolds in the aftermath of independence. Abu Rabi' posits that a multitude of Arab philosophers construe globalization as the latest iteration of neocolonialism, marking the culmination of the global rise of the capitalist enterprise and, consequentially, casting detrimental effects on the region.[29] From this perspective, post-colonialism materializes as the fraternal counterpart to neocolonialism.

Colonialism, conventionally depicted as a historical phenomenon, often implies the military subjugation of one nation by another, typically characterized by a European military occupation. Simultaneously, the direct control over natural resources assumes pivotal significance in realizing the strategic objectives of the colonizer. Abu Rabi' contends that the political elite of the fledgling nation-states have sought to modernize their societies through uncritical emulation of the Western paradigm. This elite benefits from substantial Western political and military support, thereby fortifying its enduring hold on power.[30] Noteworthy is the conspicuous evasion of scrutiny in the West concerning issues such as the absence of democracy and human rights in certain nations, illuminating the intricate dynamics at play.

The West, driven by the imperative to safeguard its strategic interests, demonstrated a willingness to compromise its moral standards. Neocolonialism, as posited by Abu Rabi', is rooted in a novel form of economic dominance that paves the way for other distinct modes of supremacy, including political, cultural, and intellectual hegemony. During the Cold War, as the global power dynamics teetered between the Soviet Union and the Western capitalist world, Abu Rabi' argued that Third World nations experienced a partial reprieve from Western cultural and political pressures, capitalizing on a semblance of freedom.[31] However, the unraveling of the Soviet Union and Iraq's military defeat in the second Gulf War altered this equilibrium. Subsequently, the Arab region and its culture found themselves wholly vulnerable to American imperialism. In the wake of the United States assuming the mantle of dominant superpower, several nations, including Cuba, Syria, and Libya, have been accused of supporting terrorism by the Center.

To comprehensively fathom the ascent of American supremacy to global preeminence after 1945, one must delve into the proliferation of Fordism, an economic system that took shape in the United States in the early twentieth century and matured post-World War II.[32] Abu Rabi' contends that Fordism exerted a profound impact on the social structure and relationships within capitalist nations, thus substantiating its role as a driving force behind the rise of American dominance.[33] This effort significantly influenced the socioeconomic structure of contemporary Arab societies, giving rise to new classes and the amplification of poverty after 1945. In response, the Gulf States undertook extensive efforts to forge a new social and economic contract with their citizens, facilitated by cutting-edge technology and the Fordist project.[34] This endeavor sought to establish a novel social contract premised on the promise of financial success and the endorsement of excessive consumption. Consequently, there was no significant movement in any of the Gulf States challenging the foundational tenets of Fordism, which reached its zenith in the 1970s and 1980s. However, two decades later, the Arab world encountered the advent of post-Fordism, which had encountered a crisis in the industrialized world during the 1970s.

For Abu Rabi' and his contemporaneous Arab intellectuals, recent manifestations of globalization are construed as efficacious instances of Americanization, promulgating a distinctive cultural and economic paradigm. Abu Rabi' asserts that the advancement of Arab nations necessitates the assimilation of Western science and technology to counteract the influence of American-inspired globalization.[35] However, he underscores the indispensable requirement of underlying cultural and ethical principles for the successful transference of Western scientific knowledge. The historical acknowledgment prevails regarding the West's utilization of culture and ideas to assert dominance over the Third World during the imperialist epoch. This strategic utilization facilitated the flourishing of phenomena such as Orientalism and missionary endeavors. Classical imperialism persisted through the concurrent deployment of Western troops, entwining both physical and intellectual conquest. In the contemporary neo-imperialistic era, characterized by profound technological advancements, the dynamics have undergone a substantial metamorphosis, imperiling the intellectual and cultural integrity of smaller nations. Historically, the overarching objective encompassed the introduction of Western educational and philosophical systems into the Third World while concurrently cultivating an indigenous cultural elite aligned with Western ideals. Colonialism engendered a pervasive ideological culture. Abu Rabi' contends that in the present-day scenario, cultural invasion goes beyond mere ideological imposition; it strives to suppress the Third World's capacity for critique and rationalism. In the specific context of Arab and Muslim societies, this cultural incursion seeks to obfuscate their distinctive and illustrious intellectual heritage.[36]

He underscores that one of the paramount contemporary responsibilities of the Third World is to achieve economic and political emancipation from this novel form of hegemony. In the realm of post-colonialism, where the principal aim is cultural hegemony and the dissemination of Western ideals in the Third World, the pivotal element in this pursuit of freedom is cultural decolonization. Given the North's insistence on Occidental values as the norm or their purported universality, and the belief that embracing these values holds the key to solving the social and economic predicaments of the Third World, there is a reluctance to engage in a substantive dialogue on cultural values with the South.[37] Post-colonialism is viewed as a tool attempting to erase cultural diversity in today's global landscape, aspiring to create a singular, universally homogenized Occidentalized culture, irrespective of its nuclear and military capabilities or economic and political dominance. The concentration of most global hot spots in Muslim countries is not deemed coincidental; rather, it stems from the West's resistance to accepting a value system different from its own. However, internal factors are also implicated in the predicament.[38] Much like other parts of the Third World, the Muslim world grapples with democratic deficits, a crisis concerning fundamental human rights, and a scarcity of democratic platforms fostering open expression of opinions.[39] The repercussions of globalization manifest in the increased production of weapons by the West, with the primary markets being in the South, Africa, the Middle East, and Afghanistan. Civil wars are on the rise, particularly in the Southern Hemisphere. Post-World War II, the West, including the now-defunct Soviet Union, gleaned a crucial lesson: avoid instigating conflicts in Europe or the Northern Hemisphere.

Abu Rabi' contends that globalization has precipitated an accelerated movement of intellectual talent from the Third World to the developed Center, a phenomenon aptly termed "intellectual hemorrhage."[40] This process, which entails the outflow of knowledge across diverse research domains, particularly impacts developing nations. Individuals migrate not only in pursuit of elevated economic and social standards but also due to the absence of visionary development processes in their home countries. This deficiency is occasionally exacerbated by thoughtless emulation of the developed North. Essentially, while the South can acquire technology, concurrent efforts to foster indigenous modernism and modernization are hampered by the ongoing departure of qualified personnel. This unfortunate circumstance has engendered a cascade of interconnected issues affecting both the Muslim world and other Third World nations, encompassing illiteracy, a paucity of rigorous scientific study, and a dearth of democratic principles.

In summation, Abu Rabi' posits that globalization is precipitating the emergence of a new world, anticipated to bear minimal resemblance to the one currently familiar to us within a few decades. This transformation is characterized by several key facets: the waning influence of socialism and the proliferation of privatization in nations like China, India, and Egypt; the ascendancy of regional powers, exemplified by the European community, following the dominance of the United States; the deepening social and economic disparities within and between countries; the global pervasiveness of exploitation as a corollary of privatization; the resurgence of ultra-nationalism, ethnic cleansing, and the concomitant emergence of new refugee crises; the globalization of criminal activities, particularly those associated with Mafia operations; the collapse of nations and states; and lastly, the emergence of new international adversaries.[41]

Arab Intellectual Responses

In his exploration of globalization, Abu Rabi' directs substantial attention to the evolving dynamics in the Arab world in response to globalization. He asserts that the economic, political, and military actions of the United States toward each Arab nation since the conclusion of World War II have exerted a profound influence on virtually every Arab nation.[42] It is imperative to contextualize the development of the Israeli state post-1948 and its profound impact on the Arab world and the Palestinian people within this framework. Isolating the Israeli element from the European and American components is overly simplistic. Prior to the establishment of Israel, Zionism made strides in achieving its political objectives through affiliations with major European nations, particularly Britain post-World War I. Following the Ottoman Empire's defeat in World War I, Britain assumed regional hegemony and instituted a colonial rule in Palestine that significantly favored the Zionist project. The founding of Israel in 1948 marked a seminal triumph for Zionism. Without the substantial financial and military aid from the United States, Israel would have struggled to sustain its occupation of the West Bank and Gaza and expand its settlement operations. Israel's formidable military prowess is a direct consequence of the substantial inflow of weapons and funding from the West. According to Rabi', as we entered a new century, the Arab world grappled with social, political, and economic disparities.[43] The setback of Arab nationalism in 1967 marked its demise, further intensified when Egypt departed from the Arab coalition in 1979 by signing a separate peace treaty with Israel. The erosion of nationalism is attributed to both external and internal factors, encompassing foreign interference, the absence of governmental structures ensuring equal treatment of all citizens irrespective of religion or economic status, and the failure of modernization.

In the twenty-first century, the Arab region finds itself confronted with deep-seated divisions. The advent of an assertive form of globalization, which prioritizes profits for international corporations over fostering positive social and economic advancements in the Arab world, further compounds these divisions. Globalization, in its contemporary aggressive manifestation, has posed fundamental challenges to the global claims of both Arabism and Islamism within the modern Arab context.[44] Thus far, neither movement has succeeded in establishing an enduring international Arab or Islamist order capable of navigating the formidable challenges of the contemporary era. The fabric of social cohesion in many Arab countries is already unraveling due to the impact of privatization. This phenomenon is concurrently giving rise to a prosperous class of compradors who play a substantial role in channeling their nations' wealth toward the global elite. The socioeconomic landscape of these nations is undergoing transformation, with implications that extend beyond their borders and exacerbate existing disparities within the Arab world.

In Abu Rabi's opinion, Arab intellectuals face a fundamental challenge beyond the observable social and economic impacts of globalization, involving the modern cultural identity of the entire Arab world, spanning the Middle East and North Africa.[45] This challenge unfolds across several dimensions. First, Arab thinkers contend that there has been a substantial political and military imbalance in the Third World since the collapse of the Soviet Union.[46] Second, the ascent of the United States to global hegemony has adversely affected the Arab political system, leading to a retreat of democracy and an upsurge in authoritarianism. Third, the poverty gap has widened in recent decades, with the governing Arab political class, particularly through collaboration with the Center, turning toward right-leaning policies. Fourth, the Zionist movement and Israel are identified as primary beneficiaries of Middle Eastern globalization. Fifth, as modernization permeates the Arab world, Islamism appears to be gaining renewed traction as a source of hope for the disenfranchised middle classes and the impoverished. Sixth, despite the inevitability of globalization, there is a call for cultural unification within the Arab world to counteract the spread of Americanization.

Abu Rabi examines three distinct trends that have emerged in response to the phenomenon of globalization within the Arab world: Marxist, Nationalist, and Islamist perspectives. The Arab Left, positioned as a vanguard intellectual force, assumes a pivotal role in presenting a coherent and comprehensive critique of globalization. Eminent figures within the Arab Left, including Samir Amin and Sadiq Jalal al-'Azm, have gained international recognition for their profound analyses of globalization. Prominent publications like the Lebanese al-Tariq and the Egyptian Qadayah Fikriyyah have also devoted considerable attention to unraveling the complexities posed by globalization. In particular, Abu Rabi focuses on scrutinizing Mahmud Amin al-'Alim's nuanced response to globalization. 'Alim posits that globalization constitutes an objective manifestation of human unity, representing a historic realization unparalleled in human history.[47] Despite its roots in Europe and the prevailing Western dominance, 'Alim contends that capitalist civilization transcends Western Europe, characterizing it as a global phenomenon. From 'Alim's perspective, capitalism has waged a relentless global war for new markets since its inception, culminating in the formation of a fiercely competitive global civilization.[48] Rabi' highlights 'Alim's complex stance on the exploitation of the Third World during the eighteenth and nineteenth centuries. While 'Alim criticizes aggressive capitalism during this period, he adopts a more measured perspective on the exploitation experienced by the Third World. Instances such as the activities of the East India Company in India and the East Dutch Company in Indonesia are cited, where the pursuit of maximizing trade earnings coexisted with endeavors to assert or alter prevailing power structures.

Al-'Alim posited that the prevailing capitalist mode of production was the driving force behind the formation of the current capitalist civilization and culture, ultimately leading to the globalization of capitalism.[49] Using the term "a worldwide capitalist civilisation," Al-'Alim characterized modern capitalism as surpassing earlier human civilizations and cultures. According to Rabi, Al-'Alim asserted that contemporary globalization has given rise to a shift toward a homogenized economic system, which is variably accepted across the globe.[50] Al-'Alim contended that the dominant capitalist civilization, shaped by the homogenized economic system, is the sole entity capable of survival in the modern world. In opposition to Samuel Huntington's proposition of an impending Clash of Civilizations, Al-'Alim rejected the idea, arguing that there exists only one global capitalist civilization governing the world.[51] Rabi raises the question of why accepting modern globalization is crucial. He highlights the Arab East's historical struggles, dating back to the eighteenth century, to find alternatives to its dependence on the capitalist West. Despite various political movements, notably nationalism aiming to break structural and economic ties with the West, no viable solutions have emerged. Al-'Alim attributed the contemporary challenges within the Arab social system to the hegemony of the United States and the global division of labor under capitalism. This division either benefits the Arab political elite or remains resistant to their attempts at favorable modification.[52] Rabi further explores whether the political elite has gained from globalization in maintaining their power and whether the modern Arab state has been undermined by globalization.[53] According to Al-'Alim, globalization has empowered the Arab political elite technologically, enabling them to exert full control over society and disseminate their version of "false consciousness" through mass media.

The permeation of capitalism in the Arab world, despite its concentration within a select few entities, has solidified its status as an integral component of the global capitalist economy. This economic paradigm engages in fierce competition with other capitalist entities, driven by an insatiable pursuit of limitless wealth and power. Within the domestic sphere, Arab capitalism adopts an assertive and unrelenting approach to secure its economic interests and perpetuate the accumulation of wealth. However, the overarching objective of capitalism in the Arab context appears to be the preservation of hegemony and the expansion of control, rather than the genuine advancement of societal progress. Notably, there is discernible evidence of leveraging widespread religious sentiments for materialistic aims, as reflected in limited investments in religious organizations. The historical coexistence of globalization and capitalism has recently undergone a qualitative departure from traditional forms. As underscored by Syrian Marxist philosopher al-'Azm, this shift is indicative of a novel phase in the interplay between capitalism and globalization. According to Rabi', since the time of Marx, a number of well-known intellectuals have investigated the nature of the global capitalist economy, most notably Paul Sweezy, Samir Amin, and Andre Gunter Frank.[54] Al-'Azm posits that the preceding model of globalization facilitated global wealth accumulation by preserving domestic industrial production resources, thereby engendering disparate circumstances in the interchange between the Center and the Periphery. Notably, the distinguishing feature of contemporary capitalism lies in its capacity to globalize the means of production, achieving industrial globalization and reproducing relations of production on a global scale.

Al-'Azm critically challenges Lenin's assertion that "imperialism is the highest stage of capitalism," contending that it has been invalidated by the pervasive tide of industrial globalization orchestrated under Western capitalism's vigilant oversight. Globalization emerges as a seismic shift within the capitalist framework, a profound metamorphosis engulfing the entire human tapestry and governed by the unequivocal dominion of an unequal trade regime. At its nucleus lies the notion that all facets of human existence should be commodified, forming the foundational bedrock upon which this innovative international economic order is built. What was once confined to local limits has now expanded its epicenter, transcending geographical boundaries. Notably, capitalism, characterized by its enduring sagacity, retains a steadfast grip on the global economic reins, adeptly reshaping itself on a grand international stage.[55] Within the domain of globalization, the resurgent prominence of the nation-state is fervently revived, its presence amplified by the widespread impact of this transformative phenomenon. Al-'Azm posits that the far-reaching effects of globalization have conferred newfound vigor and authority upon the state, particularly in the Center. It is within the folds of this revitalized state apparatus that budgetary allocations manifest, demarcated between foreign investments and the potent military machinery. Al-'Alim aligns with al-'Azm's assertion that globalization stands as an indomitable force—an unstoppable process defying restraint. Mere opposition to this formidable entity yields little, necessitating a strategic and united Arab initiative to confront its implications through coordinated economic endeavors. The very essence of Arab nations' economic interests demands safeguarding amid the turbulent currents of globalization.[56]

Al-'Azm challenges Lenin's once-hallowed pronouncement, asserting that the relentless march of industrial globalization, meticulously orchestrated under the auspices of Western capitalism, has effectively dismantled its theoretical foundations. The transformative forces of globalization, resonate globally, transcending boundaries and territories under the dominion of a complex trade system marked by inherent disparities. At the heart of this global economic order lies the notion that all facets of human existence are reducible to commodities. The epicenter, once confined to local domains, now extends its reach to encompass the global stage, enabling capitalism to deftly reinvent itself and consolidate its hegemony. Al-'Azm boldly raises the banner of the nation-state within this landscape, emphasizing the newfound strength bestowed upon it by globalization, particularly within the Center. In this realm of state power, financial resources are adeptly allocated, serving the dual purposes of foreign investments and bolstering military capabilities. In concordance with al-'Azm, Al-'Alim argues that resistance alone provides a feeble response to the inexorable march of globalization. Instead, a united Arab front, fortified by coordinated economic initiatives, emerges as the imperative shield to safeguard economic interests amid the tumultuous currents of this transformative era.[57]

Both al-'Alim and al-'Azm acknowledge the inevitability of globalization. Economist Galal Amin, while expressing apprehensions about the impact of globalization on the cultural identities of Third World nations, asserts that the contemporary Arab state is ill-prepared to mount a resistance. Notably, Amin advocates for cultural resistance in the face of globalization, yet the crucial question of leadership in such resistance remains unaddressed.[58] Amin, cognizant of the significance of economic development in the Arab world, underscores the imperative of ensuring a high material standard of living for all Arab individuals. However, the persistent issue of poverty, despite periods of wealth influx such as the 1970s and 1980s oil boom, raises pertinent questions.[59] Amin attributes Egypt's economic setbacks to its defeat by Israel in 1967, which undermined the reforms initiated by Nasser. Subsequent economic strategies, particularly Sadat's Infitah, expedited privatization, exacerbating Egypt's debt burden.[60] Amin's Marxist critique of globalization incorporates the premise that the state functions as a representative of the economic interests of the ruling class. The contemporary Arab state, according to Amin, lacks a focus on the enduring welfare of its populace, earning the pejorative label "The Soft State."[61] The trajectory toward privatization, gaining momentum after 1974, positioned Egypt as a consequential participant in globalization before the dissolution of the Soviet Union in 1991.[62]

Rabi' notes that Israel seems to have weathered the impacts of globalization favorably, despite sharing characteristics of a "soft state" with many Arab nations. The Israeli government effectively controls the free market while allocating substantial resources to the military. Shimon Peres, a former foreign minister, propagated the concept of Middle Easternism, Israel's adaptation of local globalization.[63] In critiquing Thomas Friedman's *The Lexus and the Olive Tree*, Amin raises the issue of Israel. Amin argues that Friedman not only champions the American model of globalization but also endorses the Israeli version. Muhammad Abid al-Jabiri, as highlighted by Rabi', stresses the cultural diversity of the world and the role of national culture in mitigating the adverse effects of modernity. This contrasts with al-'Alim's assertion that the world is dominated by a cross-cultural and transnational capitalist civilization.[64] Jabiri proposes eight theses to elucidate the relationship between national culture and globalization. The first thesis contends that the world comprises numerous diverse cultures rather than a singular universal culture, ensuring their continued survival and richness. Jabiri emphasizes that cultural diversity is more intriguing than the uniformity of global capitalism. His second thesis characterizes cultural identity as a fusion of three crucial elements: self, society, and nation. The interplay between these factors distinguishes national cultural identity, with its intensity rising in dynamic societies or countries. The third thesis posits that a cultural identity can actively and outwardly contribute to global cultures if rooted in the concepts of country, nation, and state.[65] Jabiri explicitly challenges the claims made by several Arab leaders, including those in Morocco, Jordan, and Saudi Arabia, that the preservation of national culture hinges on the authority of the king or other individuals in power.

Fourthly, as per Rabi', Jabiri defines globalization as a world system comprising two sets of elements: one group consists of financial and technological elements, while the other encompasses cultural, political, and ideological elements. Jabiri asserts that globalization extends beyond the continuation of capitalist modernity; it represents the dissemination of the American model of civilization. The current phase of globalization is characterized by the dominance of American cultural and ideological interests, negatively impacting the integrity of social and ethical systems in the Third World through the export of American culture. Jabiri identifies unbridled consumerism and destructive individualism as core elements of American civilization, reflecting America's pursuit of global hegemony within the overarching philosophy of globalization.[66] In his sixth thesis, Jabiri draws a distinction between universalism ('*alamiyyah*') and globalization ('*awlamah*'). While the former implies cultural openness and reciprocity, the latter signifies American domination of other cultures. Globalization initiates a complex process of infiltrating and ultimately dominating other civilizations. American ideology, driven by the ambition to rule the globe, finds substantial support from the media, which promotes individualism and materialism as foundational American values.[67]

Many Arab thinkers assert that the American mass media, with its hegemonic global presence, endeavors to shape both the material and intellectual preferences in the Third World by promoting Western concepts of consumer capitalism.[68] Frederic Jameson, in his critique of American globalization, echoes Jabiri's concerns, highlighting consumerism as the foundational core of the economic system. He emphasizes that media and entertainment industries incessantly promote this way of life through an unprecedented image and media bombardment.[69] This premise leads to the argument that embracing the moral and intellectual ideals of American culture abroad could sever ties between other cultures and their sources of legitimacy, such as homeland, nation, and state. Jabiri, as outlined by Rabi', contends that adopting these ideas results in a perilous form of globalization, overpowering various obstacles—economic, political, and cultural—through relentless American influence. Modern Arab culture and philosophy have been subject to internal division and friction since the encounter between the capitalist West and the Arab world two centuries ago. This historical interaction has polarized the cultural identity of individuals, communities, and nations.[70]

Jabiri asserts that the polarization exacerbated by globalization has intensified, enabling the Arab elite to benefit from technological advancements, while the broader population and their traditional intellectual representatives become increasingly isolated. He further argues that this division between the small, globalized elite and the rest of society opens the possibility for a comprehensive internal reconstruction of contemporary Arab culture. However, Jabiri's final thesis posits that the most effective approach to safeguarding Arab cultural identity, shaped by the interactions between country, nation, and state, is to embrace the scientific aspects of globalization without adopting the cultural baggage of modernism or modernity.[71] The challenge, as Jabiri sees it, lies in the potential contradiction between protecting the integrity of modern Arab culture and opposing both American cultural hegemony and the globalized Arab elite. He suggests that readers face difficult decisions, advocating for resistance not only against American cultural influence but also against the Arab elite itself, which has long been integrated into the globalized system. Essentially, Jabiri contends that the contemporary Arab state has failed to formulate a coherent agenda for Arab culture and utilizes the media to promote cultural manifestations incongruent with the essence of the Arab nation.[72]

It is essential to consider Islamist perspectives on globalization for a comprehensive analysis of the Arab dialogue.[73] Arab Islamists, like other intellectuals, have entered the discourse later but find the concerns surrounding globalization crucial. Two significant Islamist philosophers, Yusuf al-Qaradāwī and Muhammad Qutb, who represent the older generation of thought within the Muslim Brotherhood, play a crucial role in this context. Both were close followers of Shaykh Hassan al-Banna. Qaradāwī and Qutb share the fundamental contention with Jabiri that current globalization embodies American intellectual, cultural, and economic hegemony. They see globalization as an aggressive form of cultural invasion and a tangible expression of American arrogance.[74] Qaradāwī explicitly equates globalization with Westernization and Americanization. Qaradāwī argues that America's foreign policy toward the Muslim world aims to silence Muslim opposition voices, citing examples such as Sudan, Libya, and Iran that suffered due to UN embargoes pressured by the United States and United

Kingdom.[75] Despite his strong criticism of globalization, Qaradāwī acknowledges it as an unavoidable phenomenon, stating that escaping or resisting its grasp is beyond their power. He urges the Third World, Arab and Muslim nations, and the global community to come together in the face of globalization, although he remains vague on how to achieve such unity. Despite the drawbacks, Qaradāwī recognizes certain advantages of globalization and advocates for the dissemination of the Islamic message using cutting-edge media technologies. He believes that Islam provides the correct prescription to address the world's psychological and social ills.[76]

Regarding the benefits of globalization, Muhammad Qutb, according to Rabi', holds a less optimistic view. He sees Islam as a foreign religion in the modern world, citing the well-known *hadīth* that states, "Islam started in exile and it will start over in exile."[77] In Qutb's opinion, authentic Islam has not been practiced in society, and only those who have accepted Qur'ānic teachings as everlasting are aware of it. Unlike Qaradāwī, Qutb opposes participation in globalization, considering it based on heinous materialism and extensive exploitation. Qutb perceives no advantages and advocates for resistance.[78] Abu Rabi' draws the following succinct conclusions from the above overview of Arab perspectives on globalization: Arab Marxist theorists see globalization as a self-sustaining process that originated in the sixteenth century and developed into a major international civilization. This aligns with Robertson's definition of globalization as "both the compression of the world and the deepening of consciousness of the world as a whole." Information technology, driven by capitalism, has led to increased awareness among individuals and countries. On the other hand, most Islamists focus on the contemporary political, economic, and religious effects of globalization, emphasizing its impact on Arab culture and religion. Some Muslim scholars perceive a conflict between Western capitalism and Islamic philosophy, expressing concerns about the spread of American culture in the Arab world.[79]

Both Marxist theorists and Arab nationalists advocate for limited protectionism to mitigate the negative impacts of exposure to American culture, with Marxists viewing globalization as a natural byproduct of modernity and a continuation of their modernization efforts from the 1950s and 1960s. On the other hand, Islamists and Arab nationalists criticize the Americanization of globalization, expressing concerns about "culture invasion" and equating globalization with Americanization or American hegemony. Marxists, considering capitalist civilization as more pervasive than Americanization, are less certain about this relationship, seeing the Western world as the primary benchmark for present globalization. Arab nationalists appear particularly anxious about the role of the state in the age of globalization, with Galal Amin suggesting that the state's role may diminish, negatively impacting Arab society.[80] This perspective is not shared by Arab liberals, who argue that globalization has expanded the state's power. Islamic scholars draw a distinction between "*alamiyyah*" (globalization) and "*awlamah*" (universality), preferring the worldwide reach of Islam over the expansion of capitalism. They reject any moral acceptance of the complexity produced by the prevailing capitalist civilization, placing '*alamiyyah* at the center of their analytical endeavor.[81] Rabi' questions the rationality of comparing capitalism, fundamentally an economic and scientific system, with Islam, a religious system.[82] When contrasting narratives like capitalism and Islam are juxtaposed, a collision between the two narratives occurs. While comprehensive solutions to the challenges posed by globalization are scarce among Arab intellectuals, there is a general consensus on the need for substantial economic and political collaboration among Arab states. They advocate for a more equitable distribution of economic resources and the advancement of the status of women and disenfranchised individuals in society.[83]

Since the Industrial Revolution, the prevailing Western mindset has embraced the concept of progress, profoundly shaping the world's socioeconomic and intellectual trajectories. This notion has cultivated a belief in limitless possibilities for advancement, fostering a tendency to conquer and dominate the Third World. In the contemporary worldview, a salvational concept of development has emerged, emphasizing the paramount importance of economic expansion and technological innovation. However, the phenomenon of progress poses a significant threat to traditional cultures, their socioeconomic foundations, and their ethical worldviews. Even the most detrimental forms of progress persist in the pursuit of globalization, giving rise to novel manifestations of colonization. Rabi' draws on the insights of Hannah Arendt, who argued that the conventional understanding of progress led to a continuous accumulation of power, crucial for safeguarding an unceasing accumulation of power. This ideology of progress in the late nineteenth century foreshadowed the advent of imperialism.[84] Globalization is introducing a new, more pernicious and injurious type of colonialism, surpassing previous observations. This insidious form of colonialism unfolds as a consequence of globalizing forces, exerting influence on various aspects of society and perpetuating unequal power dynamics.[85]

Rabi emphasizes that globalization has obscured essential values in life, evident in the contemporary worldview. Traditional notions of wealth, community, connectivity, and aiding the needy have given way to aggressive new ideas that prioritize the bottom line. In the early twentieth century, the religious intelligentsia of the Muslim world viewed European progress as lacking moral underpinnings. However, some argue that Western thought, for many centuries, has been building on ethical foundations distinct from those of monotheistic revelations. This Western ethic supports the rapid accumulation of wealth and power under the influence of globalization. Today, extravagant materialism has become the norm.[86]

Richard Falk identifies the current world order crisis with multiple dimensions, including nuclearism, industrialism, materialism, and consumerism.[87] This crisis is attributed to the globalization of Western cultural influence, particularly its commitment to modernity. To comprehend and address the adverse effects of globalization, Falk suggests the development of a new collective awareness.[88] Abu Rabi' emphasizes the necessity for the Muslim community to revive Islam's social, financial, and economic ethics as a monotheistic reality in order to counteract dangerous trends. He underscores the importance of fostering a sense of community to withstand the impacts of rampant individualism prevalent in industrialized countries and satellite communities in the Third World. Abu Rabi' contends that restoring the Islamic community ethic, which advocates for righteousness and opposes wrongdoing, is indispensable given the widening divides between regions and demographics in South Asian nations and the increasing numbers of disadvantaged individuals in urban areas.[89] Thus, solutions rooted in traditional worldviews are deemed necessary to address the social and psychological devastation wrought by globalization in the Muslim world.

Conclusion

This chapter provided Abu Rabi's critical reflections on globalization. His engagement with critical theory, notably influenced by intellectuals such as Antonio Gramsci and Samir Amin, accentuates the conspicuous dearth of Muslim scholars within Western contexts capable of effectively navigating the challenges posed by modernism and globalization. Despite their advantageous position to comprehend globalization from within Western societies and articulate the perils associated with neoliberalism and market forces, these intellectuals have regrettably failed to make substantive contributions to the ongoing discourse, consequently impacting the broader Muslim world.[90] Abu Rabi discerns a significant impediment to the emergence of new intellectual voices, namely an excessive preoccupation with matters of identity, heritage, and authenticity. He posits the pressing need to transcend the established conceptual frameworks rooted in the nineteenth-century perspectives of Muslim intellectuals and cultivate a novel Islamic mode of thought that can creatively respond to the exacting standards of critical philosophical and ethical reasoning.[91] This imperative becomes especially pronounced when contending with the intricate challenges posed by globalization. Abu Rabi contends that a nuanced understanding of globalization necessitates a profound grasp of recent developments in critical theory, economic, and social thought within both the Muslim world and the West, along with an ethical response that modern Islamic thought must articulate to reaffirm its pertinence. To effectively address the multifaceted challenges of the contemporary world, Islamic thinking must integrate indispensable tools beyond religious revelation.[92]

While the trajectory of globalization may seem inexorable, Abu Rabi posits that a united Arab front holds the potential to counteract the encroachment of U.S. cultural imperialism. Moreover, he underscores the imperative of fostering closer relations among Arab nations to collectively grapple with the substantial challenges posed by globalization. In categorizing intellectuals into three primary groups—Marxists, nationalists, and Islamists—Abu Rabi unveils nuanced perspectives on this global phenomenon. For Marxist philosophers, globalization is construed as a self-sustaining process rooted in the sixteenth century that has burgeoned into a pervasive global civilization.[93] Conversely, Islamists and, to a lesser degree, Arab nationalists harbor reservations about the cultural incursion propagated by Americanization. While Marxists view globalization as a logical extension of the modernity project from the mid-twentieth century, all three factions express apprehensions about the economic and political constraints imposed by global capitalism. Islamists, represented by figures like Yusuf al-Qarādawī and Muhammad Qutb, draw a distinction between globalization and universality, positing that only Islam is ordained for universality. They contend that the global dominance of capitalism, orchestrated by the West, amounts to a usurpation of the divine status bestowed upon Islamic doctrine.[94]

Abu Rabi laments the common reluctance of Islamists to critically scrutinize the structural dynamics of globalization and arrive at meaningful ethical judgments. However, across these diverse orientations within the Arab intellectual landscape, there is a shared lamentation regarding the adverse political and economic ramifications of globalization. In summary, Abu Rabi's exploration of critical theory at the intersection of Islamic thought underscores the imperative for Muslim intellectuals to engage critically with the challenges posed by modernism and globalization. By transcending conventional frameworks, incorporating a diverse array of intellectual tools, and fostering unity and cooperation among Arab nations, the Muslim world can actively confront the unfavorable dimensions of globalization and endeavor toward a more equitable and prosperous future.

Notes

1. Ibrahim M. Abu-Rabi, "Beyond the Post-Modern Mind," *American Journal of the Islamic Social Sciences* 7, no. 2 (1990): 235–256.

2. Charlene Spretnak, *The Resurgence of the Real: Body, Nature and Place in a Hypermodern World* (New York: Addison-Wesley, 1997), 2.

3. Hannah Arendt, *The Origins of Totalitarianism* (Cleveland, OH: Meridian Books, 1963), 143.

4. David R. Griffin and Huston Smith, *Primordial Truth and Postmodern Theology* (Albany, NY: State University of New York Press, 1989), 45.

5. Akbar S. Ahmed, *Postmodernism and Islam: Predicament and Promise* (London: Routledge, 1992), 11.

6. Ian S. Markham, "Ibrahim M. Abu-Rabi (1956–2011): A Reflection," *Ilahiyat Studies* 2, no. 2 (2011): 271–273.

7. International Council for Middle East Studies, "Professor Ibrahim Abu-Rabi' (In Memoriam)." Accessed April 15, 2024. https://www.icmes.net/board-of-directors/ibrahim-abu-rabi?rq=ibrahim%20Abu%20Rabi.

8. International Council for Middle East Studies, "Professor Ibrahim Abu-Rabi' (In Memoriam)."

9. Markham, "Ibrahim M. Abu-Rabi (1956–2011)," 271.

10. Giddens, *The Consequences of Modernity*, 64.

11. Zaki al-Milad, "Islamic Thought and the Issue of Globalisation," *Middle East Affairs Journal* 1–2 (1999): 13–32.

12. Ibrahim Abu Rabi', *Contemporary Arab Thought: Studies in Post-1967 Arab Intellectual History* (London: Pluto Press, 2003), 182.

13. Abu Rabi', *Contemporary Arab Thought*, 184.

14. John Pilger, *The New Rulers of the World* (London: Verso Books, 2002), 13.

15. William K. Tapp, *The Amoral Elephant: Globalisation and the Struggle for Social Justice in the Twenty-First Century* (New York: Monthly Review Press, 2001), 101.

16. Abu Rabi', *Contemporary Arab Thought*, 179.

17. Eric Wolf, *Europe and the People without History* (Berkeley, CA: University of California Press, 1982), 76.

18. David Harvey, *Spaces of Hope* (Berkeley, CA: University of California Press, 2000), 13.

19. Wolf, *Europe and the People without History*, 103.

20. Wolf, *Europe and the People without History*, 77.

21. Susan Strange, *The Retreat of the State: The Diffusion of Power in the World Economy* (Cambridge: Cambridge University Press, 1998), 34.

22. Immanuel Wallerstein, *After Liberalism* (New York: The New Press, 1995), 15.

23. Daniel T. Griswold, "The Blessings and Challenges of Globalisation," *International Journal on World Peace* 17, no. 3 (2000): 3–22.

24. Nancy Birdsall, "Life is Unfair: Inequality in the World," *Foreign Policy* 111 (1998): 76–93.
25. Abu Rabi', "Contemporary Arab Thought," 172–173.
26. Abu Rabi', "Contemporary Arab Thought," 172–173.
27. 'Abd al-Ilah Bilqaziz, "Al-"Awlamah Wa'l Hawiyyah al-Thaqafiyyah" [Globalisation and Cultural Identity], *Al-Mustaqbal al-Arabi* 236 (1998): 92.
28. Pierre Bourdieu, *Acts of Resistance: Against the Market* (New York: The New Press, 1998), 20.
29. Antonio Gramsci, "Americanism and Fordism," in *The Prison Notebooks*, ed. Quintin Hoere and Geoffrey Nowell Smith (New York: International Publishers, 1971), 279–316.
30. Abu Rabi', *Contemporary Arab Though*, 182.
31. Abu Rabi', *Contemporary Arab Thought*, 183.
32. Abu Rabi', *Contemporary Arab Thought*, 184.
33. Abu Rabi', *Contemporary Arab Thought*, 186.
34. Abu-Rabi, "Beyond the Post-Modern Mind," 235.
35. Abu-Rabi, "Beyond the Post-Modern Mind," 236.
36. Abu-Rabi, "Beyond the Post-Modern Mind," 238.
37. Elmandjra, *Al-Harb al-Hadariyyah al-Ulah* [The First Civilizational War] (Casablanca: 'Uyun, 1994), 21–22.
38. Abu Rabi', *Contemporary Arab Thought*, 184.
39. Ibrahim M. Abu-Rabi', *Intellectual Origins of Islamic Resurgence in the Modern Arab World* (New York: Suny Press, 1995), 16.
40. Fathi Yakan, "The Islamic Movement: Problems and Perspectives," in *The Contemporary Arab Reader on Political Islam*, ed. Ibrahim M. Abu-Rabi' (London: Pluto Press, 2010), 6–20.
41. Abu-Rabi', *Intellectual Origins of Islamic Resurgence*, 17.
42. Abu-Rabi', *Intellectual Origins of Islamic Resurgence*, 18.
43. Yakan, "The Islamic Movement: Problems and Perspectives," 7.
44. Hamilton Gibb, *Modern Trends in Islam* (Chicago, IL: The University of Chicago Press, 1947), 65.
45. Abu Rabi', *Contemporary Arab Thought*, 184.
46. Nikki R. Keddi, "Is There a Middle East?," *International Journal of the Middle East* 4, no. 3 (1973): 257.
47. Abu-Rabi', *Contemporary Arab Thought*, 189.
48. Samir Amin, *The Arab Nation: Nationalism and Class Struggle* (London: Zed Books, 1983), 43.
49. Abu-Rabi', *Contemporary Arab Thought*, 189.
50. Abu-Rabi', *Contemporary Arab Thought*, 190.
51. Abu-Rabi', *Contemporary Arab Thought*, 190.
52. Abu-Rabi', *Contemporary Arab Thought*, 191.
53. Mahmud Amin al-'Alim, *Mafahim wa Qadaya ishkaliya* (Cairo: Dar al-Thaqafah al-Jadidah, 1989), 18.
54. Abu-Rabi', *Contemporary Arab Thought*, 189.
55. Sadiq Jalal al-'Azm, "Mahiya al-'Awlamah?," *Al-Tariq* 56, no. 4 (1997): 31.

56. Abu-Rabi', *Contemporary Arab Thought*, 189.

57. Noam Chomsky, "Free Trade and Free Market: Pretense and Practice," in *The Cultures of Globalisation*, ed. Fredric Jameson and Masao Miyoshi (Durham, NC: Duke University Press, 1998), 359.

58. Abu-Rabi', *Contemporary Arab Thought*, 190.

59. Abu-Rabi', *Contemporary Arab Thought*, 191.

60. Samir Amin, *Misr fi Muftaraq al-Turuq: Bayna Iflas al-Yamin, wa Mihnati al-Yasar wa Azmati al-Tayyar al-Dini* (Cairo: Dar al-Mustaqbal al-'Arabi, 1990), 9–13.

61. Amin, *Misr fi Muftaraq al-Turuq*, 12.

62. Abu-Rabi', *Contemporary Arab Thought*, 194.

63. Abu-Rabi', *Contemporary Arab Thought*, 195.

64. Abu-Rabi', *Contemporary Arab Thought*, 196.

65. Abu-Rabi', *Contemporary Arab Thought*, 197.

66. Abu-Rabi', *Contemporary Arab Thought*, 197.

67. Paul Salem, "Al-Wilayat al-Mutahiddah wa'l 'Awlamah: Ma'alim al-Haymanah fi Matla' al-Qarn al-Hadi wa'l 'Ishrin," in *al- Arab wa'l Awlamah*, ed. Markaz Dirasat al-Wihdah al-"Arabiyyah (Beirut: Markaz Dirasat al-Wihdah al-'Arabiyyah, 1998), 209–252.

68. Abu-Rabi', *Contemporary Arab Thought*, 194.

69. Muhammad Abid al-Jabiri, "Al-'Arab wa'l 'Awlamah: al-'Awlamah wa'l Hawiyyah al-Thaqafiyyah," in *al-'Arab wa'l 'awlamah*, ed. Markaz Dirasat al-Wihdah al-"Arabiyyah (Beirut: Markaz Dirasat al-Wihdah al-'Arabiyyah, 1998), 298.

Abid al-Jabiri, "Al-'Arab wa'l 'Awlamah."

70. Abid al-Jabiri, "Al-'Arab wa'l 'Awlamah," 299.

71. Abid al-Jabiri, "Al-'Arab wa'l 'Awlamah," 300.

72. Yusuf al-Qaradawi, *Al-Muslimun wa'l 'Awlamah* (Cairo: Dar al-Tawzi' wa'l Nashr al-Islamiyyah, 2000),13.

73. Abu-Rabi', *Contemporary Arab Thought*, 194.

74. Yusuf al-Qaradawi, *Al-Muslimun wa'l 'Awlamah*, 14.

75. Abu-Rabi', *Contemporary Arab Thought*, 195.

76. Abu-Rabi', *Contemporary Arab Thought*, 196.

77. Muhammad Qutb, *al-Muslimun wa'l 'awlamah* (Cairo: Dar al-Shuruq, 2000), 10.

78. Qutb, *al-Muslimun wa'l 'awlamah*, 11.

79. Roland Robertson, *Globalisation: Social Theory and Global Culture* (London: Sage, 1996), 8.

80. Abu-Rabi', *Contemporary Arab Thought*, 195.

81. Abu-Rabi', *Contemporary Arab Thought*, 196.

82. Abu-Rabi', *Contemporary Arab Thought*, 197.

83. Abu-Rabi', *Contemporary Arab Thought*, 198.

84. Isma'il Sabri "Abdallah, "Al-'Arab wa'l 'Awlamah: al-'Awlamah wa'l Iqtisad wa'l Tanmiyyah al-'Arabiyyah," in *al-'Arab wa'l 'Awlamah*, ed. Markaz Dirasat al-Wihdah al-'Arabiyyah (Beirut: Markaz Dirasat al-Wihdah al-'Arabiyyah, 1998), 371.

85. Arendt, *The Origins of Totalitarianism*, 143.

86. Abu-Rabi', *Contemporary Arab Thought*, 200.
87. Abu-Rabi', *Contemporary Arab Thought*, 201.
88. Richard Falk, *Explorations at the Edge of Time: The Prospects for World Order* (Philadelphia, PA: Temple University Press, 1992), 48.
89. Abu-Rabi', *Contemporary Arab Thought*, 200.
90. Abu-Rabi', *Contemporary Arab Thought*, 67.
91. David L. Johnston, "Chandra Muzaffar's Islamic Critique of Globalisation: A Malaysian Contribution to a Global Ethic" (Melbourne: Centre for Dialogue Working Paper, La Trobe University, 2006), 3.
92. Johnston, "Chandra Muzaffar's Islamic Critique of Globalisation," 4.
93. Abu Rabi', *Contemporary Arab Thought*, 186–187.
94. Johnston, "Chandra Muzaffar's Islamic Critique of Globalisation," 4.

Conclusion

Islam, Globalization, and Shared Prosperity

This work has brought to light that Muslims are approaching the subject of globalization with a twofold purpose. Firstly, scholars aim to reflect on the significant challenges posed by this phenomenon, and secondly, they seek to evaluate the overall progress made by Muslims over the past century. Within this discourse, scholars grapple with profound transformations across various domains, including epistemology, ethics, science, economics, and politics, induced by contemporary globalization. However, there is a palpable reluctance among Muslim thinkers to fully embrace the prevailing understanding of globalization, viewing it as a set of forces emanating from the West that exert influential effects on the political, economic, social, and cultural fabric of Islamic societies.[1] Some scholars within this discourse perceive a predicament in which the Muslim world finds itself increasingly marginalized and endangered by the forces of globalization. This situation prompts a defensive posture among numerous Muslim leaders. Additionally, scholars argue that humanity's intellectual potential has been constrained to humanism, leading to the erosion of traditional worldviews and the imposition of an ideological perspective. Ideologies, despite their efficacy in organizing human experience into guiding frameworks for social and political action, are viewed as inherently ephemeral and transient.[2] They often serve as tools to legitimize political interests or uphold prevailing power structures. Recent historical trajectories underscore that ideologies are crafted by ideologues and marginal intellectuals who aim to impose their preferred norms and values on society, thus constraining the scope of public discourse. Notably, these ideological frameworks tend to reduce the concept of truth to subjective whims, conjectures, and emotional proclivities. Ideologues assert comprehensive understandings of both science and religion, yet their narratives project a distorted perspective of human nature, communicated through compelling stories that persuade, commend, criticize, discern truths from falsehoods, and distinguish the virtuous from the malevolent.

The concept of globalism emerges as an ideology of development, contributing to social and economic unrest. This phenomenon accentuates the rural–urban divide and facilitates the dissemination of modernization and technical rationalisation on a global scale.[3] The roots of globalization can be traced back approximately 12,000 years, gaining momentum in the early modern period, particularly flourishing in Europe as religious influence gradually waned in human history.[4] Hossain Nasr asserts that, historically, religions have advocated the pursuit of virtue and avoidance of evil. However, the contemporary trend toward absolutizing the human state seeks to diminish the impact of religion on the human spirit and challenges established categories of sin and evil. In contrast to earlier civilizations where nature was revered as a reflection of the Divine, this absolutization manifests as a resistance against nature, driven by an allure for the enticing fruits of profanity.[5] In the relentless pursuit of these worldly gains, both humanity and the environment stand perilously close to catastrophic consequences. The modern scientific community, often neglecting the qualitative dimensions of human existence transformed by the globalization process, appears complacent in addressing this impending threat. Modern science imparts a worldview grounded in unquestioned presumptions, presented as highly normative, thus controlling the truth system in contemporary society. Modern ideologies frequently leverage scientific truths to bolster their positions. The Muslim world and other traditional regions are compelled to embrace the challenges of the modern world, contributing to the precarious proximity to ecological calamity without due consideration for potential moral and environmental repercussions.[6] The assertion of human autonomy from the divine, coupled with a sole reliance on material pursuits, is posited as a driving force behind environmental issues, psychological instability, urban decay, and related problems. Despite humankind's attempts to negate the influence of higher powers and assert independence, the consequences of these actions remain inescapable, representing an inevitable outgrowth of the current human condition.

The foundations of the modern world are based on fundamental contradictions that, as a result of the violent transformation of a colonized polity, not only brought humanity into a state of ecological and social difficulty but also caused enormous destruction of centuries-old traditions during the colonization period, which resulted in the rapid emergence of some fifty-seven nation-states on the global map between the two world wars. This process was not simple. A life based on principles must be revived, and religious ethics provide a feasible alternative for reintroducing transcendental ethics and morality into human society. According to Abu Rabi, a new common awareness must emerge in light of the enormous effects of globalization in order to comprehend and combat the bad trends.[7] To counteract these perilous tendencies, the Muslim community must make a concerted effort to resurrect the social, financial, and economic ethics of Islam as a monotheistic phenomenon. It is crucial to rekindle a feeling of community that can survive the assaults of individualism, which have taken over in industrialized industrial countries and its satellites in the Third World.[8] There is no way around restoring the Islamic community ethic that commands the good and forbids the wrong, because of the widening differences between the North and the South and the rural–urban divides within most southern nations. It is crucial to keep in mind that conventional worldviews and ideologies must be the foundation of solutions if they are to survive in a society that values individualism and fierce competition.[9]

Alongside knowledge and wisdom, the Qur'ān places significant emphasis on values such as justice, equality, compassion, and peace. Ideally, Islamic nations should have been exemplars of these values for the world. However, they are lagging behind. In addressing this shortfall, Muslim intellectuals, if not the traditional 'ulamā, need to engage in thoughtful deliberation and propose more effective solutions.[10] The World Social Forum, championed by social justice activists with the slogan "Another world is conceivable," advocates for a world free from exploitation. Islamic nations have the potential to take the lead in establishing standards of justice, compassion, and knowledge. Regrettably, there are no clear indications of such initiatives. Engineer suggests the promotion of discourse between various ethnicities and civilizations based on the Qur'ānic emphasis on diversity to navigate the transformations induced by globalization, particularly economic migration.[11]

Islamic universality and contemporary globalization share the goal of uniting people for a common purpose, but they diverge significantly in their motivations and methodologies. Islamic universality, rooted in the inclusive nature of Islam, transcends cultural boundaries and aims to extend its teachings worldwide. Many Muslims recognize the duty to support and promote the global spread of Islam, as emphasized in the Qur'ān on numerous occasions. The foundations of Western globalization and Islamic universality must be differentiated. Islamic universality is grounded in moral standards ordained by God, emphasizing spiritual and religious principles that serve justice, kindness, and love for all. It seeks to foster a global community where individuals enjoy freedom of choice and justice and compassion prevail, promoting a harmonious coexistence. In contrast, modern globalization, orchestrated by human control, operates as a tool for dominance, often at the behest of a select few rulers, even at the cost of personal wealth and the lives of others. Islamic universality envisions a world where people live with kindness, fairness, and harmony, encouraging individual decision-making and upholding ethical principles. Conversely, contemporary globalization transforms the world into an interconnected realm resembling a jungle, where the powerful exploit the vulnerable, perpetuating a system that widens the wealth gap. The latter becomes problematic when driven by desires for dominance and principles of greed, leading to the erosion of good morals, ethical values, and principles. In such scenarios, individuals may become mere pawns in a game of chess manipulated by the powerful to further their selfish objectives.

Muslim scholars commonly perceive the West, along with nations under its influence like Japan and certain Southeast Asian countries, as the primary architects of globalization. This viewpoint underscores the West, including nations like Japan and certain Southeast Asian entities, as pivotal in shaping the contours of globalization. Implicit in this assessment is the acknowledgment that Western economic, technological, political, and cultural centers wield considerable influence, dictating the course and nature of the globalizing process. However, this perspective also acknowledges the multifaceted challenges posed by globalization. Critics argue that rather than being a force for positive growth, globalization is perceived by millions as a disruptive agent, posing threats to established traditions, livelihoods, and even lives. The global spread of a commercial culture and materialistic values is criticized for eroding traditional norms, while globalization is implicated in the globalized nature of crimes, increased prevalence of diseases, and regulatory challenges. Moreover, the emphasis on market-driven technological skills in formal education is seen as sidelining traditional academic and moral education. Unbridled carbon emissions from affluent nations and corporations are linked to environmental degradation, including deforestation driven by profit motives.[12] Despite these concerns, the responses of Muslim scholars reveal nuanced perspectives on globalization, acknowledging both its drawbacks and benefits. Positive aspects include the facilitation of more affordable and accessible communication, contributing to the dissemination of knowledge across diverse disciplines. Additionally, globalization has played a role in spotlighting critical issues such as human rights, public accountability, corruption, and women's rights, often leading to swifter remedial actions.[13] Furthermore, globalization is recognized for fostering increased social mobility, fortifying the middle class, and stimulating trade and foreign investment, thereby engendering a sense of global solidarity, particularly in response to natural or man-made disasters.

Scholars within the Islamic tradition posit that Islam upholds a unitarian perspective in its principles and values, anchored in the concept of *tawhīd* (Divine Oneness), distinct from the tenets of modern globalization. *Tawhīd*, constituting the foundational tenet of Islam, occupies a central role in the Qur'ānic discourse, influencing discussions on Islamic law and morality. It revolves around the belief in the singular nature of God and, by extension, the essential unity of humanity. *Tawhīd* asserts the oneness of the Creator reflected in the entirety of the cosmos, rejecting distinctions in the value systems governing various facets of life. Furthermore, *Tawhīd* serves as a unifying force for the Muslim community (*ummah*) and establishes a connection with the broader human collective, laying the groundwork for the fundamental equality of all individuals.[14] The Qur'ānic narrative elucidating the creation of humanity underscores that God instilled a divine essence into Adam,[15] underscoring the shared lineage of all humans.[16] The *ummah*, as a community bound by faith, acknowledges the common ancestry of all descendants of Adam, fostering a sense of shared humanity.[17] In his Farewell Sermon in Makkah, the Prophet addressed a diverse audience, emphasizing the unity of their Creator and their shared descent from a common progenitor. Islam's perspective on humanity envisions a cohesive organism that transcends differences in origin, race, color, or nationality. All individuals, regardless of religious affiliation, merit equal application of foundational principles of justice and fair treatment, grounded in their shared human dignity.[18] Islam recognizes and acknowledges the diversity embedded in the divine plan of creation, considering it a purposeful feature. Even as disparities exist for practical distinctions, the Qur'ān emphasizes that "the most virtuous among you is the most honorable of you in the sight of God," reiterating the intrinsic equality and dignity of all individuals.[19]

The concept of social brotherhood serves as a foundational principle in the organization of Muslims, shaping their communal dynamics. In Islam, a community is viewed as a collective of individuals collaborating for mutual benefit, utilizing communal resources to achieve sustainability and innovation. The necessity of production in a society gives rise to rules and regulations, culminating in the establishment of a political system aimed at fostering harmony and peace. Islamic traditions provide a robust set of political principles applicable across diverse contexts, offering potential contributions to a globalized order that respects the unique significance of various cultural traditions.[20] Qaradāwī emphasizes Islam's recognition of two levels of fraternity: the broader human fraternity (*al-ikha' al-insani*) and the religious fraternity (*al-ikha' al-dini*).[21] According to Islam, righteous behavior is universally defined, transcending race or nationality, and all individuals are held to the same standards without bias or prejudice. The core of Islam's universalist worldview lies in its belief that humans are entrusted with the vicegerency of God, aspiring to build a human civilization on Earth (*imar al-ard*). This mission is driven by the vision of wealth and success for everyone, irrespective of gender, religious affiliation, or nationality.[22]

The challenges posed by globalization, in its multifaceted expressions, warrant a thorough analysis and the adoption of reasoned stances in anticipation of potential outcomes. This prompts the question of how the *wasatiyyah* (moderate) approach can be discerned and applied in the complex scenarios that globalization is likely to engender. The consideration of seeking moderate approaches becomes pertinent given the understanding that globalization often serves as a tool of the powerful to extend influence over the weak and powerless. While it may seem imperative to comprehend and scrutinize globalization in terms of both its overarching framework and various components, addressing this complex issue does not offer a straightforward solution. Different components may necessitate distinct responses. Selecting judiciously and making well-informed decisions regarding various aspects of globalization is a challenging task, one that is not suited for those lacking in-depth knowledge. Several key considerations should guide this endeavor. First and foremost, a comprehensive understanding of globalization is paramount. It involves a meticulous examination of its objectives, long-term plans, and its potential to facilitate the advancement of third-world civilizations in the realms of science, technology, and informatics.[23] Secondly, a thorough investigation of Islam is crucial to identify adaptable characteristics that can be modified for modernization and alignment with contemporary times. Simultaneously, psychological barriers hindering acceptance of change must be addressed. Liberating our minds from the fear of losing Islamic identity and tradition is essential to overcome decision-making paralysis and foster creativity and innovation. Facing the challenges and changes brought about by globalization requires a mindset free from the perceived threat of Western civilization, enabling a spirit of self-confidence and exploration.[24]

The current approach we are undertaking is not novel; in fact, it echoes a historical precedent. During the initial four centuries after the establishment of Islam, Muslims displayed receptivity to diverse cultures, encompassing ancient Greek, Indian, Persian, and others. Islamic culture flourished as an open-minded and unrestricted environment that embraced a wide array of ideas. Al-Shibiny asserts that by emulating this historical example, Muslims can comprehend other advanced civilizations and assimilate their progress across various developmental spheres. The objective is to harness the ongoing revolution in technology, international communications, and information sciences without necessarily succumbing to the process of Westernization, but rather advancing Islamic culture.[25]

Proposed Recommendations

Every journey must come to an end, and this intellectual journey is no different. Initially sparked by the researcher's natural curiosity whenever he thought about the future of Muslims in the globalization period, this research evolved into an effort to comprehend the nature of futures thinking by examining the ideas of Muslim intellectuals and their Western counterparts. A fundamental assumption that pervades the entirety of this study is that, for the rejuvenation of Muslim civilization in the future, contemporary Muslims must actively engage in both intellectual contemplation and pragmatic endeavors. This imperative necessitates the development and application of innovative approaches adept at addressing the authentic needs of the *ummah* in the present and future contexts. Given the undeniable inevitability and irreversibility of globalization, Muslims must fortify themselves against its multifaceted impacts. Former Malaysian Prime Minister Tun Mahathir, recognizing the urgency of action, articulated in one of his speeches to the Islamic *ummah* the imperative of safeguarding Muslim nations from marginalization—a fate witnessed during the Industrial Revolution and the Industrial Age. In the contemporary context, the stakes are even higher. Failure to keep abreast of the radical advancements in science, technology, and the evolving paradigms in human and international relations not only risks marginalization but also entails the prospect of permanent domination and hegemony. Muslim nations, he contends, cannot afford to miss this opportunity.[26]

Tun Mahathir's appeal serves as a cautionary message, urging Muslims not to underestimate or disregard the ongoing developments in various technological domains such as information technology, multimedia, e-learning, and e-commerce. Adopting a proactive stance toward acquiring and effectively utilizing new technologies for societal advancement and economic empowerment is deemed a wise and prudent strategy. Diversifying away from a heavy reliance on Western technology, particularly in multimedia and software development, is suggested as another means for Islamic nations to safeguard the *ummah* amid the currents of globalization. Recognizing that a form of colonization manifests through developing a mental dependence on the West, it is proposed that oil-rich Muslim nations redirect substantial investments from America and Europe toward the emerging and underdeveloped nations within the Muslim world.[27] This strategic shift is seen as a potential remedy for mitigating the disparities between affluent and underdeveloped Muslim nations. Such an approach aligns with the Qur'ānic emphasis on mutual assistance and is regarded as a noble deed in the eyes of God.[28]

Muslim countries need to prioritize investment in research and development to recapture the pinnacle of prosperity attained during the Golden Age of Islam. During this era, the Islamic world's capacity for research not only propelled its own prosperity but also attracted intellectuals from Europe to its centers of learning and study. However, a subsequent period of complacency led to the loss of Muslim strengths as competent researchers, allowing Europeans to surpass them. The indirect consequences of colonialism, which impoverished Muslims, further weakened the *ummah*. Despite gaining freedom from Western colonial powers, Muslims have struggled to regain their former position since the fall of Baghdad in 1258. Recognizing this historical context, Muslims who are cognizant of their situation should exert diligent efforts in research and development, breaking their mental dependence on the West in the process.[29]

Khurshid Ahmad asserts that Muslims need to recognize that robust preparation is as crucial to an Islamic strategy as unwavering faith in their purpose and obligation.[30] This preparation encompasses knowledge, character, moral excellence, economic and political power, military strength, technical proficiency, and social cohesion. To effectively play a meaningful role in the world, Muslims must first address their internal affairs and mobilize all available resources. Greater collaboration, unity, and collective self-reliance within the Muslim community are essential. Establishing regional associations, trade and finance agreements, educational and technological partnerships, and political coordination are steps toward a more just and equitable global order that maintains a balanced equilibrium among different countries, sociopolitical systems, and civilizations. In the face of uncontrolled globalization, Muslim solidarity can serve as a potent deterrent against the annihilation of Muslim nations and the erasure of their civilizational identity. The correct course of action involves global discussion, interaction, engagement, and collaboration as a community with a mission. This approach is deemed a crucial part of their strategy, as it is the only way for them to survive, leaving a meaningful imprint on history through proactive and optimistic responses to global challenges.[31]

Last but not the least, the era of globalization has revitalized the moral force of human rights as a potent tool for ensuring equality and combating injustice, irrespective of the driving force behind it. For the Muslim world, the only viable option is to reevaluate the foundations of international civil society, carving out its distinct space in this globalized world.[32] This may necessitate a paradigm shift in modern Islamic thought concerning the postcolonial world, where human rights assume greater significance in everyday life. If and when such a transition occurs, it has the potential to bring about balance and control without compromising Muslim values and ethics. In conclusion, this study underscores the imperative for a reevaluation of Islamic methodology to effectively address the challenges of the modern era. We advocate for the integration of Islamic methodology into contemporary approaches to researching globalization, emphasizing that it should not be viewed as a deterministic project but rather as a value-guided approach to thinking and acting. Rather than departing from the Islamic heritage, our research seeks to situate this dialogue within it to better comprehend globalization in Muslim communities, analyze current ways of thinking and acting, and assess the applicability of developmental paradigms promoted by globalists across the board.

Notes

1. Farish A. Noor, "The Evolution of 'Jihad' in Islamist Political Discourse: How a Plastic Concept Became Harder." Accessed April 15, 2024. https://items.ssrc.org/after-september-11/the-evolution-of-jihad-in-islamist-political-discourse-how-a-plastic-concept-became-harder/.

2. Seyyed Hossein Nasr, *Islam and the Plight of Modern Man* (London: Longman, 1975), 113.

3. Jerry Mander, "Introduction: Facing the Rising Tide," in *The Case Against the Global Economy: And for a Turn Toward the Local*, ed. Jerry Mander and Edward Goldsmith (San Francisco, CA: Sierra Club Books, 1996), 3–8.

4. Seyyed Hossein Nasr, *Man and Nature* (London: Mandala, 1968), 6.

5. Nasr, *Man and Nature*, 13.

6. Nasr, *Man and Nature*, 14.

7. Rabi, "Globalisation: A Contemporary Islamic Response?," 38.

8. Rabi, "Globalisation: A Contemporary Islamic Response?," 39.

9. Ahmad, *Postmodernism and Islam*, 22.

10. Khaled Abou El Fadl, "Qur'anic Ethics and Islamic Law," *Journal of Islamic Ethics* 1, no. 1–2 (2017): 7–28.

11. Al-Qur'ān, 30:22 and 5:48.
12. Bruce Lawrence, "Islam in the Age of Globalization," *Religion Compass* 2, no. 3 (2008): 331–339.
13. Lawrence, "Islam in the Age of Globalization," 332.
14. Mohammad Hashim Kamali, *The Dignity of Man: An Islamic Perspective* (Cambridge: Islamic Text Society, 1999), 5.
15. Al-Qur'ān: 4:1.
16. Al-Qur'ān: 38:72.
17. Ibn 'Abd Rabbih al-Andalusi, *Al-'Iqd al-Farid, li'-Malik al-Sa'id*, 3rd ed., Vol. 2 (Cairo: Matba'ah Lajnat al-Tal'lif, 1965), 357.
18. Al-Qur'ān, 16:90.
19. Al- Qur'ān, 49:13. Yusuf Al-Qaradawi, *Al-Khasa'is al-'Ammah li'l-Islam* (Cairo: Maktabah Wahbah, 1989), 84.
20. Said and Funk, "Islamic Revivalism: A Global Perspective," 324.
21. Al-Qaradawi, *Al-Khasa'is al-'Ammah li'l-Islam*, 84.
22. Kamali, *The Dignity of Man*, 208.
23. Kamali, *The Dignity of Man*, 209.
24. Mohammed El-Shibiny, *The Threat of Globalisation to Arab Islamic Culture: The Dynamics of World Peace*, (Pittsburgh, PA: Dorrance Publishing, 2005), 9–10.
25. El-Shibiny, *The Threat of Globalisation*, 11.
26. Mohd Abbas Abdul Razak, "Globalisation and its Impact on Education and Culture," *World Journal of Islamic History and Civilization* 1, no. 1 (2011): 66.
27. Amer Al-Roubaie, *Globalisation and the Muslim World* (Malita: Jaya Publishing House, 2002), 90–102.
28. Abdul Razak, "Globalisation and its Impact on Education and Culture," 66.
29. Al-Qur'ān: 3:103.

And hold fast, all together, unto the bond with God, and do not draw apart from one another. And remember the blessing which God has bestowed upon you: how, when you were enemies, He brought your hearts together, so that through His blessing you became brethren; and [how, when] you were on the brink of fiery abyss, He saved you from it.

30. Ahmad, "Globalisation: Challenges and Prospects for Muslims," 9.
31. Ahmad, "Globalisation: Challenges and Prospects for Muslims," 10.
32. Mahmood Monshipouri, "Islam and Human Rights in the Age of Globalisation," in *Islam Encountering Globalisation*, ed. Ali Muhammadi (London: Routledge, 2002), 107.

Bibliography

Abou El Fadl, Khaled. "Qur'ānic Ethics and Islamic Law." *Journal of Islamic Ethics* 1, no. 1–2 (August 2017): 7–28.
Abu Rabi', Ibrahim. *Contemporary Arab Thought, Studies in Post -1967 Arab Intellectual History*. London: Pluto Press, 2003.
Abu Sulayman, A. A. "The Islamisation of Knowledge: A New Approach towards Reform of Contemporary Knowledge." 91–118 in *Islam: Source and Purpose of Knowledge: Proceedings and Selected Papers of Second Conference on Islamisation of Knowledge 1402 AH/1982 AC*. Herndon, VA: IIIT, 1988.
Abu-Rabi, Ibrahim M. "Beyond the Post-Modern Mind." *American Journal of the Islamic Social Sciences* 7, no. 2 (September 1990): 235–256.
Abu-Rabi', Ibrahim M. "Globalisation: A Contemporary Islamic Response?" *The American Journal of Islamic Social Sciences* 15, no. 3 (October 1998): 15–44.
Adhama, Khairul Akmaliah, Saidb, Mohd Fuaad, Muhamad, Nur Sa'adah, and Yaakub, Noor Inayah. "Technological Innovation and Entrepreneurship from the Western and Islamic Perspectives." *International Journal of Economics, Management and Accounting* 20, no. 2 (August 2012): 109–148.
Ahmad, Akbar, *Journey into Islam: The Crisis of Globalization*. Washington, DC: Brookings Institution Press, 2007.
Ahmad Akbar S., and Donnan, Hastings. "Islam in the Age of Postmodernity." 1–20 in *Islam, Globalization and Postmodernity*, edited by Akbar S. Ahmad and Hastings Donnan. London: Routledge, 1994.
Ahmad, Khaliq and Hassan, Arif. "Distributive Justice: The Islamic Perspective." *Intellectual Discourse* 8, no. 2 (2000): 159–172.
Ahmad, Khurshid. "Globalization: Challenges and Prospects for Muslims." *Policy Perspectives* 3, no. 1 (January–June 2006): 1–11.

Ahmad, Akbar. *The Muslim 500: The World's Most Influential 500 Muslims*. Dabuq: Royal Islamic Strategies Centre, 2023.

Ahmed, Akbar S. *Discovering Islam: Making Sense of Muslim History and Society*. London: Routledge, 1988.

Ahmed, Akbar S. *Journey into Europe: Islam, Immigration and Identity*. New York: Brookings Institution Press, 2018.

Ahmed, Akbar S. *Postmodernism and Islam: Predicament and Promise*. London: Routledge, 1992.

Ahmed, Akbar S. *Religion and Politics in Muslim society: Order and Conflict in Pakistan*. Cambridge: Cambridge University Press, 1983.

Ahmed, Akbar S. *The Thistle and the Drone: How America's War on Terror Became a Global War on Tribal Islam*. New York: Brookings Institution Press, 2013.

Ahmed, Akbar S. and Forst, Brian. "Toward a More Civil Twenty-first Century." 3–13 in *After Terror: Promoting Dialogue Among Civilizations*, edited by Akbar Ahmad and Brian Forst. London: Polity Press, 2005.

Ahmed, Irfan, Akhtar, Muhammad, Ahmed, Ishaq, and Aziz, Saima. "Practices of Islamic Banking in The Light of Islamic Ethics: A Critical Review." *International Journal of Economics, Management and Accounting* 25, no. 3 (November 2017): 465–490.

Akbar, Ahmad. *Discovering Islam: Making Sense of Muslim History*. London: Routledge, 2002.

Akbarzadeh, Shahram. "The Globalization of Islam." 308–309 in *An Introduction to International Relations: Australian Perspectives*, edited by Richard Devetak, Anthony Burke, and Jim George. Cambridge: Cambridge University Press, 2008.

Akhtar, Shabbir. *Islam as Political Religion: The Future of an Imperial Faith*. London: Routledge, 2011.

Akoda, Winifred E. "The Contributions of Ali Mazrui to African Historical Scholarship." *International Journal of Humanities Social Sciences and Education (IJHSSE)* 2, no. 6 (2015): 65–69.

Al Faruqi, Maysam J. "Umma, The Orientalists and the Qur'ānic concept of Identity." *Journal of Islamic Studies* 16, no. 1 (January 2005): 1–34.

Al-Ahsan, Abdullah. *Ummah or Nation? Identity Crisis in a Contemporary Muslim Society*. London: The Islamic Foundation, 1992.

Al-Andalusi, Ibn 'Abd Rabbih. *Al-'Iqd al-Farid, li'-Malik al-Sa'id*. 3rd ed. Vol. 2. Cairo: Matba'ah Lajnat al-Tal'lif, 1965.

Al-Faruqi, Ismail R. and Lamya al-Faruqi, Lois. *The Cultural Atlas of Islam*. New York: Macmillan Publishing Company, 1986.

Al-Jannah, Aḥmad Ibn Ṭuwayr. *The Pilgrimage of Ahmad, Son of the Little Bird of Paradise: An Account of a 19th Century Pilgrimage from Mauritania to Mecca*. Translated by H. Norris. Warminster: Aris and Phillips, 1977.

Al-Jayyousi, Odeh Rashed. *Rethinking Sustainability: Islamic Perspectives*. March 2, 2023. https://www.ecomena.org/sustainability-islamic-perspectives/.

Al-Jurjany, A. I. M. *Mujam al-Ta'rifat* [Glossary of Definitions]. Beirut: Daru Al-kutub Al-Ilmiyyah [Scientific Books House], 1983.

Allievi, Stefano and Nielsen, Jorgen. *Muslim Networks and Transnational Communities in and across Europe*. Muslim Minorities Series, vol. 1. Leiden: Brill, 2003.

Allioui, Hanane and Mourdi, Youssef. "Exploring the Full Potentials of IoT for Better Financial Growth and Stability: A Comprehensive Survey." *Sensors* 23, no. 19 (2023): 8015.

Al-Milad, Zaki. "Islamic Thought and the Issue of Globalization." *Middle East Affairs Journal* 1–2 (1999): 13–32.

Al-Qaradawi, Yusuf. *Al-Khasa'is al-'Ammah li'l-Islam*. Cairo: Maktabah Wahbah, 1989.

Al-Qudsy, Sharifah Hayaati Syed Ismail and Rahman, Asmak Ab. "Islamic Perspectives of Creativity: A Model for Teachers of Social Studies as Leaders." *Procedia Social and Behavioral Sciences* 2 (January 2010): 412–426.

Al-Roubaie, Amer. *Globalization and the Muslim World*. Shah Alam, Malita: Jaya Publishing House, 2002.

Altglas, Veronique. "Introduction." 3–10 in *Religion and Globalisation: Critical Concepts in Social Studies*, edited by Veronique Altglas. London and New York: Routledge, 2011.

Al-Zuhayli, W. *Mawsu'ah al-Fiqh al-Islami Wa al-Qadaya al-Mu'asara* [Encyclopedia of Islamic Jurisprudence and Contemporary]. Damsyiq: Dar al-Fikr, 2010.

American University, School of International Service, Faculty. "Akbar Ahmad." Accessed April 14, 2024. https://www.american.edu/sis/faculty/akbar.cfm.

Amin, Hussain. *Al-Islam fi Alam Mutaghir* [Islam in a Changing World]. Cairo: Madbooli Bookshop, 1987.

Appadurai, Arjun. "Dead Certainty: Ethnic Violence in the Era of Globalization." *Public Culture* 10, no. 2 (October 1998): 225–247.

Appadurai, Arjun. "Disjuncture and Difference in the Global Cultural Economy." 295–311 in *Global Culture: Nationalism, Globalizationand Modernity*, edited by Mike Featherstone. London: Sage, 1990.

Appadurai, Arjun. "The Production of Locality." 208–229 in *Counterworks: Managing the Diversity of Knowledge*, edited by Richard Fardon. London: Routledge, 1995.

Arendt, Hannah. *The Origins of Totalitarianism*. Cleveland, OH: Meridian Books, 1963.

Arjomand, Sa'Id. "Social Theory and the Changing World: Mass Democracy, Development, Modernization and Globalization." *International Sociology* 19 (September 2004): 321–353.

Arnason, Johann P. "Nationalism, Globalization and Modernity." 207–236 in *Global Culture: Nationalism, Globalization and Modernity*, edited by Mike Featherstone, 220. London: Sage, 1990.

Arnett, Jeffrey J. "The Psychology of Globalization." *American Psychologist* 57, no. 10 (October 2002): 774–783.

Ashtankar, Omprakash. "Islamic Perspectives on Environmental Protection." *International Journal of Applied Research* 2, no. 1 (January 2016): 438–441.

Babayo Sule, Aminu Yahaya, Muhammad, and Ating, Rashid. "Globalization and the Muslim Ummah: Issues, Challenges, and the Ways Out." *IIUM Journal of Religion and Civilisational Studies (IJECS)* 1, no. 1 (December 2018): 7–29.

Baderin, Mashood A. "The Evolution of Islamic Law of Nations and the Modern International Order." *American Journal of Islamic Social Sciences* 17, no. 2 (July 2000): 57–80.

Badran, Margot. "Understanding Islam, Islamism and Islamic Feminism." *Journal of Women's History* 13, no. 1 (March 2001): 47–52.

Bagader, Abubaker A. "Contemporary Islamic Movements in the Arab World." 111–122 in *Islam, Globalization and Postmodernity*, edited by Akbar S. Ahmed and Hastings Donnan. London: Routledge, 1994.

Bakar, Osman. "Cultural Pluralism in a Globalised World: Challenges to Peaceful Coexistence." *ICR Journal* 1, no. 3 (April 2010): 528–531.

Baker, Oliver. "The Qur'ān on Interfaith and Inter-Civilizational Dialogue: Interpreting a Divine message for Twentieth Century Humanity." International institute of Islamic Thought Malaysia (IIITM) and Institute for the Study of the Ummah and Global Understanding (ISUGO), 2006. https://catalogue.nla.gov.au/catalog/4515723.

Barber, Benjamin R. *Jihad Versus McWorld: How Globalism and Tribalism are Reshaping the World*. New York: Ballantine Books, 1996.

Barkawi, Tarak and Laffey, Mark. "The Postcolonial Moment in Security Studies." *Review of International Studies* 32 (May 2006): 329–352.

Barry, Buzan and Wæver, Ole. *Regions and Powers: The Structure of International Security*. Cambridge: Cambridge University Press, 2003.

Bauman, Zygmunt. *Globalization: The Human Consequences*. Cambridge: Polity, 1999.

Beck, Ulrich. "The Terrorist Threat: World Risk Society Revisited." *Theory, Culture and Society* 19, no. 4 (August 2002): 39–55.

Beck, Ulrich. *What is Globalization?* Cambridge: Polity Press, 2000.

Beckford, James. "Religious Movements and Globalisation." 165–183 in *Global Social Movements*, edited by Robin Cohen and Shireen Rai. London: Athlone, 2000.

Bilqaziz, 'Abd al-Ilah. "Al-'Awlamah Wa'l Hawiyyah al-Thaqafiyyah." *Al-Mustaqbal al-'Arabi* 236 (1998): 90-125.

Birdsall, Nancy. "Life is Unfair: Inequality in the World." *Foreign Policy* 111 (Summer 1998): 95–113.

Bischof, David and Wagner, Martin. "Do Voters Polarize When Radical Parties Enter Parliament?," *American Journal of Political Science* 63, no. 4 (October 2019): 888–904.

Black, Antony. *The History of Islamic Political Thought: From the Prophet to the Present*, 2nd edition. Edinburgh: Edinburgh University Press, 2011.

Bolognani, Marta and Statham, Peter. "The Changing Public Face of Muslim Associations in Britain: Coming together for Common 'Social' Goals?," *Ethnicities* 13 (March 2013): 229–249.

Bouma, Gary, Haidar, Ami, Nyland, Chris, and Smith, W. "Work, Religious Diversity and Islam." *Asia Pacific Journal of Human Resources* 41 (May 2003): 51–61.

Bourdieu, Pierre. *Acts of Resistance: Against the Market*. New York: The New Press, 1998.

Boyer, Robert and Drache, Daniel. *States Against Markets: The Limits of Globalization*. London: Routledge.

Braudel, Fernand. *A History of Civilizations*. New York: Penguin Books, 1995.

Bruquetas-Callejo, Maria, Garcés-Mascarenas, Bianca, Penninx, Rinus, and Scholten, Peter. 2007. *Policymaking Related to Immigration and Integration: The Dutch case*. Working Paper: Country Report, No. 15. Amsterdam: IMISCOE.

Buchan, Neil, Brewer, Michael, Grimalda, Gianluca, Wilson, Robert, Fatas, Ernesto, and Foddy, Marco. 2011. "Global Identity and Global Cooperation." *Psychological Science* 22, no. 6 (May 2011): 821–828.

Butt, Nasim. *Science and Muslim Societies*. London: Grey Seal, 1991.

Buzan, Barry. "New Patterns of Global Security in the Twenty-first Century." *International Affairs* 67, no. 3 (July 1991): 431–451.

Carnegie, Andrew and Carson, Andrew. "Reckless Rhetoric? Compliance Pessimism and International Order in the Age of Trump." *Journal of Politics* 81, no. 2 (April 2019): 739–746.

Cassidy, Edward Idris Cardinal. *Ecumenism and Interreligious Dialogue*. New York: Paulist Press, 2005.

Castells, Manuel. *The Information Age: Economy, Society and Culture: The Power of Identity*. Oxford: Blackwell, 2000.

Chapra, Umer M. *The Future of Economics: An Islamic Perspective*. Leicester: The Islamic Foundation, 2000.

Chapra, Umer M. "Global Economic Challenges and Islam." *Policy Perspectives* 3, no. 2 (July–December 2006): 19–41.

Chapra, Umer M. *Islam and Economic Development: A Strategy for Development with Justice and Stability*. Islamabad: Islamic Research Institute Press.

Chapra, Umer M. "Islamic Economic Thought and The New Global Economy." *Islamic Economic Studies* 9, no. 1 (September 2001): 1–16.

Chapra, Umer M. *The Islamic Vision of Development in the Light of Maqasid Al-Sharī'ah*. Herndon, VA: The International Institute of Islamic Thought, 2007.

Chapra, Umer M. Research Centre for Islamic Legislation and Ethics. Accessed April 14, 2024. https://www.cilecenter.org/about-us/our-team/dr-umer-chapra.

Choudhury, Masudul Alam. "Financial Globalization and Islamic Financing Institutions: The Topic Revisited." *Islamic Economic Studies* 9, no. 1 (September 2001): 20–38.

Christison, Kathleen. *Perceptions of Palestine: Their Influence on U.S. Middle East Policy*. Berkeley, CA: University of California Press, 1999.

Clansy-Smith, Julia. "Saints, Mahdis and Arms: Religion and Resistance in Nineteenth-Century North Africa." 60–80 in *Islam, Politics and Social Movements*, edited by E. Burke III and I. M. Lapidus. London: I.B. Tauris & Co.

Cohn, Theodore H. *Global Political Economy*. 6th edition. New York: Pearson, 2012.

Colantone, Italo and Stanig, Piero. "The Trade Origins of Economic Nationalism: Import Competition and Voting Behavior in Western Europe." *American Journal of Political Science* 62, no. 4 (April 2018): 936–953.

Cole, Juan. "Paradosis and Monotheism: A Late Antique Approach to the Meaning of Islām in the Quran." *Bulletin of the School of Oriental and African Studies* 82, no. 3 (December 2019): 405–425.

Collins, Carole. "Colonialism and Class Struggle in Sudan." *MERIP Reports* 46 (April 1976): 3–20.

Cooley, John. *Unholy Wars: Afghanistan, America and International Terrorism*. London: Pluto Press, 2000.

Cooper, Alex and Alan, Alexandroff. "Introduction." 1–16 in *Rising States, Rising Institutions: Challenges for Global Governance*. Waterloo: Centre for International Governance Education, 2010.

Crone, Patricia. *God's Rule: Government and Islam*. Edinburgh: Edinburgh University Press, 2004.

Dahlia, Arikha. "Monetary Policy in Perspective of Umer Chapra." Accessed April 15, 2024. https://mpra.ub.uni-muenchen.de/87022/.

Dallal, Ahmad. "The Origins and Objectives of Islamic Revivalist Thought, 1750-1850." *Journal of the American Oriental Studies* 113, no. 3 (July–September 1993): 341–359.

Delanty, Gerard and Rumford, Chris. "Political Globalization." 416–417 in *The Blackwell Companion to Globalization*, edited by George Ritzer. Oxford: Blackwell, 2007.

Dessì, Ugo. *The Global Repositioning of Japanese Religions: An Integrated Approach*. London and New York: Routledge, 2017.

Dessì, Ugo and Sedda, Franciscu. "Glocalization and Everyday Life." *Glocalism: Journal of Culture, Politics and Innovation* 3 (2020): 1–13.

Dieyem, Adama. *An Islamic Model for Stabilization and Growth*. New York: Palgrave Macmillan, 2020.

Dippel, Christian, Gold, Robert, and Heblich, Stephan. "Globalization and Its (Dis-)Content: Trade Shocks and Voting Behavior." NBER Working Paper 21812. Cambridge, MA: National Bureau of Economic Research, 2015.

Donnan, Hastings, and Pnina, Werbner. "Introduction." 9–10 in *Economy and Culture in Pakistan: Migrants and Cities in a Muslim Society*, edited by Hastings Donnan and Pnina. Werbner. London: Macmillan, 1991.

Donner, Fred M. "Muhammad and the Caliphate." 2–61 in *Oxford History of Islam*, edited by John L. Esposito. Oxford: Oxford University Press, 2000.

Doz, Yves. "The Rise of Multicultural Managers." *INSEAD: Knowledge*. July 24, 2013. Accessed April 15, 2024. http://knowledge.insead.edu/career/the-rise-of-multicultural-managers-2552.

Duderija, Adis. "Toward a Methodology of Understanding the Nature and Scope of the Concept of Sunnah." *Arab Law Quarterly* 21 (September 2007): 269–280.

Dunn, Ross E. "International Migrations of Literate Muslims in the Later Middle Period." 199–212 in *Golden Roads: Migration, Pilgrimage and Travel in Modern and Medieval Islam*, edited by Ian Richard Netton. London: Routledge, 1993.

Duran, Khalid. "The Drafting of a Global Ethic: A Muslim Perspective." Accessed April 15, 2024. https://static1.squarespace.com/static/5464ade0e4b055bfb204446e/t/57211414ab48de3e8ab4eb73/1461785620458/The+Drafting+of+a+Global+Ethic+-+A+Muslim+Perspective.

Eddebo, Johan. "Tawḥīd al 'Uluhiyya, Secularism, and Political Islam." *Journal of Religion and Society* 16 (March 2014): 1–7.

Edey, Malcolm. "The Global Financial Crisis and Its Effects." 208–211 in *The Globalization Reader*, edited by Frank J. Lechner and John Boli. Oxford: Blackwell, 2000.

Eickelman, Dale F., and Piscatori, James. "Introduction." 11–16 in *Muslim Travellers: Pilgrimage, Migration and Religious Imagination*, edited by Dale Eickelman and James Piscatori. London: Routledge, 2013.

Eisenstadt, Shmuel N. "The Resurgence of Religious Movements in Processes of Globalisation." *International Journal on Multicultural Societies* 2, no. 1 (January 2000): 13–24.

El-Awaisi, Abd Al-Fattah. "The Conceptual Approach of the Egyptian Muslim Brothers towards the Palestine Question, 1928–1949." *Journal of Islamic Studies* 2 (February 1991): 225–244.

Elischer, Sebastian. "Autocratic Legacies and State Management of Islamic Activism in Niger." *African Affairs* 114 (October 2015): 577–597.

Elius, Mohammad, Khan, Issa, and Nor, Roslan. Mohd. "Interreligious Dialogue: An Islamic Approach." *Katha* 15 (December 2019): 1–19.

Elmandjra, *Al-Harb al-Hadariyyah al-Ulah* [The First Civilizational War]. Casablanca: 'Uyun, 1994.

El-Mesawi, Mohamed El-Tahir. "Religion, Society and Culture in Malik Bennabi's Thought." 249–262 in *The Blackwell Companion to Contemporary Islamic Thought*, edited by Ibrahim Abu Rabi. Oxford: Blackwell Publishing Limited, 2006.

El-Shibiny, Mohammed. *The Threat of Globalization to Arab Islamic Culture: The Dynamics of World Peace*. Pittsburgh, PA: Dorrance Publishing, 2005.

Eyerman, Ron. *The Assassination of Theo van Gogh: From Social Drama to Cultural Trauma*. Durham, NC: Duke University Press, 2008.

Ezziti, Badre. E. "The Historical Development of Constitutional Islamic Religious Text of the Legal Status of Non-Muslims in Islam." *International Journal of Innovation and Applied Studies* 23, no. 3 (June 2018): 290–298.

Fetzer, Thiemo. "Did Austerity Cause Brexit?" *American Economic Review* 109, no. 11 (November 2019): 3849–3886.

Foroutan, Yaghoob. "Ethnic and Religious Discrimination? A Multicultural Analysis of Muslim Minorities in the West." *Journal of Muslim Minority Affairs* 31 (September 2011): 327–338.

Forster, Gillian and Fenwick, John. "The Influence of Islamic Values on Management Practice in Morocco." *European Management Journal* 33 (May 2015): 143–156.

Foucault, Michel. *The History of Sexuality, Volume I: An Introduction*. Translated by Robert Hurley. New York: Vintage Books, 1990.

Friedman, Jonathan. "Being in the World: Globalization and Localization." 311–328 in *Global Culture: Nationalism, Globalization and Modernity*, edited by Mike Featherstone. London: Sage, 1990.

Gan, Peter Chong Beng. "The Problem of Cultural Identity." 7–31 in *Implications of Pluralism: Essays on Culture, Identity and Values*, edited by Göran Collste. Bangi: Institute of Ethnic Studies, Universiti Kebangsaan Malaysia, 2011.

Gawdat, Bahgat. "Managing Dependence: America-Saudi Oil Relations." *Arab Studies Quarterly* 23, no. 1 (January 2001): 1–14.

Gazleh, Mohammad Abo. "Globalization and Politics: The Effects of Globalization on Human Life Aspects." Paper Presented in the International Conference on Malaysia and Globalization, University of Malaya, Kuala Lumpur, 2001.

The Globalist. "Akbar Ahmed: When Honor is Threatened." Accessed April 14, 2024. https://www.theglobalist.com/akbar-ahmed-when-honor-is-threatened/.

Grimalda, Gianluca, Buchan, Nancy, and Brewer, Marilynn. "Social Identity Mediates the Positive Effect of Globalization on Individual Cooperation: Results from International Experiments." *PLoS ONE* 13, no. 12 (December 2018): e0206819.

Gramsci, Antonio. "Americanism and Fordism."277-316 in *The Prison Notebooks*, edited and translated by Quintin Hoare and Geoffrey Nowell Smith. New York: International Publishers, 1971.

Griffin, David R. and Smith, Huston. *Primordial Truth and Postmodern Theology*. Albany, NY: State University of New York Press, 1989.

Griffiths, Paul J. *Problems of Religious Diversity*. Malden, MA and Oxford: Blackwell, 2001.

Griswold, Daniel T. "The Blessings and Challenges of Globalization." *International Journal on World Peace* 17, no.3 (September 2000): 3-22.

Grugel, Jean and Piper, Nicola. *Critical Perspectives on Global Governance*. London: Routledge, 2007.

Habti, Driss. "The Religious Aspects of Diasporic Experience of Muslims in Europe within the Crisis of Multiculturalism." *Policy Futures in Education* 12, no. 1 (January 2014): 149–162.

Haddad, Yuonne Yazbeck. "The Revivalist Literature and the Literature on Revival: An Introduction." 4–7 in *The Contemporary Islamic Revival: A Critical Survey and Bibliography*, edited by Yuonne Yazbeck Haddad, John Obert Voll, and John L. Esposito. New York: Greenwood Press, 1991.

Haji Hasan, Ahmad Husni. "An Islamic Perspective of Interfaith Dialogue amidst Current Interreligious Tensions Worldwide." *Global Journal Al-Thaqafah* 1, no. 1 (December 2011): 25–35.

Hanafi, Hasan and Jalal al-Azm, Sadiq. *What is Globalisation?* Damascus: Dar al-Fikr, 2000.

Hannerz, Ulf. "Cosmopolitans and Locals in World Culture." 237–252 in *Global Culture: Nationalism, Globalization and Modernity*, edited by Mike Featherstone. London: Sage, 1990.

Haq, Muhammad Z. "Muslims' Participation in Interfaith Dialogue: Challenges and Opportunity." *Journal of Ecumenical Studies* 49, no. 4 (September 2014): 613–646.

Haque, Faatin. "Countering Religious Militancy through Interfaith Cooperation: An Islamic Perspective." 20–24 in *World Universities*, edited by Ali Akdemir and Oktay Koç. *Congress*. Canakkale: Canakkale Onsekiz University, 2010.

Harold, James. *The End of Globalization: Lessons from the Great Depression*. Cambridge, MA: Harvard University Press, 2001.

Harvey, David. *The Condition of Postmodernity*. Oxford: Blackwell, 1989.

Harvey, David. *Spaces of Hope*. Berkeley, CA: University of California Press, 2000.

Hasan, Mubashar. "The Concept of Globalization and How this has Impacted on Contemporary Muslim Understanding of Ummah." *Journal of Globalization Studies* 2, no. 2 (November 2011): 145–159.

Hassan, Riaz. "Globalization's Challenge to the Islamic Ummah." *Asian Journal of Social Science* 34, no. 2 (January 2006): 311–323.

Hay, Colin, and Marsh, David. "Introduction: Demystifying Globalisation." 1–17 in *Demystifying Globalisation*, edited by Colin Hay and David Marsh. New York: Palgrave Macmillan, 2000.

Hayes, Carlton J. H., Baldwin, Marshall Whithead, and Cole, Charles Woolsey. *History of Western Civilization*. New York: Macmillan Publishing Company, 1962.

Held, David. "A Globalising Society?" in *A Globalizing World? Culture, Economics, Politics*. London: Routledge, 2000 pp.5-43.

Held, David. "Realism Versus Cosmopolitanism: A Debate between Barry Buzan and David Held, Conducted by Anthony Mcgrew." *Review of International Studies* 24, no. 3 (July 1998): 387–398.

Held, David and McGrew, Anthony. *Globalisation/Anti-Globalisation*. Cambridge: Polity, 2002.

Held, David and McGrew, Anthony. *The Global Transformations Reader: An Introduction to the GlobalizationDebate*, 2nd edition. Cambridge: Polity Press, 2003.

Held, David, McGrew, Anthony, Goldblatt, David, and Perraton, Jonathan. "Rethinking Globalisation." 14–28 in *Global Transformations: Politics, Economics and Culture*. Cambridge: Polity Press and Stanford, CA: Stanford University Press, 1999.

Hinnells, John R. "The Study of Diaspora Religion." 682–690 in *A New Handbook of Living Religions*, edited by John R. Hinnells. Oxford: Blackwell, 1997.

Holten, Robert J. *Making Globalisation*. New York: Palgrave Macmillan, 2005.

Hopkins, Antony G. "The History of Globalizationand Globalizationof History?" 11–46 in *Globalizationin World History*, edited by A. G. Hopkins. London: Pimlico, 2002.

Hossain, Ishtiaq. "Muslim Ummah, International Organisations, and Human Development in the MMCs." 302–303 in *The Muslim World in the 21st Century: Space, Power, and Human Development*, edited by Samiul Hasan. London: Springer, 2012.

Howie, Emily. "Protecting the Human Right to Freedom of Expression in International Law." *International Journal of Speech-Language Pathology* 20, no. 1 (November 2018): 12–15.

Huntington, Samuel P. *The Clash of Civilisations and the Remaking of the World Order*. New York: Penguin Books, 1997.

Huntington, Samuel P. *The Clash of Civilisations and the Remaking of the World Order*. New York: Simon & Schuster, 2011.

Huntington, Samuel P. *Clash of Civilizations*. London: Simon & Schuster, 1997.

Hussain, Mumtaz, Shahmoradi, Asghar, and Turk, Rima. "An Overview of Islamic Finance." IMF Working Paper, 2015. Accessed April 16, 2024. https://www.imf.org/external/pubs/ft/wp/2015/wp15120.pdf.

Ibn Khaldun, Abd al-Rahman. *Muqaddimah*. Cairo: Al-Maktabah al-Tijariyyah al-Kubra, n.d.

Ibn Khaldun, Abd al-Rahman. *The Muqaddimah: An Introduction to History*. Translated by Franz Rosenthal. Princeton, NJ: Princeton University Press, 1969.

Ibrahim, Anwar. "Islamic Renaissance and the Reconstruction of Civilization." *Islamic Horizons* 25, no. 5 (1996): 14–15.

Inda, Jonathan Xavier and Rosaldo, Renato. "Introduction: A World in Motion." 1–34 in *The Anthropology of Globalisation: A Reader*, 2nd edition. Maiden, MA: Blackwell, 2008.

Iqbal, Muhammad Adil. *Islam, Globalism and Globalisation*. Accessed April 15, 2024. https://islamicgovernance.org/tp12/n.

Iqbal, Zafar and Lewis, Mervyn. *An Islamic Perspective on Governance*. Cheltenham: Edward Elgar, 2009.

Ishak, Muhammad Shahrul Ifwat and Nasir, Nur Syahirah Mohammad. "Maqasid al-Shariah in Islamic Finance: Harmonizing Theory and Reality." *The Journal of Muamalat and Islamic Finance Research* 18, no. 1 (June 2021): 108–119.

"Islamic Economics, Biography: Dr. Muhammad Umar Chapra: The Pioneer of Modern Islamic Economics." Accessed April 14, 2024. http://islamiceconomicsbd.blogspot.in/2011/09/biographydr-muhammad-umar-chapra.html.

Jackson, Robert and Nesbitt, Elenor. *Hindu Children in Britain*. Stoke-on-Trent: Trentham Books, 1993.

Jacobson, Robert. "The 'Austrian' School of Strategy." *Academy of Management Review* 17, no. 4 (October 1992): 782–807.

Jalil, Abdullaah. "The Significances of Maslahah Concept and Doctrine of Maqasid (Objectives) Al-Shari'ah in Project Evaluation." *The Journal of Muamalat and Islamic Finance Research* 3, no. 1 (March 2006): 171–202.

Jamil Hilal. "Rethinking Palestine." *Contemporary Arab Affairs* 8, no. 3 (July–September 2015): 351–362.

Jeannet, Jean-Pierre and Hennessey, Hubert. *Global Marketing Strategies*. Boston, MA: Houghton Mifflin Company, 1992.
Jeili, Chamsy O. and Hayden, Patrick. *Critical Theories of Globalisation*. New York: Palgrave Macmillan, 2006.
Johns, Leslie, Pelc, Krzysztof, and Wellhausen, Rachel L. "How a Retreat from Global Economic Governance May Empower Business Interests." *Journal of Politics* 81, no. 2 (2019): 731–738.
Johnston, David L. "Chandra Muzaffar's Islamic Critique of Globalization: A Malaysian Contribution to a Global Ethic." La Trobe University Centre for Dialogue Working Paper, Melbourne, 2006.
Kaba, Lansine. "Islam in West Africa: Radicalism and the New Ethic of Disagreement, 1960-1990." 189–208 in *The History of Islam in Africa*, edited by Nehemia Levtzion and Randall L. Pouwels. Athens, OH: Ohio University Press, 2000.
Kafrawi, Salahudin, Mazrui, Alamin M., and Sebuharra, Ruzima. "Globalisation, Islam and the West: Between Homogenisation and Hegemonisation." 261–274 in *Islam between Globalizationand Counterterrorism*, edited by Salahudin Kafrawi, Alamin M. Mazrui, and Ruzima Sebuharra, 268. Oxford: James Currey, 2006.
Kamali, Mohammad Hashim. *The Dignity of Man: An Islamic Perspective*. Cambridge: Islamic Text Society, 1999.
Kamali, Mohammad Hashim. *The Middle Path of Moderation in Islam: The Qur'ānic Principle of Wasaṭiyyah*. Oxford: Oxford University Press, 2015.
Kamali, Mohammad Hashim. *Shari'ah Law: An Introduction*. Oxford: Oneworld, 2008.
Karim, Khairulnizam M. and Saile, Saily A. "Inter-faith Dialogue: The Qur'ānic and Prophetic Perspective." *Journal of Usuluddin* 29 (June 2009): 65–94.
Karpat, Kemal H. "The Hijra from Russia and the Balkans: The Process of Self-Definition in the Late Ottoman State." 131–152 in *Muslim Travellers: Pilgrimage, Migration and the Religious Imagination*, edited by Dale F. Eickelman and James Piscatori. London: Routledge, 1990.
Kastoryano, Riva. "Muslim Diaspora(s) in Western Europe." *South Atlantic Quarterly* 98, no. 1/2 (March 1999): 191–202.
KAVAKÇI, Merve. "Deconstruction of Turkey's National Identity: Then And Now (A Postcolonial Critique)." *Türkiye'nin Milli Kimliğinin Yapı Sökümü: Öncesi ve Şimdi (Postkolonyal Bir Eleştiri)*, *Üniversitesi Sosyal Bilimler Dergisi* 1, no. 1 (November 2016): 49–86.
Kayaoglu, Turan. "Constructing the Dialogue of Civilizations in World Politics: A Case of Global Islamic Activism." *Islam and Christian–Muslim Relations* 23, no. 2 (April 2012): 129–147.
Keddie, Nikki. *An Islamic Response to Imperialism: Political and Religious Writings of Jamal al-Din al-Afghani*. Berkeley, CA: University of California Press, 1983.
Kempf, Arlo. "Contemporary Anticolonialism: A Transhistorical Perspective." 13–35 in *Breaching the Colonial Contract Anti-Colonialism in the US and Canada*, edited by Arlo Kempf. New York: Springer, 2009.

Kerr, Andrew Jensen. "Art Threats and First Amendment Disruption." *Duke Journal of Constitutional Law and Public Policy* 16 (April 2021): 173–212.

Khadduri, Majid. *The Islamic Law of Nations: Shaybani's Siyar*. Baltimore, MD: Johns Hopkins University Press, 1966.

Khan, M. A. Muqtedar. *Islam and Good Governance: A Political Philosophy of Ihsan*. New York: Palgrave Macmillan, 2019.

Khondker, Habibul H. "Globalization Theory: A Critical Analysis." Department of Sociology Working Paper, National University of Singapore, Singapore, 1994.

Khondker, Habibul H. "Glocalization as Globalization: Evolution of a Sociological Concept." *Bangladesh e-Journal of Sociology* 1, no. 2 (July 2004): 12–20.

Kinnvall, Catarina and Larking, Paul Nesbitt. *The Political Psychology of Globalisation: Muslims in the West*. London: Oxford University Press, 2011.

Kraidy, Marwan M. *Hybridity, or the Cultural Logic of Globalisation*. Philadelphia, PA: Temple University Press, 2005.

Kramer, Martin. *Arab Awakening and Islamic Revival*. London: Transaction Publishers, 1996.

Kurucan, Ahmet and Erol, Mustafa K. *Dialogue in Islam: Qur'ān Sunnah-History*. London: Dialogue Society, 2012.

Lang, Valentine F. and Tavares, Marina Mendes. *The Distribution of Gains from Globalization*. Washington, DC: International Monetary Fund, 2018.

Lapidus, Ira. M. *A History of Islamic Societies*. Cambridge: Cambridge University Press, 1988.

Lapidus, Ira M. "Islamic Revival and Modernity: The Contemporary Movements and the Historical Paradigms." *Journal of the Economic and Social History of the Orient* 40, no. 4 (January 1997): 444–460.

Lebl, Leslie. S. "The EU, the Muslim Brotherhood and the Organization of Muslim Cooperation." *Orbis* 57 (January 2014): 101–119.

Levitt, Peggy. "Local-level Global Religion: The Case of US-Dominican Migration." *Journal for the Scientific Study of Religion* 37, no. 1 (March 1998): 74–89.

Levitt, Theodore. "The Globalization of Markets." *Harvard Business Review* 61, no. 3 (May/June 1983): 92–102.

Lieberman, Victor. "Local Integration and Eurasian Analogies: Structuring Southeast Asian History, c. 1350-c. 1830." *Modern Asian Studies* 27, no. 3 (November 1993): 475–572.

Little, David. *Essays on Religion and Human Rights: Ground to Stand On*. Cambridge: Cambridge University Press, 2015.

Loobuyck, Patrick, Debeer, Jonathan, and Meier, Petra. "Church–state Regimes and their Impact on the Institutionalization of Islamic Organizations in Western Europe: A Comparative Analysis." *Journal of Muslim Minority Affairs* 33 (May 2013): 61–76.

Mabrūk, Muhammad Ibrāhīm. *Amerika wa al Islām al-nafi'ī* [America and Pragmatic Islam]. Cairo: Dār al Tawzī' wa al-Nashr al Islāmīyah, 1989.

Mader, Mathias, Steiner, Nils. D, and Schoen, Harald. "The Globalizationdivide in the Public Mind: Belief Systems on Globalizationand their Electoral Consequences." *Journal of European Public Policy* 27, no. 10 (October 2019): 1526–1545.

Madi, Abu al-'Ala. *Jama'at al-'Unf al-Misriyyah al-Murtabitah Bi'l islam: al-Judhur al-Tarikhiyyah wa'l Usus alfikriyyah Wa'l Mustaqbal*. Cairo: Al-Markaz al-Duwali li'l Dirasat, 1997.

Mahdavi, Mojtaba and Knight, W. Andy. "Introduction: Towards 'the Dignity of Difference?' Neither 'End of History' nor 'Clash of Civilizations'." 1–27 in *Towards the Dignity of Difference?* edited by Mojtaba Mahdavi and W. Andy Knight. Farnham: Ashgate, 2012.

Mandaville, Peter. "From Medina to the Ummah: Muslim Globalization in Historical and Contemporary Perspective." 193–215 in *World Religions and Multiculturalism: A Dialectic Relation*, edited by Eliezer Ben-Rafael and Yitzhak Sternberg. Leiden: Brill, 2010.

Mander, Jerry. "Introduction: Facing the Rising Tide." 1–18 in *The Case Against the Global Economy: And for a Turn Toward the Local*, edited by Jerry Mander and Edward Goldsmith. San Francisco, CA: Sierra Club Books, 1996.

Mann, Michael. "Globalizationand September 11." *New Left Review* 12 (November 2001): 51–72.

Maqbool, Ahmad S. "Madrasa System of Education and Indian Muslim Society." 60–69 in *India and Contemporary Islam: Proceedings of a Seminar*, edited by S. T. Lokhandwalla. Shimla, India: Indian Institute of Advanced Study, 1971.

Marranci, Gabriele. *The Anthropology of Islam*. Oxford: Berg, 2007.

Marshall, Paul. "Disregarding Religion." *SAIS Review* 18, no. 2 (October 1998): 13–18.

Maussen, Marcel and Bader, Veit. "Introduction." 9–26 in *Colonial and Post-Colonial Governance of Islam*, edited by Marcel Maussen, Veit Bader, and Anneleis Moors. Amsterdam: Amsterdam University Press, 2011.

Maussen, Marcel and Grillo, Ralph. "Regulation of Speech in Multicultural Societies: Introduction." *Journal of Ethnic and Migration Studies* 40, no. 2 (November 2014): 174–193.

Mayncs, Charles W. "America's Third World Hang-ups." *Foreign Policy* 71 (Summer 1988): 117.

Mazrui, Ali A. "From Slave Ship to Space Ship: Africa between Marginalization and Globalization." *African Studies Quarterly* 2, no. 4 (1999): 6–9.

Mazrui, Ali A. "Globalisation, Islam and the West: Between Homogenisation and Hegemonisation." *The American Journal of Islamic Social Sciences* 15, no. 2 (October 1998): 1–13.

Mazrui, Ali A. "Globalisation: Origins and Scope." October, 2001. The Center for Humanities and Arts and the Center for International Trade and Security Georgia, United States of America.

Mazrui, Ali A. "Globalizing Africa and The Commonwealth: Four Ethical Revolutions." 27–45 in *Globalizing Africa*, edited by Malinda S. Smith. Trenton, NJ and Asmara: Africa World Press.

Mazrui, Ali A. and Mazrui, Alamin M. "The Digital Revolution and the New Reformation: Doctrine and Gender in Islam." *Harvard International Review* 23, no. 1 (Spring 2001): 52–55.

McFarland, Sam Webb, Matthev, and Brown, Darek. "All Humanity is My Ingroup: A Measure and Studies of Identification with all Humanity." *Journal of Personality and Social Psychology* 103, no. 5 (2012): 830–853.

McNamara, Kathleen R. "A Rivalry in the Making? The Euro and International Monetary Power." *Review of International Political Economy* 15, no. 3 (August 2008): 439–459.

Metcalf, Barbara. "Introduction: Sacred Words, Sanctioned Practice, New Communities." 1–27 in *Making Muslim Space in North America and Europe*, edited by Barbara Metcalf. Berkeley, CA: University of California Press, 1996.

Meunier, Sophie and Czesana, Rozalie. "From Back Rooms to the Street? A Research Agenda for Explaining variation in the Public Salience of Trade Policy-Making in Europe." *Journal of European Public Policy* 26, no. 12 (October 2019): 1847–1865.

Michie, Jonathan. "Introduction." 1–13 in *The Handbook of Globalisation*, edited by Jonathan Michie. Cheltenham: Edward Elgar, 2011.

Mohiuddin, Md Golam. "Decision Making Style in Islam: A Study of Superiority of Shura (Participative Management) and Examples from Early Era of Islam." *European Journal of Business and Management* 8, no. 4 (2016): 79–88.

Momayezi, Nasser. "Islamic Revivalism and the Quest for Political Power." *The Journal of Conflict Studies* XVII, no. 2 (November 1997). Accessed April 16, 2024. https://journals.lib.unb.ca/index.php/JCS/article/view/11753/12527.

Monshipouri, Mahmood. "Islam and Human Rights in the Age of Globalization." 91–110 *Islam Encountering Globalisation*, edited by Ali Muhammadi. London: Routledge, 2002.

Moosa, Ebrahim. "Muslim Ethics in an Era of Globalism: Reconciliation in an Age of Empire." 97–113 in *Solidarity Beyond Borders: Ethics in a Globalising World*, edited by Salamon Janusz. London: Bloomsbury Publishing.

Moten, Abdul Rashid. "Islamic Thought in Contemporary Pakistan: The Legacy of 'Allama Mawdūdī." 175–194 in *Contemporary Islamic Thought*, edited by Ibrahim Abu-Rabi. Oxford: Blackwell Publishing Limited, 2006.

Moten, Abdul Rashid. *Revolution to Revolution: Jamāt-e-Islami in the Politics of Pakistan*. Kuala Lumpur: Islamic Book Trust, 2002.

Movius, Lauren. "Cultural Globalizationand Challenges to Traditional Communication Theories." *PLATFORM: Journal of Media and Communication* 2, no. 1 (January 2010): 6–18.

Mozaffari, Mehdi. "Islamic Civilization between Medina and Athena." 198–217 in *Globalization and Civilizations*, edited by Mehdi Mozaffari. London: Routledge, 2002.

Muhammad, Abid al-Jabiri. "Al-'Arab wa'l 'Awlamah: al-'Awlamah wa'l Hawiyyah al-Thaqafiyyah." 298 in *al-'Arab wa'l 'awlamah*, edited by Markaz Dirasat al-Wihdah al-'Arabiyyah. Beirut: Markaz Dirasat al-Wihdah al-'Arabiyyah, 1998.

Mukherjee, Kunal. "Islamic Revivalism and Politics in Contemporary Pakistan." *Journal of Developing Societies* 26, no. 3 (September 2010): 329–353.
Muthi, Ahmad Dawamul and El-Awaisi, Khalid. "The Contributions of Caliph Abu Bakr to The First Muslim Liberation of Islamic Jerusalem." *Journal of Islamic Jerusalem Studies* 22, no. 2 (December 2022): 133–152.
Muzaffar, Chandra. *Human Rights and the New World Order*. Penang: Just World Trust, 1993.
Muzaffar, Chandra. *Rights, Religion and Reform: Enhancing Human Dignity through Spiritual and Moral Transformation*. London: Routledge Curzon, 2002.
Naim, Asher. "Perspectives—Jomo Kenyatta and Israel." *Jewish Political Studies Review* 17, no. 3/4 (Fall 2005): 75–80.
Najjar, Fauzzi. "The Arabs, Islam and Globalisation." *Middle East Policy* XII, no. 3 (Fall 2005): 91–96.
Nasr, Hossain. *Islam: Religion, History and Civilisation*. San Francisco, CA: HarperSanFrancisco, 2003.
Nasr, Sayed Vali Reza. "European Colonialism and the Emergence of Modern Muslim States." 549–600 in *The Oxford History of Islam*, edited by John L. Espoito. Oxford: Oxford University Press, 1999.
Nasr, Seyyed Hossein. *Islam and the Plight of Modern Man*. London: Longman, 1975.
Nasr, Seyyed Hossein. *Man and Nature*. London: Mandala, 1968.
Noor, Farish A. "The Evolution of 'Jihad' in Islamist Political Discourse: How a Plastic Concept Became Harder." Essay for the Social Science Research Council, November 2001. Accessed April 2024. https://items.ssrc.org/after-september-11/the-evolution-of-jihad-in-islamist-political-discourse-how-a-plastic-concept-became-harder/.
Noor, Farish A. "Reformist Muslim Thinkers in Malaysia Engaging with Power to Uplift the Umma?" 208–226 in *Reformist Voices of Islam: Mediating Islam and Modernity*, edited by Shireen Hunter. London: M.E. Sharpe, 2009.
Nor, Mohd. Roslan. M. "Islamic Jerusalem under Muslim rule: A Study of the Implementation of Inclusive Vision on the Region." *Journal of Al-tamaddun* 3, no. 1 (2008): 186–208.
Norris, P. and Inglehart, R. *Cultural Backlash: Trump, Brexit, and Authoritarian Populism*. New York: Cambridge University Press, 2019.
Nubar, Hovsepian. "Competing Identities in the Arab World." 97–117 in *Islam and Globalization: Critical Concepts in Islamic Studies Shahram Akbarzadeh*, edited by Shahram Akbarzadeh, Volume 1. London: Routledge, 2006.
Nurullah, Abu Sadat. "Globalizationas a Challenge to Islamic Cultural Identity." *The International Journal of Interdisciplinary Social Sciences* 3, no. 6 (October 2008): 45–52.
Obstfeld, Maurice. "Globalization Cycles." *Italian Economic Journal* 6, no. 1 (March 2020): 1–12.
Onapajo, Hakeem. "Islamic Revivalism and Social Change in Muslim Societies: A Rethink of Marxist Historical Materialism." *World Journal of Islamic History and Civilization* 2, no. 4 (2012): 196–205.

Organization of the Islamic Conference (OIC). *Final Communiqué*, 1997. Accessed April 16, 2024. http://www.oic-oci.org/english/conf/is/8/8th-is-summits.htm.

Overbeek, Henk. "Global Governance, Class, Hegemony." 39–56 in *Contending Perspectives on Global Governance: Coherence and Contestation*, edited by Alice D. Ba and Matthew J. Hoffmann. London: Routledge, 2005.

Palmer, R. R. and Colton, Joel. "The Advance of Democracy: Third French Republic, United Kingdom, German Empire." 605–617 in *A History of the Modern World*, 3rd edition, edited by R. R. Palmer and Joel Colton. New York: Afred A. Knopf, 1978.

Petito, Fabio. "Khatami' Dialogue among Civilizations as International Political Theory." *Journal of Humanities* 11, no. 3 (July 2004): 11–29.

Picchi, Margherita. "Islam as the Third Way: Sayyid Quṭb's Socio-Economic Thought and Nasserism." *Oriente Moderno* 97, no. 1 (March 2017): 177–200.

Pieterse, Jan Nederveen. "Globalizationand Culture: Three Paradigms." *Economic and Political Weekly* 31, no. 23 (June 1996): 1389–1393.

Pilger, John. *The New Rulers of the World*. London: Verso Books, 2002.

Pio, E. *Longing & Belonging: Asians, Middle Eastern, Latin American and African Peoples in New Zealand*. Wellington: Dunmore, 2010.

Platt, Steve. "Sanctions Don't Harm Saddam." *New Statesman and Society* 7 (November 1994): 10.

Pratt, Douglas. "The Vatican in Dialogue with Islam: Inclusion and Engagement." *Islam and Christian–Muslim Relations* 21, no. 3 (July 2010): 245–262.

Rane, Halim. "Cogent Religious Instruction: A Response to the Phenomenon of Radical Islamist Terrorism in Australia." *Religions* 10, no. 4 (April 2019): 1–22.

Razak, Abdul and Abbas, Mohd. "Globalization and its Impact on Education and Cultur." *World Journal of Islamic History and Civilization* 1, no. 1 (2011): 59–69.

Riddell, Peter G. "Globalisation, Western and Islamic, into the 21st Century: Perspectives from Southeast Asia and Beyond." *Asian Christian Review* 2, no. 2 and 3 (Summer and Winter 2008): 133–134.

Ring, Magnus. *A Culture, a Manifesto, and an Act of Terrorism*. Unpublished Manuscript, Lund University, Lund, 2011.

Ritzer, G. "Introduction." 1–14 in *The Blackwell Companion to Globalization*, edited by George Ritzer. Oxford: Basil Blackwell, 2007.

Robertson, John C. and Tallman, Ellie. W. "Vector Autoregressions: Forecasting and Reality." *Federal Reserve Bank of Atlanta, Economic Review* 1 (1999): 4–18.

Robertson, Ronald and White, Kathleen. *Globalization: Critical Concepts in Sociology*. London: Routledge, 2003.

Rodrik, Dani. "Populism and the Economics of Globalization." *Journal of International Business Policy* 1 (2018): 12–33.

Roudometof, Victor. *Glocalization: A Critical Introduction*. London: Routledge, 2016.

Rouleau, Eric. "America's Unyielding Policy Toward Iraq." *Foreign Affairs* 74, no. 1 (January–February 1995): 59–72.

Rumeli, Ahmet. "Moral and Material Values Versus Technological Development of the Muslim World." *Journal of Islamic Academy of Sciences* 4, no. 3 (1991): 181–183.

Saat, Norshahril and Alatas, Afra. "Islamisation in Malaysia Beyond UMNO and PAS." 11 October 2022. Accessed April 16, 2024. https://fulcrum.sg/islamisation-in-malaysia-beyond-umno-and-pas/.

Sabet, Amr. *Islam and the Political*. London: Pluto, 2008.

Sachedina, Abdulaziz. *The Role of Islam in the Public Square*. Leiden and Amsterdam: ISIM/Amsterdam University Press, 2006.

Sacks, Jonathan. *The Dignity of Difference: How to Avoid the Clash of Civilizations*. London: Continuum, 2002.

Sadeq, A. H. M. "Economic Development in Islam." *Journal of Islamic Economics* 1, no. 1 (February 1987): 35–45.

Sahlins, Marshall. "Goodbye to Tristes Tropes: Ethnography in the Context of Modern World History." *The Journal of Modern History* 65, no. 1 (March 1993): 1–25.

Said, Abdul Aziz and Funk, Nathan C. "Islamic Revivalism: A Global Perspective." 312–330 in *Toward a Global Civilization: The Contribution of Religions*, edited by Patricia M. Miche and Melissa Merking. New York: Peter Lang, 1997.

Salah, Muhammad. "Kharitat Harakat al-'Unf fi Misr." *Wijhat Nadhar* 1, no. 4 (1999): 20–25.

Samier, Eugenie A. "Philosophical and Historical Origins and Genesis of Islamic Global Governance." 83–104 in *Global Governance and Muslim Organizations*, edited by Leslie A. Pal and M. Evren Tok. New York: Palgrave Macmillan, 2019.

Sara Silvestri. "Misperceptions of the 'Muslim Diaspora'." *Current History* 115, no. 784 (November 2016): 319–321.

Sardar, Ziauddin. *Islamic Science: The Way Ahead*. Islamabad: OIC/COMSTECH, 1995.

Sassen, Saskia. "Territory and Territoriality in the Global Economy." *International Sociology* 15 (2000): 372–393.

Sassen, Saskia. *Territory, Authority, Rights: From Medieval to Global Assemblages*. Princeton, NJ: Princeton University Press, 2006.

Satyakti, Yayan. "The Effect of Applying Sustainability (Maqasid Shariah) and Competition on Islamic Bank Financing." *Sustainability* 15, no. 17 (2023): 12994.

Sayyid Qutb. *Tafsir Fizilalil Qur'ān*. Accessed April 16, 2024. https://tafsirzilal.wordpress.com/2012/06/05/english-language/.

Schirato, Tony and Webb, Jen. *Understanding Globalisation*. London: Sage, 2003.

Scholte, Jan Art. *Globalisation: A Short Introduction*. New York: Palgrave Macmillan, 2005.

Sedda, Franciscu. "Glocal and Food: On Alimentary Translation." *Semiotica* 211 (May 2016): 105–125.

Sedda, Franciscu. "Semiotics of Culture(s): Basic Questions and Concepts." 675–696 in *International Handbook of Semiotics*, edited by Peter P. Trifonas. Berlin: Springer, 2015.
Sen, Amartya. "How to Judge Globalism." Accessed April 16, 2024. http://www.prospect.org/article/how-to-Judge-globalism.
Shackley, Myra. *Atlas of Travel and Tourism Development*. Burlington, VT: Elsevier, 2006.
Sharfuddin, Ibnomer Mohamed. "Toward an Islamic Administrative Theory." *American Journal of Islamic Social Sciences*, 4, no. 2 (December 1987): 229–244.
Shawqi, Dayf. *The Universality of Islam* (Trans. Abdel Wahb El-Affendi). Rabat: ISESCO, 1998.
Shepard, William E. "Sayyid Qutb's Doctrine of 'Jāhiliyya'". *International Journal of Middle East Studies* 35, no. 4 (November 2003): 521–545.
Shepherd, Melinda C. "Ali Al Amin Mazrui: Kenyan-American Political Scientist." Accessed April 14, 2024. https://www.britannica.com/biography/Ali-Al-Amin-Mazrui.
Siddiqui, Ataullah. *Christian–Muslim Dialogue in the Twentieth Century*. New York: Palgrave Macmillan, 1997.
Sinclair, Timothy. *Global Governance*. Cambridge: Polity, 2012.
Smith, Michael P., and Guarnizo, Luis Eduardo. *Transnationalism from Below*. New Brunswick, NJ: Transaction Publishers, 1998.
Snel, Erik. *De vermeende kloof tussen culturen* [The Perceived Gap between Cultures]. Enschede: Universiteit Twente, 2003.
Soguk, Navzat. *Globalization and Islamism: Beyond Fundamentalism*. New York: Rowmann and Littlefield, 2011.
Sokefeld, Martin. "Religion or Culture? Concepts of Identity in the Alevi Diaspora." Paper Presented at conference on 'Locality, Identity, Diaspora', University of Hamburg, Hamburg, 2000.
Spretnak, Charlene. *The Resurgence of the Real: Body, Nature and Place in a Hypermodern World*. New York: Addison-Wesley, 1997.
Spruit, Leen. "Intellectual Beatitude in the Averroist Tradition: The Case of Agostino." 125–144 in *Renaissance Averroism and Its Aftermath*, edited by Anna Akasoy and Guido Giglioni. Dordrecht: Springer, 2012.
Starr, Amory. "Beyond Panic: Religious Nationalism, Political Economy, and the Blockage Against Globalization." Paper Presented at Colorado State University at Lamar, 2002. Accessed April 16, 2024, http://lamar.colostate.edu/~america/panic.html.
Stearns, Peter N. *Globalizationin World History*. London: Routledge, 2010.
Steger, Manfred B. *Globalisation: A Very Short Introduction*. London: Oxford University Press, 2003.
Stevens, Paul. "The Role of Oil and Gas in the Economic Development of the Global Economy." 71–90 in *Extractive Industries: The Management of Resources as a*

Driver of Sustainable Development, edited by Tony Addison and Alan Roe. Oxford: Oxford University Press, 2018.

Strange, S. *The Retreat of the State: The Diffusion of Power in the World Economy.* Cambridge: Cambridge University Press, 1998.

Sutton, Philip W. and Vertigans, Stephen. *Resurgent Islam: A Sociological Approach.* London: Polity Press, 2005.

Swank, Duane. "The Effect of Globalizationon Taxation, Institutions, and Control of the Macroeconomy." 403–420 in *The Global Transformations Reader: An Introduction to the Globalization Debate*, edited by David Held and Anthony Mcgrew. Cambridge: Polity Press, 2000.

Tahseen, S. "Bangladeshi Muslims in Mississippi: Impression Management based on the Intersectionality of Religion, Ethnicity and Gender." Program on International Migration, 2015. http://escholarship.org/uc/item/7s77j3hk.

Tajfel, Henri. *Human Groups and Social Categories: Studies in Social Psychology.* Cambridge: CUP Archive, 1981.

Tapp, William K. *The Amoral Elephant: Globalization and the Struggle for Social Justice in the Twenty-First Century.* New York: Monthly Review Press, 2001.

Ter Haar, Gerrie. "Strangers and Sojourners: An introduction." 1–11 in *Strangers and Sojourners: Religious Communities in the Diaspora*, edited by Gerrie ter Haar. Leuven: Peeters, 1998.

Tomlinson, John. *Globalizationand Culture.* Chicago, IL: University of Chicago Press, 1999.

Toynbee, Arnold. *A Study of History.* London: Oxford University Press, 1995.

Turner, Bryan S. "Enclave Society: Towards a Sociology of Immobility." *European Journal of Social Theory* 10, no. 2 (May 2007): 287–304.

Turner, John C., Hogg, Micheal, Oakes, Penelope, Reicher, Stephen, and Wetherell, Margcrct. *Rediscovering the Social Group: A Self-Categorization Theory.* Oxford, Basil Blackwell, 1987.

US Department of State. "24th Anniversary of the 1998 Embassy Bombings." Accessed April 14, 2024. https://www.state.gov/24th-anniversary-of-the-1998-embassy-bombings/.

Van Gorder, A. Christian. *Islam, Peace and Social Justice: A Christian Perspective.* New York: James Clarke & Co, 2015.

Vertovec, Steven and Cohen, Robin. "Introduction." Xiii–xxviii in *Migration, Diasporas and Transnationalism*, edited by Steven Vertovec. Cheltenham: Edward Elgar, 1999.

Waardenburg, Jacques. "The Institutionalisation of Islam in the Netherlands." 8–31 in *The New Islamic Presence in Europe*, edited by Tomas Gerholm and Yngve G. Lithman. London: Mansell, 1988.

Wallerstein, Immanuel. *After Liberalism.* New York: The New Press, 1995.

Wallerstein, Immanuel. *World-Systems Analysis: An Introduction.* Durham, NC: Duke University Press, 2005.

Walter, Stefanie. "The Backlash Against Globalization." *Annual Review of Political Science* 24 (2021): 421–442.
Walter, Stefanie. "The Mass Politics of International Disintegration." Working Paper 105. Zurich: Center for Comparative and International Studies, University of Zurich, 2020.Wani, Hilal, Abdullah, Raihanah, and Chang, Lee. W. "An Islamic Perspective in Managing Religious Diversity." *Religions* 6 (May 2015): 642–656.
Waters, Malcolm. *Globalisation*. London: Routledge, 1998.
Waters, Malcolm. *Globalisation: Key Ideas*, 2nd edition. London: Routledge, 2001.
Weiss, Jessica Chen and Wallace, Jeremy. "Domestic Politics, China's Rise, and the Future of the Liberal International Order." *International Organization* 75 (2021): 635–664.
Weiss, Thomas and Wilkinson, Rorden. "Continuity and Change in Global Governance," *Ethics & International Affairs* 29, no. 4 (December 2015): 397–406.
Weston, Burns H. "Security Council Resolution 678 and Persian Gulf Decision Making: Precarious Legitimacy." *American Journal of International Law* 85, no. 5 (July 1991): 516–535.
Williams, Marc. "Multilateral Economic Institutions." 237–247 in *An Introduction to International Relations: Australian Perspectives*, edited by Richard Devetak, Anthony Burke, and Jim George. Cambridge: Cambridge University Press, 2007.
Wolf, Eric. *Europe and the People without History*. Berkeley, CA: University of California Press, 1982.
Yamak, Sibel., Ergur, Ali, Unsal, Artun, Uyguyr, Selcuk, and Ozbilgin, Mustafa. "Between A Rock and a Hard Place: Corporate Elites in the Context of Religion and Secularism in Turkey." *The International Journal of Human Resource Management* 26, no. 11 (June 2015): 1474–1497.
Yamamoto, Kooru. "Educational Psychology." 234–240 in *The Social Sciences Encyclopedia*, 2nd edition, edited by Adam Kuper and Jessica Kuper. London: Routledge, 1996.
Yom, Sean L. "Islam and Globalization: Secularism, Religion, and Radicalism." Accessed April 14, 2024. https://www.fes.de/ipg/IPG4_2002/ARTYOM.HTM.
Yousuf Ali, M. D. "Tawhid and its Effects on Man's Life." *Journal of Usuluddin* 23, no. 23 (2006): 1–34.
Zalloum, Abdullahy Y. *Painting Islam as the New Enemy: Globalizationand Capitalism Crisis*. Kuala Lumpur: Crescent New, 2003.
Zein, Ibrahim, al-Ahsan, Abdullah, and Zakaullah, Muhammad. "Qur'ānic Guidance on Good Governance." 8–22 in *Guidance for Good Governance*, edited by Abdullah al-Ahsan and Stephen Young. Kuala Lumpur: International Islamic University Malaysia, 2008.
Ziabari, Kourosh, and Ahmed, Akbar. "The Dialogue of Civilizations, Not the Clash of Civilizations." *Fair Observer*. Accessed April 14, 2024. https://www.fairobserver.com/region/europe/the-dialogue-of-civilizations-not-the-clash-of-civilizations-02158/#.

Index

9/11 attacks, 102, 226, 233, 239, 242, 243
1990s Balkans conflict, 226
2019 Madrid climate summit, 62

Aawa, Salim al-, 105
Abduh, Muhammad, 129, 174, 242, 244
Abdul Hamid II, 129
Abu Bakr (632-634), 94, 151
Abu-Rabi, Ibrahim M., 4, 18, 20, 27, 30, 43, 175, 279, 281, 283–88, 294, 296, 297, 305; biography, 276–78; biography and works, 276–78
academic discourse, 71, 139
Acquisti, Alessandro, 142
acts of war, 201–8
adaptability within Islam, 72
Adhama, Khairul Akmaliah, 87
adl (social justice), 75, 76, 153
Afghani, Jamal al-Din al-, 129, 173
African American Muslim role models, 238
Africans of the blood, 205
Africans of the land, 205

ahkām, 81, 82
Ahmad, Akbar S., 18, 19, 28, 174, 226, 227, 229–46; biography, 227–28
Ahmad, Khurshid, 4
Ahsan, Abdullah al-, 79
Ajmer model, 242
Akhtar, Shabbir, 73
Alawi sultanates, 126
Al-Baqarah-2:164, 87
Al-Baqarah-2:259, 87
Alexander the Great (356-323 BC), 7
Al-Ghashiya-88:17–20, 88
al-hakimiya, 151
Ali (656-661), 151
Ali, Ahmad Mohamed, 259
Aligarh model, 242
Alim, Mahmud Amin al-, 288–91
Allah, Shah Wali, 171
al-Sanusi's revivalist movement, 171
al-shurā, 153
al-siyasah al-shar'iyyah, 152
altruism, 92, 263
amanah, 153
American civilization, 292

American imperialism, 284
Americanization of globalization, 294
Americanization/Westernization, 4
American military engagements, 201–8
American Muslim identity, 238–40
American supremacy, 107
America's foreign policy, 293
Amin, Galal, 291, 295
Amin, Hussein, 179, 180
Amin, Samir, 288, 289
ancient Axial civilizations, 184
Anglo-Saxon globalization, 9–11
Annan, Kofi, 205, 232, 233
An-Nur-24:44, 88
antecedent civilizations, 8
anti-American terrorism, 203
anti-globalization forces, 52, 57–62
anti-terrorism legislation, 211
Anyouku, Emeka, 206
Appadurai, Arjun, 46
Arab engagement in Indian Ocean trade, 33
Arabic language, 34, 123, 193
Arab intellectual responses: Arab East's historical struggles, 289; Arab Left, 288; authoritarianism, 287; consumerism, 292; cultural diversity, 292; cultural identity, 292, 293; destructive individualism, 292; foreign investments, 290; Islamist perspectives, 288; Marxist, 288; military capabilities, 290; nationalism, 287; Nationalist, 288; political movements, 289; poverty gap, 287; regional hegemony, 286; social and economic impacts, 287; The Soft State, 291; Zionism, 286
Arab-Israeli conflict, 203
Arab League, 131
archaic globalization, 18, 121–26
Arendt, Hannah, 275, 295

assets under management (AuM), 97
assimilationist policy, 145
Association for the Taxation of Financial Transactions and Aid to Citizens (ATTAC), 59
Ataturk, Kemal, 10
authentic globalization, 15
avant-garde strategies, 191
Awwa, Salim al, 30
Axial civilizations, 184
ayatollah (a learned religious scholar), 229
Aziz, Shah 'Abd al-, 171
Aziz, Umar Ibn 'Abdul al-, 170
Azm, Sadiq Jalal al-, 288–91
Az-Zumar-39:21, 88
Azzuz, Mustafa Ibn, 171

Baderin, Mashood A., 152
balanced and nuanced (*wasatiyyah*) approach, 21
Bandung project, 281
Banna, Hassan al-, 174
Banna, Shaykh Hassan al-, 293
Barber, Benjamin, 45
Barkawi, Tarak, 150
Barnett, Michael, 154
Baumann, Zygmaunt, 28
Bay of Pigs invasion, 204
Beck, Ulrick, 43
Bennison, Amira, 123
Berlin Wall (1989–1991), 1
bin Laden, Osama, 177, 202, 206, 234, 236, 238
Black Stone (*Hajar al-Aswad*), 103
Blackwater, 239
Boli, John, 52
Bolkestein, Frits, 145
Bolsonaro, Jair, 58
born-again Christians, 169
Boutros-Ghali, Boutros, 205
Braudel, Fernand, 122
Breivik, Anders, 145
Brexit referendum, 58, 60, 61

British Malay, 136
Bruquetas-Callejo, Maria, 145
Buchan, Nancy, 57
Bunche, Ralph, 205, 206
bureaucracy, 6, 122
Bush, George Jr., 169
Bush, George W., 204, 205, 227, 232, 238, 239
Butt, Nasim, 178

capitalism, 3, 4, 6, 26, 37, 45, 47, 48, 96, 250, 288–90, 292, 295; corporate capitalism, 1; disorganised capitalism, 236; international capitalism, 280; laissez-faire capitalism, 27; transnational capitalism, 38
capitalist civilization, 288, 294, 295
Carey, George, 232
Carter, Jimmy, 204
caste and community identities, 168
Castells, Manuel, 43
Catholicism, 139, 217
censorship, 208–12
Chamberlain, Joseph, 204
Chapra, Umar, 18, 20, 250, 251, 253–70; biography, 251–52
Charter of Madinah, 78, 79
China shock, 60
Chinese Muslims, 9
Christianity, 44, 73, 119, 178, 195
Christian–Muslim relations, 108, 127
Christian Reformation, 178
civilizations, 19, 32, 46, 106–9, 120–22, 169, 195, 196, 216, 220, 225, 239, 260, 275, 280, 281, 297, 304, 305, 310; American civilization, 292; Axial civilizations, 184; capitalist civilization, 288, 294, 295; civilizational standards, 200; clash of civilizations, 19, 37, 50, 63, 106, 145, 149, 156, 183, 226, 232–33, 288; democratic civilization, 131; Hellenistic civilization, 8; human civilization, 108, 308; international civilization, 294; Islamic civilization, 8, 9, 125, 127, 170, 183, 244, 251, 266; Judeo-Christian civilization, 218; Muslim civilization, 8, 9, 122, 237, 242, 255, 309; non-Western civilizations, 46; religious civilizations, 48; transnational civilization, 48; Western civilizations, 4, 7, 9–11, 76, 102, 174, 199, 212, 243, 308
clash of civilizations, 19, 37, 50, 63, 106, 145, 149, 156, 183, 226, 232–33, 288
climate youth movement, 58
Clinton, Bill, 204
Coca-colonization, 45
Cohen, Robin, 143
Cold War, 10, 36, 46, 59, 106, 197, 200, 201, 206–8, 279, 283
Cole, Juan, 104
collective identity, 143, 176, 183
colonial domination, 91
colonialism, 13, 92, 133–37, 175, 200, 283, 285
colonial powers, 6, 35, 130, 132–34, 137, 138, 149, 171, 230, 310
Commission on Global Governance, 150, 154
Commonwealth, 126, 206, 207
Common Word initiative, 103
Confucianism, 33
Constitutional Amendment, 216
Constitution of Medina, 152
consumerism, 44, 169, 234, 242, 292, 296
consumption-centric lifestyle, 4
The Contemporary Arab Reader on Political Islam (Abu-Rabi), 277
contemporary Islamic thought, 278–80

corporate capitalism, 1
counterterrorism, 155
COVID-19 crises, 62
cultural convergence, 126
cultural diversity, 48, 72, 105, 124, 141, 220, 221, 260, 285, 291, 292
Cultural Forces in World Politics (Mazrui), 194
cultural globalization, 44–48, 213–15
cultural hegemony, 3, 283–86, 293
cultural heritage, 6, 15, 199, 221
cultural homogenization, 3, 45–47, 231
cultural hybridization, 48
cultural imperialism, 45, 63, 214; U.S. cultural imperialism, 297
cultural pluralism, 102
cultural reproduction, 145–48
cultural Westernization of Muslims, 217

dar al-harb (the Abode of War), 34, 101, 124, 197–98
dar al-Islam (the Abode of Islam), 34, 124, 197–98
dar al-maghrib (the Domain of the West), 197
dar al-sulh (the Abode of Peace), 197–98
Darwinian mechanism, 95
de Certeau, M., 54
decolonization process, 36, 134; French decolonization, 207
decontextualization, 3; of politics, governance, and rule, 42
defensiveness, 12, 235
deglobalization, 49, 207
degree of equity, 94
degree of protectionism, 268
degree of sustainability, 99
degrees of settlement, 146
de-Islamization, 10, 216
de Klerk, F.W., 205, 206
Delanty, Chris, 42
democracy, 6, 7, 10, 29, 43, 46, 128, 149, 150, 167, 168, 174, 194, 213, 215, 220, 241, 277, 282, 283, 287
democratic civilization, 131
demographic globalization, 195
denationalization, 43
Deoband model, 242
deterritorialization, 6, 26, 44, 55
detonation, 2
detractors of globalization, 2
dhimmi law, 105, 106
dhiya (waste), 75, 76
Dialogue among Civilisations, 106, 108
dialogue of civilisations, 226
diasporic duality, 146
diasporic identity, 145–48
dichotomy, 19, 42, 96, 150, 167
Discovering Islam: Making Sense of Muslim History and Society (Ahmad), 227
Disneyfication, 45
disorganised capitalism, 236
distinctive phase of "globalization," 8
dollars of the Middle Ages, 33
Donnan, Hastings, 28, 229
dual-pronged strategy, 93
Durkheim, E., 235
Dutch Indies, 136
Duvall, Raymond, 154
dynamics of identity, 233–34
dynamism, 2, 72

Earth stewardship, 112
economic disparities, 93, 286
economic globalization, 31, 38–42, 57–59, 62, 63, 184, 201, 202, 214, 218, 219, 250, 251, 259
economic global order, 229–30
economic imperialism, 134
economic inequality, 231
economic integration, 255; challenges, 257–59
economic justice, 91–98
economic sustainability, 99
egalitarianism, 279

egalitarian (revolutionary) movements, 2
egalitarian principles, 8
Egyptian–Syrian unity, 136
Eickelman, Dale F., 146, 148
Eisenhower, Dwight, 204
El-Awaisi, Abd Al-Fattah, 77
"enclave society" thesis, 51
Engineer, Asghar Ali, 167, 168
enlightenment concepts, 2
environmental challenge, 72, 100, 111, 112
environmental crisis and management, 100–101
environmental sustainability, 99
equality, 8, 63, 74, 105, 109, 123, 141, 151, 153, 154, 157, 176, 220, 221, 253–54, 262, 264–66, 307, 311
Ernest S. Frerichs, 146
Erol, Mustafa K., 105
ethnic identities, 137, 142
ethnic schism, 138
ethnocentrism, 2
eurocentric globalization, 128
Eurocentrism, 200
European Court of Human Rights, 58
European imperialism, 28, 129
European political frameworks, 144
European powers, 35
European Union (EU)'s endorsement, 37

faith, 7, 9, 12, 34, 72–74, 77, 86, 88, 93, 103, 104, 109, 121, 123, 127, 140–43, 146, 147, 178, 181, 193, 215, 225, 229, 233, 236, 238–41, 244, 245, 253, 254, 256, 262, 264, 265, 307, 310
faith of Muhammad, 9
falāh, 253
Falk, Richard, 296
Faruqi, Ismail R. al-, 77, 174
fatun, 182

fatwa (a public proclamation), 229
Featherstone, Mike, 47
Fields of Wheat, Rivers of Blood (Karakasidou), 209
financial globalization, 40, 41, 60
focal disparity, 7
Fong, Christina M., 142
Ford, Gerald, 204
Fordism, 1, 284
Foroutan's statistical analysis, 143
Foucault, Michel, 185
Foudah, Faraj, 179, 180
Frank, Andre Gunter, 289
freedom of movement, 129
free-market economy, 26
free-market system, 95
French decolonization, 207
Fresh Global System, 128
Friedman, Jonathan, 47
Friedman, Thomas, 243, 291
Fukuyama, Francis, 243
fundamentalism, 2, 17, 105, 149, 165–69, 214, 215, 237
The Future of Economics: An Islamic Perspective (Chapra), 251, 252

General Agreement on Tariffs and Trade, 250
al-Ghannouchi, R., 179
Ghannoushi, Rashid, 105
Ghazali, Abu Hamid al-, 89, 98, 172, 265, 266
Giddens, Anthony, 2, 3, 46, 243
Giugni, Marco, 143
global community, 13, 14, 34, 50, 74, 79, 83, 119, 125, 157, 177, 192, 207, 234, 294, 306
global consciousness, 3, 53, 235
global disparities, 2
global dynamics, 1, 18, 49–55, 120, 241
global governance, 3, 18, 42, 43, 111, 121, 148–56
global interconnectedness, 15, 123, 156
global interconnections, 229–30

globalists, 29–30, 42, 121
globalization: advancement, 25; anti-globalization forces, 57–62; augmentation of social relations, 28; backlashes, 240–42; complexity of, 31; conceptualization of, 27, 28; contemporary phase of, 36; cultural globalization, 44–48; definition, 27, 28; demographic globalization, 195; deterritorialization, 26; discursive regime, 27; driving forces of, 194–95; early modern period (1500–1750), 31, 35; early stages of, 125–27; economic consequence of, 231; economic globalization, 31, 38–42, 57–59, 62, 63, 184, 201, 202, 214, 218, 219, 250, 251, 259; Europe, 35; foundational mechanisms, 27; global dynamics, 49–55; global infrastructures, 28; globalists, 29–30, 42, 121; heightened interpenetration, 28; historical narrative of, 38; ingroup–outgroup categorization, 56, 57; initial phase, 31; intensification of flows, 28; Islamic revivalism, 26; mechanisms of, 234; modern phase (1750–1970), 31; multifaceted nature of, 37; notions of peace, 25; political globalization, 42–44, 214; political marginalization, 25; prehistoric globalization, 31; premodern indications of, 33; prosperity, 25; responses to, 26; self-categorization levels, 56; skeptics, 30; and social identity, 55–57; social transformation, 25; spatial considerations, 26; subsequent modern period (1750–1970), 35; time-space compression, 27; transformationalists, 30–31; *See also Individual entries*

global moral leadership, 205
global perception of Islam, 181–84
"global" social movements, 57
global sustainability, 91–98
global village economy, 281
global warming, 231
glocalization, 50–53, 55, 165; definition, 49; principles, 51
gnosticism, 172
Goebbels, Mastermind of the Third Reich (Rushdie), 209
Golden Age of Muslims, 120
Greek and Christian traditions, 8
Green Endowment Fund (Waqf), 100
grobalization, 52
Grugel, Jean, 150, 154

Haar, Gerrieter, 143
hadīth, 110, 150, 171, 294
halal (praiseworthy), 75, 76
Hanafi, Hassan, 180
Hanbal, Ibn, 170
Hanifah, Imam Abu, 170
haram (blameworthy), 75, 76
harem, 229
hegemonic powers, 34
hegemonization, 4, 47, 191, 215, 216; damaging effects of, 19; *vs.* homogenization, 196–97
Held, David, 28, 38
Hellenistic civilization, 8
Hennessey, Hubert D., 49
hermeneutical space, 71
Herzel, Theodor, 204
heterogenization, 46
Hijra, 177–78, 217
Hill, Christopher, 1
Hindu diaspora, 237
Hinnells, John, 143

Hobbes, Thomas, 197
homogeneity, 19, 29, 46, 102, 192, 215, 218
homogenization, 4, 19, 26, 46–48, 192, 216, 230–31; vs. hegemonization, 196–97
honor, 193, 199, 226, 229, 234–36, 238, 263
Hossain, Ishtiaq, 77
Howeidi, Fahmi, 105
human civilization, 108, 308
humanity, 2, 4, 5, 13, 14, 41, 57, 74, 76, 87, 88, 93, 96, 99, 101, 103, 107, 119, 123, 151, 153, 191, 195, 196, 206, 242, 246, 253–55, 262, 303, 304, 307
Huntington, Samuel P., 37, 46, 106, 149, 226, 243, 288
hyper-imperialism, 157
hypersensitivity, 12

ibadah, 75, 76, 85, 90, 91, 94
ibn Hanbal, Imam Ahmad, 91
Ibn Khaldun, Abd al-Rahman, 125, 193, 227, 233, 243, 255, 256, 267, 268
identity-based movements, 14
ihsan, 90, 91, 93, 153
ijtihād, 178, 215
ilm (knowledge), 75
imperialism, 3, 16, 37, 171, 173, 275, 284, 290, 295; American imperialism, 284; cultural imperialism, 45, 63, 214; economic imperialism, 134; European imperialism, 28, 129; hyper-imperialism, 157; Western imperialism, 214
individualism, 6, 14, 36, 44, 276, 292, 296, 305
Indonesian Liberal Islam Network, 181
Industrial Revolution, 178, 195, 275, 295, 309
infant mortality rate, 198

ingroup favoritism, 56
injustice, 6, 74, 78, 97, 123, 170, 175, 253–56, 261, 263, 268, 311
institutional isomorphism, 52
instrumental role of globalization, 7
intellectual hemorrhage, 285
intellectual short-termism, 31
intercivilizational interactions, 32
interest-based financial transactions, 97
interfaith, 101–10, 277, 278
International Bank for Reconstruction and Development, 39
international capitalism, 280
international civilization, 294
international community, 199
International Institute of Islamic Thought, 174
international law, 198–201
International Monetary Fund (IMF), 29, 30, 39, 40, 57, 60, 155, 252, 258, 281
International Relations and Political Theory, 106
international trade agreements, 59
interregional trade, 32, 34
intersection of Islam and western culture, 215–18
Iqbal, Muhammad, 174
Irving, David, 209
Islam and Economic Development (Chapra), 252
Islam and the Economic Challenge (Chapra), 252
Islam between Globalization and Counterterrorism (Mazrui), 194
Islam: Challenges in the Twenty-first Century (Engineer), 167
Islamdom, 138
Islamic and Hindu fundamentalism, 237
Islamic civilization, 8, 9, 125, 127, 170, 183, 244, 251, 266

Islamic cooperation and conflict, 127–29
Islamic cosmology, 180
Islamic Declaration of Istanbul, 100
Islamic "*dhimmī*" system, 105
Islamic divine law (*sharī'ah*), 79–81, 85, 89–91
Islamic doctrine, 93, 297
Islamic economic system, 20, 92, 95–97, 251, 255–57, 266–70; principles, 259–60
Islamic economic thought, 265–67
Islamic extremism, 108, 183
Islamic finance, 72, 98–99, 111
Islamic financial system, 92, 97
Islamic humanism, 182
Islamic Institute of Advanced Studies, 174
Islamic Jerusalem, 103
Islamic modernism, 128
Islamic modernization, 129
Islamic paradigm of globalization, 80; *adl* (social justice), 75, 76; *ahkām*, 81; cross-border processes, 73; *dhiya* (waste), 75, 76; economic development, 84–86; economic justice, 91–98; ethics, 84–86; global sustainability, 91–98; *halal* (praiseworthy), 75, 76; *haram* (blameworthy), 75, 76; *ibadah*, 75, 76, 85, 90, 91, 94; *ilm* (knowledge), 75; innovation, 84–86; institutional aspect of globalization, 81, 84; Islamic divine law (*sharī'ah*), 79–81, 85, 89–91; Islamic system of belief, 74; *istislah* (public interest), 75, 76; *khilafah* (trusteeship), 73, 75, 76; *mardhatillah*, 85; Muslim conviction in unity of God, 73; polity (*shūrā*), 81; Prophethood of Muhammad (PBUH), 73, 74, 86; *shahadah/kalimah* or Islamic creed, 73; *Shurātic* perspective, 81–83; *tawhīd* (unity), 73, 75–77, 79–81, 86, 88, 89; *ummah*, 74, 76–80; values-based principles, 85; *zulm* (tyranny), 75
Islamic piety (*taqwa*), 142
Islamic politics, 182
Islamic principles, 13
Islamic revivalism (*ihyā*), 17, 18, 26; critique of, 179–81; in early period, 169–70; eighteenth- and nineteenth-century revivalism, 171; and fundamentalism, 167–69; and global perception of Islam, 181–84; modern revivalism, 173–77; objective of, 169; *Tajdīd*, 172–73; technological fixes, 166–67; and technology, 177–78
Islamic revivalist movements, 181–84
Islamic scholarship, 86, 193, 215
Islamic system of belief, 74
The Islamic Welfare State and Its Role in the Economy (Chapra), 252
Islamist fundamentalism, 105
Islamization of Knowledge, 174
Islamophobia, 205
Islam's vision of equality and solidarity, 253–54
Islam Today: A Short Introduction to the Muslim World (Ahmad), 228
Israel–Palestine conflict, 102
istislah (public interest), 75, 76
Italian diaspora, 139

Jabiri, Muhammad Abid al-, 291–93
Jahilliyah, 78
Jamā'at al-Tabligh manifestos, 10
Jama'at-I-Islami movement, 175
jamaats, 185

Jameson, Frederic, 292
Jayyousi, Odeh Rashed al-, 100
Jeannet, Jean-Pierre, 49
jihad, 229, 244
Jinnah, M.A., 227
Jinnah Quartet (Ahmad), 227
Johnson, Lyndon, 204
Journey into Islam: The Crisis of Globalization (Ahmad), 225
Judaism, 73, 119, 218
Judeo-Christian civilization, 218
justice, 4, 14, 63, 72, 74, 76, 78, 91–98, 105, 107, 108, 111, 123, 151–54, 157, 176, 193, 203, 220, 221, 232–34, 236, 244, 253–58, 260–65, 267–70, 305–7

Karakasidou, Anastasia, 209
Karasneh, Samih Mahmoud al-, 87, 114n32
Kathir, Ibn, 170
Kemalist revolution, 180
Kennedy, John F., 204
Khadduri, Majid, 197
Khaldun, Ibn, 125, 227, 256, 267, 268
Khan, Sayyid Ahmad, 173
Khatami, Mohammad, 106, 107, 109, 226
Khatami, Muhammad, 232
khilafah (trusteeship), 73, 75, 76, 124
Khomeini, Ayatollah, 176
Khondker, Habibul H., 49, 51
King, Martin Luther, Jr., 206
Koopmans, Ruud, 143
Kurucan, Ahmet, 105

Laffey, Mark, 150
laissez-faire capitalism, 27
Law of Nations, 200
Lebl, Leslie. S., 141
Lechner, Frank J., 52
Levitt, Peggy, 147, 148
Levitt, Theodor, 49

Lewis, Bernard, 226
The Lexus and the Olive Tree (Friedman), 291
literary criticism theories, 181
Living Islam television series, 227
long-distance trade, 280
Lotman, Juri M., 55
Luthuli, Albert, 205, 206

Machiavellian principles, 213
macro-localization, 49, 50
Madivo, Callisto, 206
Malik, Imam, 170
Mandaville, Peter, 139
Mandela, Nelson, 205, 206
Mann, Michael, 28
maqasid, 267
maqasid al-sharī'ah, 20, 89–90, 98, 251, 263, 265–68
mardhatillah, 85
market-based risk-sharing mechanisms, 97
market Marxism, 208
Marranci, Gabriele, 77
Marx, Karl, 200
mass media, 109, 235, 292
mass migration policy, 145
Mau Mau conflict, 204
Mawardi, al-, 256
Mawdūdī, Sayyid Abul A'la, 175
Mazrui, Ali A., 4, 18, 19, 27, 30, 131, 177, 178, 195–98, 200–210, 212–16, 218–21; biography, 192–94; scholarly discourse, 191
M'Bow, Amadou Mahtar, 206
McDonald, 234
McDonaldization, 50
McGrew, Anthony, 28, 30
McWorld, 45
mechanism of evolutionary learning, 75
Medina, 105, 122, 125, 150, 170, 178; Constitution of Medina, 152
Medjauni, Mohammed, 206

Menon, Krishna, 200
Metcalf, Barbara, 146
Meyer, John W., 51
micro-globalization, 49, 50
migrating groups, 32
Mill, John, 200
modern imperial globalization, 130
modern revivalism, 173–77
Mohamad, Mahathir Bin, 41, 66n42, 233, 236, 266
monotheism, 73, 104, 110, 195
monotheistic phenomenon, 276
monotheistic religions, 121, 122
moral filter, 264
Moral Foundation, 261–65
Moroccan diaspora, 139
Muhammad, Mahathir, 266
mujahidin, 212
Mulk, Surah al-, 90
Muslim–Buddhist contentions, 102
Muslim civilization, 8–9, 122, 237, 242, 255, 309
Muslim Civilization: The Causes of the Decline and the Need for Reform (Chapra), 252
Muslim conviction in unity of God, 73
Muslim diaspora, 18, 121, 139–43, 146, 147, 236–38; dynamics of, 236–38; religious associations, 143–45; transnational ties, 143–45
Muslim immigrants, 229, 238–40
Muslim-majority nations, 13
Muslim Malay, 136
Muslim migrations, 130; migrant women in Australia, 142; migrant workers, 237
Muslim-minority nations, 13
Muslim-related threats, 239
Muslim response to globalization, 5–6
Muslim Spain, 226
Muslim universalism, 18, 121, 125–27; in postcolonial world, 129–32
Muslim world, 11–14

Muzaffar, Chandra, 27, 41, 48

Nahdah movement, 175
Napoleon's invasion of Egypt (1798–1801), 127
Nasser, Gamal 'Abd, 174
nationalism, 43, 44, 63, 127, 130, 133, 135–37, 174, 177, 214, 281, 287, 289
national particularism, 141
nation-state model, 131
neocolonialism, 10, 207, 283–86
neoliberal economic approach, 40
neoliberalism, 20, 63, 71, 153, 296
neoorthodox ideologies, 169
New World Order, 10, 128
Nixon, Richard, 204
non-Muslim Malay, 136
non-Western civilizations, 46
normative principles of Islam, 152
Nostra aetate declaration, 109
notions of righteousness, 12

Objectives of Islamic Economic Order: An Introduction in Economics and Islamic Financing (Chapra), 251
Objectives of the Islamic Economic Order (Chapra), 252
obscurantism, 183
OIC 25 agenda, 100
Organisation of Islamic Cooperation (OIC), 97, 100, 106, 108, 109
organizational leaders, 142
Organization of the Petroleum Exporting Countries (OPEC), 39
orientalism, 149, 284
Orientalist narrative, 9
orthodox Muslims, 6
Osamaphilia, 203
Osamaphobia, 202–3, 205
Ottoman caliphate, 129

Pakistani Christian diaspora, 139

pan-Islamism, 129
Pax Americana, 131
peace treaty, 78, 197, 287
Pentagon collision, 226
Peres, Shimon, 291
Pharaoh Akhenaton, 195
Pieterse, Nederveen, 46
Pio, Edwina, 142
Piper, Nicola, 150, 154
Piscatori, James, 146, 148
pluralism, 72, 101–10, 140, 146, 150, 152, 240
political-economy approaches, 166
political fragmentation, 36
political globalization, 42–44, 57, 58, 214
political integration, 261
The Political Sociology of the English Language (Mazrui), 194
The Politics of War and the Culture of Violence (Mazrui), 194
polity (*shūrā*), 81
post-9/11 invasions, 19, 150, 240, 242
postcolonial globalization, 128
postcolonial identity formation, 18, 121, 132–39
post-colonialism, 285
postmodernism, 1, 184, 244
Postmodernism and Islam: Predicament and Promise (Ahmad), 228
post-Ottoman Turkey, 10
poverty, 9, 20, 92–95, 168, 225, 231, 238, 242, 260, 266, 280–84, 287, 291
power hegemony, 3
The Power of Babel: Language and Governance in Africa's Experience (Mazrui), 194
pricing filter, 264
Prince, Erik, 239
Prince Charles, 227
principles of interpretation, 124
process of deregulation, 2
process of "maturation," 45

profit-centric models, 111
Prophethood of Muhammad (PBUH), 5, 15, 33, 73, 74, 77, 78, 86, 90, 91, 105, 110, 113n4, 122, 151–53, 177, 238
Prophet Ibrahim, 104
Prophet Noah, 104
Prophet of Islam, 103, 104, 236, 238, 242, 253, 255
Protestant Reformation, 178
proto-globalization, 126, 127, 130
public broadcasting system, 209

Qaf-50:6–8, 88
Qaf-50:8, 88
Qaradāwī, Yusuf al-, 105, 293, 294, 297
Qayyim, Ibn al-, 170
quasi-imperialist nexus, 37
Qudsy, Sharifah Hayaati Syed Ismail al-, 152
Qur'ān, 4, 5, 15, 18, 74, 75, 77, 85–89, 94, 96, 100, 103, 104, 110, 120, 121, 124, 150, 170, 172, 173, 180–82, 215, 236, 253–55; message of social integration, 260–61
Qur'ānic principles, 142
Qutb, Muhammad, 293, 294
Qutb, Sayyid, 88, 90, 174, 180

"*rabbil 'alamin*",' 104
Rabi, Ibrahim Abu, 18, 20, 27, 175
Rahman, Asmak Ab, 152
Ramphal, S. 206
Rashid, Caliph Harun al-, 256
rationalism, 6, 150, 285
Reagan, Ronald, 204
reform movements, 173
relativization process, 47
religious civilizations, 48
religious fanaticism, 168, 171
religious traditions, 5, 74, 102, 104, 119, 141

Rida, Rashid, 174
risk society, 235–36
Ritzer, G., 51, 52
Robertson, Roland, 28, 46, 47, 49, 51–53, 165, 294
Roosevelt, Franklin D., 204, 205
Roudometof, Victor, 52
Roy, Olivier, 139
Rumford, Chris, 42
Rushdie, Salman, 147, 208, 228

Sabet, Amr G., 150
Sachedina, Abdulaziz, 151
Sachs, Jeffrey, 258
Sadat, Anwar, 205, 206
Safi, Luay, 78, 79
Said, Abdul Aziz, 149
Salafism, 105
Saleh, Ali Mohammad Jubran, 87, 114n32
The Satanic Verses (Rushdie), 208–9, 228
Saudi Islam, 167
Scheffer, P., 145
Schirato, Tony, 27
Scholten, Peter W.A., 33, 55
Secretaries General of the Commonwealth, 206
secularism, 130, 131, 142, 180, 185, 262, 266
secularization, 10
Sen, Amartya, 16
September 11 attacks, 232
Serageldin, Ismail, 206
Shafiʿī, al-, 170
Shah, Reza, 176
Shahādah, 77
shahadah/kalimah or Islamic creed, 73
Shahid, Ismaʿīl, 171
Shahid, Sayyid Ahmad, 171
Shahrour, Muhammad, 180, 181
sharīʿah, 9, 10, 79–81, 85, 89–91, 98, 124, 152, 179, 180, 251, 266, 268

Shaw, George Bernard, 9
Shaye J. D. Cohen, 146
Shiite/Abbasid movement, 170
shurā, 128
shurātic, 72, 110, 111
Silk Route, 123
Sinclair, Timothy, 150, 154
siyasa, 151
skepticism, 6, 30, 58, 59, 61, 62, 64
skeptics, 25, 29, 30, 42
social identity, 56
socialism, 44, 96, 174, 264, 266, 281, 286
The Social Sciences Encyclopaedia, 27
social sustainability, 98–99
social transformation, 25, 50, 170
social unity, 93
societal uniformity, 4
sociocultural globalization, 59
socioeconomic disparities, 92, 93, 267
socioeconomic justice, 97
Sokefeld, Martin, 146
Soviet invasion of Afghanistan, 1980, 226
Soviet socialist economy, 281
Soviet Union, 9, 10, 31, 36, 40, 106, 199, 283–85, 287, 291
spiritual unity, 146
Statham, Paul, 143
Stearns, Peter, 32
sterling-based gold standard, 36
stewardship, 8, 72, 76, 111, 112, 142, 154
Streger, Manfred, 31, 36
Sufism, 171, 172
Summit Conference, 106–8, 131
Sunnah, 75, 94, 150, 153, 170, 173
Sunni-Sharīʿah-Sufi synthesis, 172
Sunni–Shia schism, 140
supra-territorialization, 55, 56
Surah Al-Ankabut-29:20, 87
Surah Al-Imran-3:137, 87
Surah Yusuf-12:111, 87
sustainability principles, 72, 100, 111

Sutton, Philip, 165
Swahili development, 33
Sweezy, Paul, 289
Syed, Jawad, 142

tahsiniyyah, 90
Tajdīd, 172–73
takāful, 97
A Tale of Two Africas: Nigeria and South Africa as Contrasting Visions (Mazrui), 194
tawhīd (unity), 73, 75–77, 79–81, 86, 88, 89, 256, 268
Taymiyyah, Ibn, 170, 244, 256
territorial fragmentation, 9
terrorism, definition, 205
terrorist attacks, September 11, 2001, 226
Third World, 9, 28, 133, 198, 206, 207, 213, 266, 275, 276, 281–88, 291, 292, 294–96, 305
"totalitarian" Islamism, 181
totalitarianism, 279
Towards a Fair Monetary System (Chapra), 251
Towards a Just Monetary System (Chapra), 252
Towards a Pax Africana (Mazrui), 194
Toynbee, Arnold, 122
trade agreements, 91
trade liberalization, 40
trade routes, 123
traditionalism, 5
traditional Muslims, 6, 242
trajectory of globalization, 2, 4, 17, 26, 36, 101, 119, 297
tranquility, 4, 88, 104, 213, 270
trans-ethnic communities, 177
transformationalists, 30–31
transformative forces, 71
transnational civilization, 48
transnational corporations (TNCs), 3, 40–43, 154
transnational Islamic movements, 12

transnationalism, 129, 143, 147, 148
transnational nationalism, 214
transnational politics, 43
transnational religions, 44
trans-Saharan trade networks, 126
trans-state migrations, 124
The Trial of Christopher Okigbo (Mazrui), 194
Trinity in Christianity, 73
true Islam, 214
Truman, Harry, 204
Trump, Donald, 58, 61, 62
Turkish secularism, 180
Turner, Bryan S., 51, 56
Tutu, Desmond, 205, 206

Umar (634-644), 151
Umar, Suhail, 76
Umayyad dynasty's integration of Islamic principles, 18
Umayyad era/Umayyad period, 170
ummah, 14, 18, 34, 72, 74, 76–80, 92, 106, 109–11, 122, 124, 129, 135, 136, 146, 174–77, 184, 214, 216, 255
unemployment, 20, 39, 258, 260
UNESCO, 206, 207
United Kingdom's legal framework, 211
United Nations (UN), 29, 36, 43, 134, 150, 154–56, 199, 204, 205, 207, 261, 293; General Assembly, 106; international law, 200; official languages, 199; responsibility, 200; Secretaries-General, 206, 232, 233; Security Council, 198, 199; Year of Dialogue among Civilizations, 106, 108
United States–Israel alliance, 203
unity and equality, 8
Unity of God, 4, 73, 75, 79, 255
unity of humanity, 5
UN's Declaration of 2001, 108

U.S. Constitution, 210
U.S. foreign policy, 243
U.S. policy, 226
Uthman (644-656), 151

Vasco da Gama, 195
Vertigans, Stephen, 165
Vertovec, Steven, 143
Vietnam conflict, 204
Vietnam War, 204, 205
violence, 29, 78, 102, 155, 179, 202, 210, 212–13, 215, 225, 231, 235, 238, 244, 255, 266

Waardenburg, Jacques, 147
Wahab, Muhammad ibn 'Abd al-, 171
WaliAllah, Shah, 129
Wallerstein, Immanuel, 34, 166, 281
Warner, Stephen, 146
war on terror, 239
Warsaw Pact, 207, 208
Washington Consensus, 40
Waters, Malcolm, 48
Wayne, John, 193
wealth disparities, 41, 266
Webb, Jen, 27
Weiss, Thomas G., 154
Western Christian calendar, 217
Western civilizations, 4, 7, 9–11, 76, 102, 174, 199, 212, 243, 308

Western cultural imperialism, 214
Western culture, 3, 4, 19, 44, 45, 48, 192, 208–12, 215–18, 220, 243
Western-dominated globalization, 20
Western educational system, 174
Western hegemony, 15, 19
Western imperialism, 214
Westoxification, 45
Westphalian state system, 35
White, Andrew D., 51, 193
White, Kathleen, 51
Wilkinson, Rorden, 154
World Council of Churches (WCC), 109
A World Federation of Cultures: An African Perspective (Mazrui), 194
world-systems theory, 166
World Trade Center, 226
WTO dispute settlement system, 57, 58

yudabbiru, 152
Yusuf, Abu, 256

Zakat, 92, 95, 99; beneficiaries of, 93; funds, 94, 95; payment of, 94; revenues, 95
Zionist movement, 203–4
zulm (tyranny), 75

About the Author

Asif Mohiuddin is a Lecturer in the Department of Moral Studies, Civics and Character Building at the Faculty of Human Sciences, Sultan Idris Education University, Malaysia. Previously, he worked as a Postdoctoral Academic Officer at the same institution. He is the author of the book *Navigating Religious Authority in Muslim Societies: Islamist Movements and the Challenge of Globalisation* (2023). From 2021 to 2022, he served as a Post-Doctoral Fellow in the Faculty of Theology at Sakarya University, Turkey. Before joining Sakarya University, he was a Lecturer in the Department of Higher Education, Government of Jammu and Kashmir, India. He earned his PhD from the University of Kashmir in 2018. His research interests include globalisation and Islam, intersection between politics and religion in the Middle East, human rights law, Islam and the West and Muslim minorities in multicultural societies (Europe and South Asia).

www.ingramcontent.com/pod-product-compliance
Lightning Source LLC
Chambersburg PA
CBHW032013300426
44117CB00008B/1011